SHAKESPEARE AND THE DRAMATURGY
OF POWER

Shakespeare AND THE DRAMATURGY OF POWER

&❧ JOHN D. COX

PRINCETON UNIVERSITY PRESS

PRINCETON, NEW JERSEY

Copyright © 1989 by Princeton University Press
Published by Princeton University Press, 41 William Street,
Princeton, New Jersey 08540
In the United Kingdom: Princeton University Press,
Guildford, Surrey

This book has been composed in Linotron Trump type

Clothbound editions of Princeton University Press books are
printed on acid-free paper, and binding materials are chosen for
strength and durability. Paperbacks, although satisfactory
for personal collections, are not usually suitable
for library rebinding

Printed in the United States of America by Princeton
University Press, Princeton, New Jersey

Library of Congress Cataloging-in-Publication Data
Cox, John D., 1945–
Shakespeare and the dramaturgy of power / John D. Cox.
p.   cm.
Bibliography: p.
Includes index.
ISBN 0-691-06765-1 (alk. paper)
1. Shakespeare, William, 1564–1616—Political and social
views. 2. Shakespeare, William, 1564–1616—Knowledge—
Literature. 3. English drama—To 1500—History and criticism.
4. Power (Christian theology) in literature. 5. Power (Social
sciences) in literature. I. Title.
PR3017.C68 1989
822.3'3—dc19   88-29311

For Karen, Anna-Lisa, Jonathan, and Amelia

CONTENTS

PREFACE ❧ POWER AND THEORY

The primary task of this book is to reexamine Shakespeare's plays in the context of his medieval dramatic heritage. While my discussion of Shakespeare is therefore organized according to the dramatic genres that have come to be recognized in his work—comedy, history, tragedy, and romance—my purpose in dealing with each genre is to examine it anew in light of what Shakespeare inherited from his immediate predecessors on the English stage. The book does not pretend to be comprehensive: I discuss those plays that I think are best illuminated by the particular approach I have chosen. *All's Well That Ends Well* and *Measure for Measure* are thus given a chapter apiece, while the tragedies are dealt with in a single chapter, because this book is not about a particular dramatic genre but about how Shakespeare adapted and shaped the tradition that I believe adapted and shaped him most profoundly.

What distinguishes this study from other studies of Shakespeare against his medieval background is my secondary purpose and my primary debt. For this book approaches Shakespeare's medieval dramatic heritage for the first time in a new way—according to the methodology that has come to be called New Historicism. In all frankness, without the benefit particularly of work by Jonathan Dollimore, Stephen Greenblatt, Louis A. Montrose, and Frank Whigham, this book would not exist.[1] Its argument is informed throughout by the New Historicist insight that literature is a cultural artifact—"the expression of the codes by which behavior is shaped," as Greenblatt puts it (*Self-Fashioning*, p. 4)— and that literature therefore perpetuates specific cultural values—values of class, wealth, power, gender, and indeed of literacy itself. In some abstract sense, this book could in fact be said to deal with the effects of literacy as an emerging criterion for social advancement in the sixteenth century. For literacy has not always had the privileged position it enjoys today: even during the European Middle Ages, which are often thought of as the age of the book, literacy had less to do with social standing than it has today in any of the so-called emerging nations, and literacy only has such status now because it is a principal criterion for "emergence." I do not mean that the rising prestige of literacy in early modern England is always and everywhere the subject of my argument. The issue is addressed explicitly for the first time only in chapter 3 and then referred to occasionally thereafter. But it is assumed throughout as the context in which I interpret Shakespeare's debt to his medieval predecessors.

In spite of my debt to New Historicism, I need to emphasize from the outset that this book also entails a sustained critique of New Historicist assumptions. Put in the simplest terms, my argument is that New Historicists are right, but for inadequate reasons. In making this case, I have benefited greatly from Raymond Williams's ideas about cultural change.[2] His suggestion that culturally dominant ideas are always in dialectical relationship with both residual and emergent ideas is an insight that I have found fruitful as a way of approaching English Renaissance drama, particularly as it developed out of the religious drama of the Middle Ages and as it gave rise, in turn, to the neoclassical preoccupations of the late seventeenth and eighteenth centuries. These changes are not merely esthetic or intellectual; they are deeply involved, as I hope to show, with social and political changes between the fifteenth and seventeenth centuries.

Since Raymond Williams is also a formative figure in New Historicism (see especially Dollimore's *Radical Tragedy*), my claim to be using his ideas as a means of qualifying New Historicist assumptions clearly demands explanation. What I have learned from Williams is the tripartite dialectic I have just mentioned; where I differ from him and the New Historicists he has inspired, however, is in the application of that dialectic to the Renaissance. A paradigmatic example (which Dollimore in fact represents in many details) takes Christian idealism in this period as dominant: it is manifest in the theological discourse of Reformer and Counter Reformer alike, and in Christian defenses of monarchical absolutism in the emerging nation states. In this view, what is residual is the materialism of popular culture, which Christian idealists and royal absolutists regard as subversive and attempt in various ways to suppress and contain. What is emergent is philosophical materialism—implicit in the cosmology of Copernicus and Galileo, more or less explicit in the political theory of Machiavelli and Hobbes (who was inspired by Galileo's theories of mechanical motion), and in the ontology, physics, and psychology of Descartes. Like the residual materialism of popular culture, emerging philosophical materialism is also regarded as subversive and is also the object of attempts to suppress and contain it. One could cite, for example, the English response to Machiavelli in the sixteenth century and the Counter Reformation response to Galileo in the seventeenth.

What I offer in the following pages is quite a different version of Williams's tripartite conception. I agree that philosophical materialism is in some sense emerging in the Renaissance, but I think to *call* it materialism in this period is a question-begging oversimplification that collapses the past into the future. Hobbes is the period's prize exhibit of explicit materialist thinking, but his ideas cannot be confused with modern cultural materialism, since they took him in the direction of royal absolutism, not political radicalism. It would be more accurate to say that what is emergent in the Renaissance is philosophical rationalism, in which the seeds of a full-blown materialism in the nineteenth-century sense can sometimes be found, but not very often. The most important point I have to make vis-à-vis the New Historicism, however, is that emergent rationalism is often very difficult to distinguish from what I would argue is truly residual—not popular materialism but what I propose to call Christian political realism. As I point out in chapter 1, this complex view of the human social and political situation is formulated most impressively in Augustine's *City of God*, a work that seeks to articulate a distinctively Christian response to the centralized power of ancient Rome. Augustine's is a minority opinion when he first enunciates it, and it never becomes culturally dominant in the Middle Ages, let alone any later age. But as I argue in chapter 2, Augustine's political realism is formative in medieval religious drama: indeed, the politics of that drama cannot be understood apart from Augustine.

In my understanding of Williams's historico-cultural analysis, what is dominant in the Renaissance is misleadingly described as Christian idealism and more accurately as neopagan political idealism, which gains strength in pace with the rapid centralization of power. By using "neopagan" I do not mean to deny that what becomes culturally dominant in the Renaissance is described and defended in the language of Christian belief; what I mean is that to construe that language as authentically Christian is misleading, because the ideas it clothes originate not in Judeo-Christian tradition but in Plato, Aristotle, the Stoics, and Hellenistic ideas of kingship. It was this same package of classical ideas about human political and social order that Augustine came to oppose, and I shall argue in chapter 3 that the rapid reascendance of these ideas in the sixteenth century decisively eclipsed not only Christian political realism but a distinctively Augustinian rhetorical conception that was its counterpart. Rhetorical, stylistic, and dramaturgical transformations are thus constituent elements of contemporaneous political and social transformation. This book aims to explore how Shakespearean drama at once contributes to these changes and yet opposes them in the specific way it embodies power relations.

To borrow someone's ideas (in this case, Raymond Williams's) and at the same time to redefine them as thoroughly as I propose to do may seem capricious and arbitrary, and I should therefore explain why I am doing it. Williams insists that if human beings make anything it is their history, and he sees little hint of this insight before the advent of eighteenth-century "Universal History," which "was the crucial step beyond

the relatively static ('timeless') conception of history which had depended on religious or metaphysical assumptions" (*Marxism and Literature*, p. 13). Part of the history human beings have made, in other
words, is the Enlightenment recognition that they make their own history. My reservations about this claim are both practical and theoretical.
My practical reservation is that the insight Williams identifies with
eighteenth-century Universal History in fact informs Shakespeare's history plays in the late sixteenth century, as I argue in chapters 5 and 6.
For it is the secular character of these plays as history that distinguishes
them from the only model for staging history that Shakespeare knew,
that is, the medieval biblical cycles. Virtually everything about Shakespeare's history plays indicates that the human knowledge of history is
limited to what we ourselves make of it and does not include history's
being made for us (as it is made in medieval religious drama) through
decisive divine undertaking with implicit eschatalogical significance.

This practical reservation leads naturally to my theoretical reservations about Williams's claim (and it is an implicit New Historicist claim
as well) that human thinking about history evolved in a radical new way
in the nineteenth century. For the practical reservation I have just cited
can be met with the rejoinder that Shakespeare's histories anticipate
eighteenth-century Universal History because historical empiricism is
emergent in Shakespeare: he merely foreshadows the promise revealed
faintly in Gibbon and Hume and fully in Marx. But my response to this
objection is that it is impossible to establish unambiguously, because
Shakespeare's secular history not only looks forward to the Enlightenment but also backward to the residual political realism of Augustine.
As R. A. Markus argues, Augustine's conception of the *Civitas Terrena*
is that it is a *secular* "city": human political and social life is distinguished not only by the structural failure of *caritas* (which is the co-
hesive principle of the *Civitas Dei*) but by the absence of the definitive
prophetic insight that shapes sacred history.[3] Augustine's understanding
of the Earthly City and its history thus has an empirical bent, as his
survey of Roman history in books 2 to 4 of *The City of God* demonstrates, and it is this empiricism that Shakespeare's history plays look
back to. My point is not that Shakespeare can be collapsed back into
Augustine—much less that he should be—but that the attempt to make
Shakespeare look forward is inevitably complicated by a residual tradition that antedates Shakespeare himself by more than a thousand years.

Because Jonathan Dollimore's recent and influential book focuses
on Shakespeare, I have given primary attention to Dollimore in the following pages. Any book that makes New Historicist claims must be indebted to Stephen Greenblatt as well, however, and I should therefore
clarify briefly how my qualifications of New Historicism relate to his
work too. *Renaissance Self-Fashioning* sets out to explicate a changing

sense of self in the changing political and social climate of the Renaissance. The notion that the self could be fashioned is an innovation—or at least a new emphasis—Greenblatt claims, and in support of his claim he cites evidence from early modern English (the new use of "fashion" in relation to the self) and the evidence of intellectual history, exemplified in Augustine's warning, "Hands off yourself. Try to build up yourself and you build a ruin" (*Self-Fashioning*, p. 2).

In brief, my reservations about this claim are again practical and theoretical. In practical terms, Greenblatt's citing of Augustine is a historical blunder, because Augustine's sense of self is extraordinarily complex and subtle—enough so, certainly, to encompass what Greenblatt is thinking of as self-fashioning.[4] Even a cursory reading of *The Confessions* is enough to dispel the idea that the one sentence Greenblatt quotes from Augustine can do justice to Augustine's sense of self. Considered rhetorically, *The Confessions* can in fact be described as an extended exercise in self-fashioning of a particular kind, and because of this exercise we know more about Augustine as an individualized human personality than about anyone else in the ancient world. With *The Confessions* in mind, Greenblatt's assertion that the ancient elite understood self-fashioning, while Christianity was suspicious of it (p. 2), is difficult to credit. Again, then, my practical reservation is that what Greenblatt points to as a Renaissance innovation is in fact preceded by a residual tradition originating in Augustine.

My theoretical reservation about Greenblatt's argument is that it takes the same implicit form as Williams's and Dollimore's: something innovative that emerges in the Renaissance only achieves its perfection in the nineteenth century. For Greenblatt could hardly see what he sees in the Renaissance were it not for Marx and Freud, two members of the triumvirate that Paul Ricoeur calls the "school of suspicion" in the nineteenth century (the third being Nietzsche).[5] "Suspicion" certainly fits Greenblatt's idea of Renaissance self-fashioning, as I argue in chapter 4: one so frequently makes and remakes one's self in theatrical response to the threatening challenge of changing power relations that identity is immersed in layers of ambiguity and self-deception. Edward Pechter has characterized Greenblatt's implicit view of the world with the statement, "It's a jungle out there," but this summary misses Greenblatt's point about the Renaissance self: one knew it was a jungle out there because one knew oneself to be a ravening beast.[6]

While this grim epistemology of self and society achieves its most penetrating expression in the nineteenth century, we cannot conclude with certainty that it is newly emergent in the Renaissance because it is residual in biblical and patristic tradition. That human beings devour one another like monsters of the deep is a patristic commonplace "culled from rabbinic tradition," and it underlies Augustine's thinking about human social and political life.⁷ This is a point that Max Weber understood. In opposing the premise that political good follows from political good and evil from evil, Weber points to the early Christians, who "knew full well the world is governed by demons and that he who lets himself in for politics, that is, for power and force as means, contracts with diabolical powers, and for his action it is *not* true that good can follow only from good and evil only from evil, but that often the opposite is true. Anyone who fails to see this is, indeed, a political infant."⁸ The counterpart to this sense of political life is what Augustine recognizes about the self in *The Confessions*: that our fundamental instinct is to hide what we know about ourselves even from ourselves, and the divinely unaided quest for self-knowledge is a delusion.

In summary, my reservations about Greenblatt derive from a historical skepticism that also informs my reservations about New Historicism in general. This book should not be construed as an argument that Shakespearean drama is an allegorization of Augustinian theology, but I do take Augustine as a point of departure in questioning the implicit teleology of New Historicism. Unlike most New Historicists, I am not committed to finding that either cultural poetics or cultural materialism is the ripening paradisal fruit on the intellectual tree planted by early modern rationalism. Williams's assertion that we make our own history is fine as a description of secular history but inadmissible as a historicist claim, that is, as a claim that we (and especially we New Historicists or Cultural Materialists) are the purpose toward which history has been moving and continues to move. Behind that implicit teleology is the habit of mind that transforms historical change into moral change—"what is" into "what ought to be"—and in comparison my conception of historical change is indeed "relatively static." Remarkable changes have certainly occurred since the seventeenth century, and they have sometimes enriched and complicated our moral understanding. Moreover, they frequently have antedecedents in the Renaissance. I am not persuaded, however, that as imperatives to human action (that is, as moral signifiers) the mere facts of modern history are radical advances over the past. Nor do they provide grounds, I think, for concluding either that the human race only began to be seriously aware of injustice, oppression, exploitation, greed, and self-deception in the sixteenth century or that we have successfully determined how to eradicate any of those sad and dismal aspects of our lives.

I HAVE MADE a conscious effort in the following pages to use inclusive language wherever possible, including quotations. I have thus silently emended the generic "man" or "mankind" to "humankind" or "human beings," even in modern translations of ancient texts. I am well aware that such emendation falsifies subtleties of Latin meaning, but at this point in human history and in a book that is not about ancient linguistics, the connotations for modern readers are more important than niceties of Latin distinction. In early modern vernacular texts, emendation to achieve inclusive language is more difficult, particularly in poetry, but I have found little need for it in such contexts anyway. I have consistently modernized archaic orthography and punctuation in early modern texts in English, primarily because my quotations from Shakespeare are modernized in this way, and I see no virtue in inconsistency on this front. I have used the glosses and translations provided by David Bevington in his anthology called *Medieval Drama*, and when quoting passages not in his anthology, I have used his method of transcribing Middle English and supplied glosses like his, on the assumption that this book will be read mostly by those who will find such an apparatus helpful. Biblical quotations are from the Geneva Bible, edited by Lloyd Berry (Wisconsin, 1969), because it is the most important translation for Shakespeare. Quotations from Shakespeare are taken from *The Complete Works of Shakespeare*, ed. David Bevington (Scott, Foresman, 1980).

ACKNOWLEDGMENTS

Throughout the time this book was written I have been deeply involved in the life of an undergraduate liberal arts college as a busy teacher and part-time administrator. I am grateful to colleagues at Hope College for the interdisciplinary stimulation that such an atmosphere provides. I am also very grateful for generous assistance from many sources that have given me the time required for bringing a project like this to completion. The bulk of the book was written during a year's leave of absence in 1985–86, made possible by a Fellowship for College Teachers from the National Endowment for the Humanities. Hope College has been generous with support in the form of faculty development grants in the summer of 1982, 1983, 1984, 1986, and 1987. I was also assisted by a Summer Seminar grant from NEH in 1981, when I had the pleasure of working with Arthur Kirsch at the University of Virginia, and by a grant from the Huntington Library, in San Marino, California, in 1983. "Occasional grants" provided by the University of Chicago Midwest Faculty Seminars have made the Regenstein and Newberry Libraries much easier for me to get to than they would have been otherwise. Portions of two chapters have appeared in print in earlier versions: chapter 5 in *Comparative Drama* (1978), and chapter 8 in *Modern Philology* (1983). I thank each of these journals for permission to use material that they first published. I am also grateful for permission to quote a passage from *Bartolomé de las Casas: A Selection of His Writings* by Bartolomé de las Casas; translated by George Sanderlin. Copyright (c) (1971) by Alfred A. Knopf, Inc. Reprinted by permission of the publisher.

I have also been treated generously by the organizers of academic conferences who have invited me to present portions of this book. These include the Congress on Medieval Studies, Kalamazoo, the Iowa Shakespeare Symposium, the Michigan Academy of Science, Arts, and Letters, the Michigan College English Association, the Midwest Modern Language Association, the Modern Language Association, the Shakespeare Association of America, and the 1986 World Shakespeare Congress in Berlin. Individuals too numerous to mention have been helpful and stimulating in their responses to my work in these conferences. Particularly memorable is David Bergeron's caveat about Perdita's flowers in

ACKNOWLEDGMENTS

The Winter's Tale and Keir Elam's suggestion of a title for chapter 4—a suggestion I was glad to take. I have worked in many libraries and been assisted by many able librarians, including those at the British Library, the Cambridge University Library, the University of Chicago Libraries, the Henry E. Huntington Library, the Newberry Library, and the Houghton and Widener Libraries at Harvard. I am grateful to Meiji Gakuin University in Tokyo for an invitation to present three lectures in June 1988, based in part on this book.

Other personal debts require mention. Henry ten Hoor first introduced me to the serious study of Shakespeare, and David Bevington taught me how to understand more than I ever thought I could, not only about Shakespeare and his medieval dramatic heritage but about friendship and the creative juggling of familial and academic responsibilities. Theodore DeWelles generously assisted me in securing a copy of his dissertation when I was not in a position to secure it otherwise. Sam Schoenbaum and Peter Rudnytsky read the manuscript for Princeton University Press. Like good teachers, they were generous in their support and unfailingly helpful in their suggestions for improvement. Others who have assisted this study in various ways include Edward Berry, Muriel Bradbrook, Cedric Brown, Elton Bruins, Gail Gibson, Charles Huttar, David Jeffrey, David Kastan, Nikola Koljevich, Jacob Nyenhuis, Oliver O'Donovan, Peter Schakel, and Sanford Schwartz. Myra Kohsel has been faithful, prompt, cheerful, and efficient in her unflagging clerical assistance. My greatest debt is acknowledged in the dedication to my family. Without much choice in the matter, they have endured the pain of this book's preparation and have been quick to delight in its pleasure. Above all, I am grateful for their charity.

SHAKESPEARE AND THE DRAMATURGY
OF POWER

CHAPTER 1 ❧ CENTRALIZED POWER AND CHRISTIAN POLITICAL REALISM: FIFTH CENTURY AND SIXTEENTH

Politically and socially the most momentous change in the Renaissance is the growth of centralized power. Even in countries where this growth was not very successful, as in Italy and Germany, people acted as if it were. Machiavelli's penetrating analysis of power in action is based on what he saw of Medici control in Florence, even though the Medicis ruled only a small territory and Italy would not become a unified nation for another four centuries. Machiavelli's realism contrasts with the cultivated neo-Platonic idealism of the Medici court, but both are direct reflections of an emerging political model that emulated ancient Rome because of its impressive achievements in successful hegemony. The expansion of Rome was also the putative model for the unprecedented territorial expansion of European regimes, so that the innovative marvels of the New World were assimilated to an ancient pattern. An entire Brazilian forest (including imported Indians) greeted Henri II in 1550 when he made his neo-Roman triumphal entry into Rouen: the new and the old alike were pressed into the service of centralized power.[1] In European countries like England, where this power was a reality and not merely a coveted aspiration, the changes it produced were enduring and profound.

Inevitably these changes were resisted, and resistance took many forms. Most obvious was the resistance of provincial power centers that were directly threatened by the gathering of the reins into royal hands. Another kind of resistance was produced by the Reformation, when the explosive foment of religious conscience within the church ignited hope of social change on a broad scale. Yet religious conflict became increasingly difficult to distinguish from conflicts of political survival or ambition, and Luther took the side of the princes against peasants while Calvin set up a centralized theocratic regime in Geneva.[2] The self-styled imperial expansion of European power in the New World met with the resistance of sheer bewilderment and outraged injustice, whose only rec-

3

ord is preserved for us in the annals of the destroyers. The Eskimo couple who were imported to England in 1577 by Martin Frobisher and invited to set up housekeeping on the banks of the Thames must have lived in a state of nearly constant shock, which is probably what killed them after only a few months of English hospitality.[3] Such mute resistance to the expansion of European power was a matter of curiosity to Europeans. Yet New World opposition to Old World hegemony is not uniformly dumb: even in a context like the Spanish colonial settlements before the Reformation, one finds striking conscientious resistance to the neoimperial claims of the conquistadors.

Consider, for example, the case of Bartolomé de las Casas, the first secular priest to be ordained in the New World. A wealthy landowner and possessor (like all his fellow Spaniards) of enslaved Indians, Las Casas suddenly decided to emancipate his slaves in 1514. He narrates the incident in his own words:

> The cleric Bartolomé de las Casas . . . was going about preoccupied with his enterprises. Like the others, he was sending Indians of his *repartimiento* [encomienda] to the mines to extract gold, and to the fields to sow, and he was profiting by them as much as he could, although he always took care to support them as well as possible, to treat them gently, and to sympathize with their miseries. But he gave no more consideration than the others to remembering that they were pagan men and to the duty he had to provide them with religious instruction and bring them within the pale of Christ's Church.
>
> Diego Valázquez . . . left the port of Xagua to establish a town of Spaniards in the province, where one called Espíritu Santo was founded. And since, except for one in the town of Baracoa, there was not a cleric or friar in the whole island but the said Bartolomé de las Casas, when Pentecost came [Las Casas] decided to leave his house on the river Arimao . . . where he had his estate and go say Mass and preach that Pentecost in Espíritu Santo.
>
> Studying the sermons he had preached last Pentecost, or other sermons for that time, he began to turn over in his mind certain texts of the Holy Scripture. And if I have not forgotten, the principal one was from Ecclesiasticus, Chapter 34: "Tainted his gifts who offers in sacrifice ill-gotten goods; mock presents from the lawless win not God's favor. The Lord is the salvation of those sustaining themselves in the way of truth and justice. The Most High approves not the gifts of the godless, nor does he have regard for the offerings of the wicked; nor for their many sacrifices does he forgive their sins. Like the man who slays his neighbor is he who offers sacrifice from

the possessions of the poor. He who sheds blood and he who defrauds his servant are brothers."

He began, I say, to reflect on the misery and servitude that those peoples suffered. In this connection, what he had heard and experienced in this island of Hispaniola benefited him—the preaching of the Dominicans that Spaniards could not in good conscience possess Indians, and that the Dominicans did not wish to confess and absolve those who held Indians, which the said cleric did not accept.

And once, while he possessed Indians in this island of Hispaniola, as thoughtlessly and ignorantly as later in the island of Cuba, he wanted to confess to a Dominican whom he found in a certain place. But the Dominican did not wish to confess him. When he asked why not and was given a reason, the cleric refuted it with frivolous arguments and vain solutions, although with a certain seeming probability, so that the Dominican said to him: "I have concluded, father, that truth always encounters much opposition and a lie has many helpers."

The cleric then yielded, because of the reverence and honor he owed the religious, who was a venerable and very learned person, much more learned than the father cleric. But as for giving up his Indians, the cleric didn't care for his opinion.

So it was worth a great deal to him to remember that dispute of his, and even the declaration he had made to the religious, in order to attain a better view of the ignorance and danger he was in, holding Indians like the others and not hesitating to confess those who possessed them or intended to possess them. . . .

After he had spent a few days with these thoughts and had each day become more and more sure, from what he read of [natural and divine] law, and from the events he witnessed—applying the first to the second—he decided for himself, convinced by truth, that everything done to the Indians in these Indies was unjust and tyrannical. He found that all he read tended to confirm this, and he was accustomed to assert that, from the first hour when he began to dispel the darkness of that ignorance, he never read a book in Latin or Spanish—and there were an infinite number in forty-four years—in which he did not find either an argument or a text to prove and corroborate the justice of these Indian peoples and to condemn the injustices, wrongs, and injuries done them.

Finally, he decided to preach that. And in order to freely condemn the repartimientos or encomiendas as unjust and tyrannical, and because if he retained his Indians he would then have in his hand a reproof of his sermons, he decided to give up his Indians and surrender them into the hands of the governor, Diego Velázquez. Not that they would be better off in Velázquez's power, for the cleric treated them with more compassion . . . and he knew that if he relinquished them they must be given to an oppressor. . . . But as . . . he would never escape defamations like "After all, he has Indians; why doesn't he give them up since he asserts it is tyrannical to hold them?" he decided to surrender them completely.

For all this to be better understood, it is well to recall here the partnership and close friendship between this father and one Pedro de Rentería, a prudent man and a very good Christian. . . . As they were not only friends but partners in their estate, and both had their repartimientos of Indians combined, they agreed between themselves that Pedro de la Rentería should go to the island of Jamaica, where he had a brother, to bring back swine to raise and maize to sow, and other things they did not have in Cuba. . . . And for this journey they chartered one of the king's caravels for 2,000 castellanos.

Now as Pedro de la Rentería was absent and the father cleric had decided to give up his Indians and preach what he felt he ought to . . . , he went one day to the governor, Diego Velázquez, and told him what he felt about his own condition, the governor's, and that of the others. He declared that they could not be saved in that state, and that to escape from the danger and do his duty by his office, he intended to preach this. Therefore, he had decided to surrender his Indians to him. . . . So Velázquez could consider them unclaimed and do with them what he would.

But the cleric asked him as a favor to keep that a secret and not to give the Indians to someone else until Rentería returned from his stay on the island of Jamaica. For the Indians and the estate, which both held indivisibly, would suffer loss if someone to whom Velázquez gave the father's Indians should undertake them and the estate before Rentería came.

The governor was perfectly astounded at hearing such a novel and, as it were, monstrous matter. First, because the cleric . . . was of the opinion of the Dominican friars, who had first brought up that business, and that he should dare proclaim it. Second, that he should so justify it and should have such contempt for temporal wealth when he was so well prepared to become rich shortly. . . . And the governor said to him: "Reflect on what you are doing, father, lest you repent. For by God I would wish to see you rich and prosperous, and therefore I do not accept your relinquishing your Indians. And that you may think better of it, I give you fifteen days to consider it carefully, after which you may return to tell me what you decide."

The father cleric replied: "Sir, I receive great honor from your desiring my prosperity, along with the other kindnesses that your honor does me. But count the fifteen days past. And please God, if I repent of this purpose that I have made known to you, and wish to possess Indians, and if you because of your love for me want to entrust or to give them to me anew . . . , may it be God who will severely punish you and not forgive you this sin. I only ask your honor that all this may be secret and that you do not give the Indians to anyone until Rentería comes, so that his estate will not be damaged."

So Velázquez promised him that and kept his promise. And from then on he had much more respect for the said cleric. . . . And all the others in the island began to hold a new concept of him, different from what they had held before, as soon as they knew that he had given up his Indians—something considered, then and always, as the strongest possible evidence of saintliness. So great was, and is, the ignorance of those who have come to these parts.

This secret was revealed in this way. The said cleric preached on the day of the Assumption of Our Lady, in that aforementioned place Espíritú Santo, and discussed the active and contemplative lives, the subject of the gospel for that day, touching on the spiritual and temporal acts of charity. It was then necessary for him to show them their duty to carry out and perform these acts among those people, by whom they were so cruelly profiting, and to reprove their neglect and omission of these acts. For this, it became pertinent to reveal the secret agreement that he had made with the governor, and he said: "Sir, I give you license to tell everyone you want to what we agreed on in secret. And I will permit myself to tell it to those who are present."

Having said this, he began to declare their ignorance, and the injustices, tyrannies, and cruelties they were committing among those gentle, innocent peoples; how they could not be saved while holding the Indians in encomiendas, nor could the one who distributed them; the obligation to restitution by which they were bound; and that he, from understanding the danger in which he lived, had given up his Indians—and many other things on the subject.

All were astonished, and even frightened, at what he told them. Some were repentant, others behaved as if they were dreaming— hearing something so novel as a declaration that they could not, without being considered sinners, possess Indians. They did not believe it, as if it were said that they could not make use of the beasts of the field.[4]

Las Casas repeatedly describes what he is resisting as "tyranny," yet very little in his account seems political in the modern sense, and his motives resist the kind of analysis we are accustomed to bringing to human behavior. Writing in the first person about himself as if he were a third person ("the cleric"), he attaches such importance to an event we would now think of as private and subjective that he makes it central in his history of the first seventy-five years of Spanish colonization in the New World. This is anything, in short, but an objective or impersonal account, and this is not what we normally think of as written history. Yet, on the other hand, it is not how we usually think of autobiography either—written in the third person, with total disregard for the affective life, as if the subject were an intelligent machine for whom a momentous and materially ruinous life decision is a matter of detached intellectual analysis. As a historian, Las Casas includes too much, making his own experience the center of a vast, heterogeneous, and complex series of events; as an autobiographer he includes too little, depicting himself as motivated purely by the weight of reason in resolving what was, by any reckoning, the major crisis of his life. That event, moreover, while being clearly a religious event of a life-changing order, occurs in the experience of a man and a culture already steeped in religious belief and practice. As a conversion, it involves a change not from unbelief to faith but from one order of faith to another within the same religious context. This is what Las Casas' auditors found so unsettling when he preached to them on Pentecost, 1514. Their astonishment and fear, their disorientation—"as if they were dreaming"—derives from his persuading them that what had always given them cosmic assurance, direction, and meaning was in fact the source of doubt, misdirection, and moral chaos in their lives, "that they could not, without being considered sinners, possess Indians."

Yet for all its religious motivation, Las Casas' experience is undeniably social and political in its impact. In many ways his change of direction closely resembles the much better known experience of Martin Luther, which was happening at almost exactly the same time: both are highly cognitive; both take their impetus from careful study of authoritative sacred texts; both involve a change in the quality of faith rather than a change from unbelief to faith; both resolve agonies of conscience in the convertite's life; despite their order as highly cognitive experiences, both conversions strike us in retrospect as deeply involved with the affective life of the individual; both result in immediate and extreme action that runs directly counter to almost everything the convertites had stood for prior to their conversion. The difference for Las Casas, however, is that his conversion results not in new cognitive formulations, as Luther's does, but in social action that has the potential to destroy the social order he has known and by means of which he has prospered. It is almost as if Luther had been converted to the social equality of the German peasant, in addition to justification by faith. In 1516, the same year Thomas More published his *Utopia*, Las Casas drew up exhaustive and far-sighted proposals for political and social reform in the Spanish colonies. In 1520, he sought to put his proposals into practice at Cumaná, a colony on the coast of what is now Venezuela; in 1537, he demonstrated the success of his proposals regarding the peaceful (as opposed to forcible) conversion of as yet uncolonized Indians in Tuzulutlan; in 1543, he accepted royal appointment as the bishop of Chiapa, where he again attempted the radical reform of the colonizers' treatment of native peoples. Returning to Spain in 1547, at the age of seventy-three, Las Casas embarked on a vigorous life of disputation and publication on behalf of the people he had actively championed in the New World. His public debate with the humanist Juan de Sepulveda, in 1550, is a model of Thomistic theology being used to oppose a neo-Aristotelian defense of slavery as a natural institution.[5] Las Casas' *Most Brief Account of the Destruction of the Indies* (written in 1542, published without license ten years later) is a highly polemical but widely influential indictment of Spanish exploitation in the New World. Translated into six other European languages by 1626 (English in 1583), it became the single most important source of information about colonial barbarity in the New World. Because of it, Spain still retains a reputation for unrivalled cruelty in her colonies, whereas if other European nations had had a Las Casas, they would all stand under the same indictment, or worse.

The similarities between Las Casas' conversion and Luther's can be explained in part against the background of late medieval culture in which each occurred: a profound crisis in their lives took the shape that they expected a crisis to take, yet was no less a crisis for all that. In neither case is the incident characteristic of midlife crises with expected shapes in modern experience, including their predominantly affective emphasis and low cognitive content. Rather, for both Luther and Las Casas (who was forty at the time of his conversion), the focus is interior and moral—on one's life stance toward ideas and practices that define one's culture as the very thing it is. For Las Casas, centering a history of the Spanish New World on himself is analogous to the medieval *mappa mundi*, which seeks not to symbolize the world with mathematical precision in two dimensions but to reveal the sacred orientation of the world—with Jerusalem in the east, for example, not because Jerusalem "is there" but for the same reason that church altars are in the east: that is a sacred direction. Las Casas' conversion in 1514 was, for him, the primary indicator of sacred direction in the course of events in the New World. Formally, Las Casas' *Historia* thus bears comparison with Dante's *Commedia*, which also puts its author's experience (a conversion described in the journey of a fictitious pilgrim) at the center of a universal history that constructs a symbolic cosmos. Both Luther and Las Casas (Dante too, for that matter) show the strong impression of late medieval scholasticism as well. Las Casas' meticulous account of how he deduced principles from natural and divine law and applied them to events he witnessed is a succinct description of scholastic deductive procedure, which also helps to account for his somewhat dry intellectualism. Again, the fact that both Luther and Las Casas were deeply impressed by Saint Augustine helps to explain the similarity of their experiences. Augustine's dramatic *conversio* in *Confessions* 8 has many of the features we have seen in Las Casas, including the intellectualism, the meditation on sacred texts, and the translation of what is perceived to be a sacred encounter into life-reorienting action with unstoppable momentum.

Yet when all the relevant cultural factors have been considered, Las Casas' conversion remains somehow irreducible. An event whose consequences are so contrary to cultural continuity is *ipso facto* difficult to explain entirely in terms of cultural continuity. In any case, Las Casas' resistance clearly does not fit the dominant cultural paradigm of imperial expansion and control. His attempts at practical reform in 1520 and 1543 met with complete failure and left him deeply discouraged, not merely because the reforms were inadequate or ill conceived but because he was struggling against such overwhelming opposition. However radical the reorientation of his own life may have been, Las Casas was unable to persuade others that they should reorient theirs in the same way. Material interests, social structure, and an ideology backed with formidable learning in defense of both proved to be an unbeatable combination. This is not to say that Las Casas was deficient in learning himself, for he was an accomplished scholar who read widely, thought incisively, and conducted himself with effective political acumen as the officially appointed protector of the Indians during the last two decades of his life. His public debate with Sepulveda in 1550 (when Las Casas was seventy-six) reveals an intelligent, alert, and learned mind. Indeed, Las Casas was sufficiently forceful that a royal order was issued forbidding the publication or sale of Sepulveda's book in the New World. Yet this did little to assist the people Las Casas had ably defended. As Lewis Hanke remarks, Las Casas' ideas were simply too radical: the Spanish crown could not promulgate them "without provoking a revolution in America."[6] The age of revolution was still more than two centuries away.

No matter how radical Las Casas may appear to be, however, he is an unlikely herald of emergent rationalism.[7] The title of Hanke's book, *All Mankind Is One*, is a quotation from Las Casas, and the idea looks promising for liberal humanitarianism—that is why Hanke chose it. But Las Casas actually had a very deficient sense of human equality, no sense of progress, and an uncritical acceptance of royal power in Spain. Moreover, he had no material motive for his conversion: as a member of the upper class in the New World he was wealthy and powerful, and as a member of the intelligentsia, he was steeped in the ideology that perpetuated the system he worked untiringly to dismantle throughout the second half of his life. He was not racially, economically, or politically marginalized; on the contrary, the decision he came to regarding native peoples was a direct threat to the prosperity and privilege he enjoyed, as Velázquez sternly warned him. Las Casas' perception of astonishment and fear in his auditors when he first preached his radical ideas suggests that he might have understood Marx's famous dictum about religion being the drug of the people, yet Las Casas' change of heart was profoundly religious itself, as we have seen. Moreover, he was slow to realize the implications of his own ideas. His 1516 proposals for political reform in the New World provided for every Spanish colonist to own black slaves, as Spaniards had done in the Old World since the defeat of the Moors. Only much later did Las Casas recognize the inconsistency of liberating Indians and providing for the continued enslavement of blacks. His slowness to realize this point highlights his relative myopia regarding the Old World. No matter how radical his proposals were for New Spain, they had no carryover to Spain itself. Las Casas' effectiveness in the latter part of his life derived from his loyalty to the crown and ability to work within a system that he had no thought of changing. He would not have been at home in the age of revolution anyway.

What I want to suggest in this book is that Las Casas' ambiguous resistance to centralized power is not unique in the Renaissance; rather, it represents an important residual tradition in European culture. Indeed, Las Casas' experience is a paradigm for a particular kind of experience that we can also find on the Elizabethan scene, especially in Shakespeare, and especially when Shakespeare's heritage in medieval religious drama is given serious attention. I am not proposing that Shakespeare is a religious playwright, as Las Casas is clearly a religiously motivated reformer. Rather, I am proposing that the paradigm Las Casas represents is a more credible explanation for political power in Shakespearean drama than the model that regards this period as the gestation of emergent materialism. Shakespeare's relation to medieval religious drama is important, as I shall argue, because the dramatic enactment of political power and social privilege by Shakespeare's predecessors manifests many of the same anomalies that we have seen in Las Casas and that are still at work in a poet like John Milton. Shakespeare's sensibility is very different from that of his predecessors, of course, and it is very different from Milton's, but what I am attempting to elucidate in the following pages are not so much the differences that are apparent to everyone but a shared continuity that has not been adequately recognized or understood.

The sources and motives of cultural resistance are complex and varied in any period, and this includes the Renaissance, but for Las Casas the most important direct source is Saint Augustine, who is indirectly the most important source for Shakespeare as well. We noticed that Augustine's conversion was a formative precedent to those of Luther and Las Casas, but Augustine also serves to reveal profound differences between the two reformers. For Las Casas took from Augustine practically his whole motive for translating religious experience into social and political action, whereas Luther was largely blind to this dimension of Augustine.[8] (Among European reformers, Calvin comes closest to Las Casas in this regard.)[9] To be sure, Augustine's staunch advocacy of imperial coercion in ecclesiastical affairs has earned him the reputation of a proto-Inquisitor, which makes him seem an unlikely source of inspiration for resistance to imperial expansion in the Renaissance.[10] There is no denying this dismal aspect of his episcopal administration in North Africa: it was a policy he adopted with increasing vigor over the course of time and maintained with undiminished certitude until his death. Indeed, his late *Retractiones* include a rejection of his earlier claim that Christ did nothing by force but only by persuading and admonishing; on the contrary, the old bishop asserts: Christ drove the money changers from the temple, and in a parable about the kingdom of God, Christ said, "Compel them to come in" (Brown, "Religious Coercion," p. 108).

To focus exclusively on Augustine's use and defense of coercion, however, is to ignore other aspects of Augustine that inspired Las Casas as he resisted the enslavement of Indians in the New World. From the privileged position of historical hindsight (which always carries a degree of moral hindsight with it), neither writer is wholly satisfactory, but whether their cups are half full or half empty is a matter of emphasis. Despite his advocacy of coercion, Augustine's mature political position in *The City of God* is anything but an idealization of imperial ambition. He is virtually unique in the ancient world in arriving at a generic sense of social and political order as defined by the struggle for power: "The city of this world ... aims at domination, which holds nations in enslavement, but is itself dominated by that very lust of domination."[11] This conception can certainly be faulted for its lack of an ameliorative principle in political life, but that lack must be understood in context. Augustine defines the Earthly City in the way he does because he is concerned to refute the classical conception of social and political life as the source of human perfectibility.[12] Such a conception dominates Plato's *Republic*, informs Aristotle's definition of the human being as "a political animal" (i.e., an animal who is designed to realize its full potential in the *polis*), and explains Cicero's definition of *res publica* in terms of justice (following Plato). Augustine's rejection of this conception explains his eloquent sarcasm in *The City of God* 4.4:

> Remove justice, and what are kingdoms but gangs of criminals on a large scale? What are criminal gangs but petty kingdoms? A gang is

a group of men under the command of a leader, bound by a compact of association, in which the plunder is divided according to an agreed convention.

If this villainy wins so many recruits from the ranks of the demoralized that it acquires territory, establishes a base, captures cities and subdues peoples, it then openly arrogates to itself the title of kingdom, which is conferred on it in the eyes of the world, not by the renouncing of aggression but by the attainment of impunity.

For it was a witty and a truthful rejoinder which was given by a captured pirate to Alexander the Great. The king asked the fellow, "What is your idea, in infesting the sea?" And the pirate answered, with uninhibited insolence, "The same as yours, in infesting the earth! But because I do it with a tiny craft, I'm called a pirate: because you have a mighty navy, you're called an emperor."

As David Brading points out, the Spanish translation of *The City of God* uses the same terminology in the passage just quoted that was used on the political scene in the New World: "leader" (Latin *princeps*) is *caudillo*; and "compact of association" (Latin *pactus societatis*) is *compañia*.[13] The passage would therefore have had special relevance to Las Casas, who cites it in relation to the New World in his memorial to the Council of the Indies in 1531.[14]

Augustine's dim view of political life cut both ways—not only against classical political conceptions but also against contemporary Christian claims that the Theodosian settlement would bring the kingdom of God to earth by combining the destinies of church and empire.[15] On the contrary, Augustine claimed, Rome at its best has never achieved more than an endless struggle for power (this is his point in surveying Roman history in books 2 to 4 of *The City of God*), and Rome can never hope to do more than that, no matter who rules it, because the struggle for power is inherent in political order. Taken at face value, such a position looks forward to Hobbes's explicit materialism, from which emerges a view of the human political situation that in some features resembles Augustine's.[16] Indeed, Augustine's demystifying survey of Roman history frequently goes beyond Hobbes in its anticipation of cultural materialism. Augustine sounds like Marx, for example, in his observation that Roman state religion was employed to contain subversion:

Take Romulus. The fulsome legend of his reception into heaven can look after itself! So can the tales of those Roman authors who allege that he was torn to pieces by the senators because of his brutality, and that someone by the name of Julius Proculus was suborned to say that Romulus had appeared to him and sent a command by him to the Roman people that he should be worshipped among the divinities; by this means, they say, the people, who had begun to swell in revolt against the senate, were restrained and subdued. (3.15)

Also in keeping with his demystifying aim are Augustine's observations about class struggle, which sometimes read like a background synopsis of *Coriolanus*, one of Jonathan Dollimore's setpiece examples of Shakespearean demystification:

> I am sick of recalling the many acts of revolting injustice which have disturbed the city's history; the powerful classes did their best to subjugate the lower orders, and the lower orders resisted—the leaders of each side motivated more by ambition for victory than by any ideas of equity and morality. (2.17)

One of Augustine's favorite rhetorical devices is to quote a Roman historian against Rome itself. Here, for example, he quotes Sallust to make his own point about class exploitation in the Roman republic—a period (Sallust had claimed) of "equity and just restraint in the government of the commonwealth":

> After that, the patricians reduced the plebians to the condition of slavery; they disposed of the lives and persons of the *plebs* in the manner of kings; they drove men from their lands; and with the rest of the people disenfranchised, they alone wielded supreme power.[17]

Despite Augustine's points of contact with modern materialist theory, one would be hard pressed to defend the thesis that materialism is emergent in Augustine. It makes much better sense to recognize the empirical cast of Augustine's political thought and to call it precisely what it is, namely, Christian political realism. For Augustine is skeptical of political order not because he is a materialist but because he rejects the perfectibility of human nature in any other context than the City of God. Since the citizens of that city are temporally inextricable from the citizens of the Earthly City, secular order can only be described empirically—not in terms of philosophical idealism (as in the classical tradition) or in terms of eschatalogy (as in the Christian imperialist tradition). Augustine's empiricism is admittedly deficient by modern standards, because he is interested only in the broad principles of the Earthly City, not in its details; nonetheless, he is capable of considerable political insight, as we have just seen. The most important principle that distinguishes the two Cities is what their citizens love, for identity, in Augustine's view, is shaped by desire (here his neo-Platonism is at work). If power and wealth are what we want, then we define ourselves in terms of those things, in however large or small a sphere—whether in world conquest, or piracy, or merely in personal relationships. Unlike Freud, who sees civilization as the containment of *libido*, Augustine sees *libido* itself as constituting such social order as we know, and that is not very much, nor can it, by the nature of the case, be any more. If we desire more than the Earthly City provides, then we define ourselves in terms of that desire too, but it can only be fulfilled in the City of God and only if what we really desire is God, the love for whom is not *libido* but *caritas*.

Augustine's political view is a minority opinion from the outset, and it is therefore more accurately described as residual political realism than emergent rationalism. His view remains vital in residual form throughout the Middle Ages, acquiring particular force in religious drama, as we shall see in chapter 2. The rediscovery of Aristotle in the late Middle Ages produced Saint Thomas's political theory, which can with considerable accuracy be called Christian idealism, especially in contrast to Augustine.[18] For Augustine does not regard political dominance as "natural"; it is purely a consequence of human evil. In their natural condition, which Augustine imagines as a prehistorical reality, human beings lived in peace with each other, with God, and with the world around them. What enabled this pacific society was its obedience to God, who had established the principles of social maintenance. When Adam and Eve violated these principles, however, they destroyed the fabric of what was, in Augustine's view, the only natural society human beings have ever known, introducing the struggle for power by imitating Satan's attempt to dominate the universe in God's place. *Libido dominandi* then manifested itself almost at once in human society when Cain murdered Abel. For Augustine, then, political order might be said to be postnatural, or subnatural, and political relationships are designed merely to contain the chaotic human lust for power and property—even as they express those lusts and therefore deserve just censure. Augustine, in short, would have understood Walter Benjamin's remark (though he would have explained it very differently): "There is no document of civilization which is not at the same time a document of barbarism."[19]

Saint Thomas, in contrast, under the influence of Aristotle, reintroduced a large measure of classical idealism about the state into Christian thought and went much further than Augustine in explaining political life as a natural good. This change of emphasis looks forward to the Renaissance revival of the classical notion that the purpose of government is to foster virtuous citizens—"to fashion a gentleman in virtuous and noble discipline," as Spenser puts it in describing his purpose as a poet serving the monarch. In drama, this conception lay dormant until the Platonic revival and the centralization of power combined to produce a thoroughgoing idealist interpretation of power—a development that reached its esthetic apex almost simultaneously in early Italian opera and the Stuart court masque. The immediate effect of Aquinas's new emphasis was to reclaim the state as a semiredemptive natural agency in its own right and thereby to move further in the direction of idealizing the existing social and political order than Augustine's theories had allowed. This effect is evident, for example, in Dante's *De monarchia*, a Ghibelline idealization of temporal power, and in Dante's vision of the Holy Roman Empire in the *Paradiso*.

Augustine's analysis of secular power illustrates how much the residual and the emergent resemble each other in the Renaissance. In any given case, we may be looking at a strain of Christian political realism going back to Augustine or at a nascent rationalism that looks forward to the Enlightenment. In the case of Las Casas the two are relatively easy to distinguish: despite his claim that "all men are one," he has very little in common with eighteenth-century egalitarianism, while his debt to Augustine is explicit and direct. Later in the sixteenth century the distinction is not so clear. New voices that advocate rebellion against tyrants would appear to look forward to Locke and the Glorious Revolution; at least, one can find no justification for such a position in Augustine, who formulates the often repeated argument that all rulers are to be endured, not resisted, because they are part of God's plan for constraining human wickedness.[20] But when one looks closely at a classic sixteenth-century text like Philippe de Mornay's *Vindicae contra tyrannos* (1579), one has a disorienting sense of double vision. For De Mornay has a clear notion of the supremacy of law (inherited from early Germanic kingship), but his way of thinking about it is indelibly theological:

> So often, therefore, as any prince shall so much forget himself, as insolently to say in his heart, I will ascend into heaven, I will exalt my throne above the stars of God; I will sit upon the mount of the congregation in the sides of the north; I will ascend above the heights of the clouds, I will be like the Most High: then, on the contrary, will the Almighty say, I will rise up more high, I will set myself against thee; I will erase thy name and all thy posterity, thy counsels shall vanish into smoke, but that which I have once determined shall remain firm, and never be annihilated.[21]

Where one might expect to find a rationalist cast of mind, one in fact finds an adaptation of Augustine's argument about the fall of Lucifer. For De Mornay here borrows an argument that was the linchpin of Augustine's theodicy: what God made was perfectly good until Lucifer willfully displayed archetypal *libido dominandi* (*City of God* 11 and 12). De Mornay's description of the tyrant is laced with allusions to Isa. 14:12–14, which patristic commentators (including Augustine) had construed as an account of Lucifer's rebellion.[22] A similar description is advanced by Fulke Greville, whose intellectual radicalism has recently been pointed out by David Norbrook and Jonathan Dollimore.[23] Perhaps in echo of De Mornay, Greville also describes resistance to tyrants in neo-Augustinian terms: "tyrants be not nursing fathers but step-fathers *and so no appointed deputies of God*, but rather lively images of the dark Prince, that sole author of discreation and disorder, who ever ruins his ends with overbuilding."[24] This is a clever passage, because Greville buries his heterodox denial that tyrants are divinely appointed in his description of an expedition Sidney planned to the New World, supposedly with the aim of doing better by the Indians than detestable Spanish tyrants had done. Nonetheless, Greville's message is undeniably radical where tyrants are concerned, and the radicalism derives from a slight adjustment in standard arguments drawn from residual Christian realism.

The vitality of Augustine's political ideas in the sixteenth century can best be understood against the dominant ideology of centralized power. Augustine had formulated his demystifying description of the Earthly City against the background of a similar ideology, namely that of the late Roman Empire, whose imminent demise was by no means so clear to contemporaries as it is to us. When centralized power again became fashionable and successful in the Renaissance, the quest to establish hegemony led to a search for justifications of power that were less ambiguous than Augustine's. In this context, Saint Thomas's arguments made greater sense, but even more appealing was the precedent of Rome itself and the ideology that had supported Roman dominance. That the so-called rebirth of learning in the Renaissance was primarily Latin rather than Greek is no coincidence, because Latin was the language of ancient Rome and therefore invested with unsurpassed prestige in the new cultural context. It is no coincidence, either, that apologists for the Tudor regime revived conceptions like Dante's of the Holy Roman Empire, as they sought to defend the Elizabethan settlement.[25] Conversely, Las Casas relied heavily on Augustine in opposing the legitimacy of Roman power, as he answered Francisco de Vitoria's argument that the precedent of Rome sanctioned Spanish conquest in the New World.[26] Given the rising prestige of Roman culture in the Renaissance, the resemblance between Augustine and Hobbes need not be the result of direct influence: it might well be the consequence of two observant realists working in very similar circumstances. Both lived in states with nearly absolute centralized power; for both, that power was bolstered with an idealist religious ideology (specifically Platonic in inspiration); and both read the same histories of Roman power and its profound ambiguities.

What I hope to do in the following pages is to establish Shakespeare's access to Augustinian political realism through his medieval dramatic heritage. My argument, in brief, is that Shakespeare's debt to that heritage enables us to understand his plays as informed no less credibly by residual political realism than by a putatively emergent materialism. Before turning directly to that argument, however, I would like to consider briefly the case of More's *Utopia*, not as a direct parallel to Shakespeare but as another instance of Augustine's enduring vitality in the sixteenth century and the consequent difficulty of distinguishing residual Christian realism from nascent rationalism.

What makes More particularly relevant here, of course, is his vision of a propertyless society, which has long been claimed by some modern interpreters as a herald of socialist materialism. There is no denying that More's concept anticipates ideas that emerged three centuries later, but a close look at More suggests that he is not much more promising than his Spanish contemporary, Bartolomé de las Casas, as a visionary materialist. To begin with, like Las Casas, More was directly and explicitly indebted to Augustine. Indeed, More first came to the attention of European humanists as a result of his lectures on *The City of God*, delivered at St. Lawrence Jewry in response to the invitation of the rector, William Grocyn, while More was studying law at Lincoln's Inn in the late 1490s. More's most recent biographer is emphatic about Augustine's influence on More: "Augustine was always his favorite saint, the writer who more than anyone else influenced the shaping of his mind. He knew Augustine almost by heart, and *The City of God* is more often quoted in his works than anything else in the Augustinian corpus."[27] What Augustine has to say about justice would have been particularly important to More as a law student, and it may have shaped his view in *Utopia*, written about fifteen years later. More's realistic pessimism about the political situation in contemporary Europe is very much in the spirit of Augustine's favorite comparison: the kingdom as a band of robbers. Certainly the *Utopia* evinces very little of the growing idealization of the monarchy that would eventually become Tudor orthodoxy:

> When I consider and turn over in my mind the state of the commonwealths flourishing anywhere today, so help me God, I can see nothing else than a kind of conspiracy of the rich, who are aiming at their own interests under the name and title of the commonwealth. They invent and devise all ways and means by which, first, they may keep without fear of loss all that they have amassed by evil practices and, secondly, they may then purchase as cheaply as possible and abuse the toil and labor of all the poor.[28]

Nor is it clear from the *Utopia* that More believes much can be done to change the situation: like Las Casas, More embarked on a career of political action, but the realities of centralized power quickly impressed themselves on his reforming zeal, as they did on that of his New World contemporary, and More's reforming vision may be no more than a vision, as his ascribing it to an imaginary philosopher suggests. Whether a real philosopher can make a difference in the real world is not so clear.[29]

In the face of Hythlodaeus' argument that philosophers waste their time in serving kings, "More's" counter claim for ameliorative political action is minimal: "What you cannot turn to good you must make as little bad as you can."[30] In *The City of God*, Augustine also confronts "the philosophers" (in this case the Stoics) on the question of public service in the interest of justice (19.6). While he does not imagine their refusing to serve (as More does with Hythlodaeus), Augustine claims they would compound injustice with ignorance born of false confidence, and he contrasts their attitude with one that strikingly anticipates More's ambivalence about social amelioration, in the imagined dispute between Hythlodaeus and "More":

> How much more mature reflection it shows, how much more worthy of a human being it is when one acknowledges this necessity [for public service] as a mark of human wretchedness, when he hates that necessity in his own actions and when, if he has the wisdom of devotion, he cries out to God, "Deliver me from my necessities!" (19.6)

Honestly to accept public service as an imposed necessity (as More seems prepared to accept it in *Utopia*) is the surest way not to seize it out of the lust for power. But the honesty, of course, is between the public servant and the God he cries out to, for even the reluctant acceptance of secular office can be cleverly pretended, as More demonstrates in his life of Richard III, whose display of cunning political dissimulation inspired Shakespeare's memorable play on the last Plantagenet king.

What, then, of More's proposal regarding communal ownership? The motive for abolishing private property is actually much clearer in *Utopia* than the advocacy of communal reform. "More" and Hythlodaeus agree that the competition for private property is a primary source of social evil: in J. H. Hexter's memorable sentence, "It is the rich black rottenness in which man's sins most abundantly flourish."[31] Only Hythlodaeus advocates abolishing private property, however, and he refuses to put his proposal into action, while "More" finds it incredible. The point on which the interlocutors agree, then, is human greed, and that in itself is hardly a revolutionary insight. Augustine had long since argued that the desire for property is closely related to the desire for power as a defining characteristic of human social relations.[32] More almost certainly follows Plato in citing private property as the root of social injustice, but he may well have been drawn to Plato in the first place because of what he saw in contemporary England. R. H. Tawney pointed out many years ago that the exploding market economy of the late Middle Ages fostered a new goal of individual prosperity and seriously undermined the communal assumptions that had dominated the medieval sense of social cohesion until the Black Death produced serious demographic upheavals and new opportunities for private ownership and individual wealth.[33] For More, in other words, Plato's communist aristocracy may well have been another example of the pagan philosopher's anticipating Christian ideals that More himself affirmed. Theodore DeWelles relates the innovative expectation of private ownership in the fifteenth century to the Towneley *Mactatio Abel* and its depiction of Cain as a grasping, assertive, and industrious peasant: "The playwright goes beyond mere convention and turns his protagonist into something quite unique in medieval literature—a hard-working, not a lazy 'bad' peasant."[34] The old communal ideal can be seen at work again in opposition to private ownership in Bartolomé de las Casas' proposals for reform in the New World, where land is to be held in common by Spaniards and Indians. (The Indians had been admired from the beginning as embodiments of the Golden Age ideal for their lack of a sense of ownership. Amerigo Vespucci praises them in these terms, and Peter Martyr writes in *De orbo novo* [1530]: "It is proven that amongst them the land belongs to everybody, just as does the sun or the water. They know no difference between *meum* and *tuum*, that source of all evil.")[35] As we noticed earlier, Las Casas' proposals for reform in New Spain are exactly contemporary with *Utopia*, and More's format of the traveller's tale was almost certainly influenced by idealistic reports coming back from the New World.

In context, then, More's communist proposal appears to look backward at least as much as it looks forward, if not more so. Hexter claims that it has more affinity with Enlightenment egalitarianism than with radical socialism, and he thus illustrates, again, the difficulty of distinguishing the residual from the emergent in the Renaissance.[36] Yet the distinction can, I think, be made in More's case. Augustine's realism defines the temporal *saeculum* as that which needs to be taken with instrumental seriousness: one cannot simply dismiss it, but one should only engage it as a means to something better, which is temporally unrealizable, i.e., the City of God. More's secular proposal is consistent with this conception: he offers it tentatively, ironically—perhaps merely as a vision—and he accompanies it with the skeptical reminder that real political engagement can only restrain evil, not promote goodness. An ameliorative proposal made in this spirit is quite foreign to the optimistic secular rationalism of the Enlightenment. Augustinian realism is both more pessimistic and more radical than later philosophical rationalism. After all, many of the *philosophes* were more content in the service of absolute monarchs than More was, and Thomas Jefferson, for one, would have been happier with Juan de Sepulveda's defense of slavery as a natural institution than with Las Casas' defense of abolishing slavery. More's inclinations were ascetic, as his four years in the London Charterhouse, his hair shirt, and his late wish for a "strait room" all indicate. These inclinations point to his close identification with monastic ideals and probably suggest a resulting ambivalence about the source of his own success in a turbulent new world of rapidly changing values.[37] His refusal to turn his resistance against tyranny into political action is certainly consistent with Augustine, just as More's death is consistent with an instrumental view of the *saeculum*—neither refusing its claims nor regarding it with ultimate seriousness.

Whatever influence Augustine may have had on More, it was certainly very different for Shakespeare, who never went to university or studied at the Inns of Court and who remained in a lower social stratum than More all his life. In that stratum, however, Shakespeare had indirect access to Augustine's political realism through the popular dramatic tradition, whether he read *The City of God* or not. For medieval religious drama, both liturgical and vernacular, is a principal repository of the residual realism that originates with Augustine. Before turning directly to Shakespeare, it will therefore be necessary to consider how medieval religious playwrights enacted power and social relations. Their example is richly transmuted in Shakespearean drama, as we shall see, but Shakespeare's qualified affirmation of social privilege in the late sixteenth and early seventeenth centuries cannot be properly understood apart from his medieval dramatic inheritance.

CHAPTER 2 ❧ LIBIDO DOMINANDI AND POTENTIA HUMILITATIS: *THE MEDIEVAL DRAMATURGY OF POWER*

When one thinks of medieval attempts to stage political power, the first image that comes to mind is the ranting Herod, and it is instructive to realize that Shakespeare's few overt references to medieval drama include two allusions to this character. True, Shakespeare's portraits of tyranny far surpass their medieval forbear in complexity and psychological subtlety, and both his allusions to Herod are derisive—one in Hamlet's advice to the players, the other in Mistress Page's characterization of Falstaff's rhetoric. Nonetheless, Herod's impressive theatricality is what both allusions register, and if Shakespeare saw the Coventry mystery plays—as he could easily have done any number of times before he was sixteen—he would have witnessed the liveliest and most memorable of the Herods, whose stage direction tells him to rage "in the pagond and in the strete also."[1] Moreover, Herod is part of a pattern of power and social privilege in medieval drama, and it is this pattern, rather than any particular ranting tyrant, that illuminates Shakespeare's own way of enacting power in drama.

The theme on which Herod plays variations can be stated simply, but it has multiple implications, many of them complex and profound: Herod's power makes him God's enemy, while the friends of God, who possess spiritual and cosmic strength, are nearly always marked by disfranchisement and social deprivation. To be sure, the plays contain examples of social privilege on God's side (the three kings who visit the Christ child, for example, or King David, who appears occasionally in the *ordo prophetarum*), but the stated humility of such characters identifies them spiritually with the majority of God's friends, whose humility is also social. In this dramatic tradition, certainly the most spectacular and memorable examples of power and privilege belong to the pattern Herod manifests. Herod himself is already *furor accensus* in the eleventh-century Christmas drama from Fleury, where his enmity with God emerges in his arrogant and jealous reaction to the wise men's news of the Incarnation.[2] "Bid, O father, your son / To begin this combat," begs Herod's bellicose offspring (73–74), in pointed contrast to the peasants who greet each other pacifically in response to the angels' announcement that a new reign of peace has arrived (1–10). "God resists the proud, but he gives grace to the humble," Augustine recalls (quoting James 4:6) in the preface to *The City of God*, and his comment can be taken as a gloss on the Fleury Christmas play:

> I know how great is the effort needed to convince the proud of the power and excellence of humility, an excellence which makes it soar above all the summits of this world, which sway in their temporal instability, overtopping them all with an eminence not arrogated by human pride, but granted by divine grace.[3]

The portrait of the powerful in medieval religious drama is in fact constructed on the principles of the City of Humankind, as Augustine describes it. Herod's jealousy of the Christ child expresses his essential *libido dominandi*—his inability to tolerate rivalry. The same motive animates other kings—Getron (in the Fleury Nicholas play), Pharaoh, Pilate, Caesar—as well as powerful ecclesiastics, such as Caiaphas and Annas or the abstraction Archisynagogus in the Benediktbeuern Christmas Play, and even the relationship of peasant brothers, like Cain and Abel. Although Cain lacks Herod's scope for exercising power, he nonetheless defines himself by his obsession with power and wealth in the circumscribed world of the primal family. His portrait is developed with particular brilliance in the Towneley *Mactatio Abel*, where Cain's apocryphal servant, Pikeharnes, primarily functions to highlight his master's tyranny, while Abel's openness and generosity clarify Cain's comic tight-fistedness. "Anyone whose aim was to glory in the exercise of power," Augustine writes in *The City of God*,

> would obviously enjoy less power if his sovereignty was diminished by a living partner. Therefore, in order that the sole power should be wielded by one person, the partner was eliminated; and what would have been kept smaller and better by innocence grew through crime into something bigger and worse. (15.6)

In this passage he is discussing Romulus' murder of Remus—an archetype, as he says, of Roman political relationships. But he immediately turns to Cain and Abel with this comment:

> Thus the quarrel that arose between Remus and Romulus demonstrated the division of the earthly city against itself; *while the conflict between Cain and Abel displayed the hostility between the two cities themselves, the City of God and the City of Humankind.* (15.6, my emphasis)

Understanding power in the English mystery plays is also facilitated by Augustine's account of how evil entered the cosmos with the revolt of Satan, an episode in cosmic theology that was first systematically explained in books 11 and 12 of *The City of God*, as we noticed in chapter 1. Augustine adumbrates Satan's revolt at considerable length for two principal reasons: he makes it the starting point of his historical theodicy, and he uses it to demystify the claim that Roman power had been sanctioned by the gods of Rome, since Augustine maintains that all pagan gods are merely Satan and his revolted angels in disguise—for him, they are the real mechanism, as it were, behind pagan mythologies of power. We have glimpsed this argument briefly in De Mornay and Greville on tyranny, and Milton uses it later with Stuart tyranny in mind in *Paradise Lost*. The same reading of Augustine is implicit in medieval drama, for Satan's challenge to God is manifestly a primordial expression of *libido dominandi*, and Satan is therefore the paradigm for citizens in the City of Humankind: all those who desire power for its own sake are ironically assimilated to Satan. Augustine thus distinguishes the two companies of angels by their desire, as he distinguishes the citizens of the heavenly and earthly cities:

> The one company burns with holy love of God; the other smoulders with the foul desire for its own exaltation; and since "God resists the proud, while he gives grace to the humble," the one dwells in the heaven of heavens, the other is cast down in confusion to inhabit this air, the lowest region of the sky. The one enjoys tranquillity in the bright radiance of devotion; the other rages in the dark shadows of desire. The one brings merciful aid, or just punishment, in obedience to God's bidding; the other seethes with the lust to subdue and to injure, at the behest of its own arrogance. (11.33)

Satan's lust to subdue is dramatized in the cycle plays by the simple device of having him literally usurp God's throne, while God is momentarily "absent." "I am now set as ye may see," Lucifer declares in the N-Town play,

> Now wurchyp me for most my[g]hty,
> And for your lord honowr now me
> Sitting in my sete.[4]

"If that ye will behold me right," Lucifer argues in the Towneley cycle, "This mastré longys to me ... Agans my grete myght / May [no]thyng stand [ne] be."[5]

"Devil with devil damned firm compact holds," Milton comments in *Paradise Lost*, echoing the *pactus societatis* of *City of God* 4.4 and expressing an essentially Augustinian sense of political community as defined by common desire—the same sense that governs the portrayal of demons in the mystery cycles. In this regard, too, the fallen angels model

social relations in the City of Humankind: both have the same coherence that characterizes a band of robbers, and for both this peculiar coherence identifies the lust for power with enmity against God. Cain's
hatred of Abel and Herod's hatred of the Christ child thus have a generic
affinity not only with each other but with Satan's usurpation of God's
throne and with demonic resistance to the harrowing of hell. This affinity becomes identity in the Doomsday plays, when the devils' well-prac-
ticed understanding of power relations enables them to detect their human compatriots with alacrity. "Thise rolles / Ar of bakbitars / And fals
quest-ditars," exclaims Secundus Demon in the Towneley *Judgment*,
"Faithe and Trowth, ma fay, has no fete to stande; / The poore pepyll
must pay, if oght be in hande" (183–90).

A specifically Augustinian moment occurs in the N-Town play of
Lucifer's fall, when Lucifer suddenly discovers the limitations of his unexpected incarnation:

> Now to helle the way I take,
> In endeles peyn ther to be pyht. *pight, pitched*
> For fere of fyre a fart I crake,
> In helle donjoon myn dene is dyth. *den / made ready*
> (79–82)

That powerful emotion (in this case fear) prompts involuntary physical
response is an insight that depth psychology affirms and should be able
to respect in so archaic a context. But the origin of the insight is not
Freud but Augustine, who argues that the bodies of fallen creatures have
incurred the penalty of losing voluntary self-control. The unfallen bodies
of Adam and Eve, in contrast, were subject to perfect volition, with the
result that sexual relations, for example, were never troubled by passion
(14.23).[6] (This is an argument that Milton rejects in *Paradise Lost*, in
favor of a more complex portrait of unfallen perfection.) With regard to
the particular loss of volition that Satan comically suffers in the N-
Town cycle, Augustine asserts that his argument about the power of the
unfallen will in Paradise is not incredible, since imperfect vestiges of it
may still be seen. He cites those who can wriggle their ears, move their
scalp, imitate the cries of animals, or sweat whenever they choose. "A
number of people," he concludes triumphantly, "produce at will such
musical sounds from their behind (without any stink) that they seem to
be singing from that region" (14.24). The N-Town Lucifer clearly has not
been blessed with this particular vestige of prelapsarian willpower.

As the demons model citizenship in the City of Humankind, then,
so the unfallen angels model citizenship in the City of God by their defining qualities: gratitude to God, obedience, and humility. These are
the same qualities that define all the human protagonists in the English
mystery cycles—with the important addition of powerlessness and social deprivation in the majority of cases. Their archetype, of course, is

Christ, "whose weakness resulted from his power," as Augustine puts it (14.9). Material weakness thus becomes an emblem of spiritual strength, a paradox that bestows an unexpected dignity on the socially marginal and dispossessed—unexpected, that is, in a culture whose rigid social hierarchy had overwhelming religious sanction. "Humility is highly prized in the City of God," Augustine explains, "and especially enjoined on the City of God during the time of its pilgrimage in this world; and it receives particular emphasis in the character of Christ, the king of that City" (14.13). The power of this king is what Augustine calls *potentia humilitatis*, and Christ's display of his power in his victimization by tyrants represents an important vindication of others who are victimized in the same way. That God humanly suffered like a criminal and outcast is crucial to understanding the mystery plays' sympathetic attitude to the peasantry and their openness to elements of popular folk culture that were otherwise marginal and suppressed in a hierarchical society. To read the suffering Christ as a masochist, in Dollimore's terms, is not only to psychologize character where characterization is virtually irrelevant but also to miss the social message encoded in the potent image of a crucified peasant.[7]

Recognizing how power is symbolized in medieval drama clarifies the residual tradition it belongs to. From a materialist perspective, the cultivation of obedience and humility is a transparent mystification of hierarchical power relations, supporting the feudal social structure and discouraging amelioration. Such a viewpoint is bound to identify the plays with the dominant feudal pattern.[8] Images of suffering preempt solutions to the causes of suffering, identifying them only with the moral failure of the wealthy to share with the poor. The Towneley *Second Shepherds Play* can be taken as a pertinent example. As everyone recognizes, this pageant treats fifteenth-century peasants with a deeply sympathetic realism, protesting the heavy tax burden of the poor, the violence of the wealthy, the repressive custom of "maintenance," and low wages deliberately paid late—altogether "perhaps the most poignant protest against oppression in medieval English literature," as Arnold Williams calls it.[9] Both the Towneley shepherds' plays are famous, too, for embracing elements of popular folk culture: in this and in their social realism they exemplify the medieval dramatic impulse to identify the humility of Christ with the humblest elements of contemporary society. Yet the spiritualized understanding of Jesus' declaration to Pilate lies heavy on these plays, as it does on all medieval religious drama: "My kingdom is not of this world."[10] Christ's humble kingship in medieval drama is a model of citizenship in the City of God, but a citizen's material privileges are all deferred, and the best one can do in the earthly city is to recognize its limitations and try to minimize them by submitting to the political status quo, as Christ did, no matter how unjust it might be. Power relations in religious drama are effectively summarized in one sentence by Augustine: "In this wicked world and in these evil times, the Church through her present humiliation is preparing future exaltation" (18.49). "[May] he kepe you fro wo," Mary tells the shepherds at the end of the *Second Shepherd's Play*, thus unburdening the long list of their real woes onto the baby they have come to worship and thereby producing a luminous moment of insight into the significance of this pageant. Yet no word is spoken about how the social institutions that have produced these woes might be changed to the real benefit of those who suffer.

What a materialist critique reveals, then, is the extent to which religion in medieval drama takes away with its left hand what it gives with its right, thus illustrating Marx's thesis that religion acts on behalf of existing power as an instrument for containing subversion. Medieval drama is in fact open to the charge that it is an unusually sophisticated example of repression at work: it invites sympathetic identification with the victims of social deprivation only to deny any redress of their wrongs, with the result that subversive potential is palliated so that it can be contained. In his sociological study of the English Corpus Christi plays, Mervyn James registers surprise at their "ridiculing of authority" and their elements "of unrestrained and coarse humour, of satire and criticism."[11] His suspicion that these aspects of the plays are muted expressions of social discontent stops short of a thoroughgoing materialist analysis. For if the plays exist to affirm the social body, as James argues, then their expressly subversive sentiments ultimately serve their central purpose. The opposition is allowed a voice only to sedate it and finally to overwhelm it with the total vision of corporate social wholeness that the procession and the pageant aim to celebrate.

While identifying medieval religious drama with the dominant cultural paradigm is theoretically elegant, it offers little foothold for commentary on the plays. For if what appears to be social protest is taken as a sophisticated form of social affirmation, then this drama is univocal, and one can say little more about it than that. If, on the other hand, the plays' social protest is regarded as culturally residual, then the form of their resistance needs to be identified and explained. As I have been suggesting, the plays are illuminated by a tradition of Augustinian political realism. At the center of all the English mystery plays—literally and thematically at the center—is the Magnificat, a gathering of statements about God's vindication of the oppressed from centuries of ancient Hebrew tradition:

Myght in his armes [God] wroght,
And destroyed in his thoght
Prowde men and high berand.
Myghty men furth of sete he dyd,
And he hyghtynd in that stede

The meke men of hart;
The hungry with all good he fyld,
And left the rich out shyld,   *shelled out, empty*
Them to unquart.[12]   *harass, render harmless*

Despite the rampant anti-Semitism of medieval religious drama, it ironically emphasizes a viewpoint produced by the realities of Jewish suffering and social marginalization. Mary's song borrows heavily from Hannah's in 1 Sam. 2:1–10, which in turn belongs to a long ancient Hebrew
tradition that God especially favors the poor and oppressed.[13] Augustine's notion of *potentia humilitatis* thus represents a perceptive reading
of Christianity's Jewish heritage, even if Augustine's hermeneutic is itself allegorical in emphasis, not historical.

While the idea that humility engages cosmic power can be dismissed as the ultimate form of religious false consciousness, then, it
should be assessed in light of its actual effects, not merely for its theoretical merits—or demerits—as an account of power relations. One of
these effects is religious drama's marked deemphasis on the virtues of a
"natural" social hierarchy. We noticed in chapter 1 that Augustine's political realism and his conception of power relations as "unnatural"
eventually gave way to late medieval idealizations of political order and
the Thomistic argument that vestiges of the divine plan are evident in
nature, including "natural" hierarchical social and political relationships. In view of this shifting emphasis, what is noteworthy about medieval religious drama is that the image of power that impresses us, as it
appears to have impressed Shakespeare, is the image of insanely cruel
and raging tyranny, not of a cosmic natural hierarchy embracing and val-
orizing human society. In short, while the divine right of kings is a product of dominant medieval ideology, one would scarcely guess that fact
from medieval religious drama. Claims to social superiority always appear in struggles for power or in bombastic claims to absolute power. An
example of the latter is made by the Chester Octavian, who eventually
becomes one of the rare examples in these plays of Herod's opposite—a
good king. Octavian begins with a boastful claim to hierarchical power:

All this world, withowten were—
King, prynce, baron, batchlere—
I may destroy in great dangere
Through vertue of my degree.[14]

But Octavian becomes uncharacteristically troubled by his mortality
and eventually asks the sybil whether any earthly king will ever surpass
him. She answers with a prophecy of Christ's birth—a prophecy immediately fulfilled in the play's action, with Octavian incongruously look-

ing on (ostensibly seeing it in a vision). When he has witnessed it, he is a changed man, recognizing now that God is "most mighty":

> Sycker yt may non other be
> *But this child is prince of posty*　　　　　　　　　　　　*power*
> And I his subject, as I see.
> He is most worthy.
>
> (671–74, my emphasis)

What finally makes Octavian a good king is not prominence in the social hierarchy but his taking on the defining qualities of a citizen in the City of God: gratitude and obedience to God, exemplified in humility. Augustine's observation is apt: the power of Christ is *potentia humilitatis*. The effect, then, of including Octavian's conversion in a nativity play is to enact the quality of Christ's kingship, which makes bellicose claims to dominance in the earthly city appear empty by comparison. The consistent bombast of these claims is a rhetorical sign of their emptiness: an affected high style makes those who use it laughable, like Bottom the weaver, even when they are kings. If, as Sidney complains, the mingling of kings and clowns is indecorous, then much more indecorous is the religious drama's presentation of kings *as* clowns.

Medieval drama's fascination with larger-than-life tyrants has long been recognized, of course, but the social implications of that fascination have not been adequately dealt with. Herod is like the Chester Octavian not only in his style but in his claims to social and political superiority. The Coventry Herod asserts that he is the maker of heaven and hell and mystifies the trappings of rank with claims to life-giving power:

> My fawcun and my fassion, with my gorgis araye,　　　　*falcon*
> He that had the grace allwey theron to thynke,
> Lyve [he] might allwey withowt othur meat or drynke.
>
> (*Shearmen and Taylors*, 511–13)

All princes are beneath him, he claims (519), as the Chester Octavian does. The N-Town Herod cautions his courtiers that the social scale is challenged by news of Jesus' birth:

> I warn yow my knyghtes,
> A barne is born I plyghtys
> Wolde clymbyn kynge and kny[gh]tys
> And lett my lordly lay.
>
> (*Massacre of the Innocents*, 37–40)

His response to perceived subversion is to order the slaughter of the innocents—a hamfisted paradigm of containment. Thereafter he is able to dine in the contentment of having preserved the hierarchy: "Now am I sett at mete / and wurthely servyd at my degré" (155–56). The context of this claim makes it heavily ironic, since the scene concludes with Herod's sudden unexpected death and Mors's levelling observation:

> For all his boste of blysse ful bare
> He lyth now ded here on his syde.
>
> . . . .
>
> His lordchep is al lorn.
> Now is he as pore as I.
> Wormys mete is his body.
>   (248–55)

The irony of mortality is a reminder that power ultimately belongs to God, since Mors acknowledges God as his master (177–81). "Nothing is superior to God," Augustine argues, "and that is why humility exalts the mind by making it subject to God. Exaltation, in contrast, derives from a fault in character, and spurns subjection for that very reason. Hence it falls away from him who has no superior, and falls lower in consequence" (14.13). The culminating irony produced by Mors in the N-Town *Death of Herod* is therefore anticipated thematically by the slaughter of the innocents, for their suffering at the hands of tyranny is an emblem of *potentia humilitatis* and identifies them as friends of God. This point is explicit in the Fleury *Slaughter of the Innocents*, where the innocents follow the lamb and sing:

> To the hallowed lamb slain for us,
> To Christ, we consecrate, under this banner of light,
> The splendor of the Father, the splendor of the virgin birth.
> In order that we, whom the wrath of Herod seeks out by numerous
>   means,
> May be delivered by the lamb, we will die together with Christ.[15]

Whatever false consciousness may be at work in these plays, they make no attempt to justify power or its effects, while they offer the victims of a heavily repressive society a hopeful vision of cosmic vindication and a realistic rendering of power in comic caricature. Strictly speaking, the result is neither submissive nor subversive, since political power is viewed with profound skepticism (making the drama appear subversive) but with no hint of alternatives that might supplant existing structures (a lack that makes it seem submissive).[16]

   The actual effect of Augustine's residual realism in medieval drama is not only negative (in deemphasizing hierarchy) but also positive, in consistently accommodating contemporary political and social reality. This is not to say that religious drama is topical as that term has usually been applied. The traditional search for explicit political commentary in drama, or even for intentional allegorical commentary about politics, is too narrow. If ideology is "a cultural system," in Clifford Geertz's phrase, then symbolic expressions of ideology—intentional or otherwise—are enacted in every aspect of culture.[17] To regard plays as apolitical simply because they seem to be concerned only with the soul's destiny is, in effect, to regard them as devoid of ideology, which is a position few would be willing to defend.[18] What needs to be asked is not whether they are "political" but what kind of ideology they enact and therefore what kind of politics they symbolize. One virtue of this approach is that it reveals the same kind of continuity in drama that was characteristic of early modern culture as a whole. Rather than sacred culture suddenly giving way to secular, what we find is a gradual transformation of ideology that accompanies the transformation of social and political relations.

Let us take a specific example from the mystery plays. One of the most explicit dramatic descriptions of late medieval wealth and social aspiration appears in the N-Town *Passion Play 1*. The context of this description is Satan's prologue to the audience, as the fiend gloatingly prepares for his entrapment of Christ. In terms of abstract doctrine, or the mere dramatic rendering of biblical narrative, the social satire is irrelevant and unnecessary. Satan can make his point about planning to destroy the man who pretends to be God's son without having to refer to the fifteenth-century social scene. Yet pointed social satire comprises about two-thirds of what he says. The question, then, is what ideology is enacted in this scene, where biblical history is staged with complex theological interpretation built into it, as well as a large measure of satirical social realism. In the brief critical history of medieval drama, three ways of answering this question are discernible. The early twentieth-century "evolutionary" answer is that the drama was becoming secular, so that doctrine and social realism are in tension with one another, a tension that would eventually result in the flowering of secular drama in the sixteenth century.[19] This response was critically identified and refuted in a series of revisionist arguments beginning in the 1960s.[20] The revisionist position is that a better understanding of the plays' hermeneutical context (i.e., late medieval theology) reveals their "artistic integrity" from a Christian point of view. This revision has recently appeared to discredit itself with the advent of New Historicism, which has recuperated a more sophisticated version of the first response. For in retrospect, the theological revisionists are too closely tied to the ostensibly apolitical organicism of the New Criticism. Kolve's brilliant chapters on goodness and evil take "the creature we shall call natural man" as a univocal abstraction, as if the class differences repeatedly acknowledged in the drama itself did not exist.[21] "Order has to be imposed from above," Kolve remarks as a generalization about the plays (p. 212), and he describes Cain as "a creature cut off from God by his own unregenerate vitality" (p. 211), thus reading the drama from the perspective of the aristocratic high culture that determines the dominant voice in Elizabethan drama. New Historicism enables one to identify the tacit conservative commitment of this approach.

Yet New Historicism—as the phrase implies—demonstrates the continuing vitality of historicist thinking, for it reintroduces the old evolutionary argument that Hardison exposed as a nineteenth-century cultural vestige.[22] The most explicitly Marxist critics (Weimann and Cohen) have much in common with Chambers and Young, because Marxism is a classic form of nineteenth-century social evolution, and the determinism and developmental teleology of neo-Marxist critics are the tokens of their neoevolutionary approach, albeit devoid of the cultural triumphalism of early twentieth-century critics. Michael Bristol's Marxism is less explicit, but he identifies radical continuity in popular culture that manifests itself subversively in "clowning and devilment," of which the N-Town Satan is presumably an example.[23] In this view, dominant culture, represented by Christian orthodoxy, is at odds with residual popular culture and its strategies for enduring social marginalization and political oppression.

It may seem a hairsplitting distinction to insist that what is residual in medieval drama has more to do with Augustinian political realism than with popular culture, but in fact the difference is illuminating when one turns to the plays themselves. The N-Town Satan is a case in point. In his direct address to the audience, his exaggerated mimicry of courtly fashion, and his mere identity as a devil, this figure conforms precisely to what New Historicism would identify as a vestige of subversive popular culture in an otherwise theologically orthodox context. The dramaturgy of this Satan, in other words, would appear to be subversively at odds with the theology he ostensively represents. But such an analysis is problematic. For the N-Town Satan consistently displays all the hallmarks of aristocratic culture, not of popular culture. He describes his costume in detail, for example, and the description is that of a fifteenth-century courtier. Moreover, he "advises" his auditors about how to behave, and his advice is consistent with the materialism, social ambition, and defensive arrogance produced by the new wealth in the late Middle Ages: "thow it ryme nowth, / Yet loke that thou desire to an [own] the newe faccion. . . . loke thou make comparison / Unto all degrees daily that passe thin[e] astat. . . . And all beggerys and pore pepyll, have hem en despite" (*Passion Play 1*. 79–88).

The evil represented by Satan, then, seems to have the specifically innovative character of newly powerful privilege on the contemporary scene. The ideology that animates this devil for satirical purposes is arguably conservative, since it does not seem to reject authority per se, or the hierarchy of inherited privilege, or the traditional communal ideal.

Yet insofar as it challenges social privilege and de facto power, it has a clear affinity with the kind of residual realism one finds in *Utopia* or in Las Casas' *History of the Indies*. Similar concern about innovative social oppression is evident everywhere in the fifteenth century. Peter Idley, himself a defender of acquisitiveness and a beneficiary of the new wealth, nonetheless attacks new attitudes in terms that are identical to those of the N-Town Satan:

> Thow shalt fynde the fende full loose in the hafte
> If he may have the[e] under his dominacioun.
> He sheweth feire semblant of the new facion
> To bryng the[e] in by som pleasaunt baite;
> But ever to begile the[e] he lith in a wayte.[24]

The morality play, *Wisdom*, includes stage directions to indicate that Lucifer is costumed like his counterpart in the N-Town *Passion Play*: "And aftyr the songe entreth Lucyfer in a dewyllys aray wythowt and wythin as a prowde galonte," and later: "Her[e] Lucyfer dewoydeth and cummyth in ageyn as a goodly galont."[25] "Wat synne ys in met, in ale, in wyn? / Wat synne ys in ryches, in clothing fyne?" he demands of the innocent Mind (473–74), thus advocating the same worldly-wise attitude toward extravagant consumption as the N-Town Satan. *Mankind*, the most striking of the late fifteenth-century moralities, associates the same characteristics with the Vices: social pretension, worldly-minded materialism, and self-serving attitudes that threaten traditional communal bonds. "Nowadays" and "New Guise," the names of two of the Vices in *Mankind*, are variants of the "new fashion" advocated by the N-Town Lucifer and warningly described by Peter Idley. The joke they play in their grotesque tailoring of Mankind's coat is a satirical treatment of outlandish courtly fashion affected by the upwardly mobile: Mankind is a rural peasant discovering the dubious pleasures of the "new fashion" in urban life. The Vices' association with overweening power is enacted in their subordination to the devil, Titivillus, who enters with the same boast that is used by tyrants in the mystery plays: "*Ego sum dominantium dominus*"—"I am the Lord of Lords."

In short, to describe devils and Vices as radical manifestations of popular culture is not enough: one also needs to ask what social task those manifestations actually perform in the drama as we have it. They appear to be one means whereby the playwrights accommodate contemporary concern about rapid social change and ominous new forms of social oppression: "all beggerys and por pepyll have hem en despite." The point is that the devils' and Vices' satirical enactment of resistance to oppressive power is in keeping with the plays' Augustinian orthodoxy, not in opposition to it. If anything is emergent in these plays, it is not rationalism (let alone materialism) but what the playwrights themselves call "the new fashion," that is, the wealth and social ambition that were breaking up the communal ideal and providing the means for an eventual effective centralization of power and the neoclassical political ideology that came with it. The N-Town Satan begins in a vein like Herod's, using three specific designators of political and social privilege, and thereby proclaiming his *libido dominandi*: "I am your lord Lucifer, that out of helle cam, / Prince of this wer[l]d and gret duke of helle" (*Passion Play 1. 1–2*). What makes the theology of his speech and appearance coalesce with the social satire of his prologue is his authorship of all evil, including contemporary social evil that is one of the playwright's major concerns. Given the fact that Satan is dressed as a gaudy court gallant and Jesus as a peasant, it is difficult to see how anyone could construe this devil as a radical popular subverter of oppressive orthodox authority. A similar contrast appears in *Mankind*, where the gaudily arrayed New Guise and Nowadays taunt Mercy, who is costumed as a country parson. Mercy is not merely a personification allegory but also a reenactment of the peasant Jesus and contemporary social reality, in the literary tradition of *Piers Plowman* and *The Canterbury Tales*.

Careful attention to the social dimension of devils and Vices thus suggests that popular culture is not a definitive factor in their formation but instead plays a minor part. Consistently directed at upper-class viciousness, these figures would appear to be the product primarily of theological reflection, secondarily of the particular social circumstances of the fifteenth century, and finally of an existing folk dramaturgy that the playwrights appropriated for its subversive energy in their dramatic rejection of the "new fashion." Regarding devils and Vices this way reveals their affinity with the plays' raging tyrants as well—even with a small-time tyrant like Cain. *Libido dominandi* is the common theological link, enacted in comically exaggerated gestures of oppressive power. The Coventry Herod boasts about "my fassion, with my gorgis araye" (*Shearmen and Taylors*, 511), as the N-Town Satan does, and Herod's ordering the slaughter of the innocents may well enact aspects of "bastard feudalism" and the rising incidence of aristocratic violence in the fifteenth century.[26] Such a character has a very close affinity with the mercenaries of Pieter Bruegel's *Massacre of the Innocents*, painted in the Netherlands in the mid-sixteenth century. To all appearances the painting is a scene of random small-town violence in a contemporary setting, but it nonetheless depicts an episode from salvation history, suggesting the enduring significance of the event by deliberate anachronism and its contemporary social significance through peasant realism. Roger Marijnissen discusses Bruegel's probable political position in terms that could equally apply to the playwrights of religious drama in England a hundred years earlier: "Unquestionably Bruegel wanted to bring home to his contemporaries human brutality, but does that make him what would today be called a member of the resistance?"[27]

Residual resistance to the "new fashion" is also discernible in another form of medieval expression that is closely related to drama, namely, preaching. The late fourteenth-century preacher, Robert Rypon, constructs a brief history of clothing—from nakedness to silk—in terms of social competition: all kinds of sumptuous raiment "are now rather for vain-glory and worldly pomp than for the necessity of nature."[28] The Dominican bishop, John Bromyard, is also moralistic about luxurious clothing, but his basic insight is that of the social anthropologist—that clothing is a sign of power:

> So it befalls that amongst such folk no fashion pleases them for long; because, inasmuch as that piece of singularity or elegance which originally was but rarely seen begins to be used and seen by many, it begins to displease them when the cause of its singularity and vanity ceases along with the admiration of others. . . . Whence it comes about that they devise some new piece of foppery to make people gaze at them in wonderment anew. (Owst, p. 408)

Nothing changes fashion so quickly, he notes, as the appearance among "ribalds and vile persons" of sumptuous innovations once reserved to the nobility. When this happens, the nobility scorn their own inventions "as too common and therefore unworthy of admiration, as is evident in the case of garters and the like" (Owst, p. 408). These comments are specific enough to be very likely based on the actual observation of innovative social competition. But the class consciousness of costume display is not all Bromyard notices. The concentration of wealth required to support such display, he points out, invariably means that it is possible only at the cost of impoverishing others (Owst, p. 409). He brings a similarly hardheaded analysis to bear on such noble pursuits as the tournament:

> The tournament of the rich is the torment of the poor: for, while the former are spending lavishly upon such amusement, they either torture their subjects with tallies and exactions, or else, where they pass by, pay nothing to them save "wooden money." At the same time, along with this, they bring with them a host of malefactors, all of whom must have hay and oats, food and drink on account, like their lords, while they are on the road. . . . Little wonder, therefore, that they indulge freely in such amusements, for the purpose of which they seem to have so much without paying for it. (Owst, p. 335)

The habit of mind that could easily convert this kind of social critique into biblical drama (or Bruegel's paintings of biblical scenes) is illustrated in Bromyard's remark that "the greater, richer and falser men, whom the Apostle calls 'enemies of the cross,' indulge in those things which are contrary to Christ, in taverns, assizes, traffickings and falsities, 'crucifying afresh the Son of God' " (Owst, p. 573).

Medieval preaching offers persuasive evidence that the powers of observation and habit of mind were not lacking in the fifteenth century to assimilate specific aspects of social reality to biblical drama by means of residual Christian realism. In this regard, medieval preaching is quite different from sixteenth-century homiletics, which were much more aquiescent to dominant Renaissance culture. Indeed, sixteenth-century preaching initially drew modern critical attention as a supposed guide to Shakespeare, as if his plays merely staged the commonplaces of Elizabethan official homilies and their open support of the regime. Elaborating the hierarchical order of cosmos and society, advocating absolute civil obedience, and denouncing rebellion, these homilies are a striking contrast not only to medieval drama but to medieval preaching. Like courtiers and academic humanists, Elizabethan preachers were personally indebted to the crown for their education, livelihood, and upward mobility. This is one of the many complex consequences of the centralization of power, including the monarch's controlling the church, a policy introduced by Henry VIII and politically perfected by his daughter. "Nay," Elizabeth exclaimed to her bishops, "I have heard there be six preachers in one diocese the which do preach six sundry ways. I wish such men to be brought to conformity," and her recommended means of conforming them was to make them read the homilies, for "there is more learning in one of those than in twenty of some of their sermons."[29] As the queen's biographer notes, Elizabeth's objections to dissenting preaching were political: "It consorted not at all with monarchy, involved revolutionary changes in the structure of society, and struck at her prerogative, replacing her authority over the church by subjection to it" (Neale, *Queen Elizabeth I*, p. 309).

The success of Elizabeth's policy justifies Dollimore's observation that preaching was a key factor in containing Elizabethan subversion.[30] But this observation is historically relative: it cannot be elevated to the status of a universal social principle about preaching and power. Dissenting preachers in Elizabethan England were in fact the inheritors of the mainstream in medieval preaching. Those who doubt the credibility of religious social protest in medieval drama should be set the penitential exercise of reading G. R. Owst's books on medieval preaching.[31] To be sure, Owst claims too much for the literary influence of the pulpit, but he says more than enough to make the contrast with Tudor preaching clear. Like contemporary dramatists but unlike their Tudor successors, medieval preachers emphasized a message that was sharply critical of established power: they denounced oppression and corruption at every level—from the papacy to the parish priest, and from the court to the local bailiff. Moreover, the preachers themselves represented every hierarchical level—from prelates like John Bromyard and Thomas Brinton of Rochester to anonymous members of the secular clergy.[32]

Like the preaching of sixteenth-century religious dissenters, medieval preaching was politically explosive, as Owst points out, but it was more difficult to contain because the church was independent of the state, and the preachers were as often as not men with power and prestige in the church. This is not to say that they preached a papal party line, like the denunciations of secular power by Gregory VII, because they attacked ecclesiastical as well as secular power.[33] In addressing the theoretical structure of society, medieval preachers have no more to offer than familiar hierarchical platitudes (in this regard their message is ostensibly quiescent, like the social message of religious drama), but the burden of their preaching is an egalitarian denunciation of power and greed. Variants of the couplet attributed to the preaching of John Ball ("When Adam delved and Eve span, Who was then the gentleman?") appear in other medieval sermons, and its implications are spelled out by Bishop Bromyard:

> All are descended from the same first parents, and all come of the same mud. For, if God had fashioned nobles from gold, and the ignoble from mud, then the former would have cause for pride. But whereas all are of one material, in that fact "thy boasting is excluded." . . . True glory does not depend upon the origin or beginning from which anything proceeds, but upon its own condition. For thus, if it were not so, lice and other worms, which derive their origin from humankind, would be noble. (Owst, p. 292)

These sentiments are not designed to cool subversive fever, and Owst is surely right to interpret them in the context of the Peasant's Revolt of 1381, which was instigated by millenarian preachers like John Ball. The rich are like pigs, Bromyard says: they are of profit only in their death (Owst, 294). He is perceptive about the concentration of wealth in the hands of the few, and his comments about it are again inflammatory. Many of the rich, he says,

> if they restored what did not belong to them, would have less than a beggar, because they would have no clothing at all to cover them; because, although they ride great horses and live splendidly and nobly in the world's eyes, yet this is not of their own goods, but of the goods of others, either borrowed for the period that ends at General Judgment or wrongfully seized in some other way. It would be far better, therefore, for their soul *that they should be drawn by*

horses to the gallows of the world, than that they should ride thus
to the gallows of Hell. (Owst, pp. 302–3)

Only a medieval preacher would hint at revolutionary violence as a favor
to the souls of its victims.

Indeed, rhetoric like Bromyard's is a reminder that his ideology is
anything but modern, no matter how radical it sounds; it was, in fact,
the theology of power that we have seen at work in medieval drama.
"The lesse joye that thou haste in this worlde, the more thou shalte have
in heven," writes a vernacular preacher; when a poor man "comyth to
the deth with pacience, then shall he be a kyng in heven with the kyng
of pore men" (Owst, p. 297). Here is the same impulse to bestow cosmic
power on the poor that we have seen at work in the Magnificat and in
medieval dramatic treatments of the slaughter of the innocents, or in
Bruegel's painting of the same incident. The dramaturgy of power in medieval pageants of Moses and Pharaoh is, in effect, explained by an English vernacular preacher:

> This wickede pride amonge lordes and knyttes, that causeth this
> oppressinge of the pore peple, maketh now so gret a noyse and soun,
> that it is a gret clamour in al this rewme, in everi schire therof, of
> the extorcioneris that dwellen therinne, which beth as tiraunte
> kynges, overledynge the peple, as Pharao ladde the childern of Israel.
> . . . The tirauntie and wrongful overledynge on the pore peple . . . of
> this tirauntes is so gret and peinfeul to bere, that the noyse and the
> cri of here preyeris is herd into the heres of god in hevene, as it was
> of the cheldern of Israel, for the wrongful oppressinge of kyng
> Pharao in Egipte. (Owst, p. 320)

Comments like these make clear that more than quaint anachronism is at work in the many allusions to contemporary life in medieval
religious drama. What looks like anachronism is in fact evidence that
the dramatists' ideological perception of power relations is closely related to Augustine's theology of power and probably indebted to it. "It is
the same with the Justice of the English," says Bishop Brinton, "as it was
with the Justice of the Jews at the time of Christ's passion" (Owst, p.
339), a comment that explains why the trial of Jesus is almost invariably
staged with all the trappings of fifteenth-century legal procedure. "For
bothe Cristen courte and seculere courte . . . goon for gold and yeftes,
and trewthe is forsaken" remarks a vernacular preacher (Owst, p. 341).
Homiletic analogies between contemporary social oppression and biblical events have simply been turned around by the dramatists (who in
most cases were very likely preachers anyway): they stage biblical
events as if they were examples of contemporary social oppression. To
take a specific instance, the N-Town *Passion Plays* involve a precise and

detailed portrait of fifteenth-century legal abuses, as Lynn Squires has pointed out. Her summary is worth quoting in full:

> The councilmen conspire to convict Jesus, they send out spies to gather evidence against him, and they pay Judas to be their false witness. These pretrial proceedings against Jesus are described in extra-scriptural detail (the council scenes in *Ludus Coventriae* number a total of 242 lines as compared to the biblical 2) because these formed the weakest link in common law procedure at that time. . . . Those in power, particularly the king, tampered with legal process only where no proper rules existed, that is, most especially with the machinery for indictment. Thus, in the fifteenth century, we find the king's legal advisers increasingly framing indictments and conducting extensive interrogations in order to get a confession before putting a defendant on trial . . . which is precisely the situation presented in *Passion 1*. This covert form of pressure is protested most strongly in the council scenes. These scenes, reflecting as they do the range of authority in a late medieval town, contain severe criticism of the fifteenth-century legal establishment as a whole—an establishment which is shown to be prone to bias, to perversions of procedures, to hypocrisy, to brutality.[34]

It is easy to forget that "medieval" social criticism like this was perpetuated in drama until well into the second half of the sixteenth century. That Shakespeare saw the Coventry mystery plays as a child and adolescent is highly probable, as we noticed at the beginning of this chapter, and in this regard the unusual lavishness and national reputation of the Coventry plays are important to bear in mind.[35] Moreover, the Coventry fragments embody trenchant social criticism and the traditional dramaturgy of power as effectively as any fully extant cycle.[36] The mystery plays are therefore important background, in addition to the morality play, when considering the many characters in Shakespearean drama whose inspiration is traceable to medieval devils and Vices.[37] A remarkable number of these characters are social climbers, or to put the point another way, politically and socially ambitious characters in Shakespeare almost invariably share Vice characteristics, from the bishop of Winchester and Richard duke of Gloucester in the early history plays, to Edmund in *King Lear* and Iago in *Othello*. Dramaturgical continuity thus parallels social continuity. Peter Idley advises his son to "put aside al fals dissimulacion / And also fained countenance of this new fassion" (pt. 1, ll. 580–81), and dissimulation and false countenance continue as the hallmarks of ambition in Shakespearean drama, particularly the kind of duplicitous ambition that models itself on Italianate fashion—the Renaissance "new fashion." As we shall see in later chapters, however, Shakespeare's choice to follow the popular and medieval dramatic tradition identifies him, both ideologically and stylistically, with residual political realism, as the sixteenth-century equivalent of the new fashion becomes increasingly dominant in Tudor culture. His dramaturgy is conservative, in other words, because of its archaism, yet its archaism stands in opposition to new forms of power and in that regard can arguably be called subversive. The combination of forces that transformed English culture in the course of the sixteenth-century—and that led to Shakespeare's peculiar kind of subversiveness—will be our concern in the next chapter.

CHAPTER 3 ❧ TUDOR POWER AND
THE NEW FASHION

When Francis Meres assessed English literature in 1598, he did so consistently in terms of the Greek and Latin classics, making in the process what has come to be an often quoted comment about Shakespeare: "As Plautus and Seneca are accounted the best for comedy and tragedy among the Latins, so Shakespeare among the English is the most excellent in both kinds for the stage."[1] This passage has drawn attention chiefly because Meres follows it with a list of the plays he knew by Shakespeare—a list that has become a benchmark in efforts to establish the early canon and its dates. But more important for present purposes is Meres's insistence on finding classical precedent for vernacular literature. To be sure, most of his pairings are uninspired and inaccurate; the point is not the quality of his comparisons but the fact that he feels compelled to make them in the first place. For what his endeavor demonstrates is the emergence of classical literary models as unquestioned standards for judging subsequent literature. Such a standard had not been recognized by playwrights a hundred years earlier, yet by the end of the sixteenth century it had become commonplace. Ironically, over the next several decades, this neoclassical standard would gain increasing prestige until it would eventually lead to the rejection of Shakespeare's drama as an example of excellence—precisely the opposite of Meres's conclusion.

Such shifts of taste are familiar enough (this one in particular) and have usually been treated as the simple data of literary history—signposts not to be explained but to be used in interpreting texts. C. S. Lewis throws up his hands when it comes to explaining a parallel shift from what he calls "drab" to "golden" poetry and prose in the sixteenth century: "I do not claim to know why there were many men of genius at that time."[2] But his disclaimer is disingenuous: he posits the confluence of genius itself as an explanation for golden poetry in order to discredit the presumed paucity of genius that produced drabness. If one looked at the same shift of taste with the eyes of Hugh Latimer, Thomas Cranmer, or Robert Crowley, one might well see a decline in genius rather than a rise. For what Lewis is describing, without acknowledging it, is not merely a shift in taste: he fails to recognize that the shift is the sign of a profound social change in the sixteenth century. He almost says as much: the culture at century's end, he observes, "was to last through most of the seventeenth century and to enrich the very meanings of the words *England* and *Aristocracy*." But Lewis was too committed himself to the outcome of that change to see the significance of his own words. The taste that governed literature at the end of the sixteenth century was literally the taste of the governing class in a stratified and newly centralized society. The constituent elements of this taste—including neoclassical standards but not confined to them—were rapidly on their way to becoming what Marx calls "ruling ideas"—or a developed ideology promulgated by those in power as a means of defining and defending their exclusive social position.[3]

Before considering the impact of this innovative ideology on drama in particular, let us first see how it came into being and how it stands over against the residual Augustinian social critique that we have seen at work in medieval preaching and drama. The centralization of power under the Tudors is a subject too well known and too thoroughly studied to require extensive development here.[4] Briefly, the Tudor monarchs successfully stabilized the kingdom, after the chaotic baronial wars of the fifteenth century, by consolidating power in their own hands. They employed a number of methods in doing so, but perhaps the most important for our purpose was the creation of a civil service staffed by humanists who owed their upward mobility directly to the monarchy and to their education. One such employee was Thomas More, but he was one of many, and their numbers increased throughout the sixteenth century. Owing their position to the crown, they were more dependable supporters of crown policy than the old landed aristocracy—indeed, as often as not, humanists were themselves the formulators of crown policy. Wolsey, a butcher's son who rose to dizzying prominence, is an important early example, and his eventual destruction in a futile attempt to compete with the very power that had made him what he was in the first place is sobering evidence of the growth of that power.

The new civil servants were also tied to the crown by their innovative humanist education, for it demarcated them from the old aristocracy and thereby quickly became an important sign of privilege.[5] The surest indication of its success is the fact that the old aristocracy began to educate its scions in the same manner, but the new sign of privilege was not established without a struggle. Just one year before Henry VII's accession, Caxton was still extolling the virtue of the old chivalric education for the social elite and deploring what he regarded as inattention to its models—"the noble volumes of saynt graal, of lancelot, of galaad, of Trystram, of perse forest, of percyval, of galaad, and many mo."[6] Roger

Ascham's condemnation of Malory, less than ninety years later, as nothing but "open manslaughter and bold bawdry" is an indication of the struggle between competing educational conceptions that were the signs of a deep-seated social struggle.[7] "I hear say," Ascham remarks, "some young gentlemen of ours count it their shame to be counted learned" (p. 49), and whether he literally heard it or read it is of little consequence: he was conscious of a struggle in either case. What Ascham may well have read is Richard Pace's letter to Colet, printed in Pace's *De fructu qui ex doctrina percipitur* (1517):

> Now there happened to be a certain person there [i.e., at a banquet Pace had attended], a nobleman, or so we call them who always carry horns hanging down their backs as though they were going to hunt while they ate. When he heard us praise learning, he became wild, overwhelmed with an uncontrollable rage, and burst out, ". . . I'd rather see my son hanged than be a student. Sons of the nobility ought to blow the horn properly, hunt like experts, and train and carry a hawk gracefully. Studies, by God, ought to be left to country boys."[8]

In Pace's account of this incident, the nobleman is boorish and only faintly ridiculous, but as an unlettered aristocrat he is literature's social progenitor of Pope's inarticulate drone, "Sir Plume, of amber snuffbox justly vain," a caricature drawn with an acid pen two hundred years later by a poet who still felt unsure of his success in the struggle for prestige by literacy and eloquence. Sixteenth-century humanists were fond of contrasting the new learning with scholastic ignorance, but their motives in doing so were not socially disinterested: the more they looked like mere clerics, the harder it was for them to compete with the nobility, whose status was superior to clerics under the system the humanists aimed to transform.[9]

That humanists were aware of their means to social mobility is evident in the claims they make both for themselves and for the new learning. "The fault is in yourselves, ye noblemen's sons," Ascham asserts, in declaring that the nobility should be educated in the new manner, "and therefore ye deserve the greater blame that commonly the meaner men's children come to be the wisest counselors and greatest doers in the weighty affairs of this realm" (*The Schoolmaster*, p. 40). Ascham does not add that he is himself an example of a meaner man's son who had become a great doer in England's weighty affairs by means of the very education he recommends to the nobility. Sir Thomas Elyot was one of the most ambitious humanists in the early part of the century, though his ambitions were seldom equalled by either the political success or financial reward he actually achieved.[10] In the *Governour* he is frankly self-serving in his claim that understanding "is the most excellent gift that man can receive in his creation, whereby he doth aproach most nigh unto the similitude of God," for as one advances in degrees of this similitude, "so should the estate of his person be advanced in degree or place where understanding may profit," namely in the "governance of mankind."[11] How such governance operates is clear in Elyot's assertion that understanding is used "to the detaining of other within the bounds of reason"—reason, of course, being the interest of those who govern. Impressive classical authority was available for arguments like this— particularly the authority of Plato; but to assume that humanists turned to such authorities in a disinterested quest to liberate new domains for the human mind is to ignore the extent to which the authorities they chose served the purpose of humanist social privilege. The Platonic re- vival, both in Italy and in England, occurred among a coterie of educated humanists who focused their hopes and ambitions on a single powerful figure—signorial in one case, monarchical in the other.[12] The idealist terms that had been used to defend Roman government were thus rein- troduced into European politics when a context was created that gave them sufficient social force to become quite literally a ruling idea.

In the new education, nothing so clearly served the interest of the new governing class as the rhetorical theory formulated most influen- tially by Cicero in the late republic and Quintilian in the empire. Cou- pled with the social structure and centralized power of Rome itself, this rhetorical theory accounts as much as anything does for the extraordi- nary appeal of Roman culture in the Renaissance. For one thing, rhetoric provided skills in the power to persuade, and that power was regarded as essential to a class that aimed to detain the rest of society within the bounds of reason. Immediately after a student is introduced to oratory at the age of fourteen, Elyot prescribes, "the art of rhetoric would be semblably taught . . . and instructing diligently the child in that part of rhetoric principally which concerneth persuasion, forasmuch as it is most apt for consultations" (*Governour*, pp. 72–73). Twenty years later, Thomas Wilson worked out the implications of rhetorical theory for governors more carefully than Elyot had done, but to the same effect: "Such force hath the tongue and such is the power of eloquence and reason that most men are forced even to yield in that which most stand- eth against their will."[13] This is power indeed. Wilson in effect com- mends what is now called false consciousness—the state of mind of a populace that has been persuaded to affirm what is in the interest of its governors:

> For what man, I pray you, being better able to maintain himself by
> valiant courage than by living in base subjection, would not rather
> look to rule like a lord than to live like an underling, if by reason he
> were not persuaded that it behooveth every man to live in his own

44

vocation and not to seek any higher room than whereunto he was at the first appointed? Who would dig and delve from morn till evening? Who would travail and toil with the sweat of his brows? Yea, who would, for his king's pleasure, adventure and hazard his life, if wit had not so won men that they were more bounden than here to live in their duty and to train their whole life according to their calling? (pp. 19–20)

Like other humanists, Wilson himself rose to power from a humble social origin: his father was a Lincolnshire yeoman. He quickly absorbed the lessons of status, however, and took pains in the *Arte of Rhetorique* to signal adroitly how far he had come from his provincial background: "The shire or town helpeth somewhat towards the increase of honor: as it is much better to be born in Paris than in Picardy, in London than in Lincoln, for that both the air is better, the people more civil, and the wealth much greater, and the men for the most part more wise" (pp. 45–46). Given the rapid increase in urban poverty and overcrowding in the sixteenth century, Wilson's view of clean air, wealth, and wisdom in London is clearly partial, as is his view of social prestige. Frank Whigham points to the *Arte* as a classic defense of limited upward mobility: "Wilson makes possible a new conception of the hierarchical social order: not as a set of sealed ranks, nor even as an order based on merit (another new strategy with its own problems), but as a system dominated by those who can convince others that they ought to submit. He effectively uncouples the existing order from transcendental authority and refounds it on the sheerly formal, learnable, vendible skills of persuasion."[14]

In view of the social importance attached to classical rhetoric in the Renaissance, the rising prestige of neoclassicism is easier to understand. For ancient rhetorical theory had been formulated in stratified societies, and the extent to which rhetoric reflected its social context made it appealing to a literate class who were anxious to justify their new status. The well-known levels of style had been socially defined, as the literary genres had been: tragedy properly dealt with persons of high estate in a high style; comedy, with the lower orders in a vulgar style. This suffusion of social relations throughout rhetoric—and the literature that more or less followed its dictates—better served the purpose of aspiring humanists and courtiers than literature that followed other social models. Sidney's condemnation of English drama for "mingling kings and clowns" is a clear example of humanism's social preoccupations and its responsiveness to classical stratification: "But besides these gross absurdities . . . all their plays be neither right tragedies nor right comedies, mingling kings and clowns, not because the matter so carrieth it, but thrust in clowns by head and shoulders, to play a part in majestical matters with neither decency nor discretion."[15] Given Sidney's aspirations at court, it is by no means certain that he would have responded any more favorably to Shakespearean drama, had he known it, than he did to earlier drama. Francis Meres no doubt did Shakespeare a social favor in equating his comedy and tragedy with that of Plautus and Seneca, but Sidney's discernment was much keener than Meres's, and his ambition to succeed at court much stronger. That he would have done the same favor Meres did for a Warwickshire glover's son who had never been to university is therefore open to question.

In appropriating the social implications of classical rhetoric, humanists implicitly rejected both the residual political realism of Augustine and the rhetorical theory that complemented it. For Augustine had opposed not only the idealist defenses of Roman power, as we saw in chapter 1, but also the social stratification that defined Ciceronian rhetoric. His reason for opposing the latter, as Erich Auerbach has pointed out, was that the Bible did not conform to the strictures of Cicero—either in subject or in style.[16] Augustine recalls in *The Confessions* that this lapse in Judeo-Christian taste initially repelled him to such a degree that he rejected the Christian religion because of it (3.5). By the time he wrote *On Christian Doctrine*, however, he had reversed his early opinion: the incompatibility between the Bible and Cicero had compelled him to redefine rhetoric. In doing so, he did not reject the levels of style, but he rejected their social correlatives: any subject, no matter how "high" or "low," could be appropriately treated in any level of style. What called for varying levels of style, then, was not the social status of the subject being treated, as Cicero had prescribed, but solely the speaker's or writer's immediate purpose at hand—to teach (low style), to praise or blame (middle style), or to persuade (high style).[17] By redefining rhetoric in this way, Augustine allowed for what he saw as a mixture of styles and subjects in the Bible. His accommodation of classical rhetoric and Christian teaching was immeasurably assisted by what had been a gradual semantic revaluation of the word *"humilis"*: used as an adjective to describe the low style (*"sermo humilis"*), it had been transformed by constant association with the impoverished life of Christ and the criminal's death to which he was sentenced, so that it had come paradoxically to connote the vulgar and the sublime at once.[18]

Augustine's redefinition of rhetorical theory has deep affinities with the political revaluation that we noticed in chapter 1. Augustine could not have regarded social hierarchy as an unnatural consequence of the Fall without fundamentally redefining the social stratification of style that dominated classical rhetorical theory. His dismantling of the high style is therefore a semiotic counterpart to his demystification of Roman history, for the high style could no more be inherently suited to nobility than Roman society could be defined in terms of justice, given the dismal record of patrician exploitation and a social order based on the desire for power rather than justice. Augustine's refusal to allow exclusive aristocratic claims to the high style is analogous to his identifying pride and the lust to dominate as the only values that really count in human social order. By the same token, his bestowing sublime dignity on *sermo humilis* parallels his claim that in the kingdom of God the primary value is humility, which paradoxically appropriates cosmic power by modelling itself on the humility of Christ.

If Augustinian realism is residual in the Middle Ages, we can see why it continued to be so in the sixteenth century, given momentous political changes together with attendant changes in social attitudes and the gradually increasing prestige of classical rhetoric. The late medieval ideal of spiritually ennobling poverty appears in literature across a wide social spectrum—not only in popular literature like the mystery plays, *Piers Plowman,* and the late fifteenth-century morality play, *Mankind,* but also in a débat like *Dives and Pauper* and in courtly poetry like *The Canterbury Tales.* An important shift away from this ideal is already apparent in More's *Utopia.* Presumably as a stroke against the idle aristocracy, More stipulates that in Utopia everyone is required to perform agricultural labor. But then he makes a crucial exception to the rule he has just formulated:

> The same exemption [from manual labor] is enjoyed by those whom the people, persuaded by the recommendation of the priests, have given perpetual freedom from labor through the secret vote of the syphogrants so that they may learn thoroughly the various branches of knowledge. But if any of these scholars falsifies the hopes entertained of him, he is reduced to the rank of workingman. On the other hand, not seldom does it happen that a craftsman so industriously employs his spare hours on learning and makes such progress by his diligence that he is relieved of his manual labor and advanced into the class of men of learning. It is out of this company of scholars that they choose ambassadors, priests, tranibors, and finally the governor himself. . . .[19]

The exemption More allows describes precisely the high-minded ideal of the new learning. Whether he is advocating this ideal or ironically undercutting its pretension is not easy to say, but in either case he places a premium on intellectual labor in Utopia that gives it social mobility, prestige enjoyed by very few others, and exclusive access to power. Since intellectual labor also expropriates wisdom in Utopia, as it does in Plato's Republic, the Augustinian association of spiritual insight with social inferiority is negated: the manual laborer with intellectual gifts and the willingness to cultivate them rises to a position whose rewards are freedom from manual labor and access to power, so perpetual stratification is guaranteed. Utopia may have been nowhere for More, but for later, lesser humanists, captivated by just such a vision of the new learning and of themselves, Utopia was not nowhere: they were living in it.

The understated social elitism that More describes in Utopia has a stylistic counterpart. More's decision to write the work in Ciceronian Latin probably implies more than a wish to avoid official censure: it may also say something about More's conception of what such a style was suited for, since the *Utopia* is a work of serious political philosophy, clearly modelled on Plato's *Republic*. In any event, More disagreed with Erasmus about use of the vernacular, particularly in translating the Bible.[20] In this regard, as in so many others, More was at odds with the Protestant reformers, who wanted to make everyone literate—including manual laborers—in order to give them direct access to the Word of God. This Protestant ideal opposed the high-minded equation between understanding and social prestige that became increasingly characteristic of humanism, and Protestant affirmation of the vernacular also had affinities with Augustine's redefinition of classical style. Thomas Cranmer in fact speaks of style in neo-Augustinian terms in his prologue to the 1540 edition of the Great Bible:

> For the Holy Ghost hath so ordered and attempered the Scriptures that in them as well publicans, fishers, and shepherds may find their edification as great doctors their erudition, for those books were not made to vainglory, like as were the writings of the Gentile philosophers and rhetoricians, to the intent the makers should be had in admiration for their high styles and obscure manner of writing, whereof nothing can be understand[ed] without a master or an expositer. But the apostles and prophets wrote their books so that their special intent and purpose might be understanded and perceived of every reader.[21]

One of the revealing ironies of Tudor power is that Cranmer's idea to make the Scriptures understood by every reader led to his commissioning the homilies: originally designed to share a culture's highest wisdom with publicans, fishers, and shepherds, these sermons eventually became one of the primary means of Tudor political constraint.

The social implications of stylistic levels were well understood by humanists. Elyot devotes considerable attention to the advantages of oratorical ability for governors: "Moreover, toward the acquiring of majesty, three things be required to be in the oration of a man having authority: that it be compendious, sententious, delectable, having also respect to the time when, the place where, and the persons to whom it is spoken."[22] This is a succinct description of the high style, and Elyot tellingly follows it with a chapter on clothing, for "apparel may be well a part of majesty." Elyot understands the social reality that style is a semiotic indicator of status both in how one speaks or writes and in how one dresses.²³ The social implications of sumptuary style are also recognized by medieval preachers, as we noticed in chapter 2, but the humanist evaluation of those implications is different from the evaluation in medieval sermons. Bishop Bromyard deplores the change of privileged fashion in the face of imitation by lower classes, for example, because such changes are luxurious and exploitative. Thomas Wilson, on the other hand, refers to fashion as a positive symbol of status, linking it, as Elyot does, to maintaining consistency in levels of style: "We must ever make our words apt and agreeable to that kind of style which we first gan to use. For as French hoods do not become lords, so Parliament robes are unfitting for ladies. Comeliness therefore must ever be used, and all things observed that are most meet for every cause."²⁴ Not surprisingly, Wilson prefers eloquence to learning, for the learned, if they speak without eloquence, "do like some rich snudges, that having great wealth go with their hose out at heels, their shoes out at toes, and their coats out at both elbows. For who can tell if such men are worth a groat, when their apparel is so homely and all their behavior so base?" (p. 324).

The social elitism of humanist style is in clear contrast to Cranmer's populist literary ideal, whose social counterpart was the early reformers' relentless social criticism, inherited from the critique of medieval preachers, as we noticed in chapter 2. In the popular preaching of Hugh Latimer, for example, appear the informal style, the use of the vernacular, the social critique, the emphasis on spiritually ennobling poverty that were characteristic of medieval preaching, as well as medieval religious drama: "For preaching of the gospel is one of God's plow works, and the preacher is one of God's plowmen. Ye may not be offended with my similitude in that I compare preaching to the labor and work of plowing and the preacher to a plowman; ye may not be offended with this my similitude, for I have been slandered of some persons for such things. . . ."²⁵ Latimer applies the simile primarily to priests, who should be as diligent in all seasons as the plower. In a manner that recalls Langland, Latimer thus constructs a portrait of the agricultural laborer as a model for his social betters—not without specific attention to social reality. In dealing with the rural scene, he addresses the evils of enclosure: "The bodily plowing is taken in and enclosed through singular commodity [private profit]. For what man will let go or diminish his private commodity for a commonwealth?" (p. 37). Turning to the court, Latimer castigates clerics who neglect their cures to work for the civil service:

> They are so troubled with lordly living, they be so placed in palaces, couched in courts, ruffling in their rents, dancing in their dominions, burdened with ambassages, pampering of their paunches, like

a monk that maketh his jubilee, munching in their mangers, and moiling in their gay manors and mansions, and so troubled with loitering in their lordships, that they cannot attend it. They are otherwise occupied, some in the King's matters, some are ambassadors, some of the Privy Council, some to furnish the Court, some are lords of Parliament, some are presidents, and some comptrollers of mints. . . . Is there never a nobleman to be a lord president but it must be a prelate? Is there never a wise man in the realm to be a comptroller of the mint? . . . If there be never a wise man, make a water-bearer, a tinker, a cobbler, a slave, a page comptroller of the mint. Make a mean gentleman, a groom, a yeoman, make a poor beggar lord president. (pp. 38–39)

Latimer thus arrives at the opposite position from the one More describes in Utopia: better have laborers govern than the wise, if the wise do so at the expense of their parishioners.

The reality of centralized power, however, made Latimer's kind of critique increasingly difficult to articulate. The reformers' commitment to the monarchy as the source of reformation was profoundly ambiguous, for what that power gave, it could also take away. Latimer himself modified his style when preaching before the king, a sensitivity to power not allowed for in Augustine's redefinition of style but clearly specified in Elyot's direction that the orator "have respect" to the person to whom he speaks (*Governour*, p. 16). The effect of power was not always so subtle. Latimer was silenced altogether by the Act of Abolishing Diversity of Opinions in 1539, and he did not preach again until the accession of Edward VI in 1547. A long anonymous poem, "Vox populi, vox Dei," almost certainly written to protest the 1539 Act, deplores the silencing of preachers and carries forward their social critique in Skeltonic rhyme, a popular vehicle for protest that would itself be silenced by the prestige of the "golden" high style at century's end:

And yet not long ago
Was preachers one or two,
That spake it plain enow
To you, to you, and to you,
High time for to repent
This devilish intent
Of covetous the convent.
From Scotland unto Kent
This preaching was bysprent;
And from the east front
Unto Saint Michael's Mount,
This saying did surmount
Abroad to all men's ears

And to your grace's peers,
That from pillar unto post
The poor man he was tossed;
I mean the laboring man,
I mean the husbandman,
I mean the plowman,
I mean the plain true man,
I mean the handicraftman,
I mean the victualing man,
Also the good yeoman.[26]

In the long run, the seductive lure of increased power and prestige was even more damaging to the articulation of social criticism than outright repression, for clerics were no less affected by the scramble for upward mobility than were humanist courtiers, as Latimer recognizes in his sermon on the plowers. The more deeply indebted one became to the system, the harder it was to criticize, while continued criticism could easily have the effect of relegating one to the margins of power and society, where one's voice could be less easily heard. For the most part, however, clerics seem to have held out longer than courtiers and academic humanists against the compromising effects of status. When Sir John Cheke responded to the rising of 1549, for example, in *The Hurt of Sedition*, he laid full blame on the rebels, castigating them for unjustifiable resistance in terms that look forward to the Elizabethan *Homily against Disobedience and Willful Rebellion*. Both Cranmer and Latimer, on the other hand, were evenhanded, designating the covetousness of rich and poor alike as the source of the rebellion.[27] Latimer, preaching boldly before Edward VI, dwells at greater length and more feelingly on the exploitative avarice of the rich than on the envious avarice of the poor. Robert Crowley, a radical Protestant divine who published his own protesting pamphlets, went further than his more prestigious clerical colleagues, blaming the entire rebellion on the oppression of the poor by the rich.[28] Crowley was unhappy with Protestant venality, particularly after the dissolution of the monasteries, and he attacked the new elite in *Philargyrie* (1550), a poem modelled on *Piers Plowman*, whose frontispiece depicts a richly dressed Protestant using a Bible to scrape golden coins into a sack.[29] Crowley fled England during the Marian persecutions and returned hopefully when Elizabeth came to the throne, accepting multiple benefices and rising rapidly in the ecclesiastical hierarchy. But like many radical reformers, he became disillusioned again and issued a protesting pamphlet he had written in 1546 but not published, *The Opening of the Wordes of the Prophet Joell* (1561). Eventually his disenchantment even with the monarchy and his sympathy to the growing Puritan movement led to the loss of his ecclesiastical living, so that when he died in 1588, he was so poor that his widow was allowed a pension of four nobles a year.[30] Few members of the established English clergy could endure such official pressure, and increasingly the voice of conformity replaced the voice of protest, which was taken up by marginal groups, most notably the Puritans.

Paralleling the decline of social criticism was the decline of the Protestant plain style, as John King has pointed out, and the eventual emergence of an aureate high style in the 1580s. The fate of the plower as a social model is a token of this transition. Robert Crowley published the first printed edition of *Piers Plowman* in 1550, because he interpreted its social protest as a prophetic heralding of Protestant reform. The poem went through four editions, but the last was in 1561, and it was not printed again until the nineteenth century (King, *English Reformation Literature*, pp. 319–39). When Puttenham published a definitive guide to courtly style in 1589, he rejected Langland's verse as "but loose meter and his terms hard and obscure, so as in them is little pleasure to be taken."[31] A poet shall not "follow the speech of a craftsman or carter or other of the inferior sort," Puttenham prescribes. "But he shall follow generally the better brought up sort, such as the Greeks call *charientes*, men civil and graciously behavoured and bred. Our maker therefore at these times shall not follow *Piers Plowman* . . ." (pp. 144–45). Hugh Latimer frankly declared his lowly social background in a sermon preached before Edward VI in 1549: "My father was a yeoman and had no lands of his own, only he had a farm of three or four pound a year at the uttermost, and hereupon he tilled so much as kept half a dozen men. He had a walk for a hundred sheep, and my mother milked thirty kine" (*Selected Sermons*, p. 67). Four years later, Thomas Wilson published *The Arte of Rhetorique*, in which he cleverly distanced himself from his own provincial background and when illustrating linguistic solecisms took frequent opportunities to put them in the mouths of anonymous "country fellows" who blunder about awkwardly in his anecdotes before their social betters. Given the fact that "throughout the sixteenth century the overwhelming majority of the country's inhabitants were engaged primarily in providing from the land, for themselves and their families, the basic needs of food and shelter," this innovative scorn for agricultural labor on the part of those who grew up dependent on it is an indication of their anxiousness to define themselves as privileged by their economic dependence on literacy and intellectual labor.[32]

Faced with Wilson's kind of eloquent dismissal, no plower could long stand as a model of anything except what one wanted least to be. In John Ferne's *Blazon of Gentry*, a courtesy book published in 1586, a plowman called Columell is included among the six interlocutors, all the rest of whom are gentlemen. Yet Columell is permitted to speak only eighteen times in the book's 470 pages, and he is the only speaker who is distinguished by his accent—a Somerset dialect of the sort used on the Elizabethan stage to demarcate peasants. When Columell complains at one point of his young master's cruelty, Paradinus (the herald) addresses his response to the other gentlemen: "the ass that beareth the burden must have leave to bray under the load."[33] The consequence was observed in 1583 by Thomas Smith in an often quoted passage from *De Republica Anglorum*: "As for gentlemen, they be made good cheap in England. For whosoever studieth the laws of the realm, who studieth in the universities, who professeth liberal sciences, and to be short, *who can live idly and without manual labor*, and will bear the port, charge, and countenance of a gentleman, he shall be called master."[34]

That drama was profoundly affected by this momentous stylistic and social shift has long been recognized. Indeed, drama is where literary historians first observed the increasing social demarcation in sixteenth-century England, partly because the drama of the period has been studied more intensively than any other form of cultural expression as scholars have worked to elucidate Shakespeare, and partly because the struggle between competing styles became overt in drama itself in the so-called war of the theaters at century's end.[35] David Bevington has traced this bifurcation through the entire century, identifying a "popular canon" of plays before the opening of the Theatre in 1576—a canon that can be distinguished dramaturgically from contemporary plays written for elite auspices.[36] What Bevington discovered about the drama, in other words, fits the pattern of an emerging high or ruling style in Tudor culture as a whole. The first play written in iambic pentameter and self-consciously employing neoclassical five-act structure is *Gorboduc*, produced at considerable expense by members of the Inner Temple for a unique performance before Queen Elizabeth in 1561. *Gorboduc* is also the only English play Sidney singles out for commendation in his *Apology for Poetry*, written two decades later. The dramaturgy Sidney rejects in the *Apology* is characteristic of Elizabethan popular dramatic romance, whose structure, as Bevington points out, was deeply indebted to the late medieval morality play and therefore innocent of neoclassical demands.[37] Such plays were produced cheaply by groups of travelling actors and most frequently performed before audiences of commoners.[38] This explains their receptiveness to elements of popular culture, a feature that makes them roughly comparable, vis-à-vis the emerging high style, to the sermons of early reformers and the pamphlets of Protestant gospellers like Robert Crowley. That the popular canon survived the pressure of social conformity to which humanists and ecclesiastics succumbed may be simply because the plays *were* popular: they belonged to a level of the social order that did not conform to the emerging ruling idea, because it did not aspire to the prestige that that idea represented.

To be sure, sixteenth-century drama is complex, and claims for its reflection of social prestige need to be made with care and tact. A play like *Gentleness and Nobility* (printed about 1525), for example, comes from the group of plays with elite auspices, yet it contains social criticism that is the most candid and radical of any play in the century.[39] Its plainspeaking Plowman belongs to the tradition of Langland, Latimer, and Crowley, and the play's arguments about social structure frequently recall Augustine: society was originally peaceful and possessions were held in common, but the social order was based on superior oppressive force that made "laws marvelous strait and hard" to its own advantage and the disadvantage of those it had dominated.[40] The full force of the Plowman's position, however, is blunted by his being only one in a three-way conversation between himself, a knight, and a merchant, each of whom consistently maintains his own interest, so that the final effect is a disinterested "play of mind," as Joel Altman felicitously calls it.[41] The play explores social issues without endorsing a particular point of view beyond the necessity for social hierarchy, as things now stand, and the need for the estates to cooperate. The overall effect is therefore one of sophisticated theoretical reflection—a decorous effect for an audience that prided itself on the *negotium* of intellectual labor. True, the Philosopher who sums up the débat at the end quite emphatically stresses virtue as the criterion for nobility, but this idea was a commonplace and had been endorsed by Italian humanists in self-serving arguments for their own social advancement.[42] These arguments had in fact been incorporated in English humanist drama by Henry Medwall as early as 1497: his *Fulgens and Lucrece*, a reworking of Buonaccorso's *De vera nobilitate*, curiously portrays the old aristocracy in the same stage conventions that popular dramatists had devised to caricature the "new fashion." Excessive apparel in *Fulgens* is the mark of Publius, whose decadent nobility is inherited: he is the one who displays "a new maner of fascyon now a day," whereas Gaius, who is in effect the Tudor "new man," dresses soberly and discreetly.[43]

These early humanist plays thus bear out the observation of a social demarcation in drama after all, despite their apparent radicalism, and in this regard, they are closely parallel to the *Utopia*. Among the twenty-odd plays that Altman discusses as examples (like *Gentleness*) of noncommittal "explorative" dramaturgy, only one (Heywood's *Four PP*) comes from the popular canon before 1576, and only three can be identified with the commercial theater thereafter.[44] That the model for explorative drama derives from Aristotle, Cicero, and Quintilian, in Altman's view, fits the picture of humanist preoccupation with classical rhetoric as a sign of prestige. Certainly that sign was never taken as seriously in England as it was in Italy and France: native English drama remained as a leavening influence (or contaminating influence, depending on one's viewpoint) throughout the heyday of neoclassicism, particularly in comedy. Nonetheless, a social bifurcation is evident in sixteenth-century drama, and the characteristics of plays written for elite auspices consistently suggest a pattern of social ambition and privilege.

The fate of biblical plays in the sixteenth century is a revealing indication of how the innovative sense of stylistic decorum affected drama. Given the inherent contradiction noted by Augustine between classical rhetoric and biblical style, we should expect to see the mixed style of medieval drama in retreat as classical rhetoric gained in prestige. And this is almost exactly what did happen. Until the reign of Elizabeth, the picture is rather confused, as it is elsewhere in Tudor culture outside handbooks of rhetoric and manuals of instruction in courtly behavior. On one hand, the mystery plays continued as popular civic celebrations in many parts of England. Moreover, reformers like John Bale did not hesitate to use these traditional forms, pouring the new wine of Protestant dogma into the old wineskins of medieval dramatic structure, untroubled by niceties of style. On the other hand, humanists recognized the impure style of popular bibilical drama and rejected it. They also tried to improve on it by writing biblical drama themselves that conformed to neoclassical expectation. As Rosemary Woolf has shown, their highbrow efforts are inept dramatizations of the Bible, when compared with the popular scriptural plays they were supposed to supplant.[45] Their choice of subject, moreover, was frequently aimed at royal flattery or advice, in the manner of the classically correct secular play, *Gorboduc*. Nicholas Udall's *Ezekias* (1539), for example, almost certainly drew on parallels between Henry VIII and Hezekiah, the reforming king of ancient Israel: Udall's preface to his translation of Luke's gospel praises Henry in precisely these terms, and the revival of *Ezekias* during a state visit of Elizabeth to Cambridge in 1564 was described by Abraham Hartwell in sufficient detail to make its flattering intention clear.[46]

Such erudite biblical plays manifest a very different dramaturgy of power from their popular vernacular counterparts. The image of the monarch is elevated and hieratic, the awesome repository of divine majesty and power on earth: the mystification of power is just what such plays aim to achieve. Yet their flattery should be understood as a function of social mobility, for the tribute they pay is not free: its price is the monarch's recognition of the one offering the tribute and an implicit enhancement of his power—with the hopeful expectation for explicit and tangible enhancement as well. "Courtly entertainments," as Louis Montrose observes, "constitute an elaborate sign system, a formation of figurative persons, actions, and topics in which loyal subjects may obliquely consider matters of state and subtly manipulate the royal will."[47] The stylistic counterpart to the mythologizing of power is rhetorical finesse. Thus in the continental *Tragedy of Abraham's Sacrifice*, by Theodore Beza (Englished by Arthur Golding in 1577), Isaac engages in a sophisticated theological flyting with the devil, who finally admits defeat because of Isaac's superior rhetorical skill—not because of his faith, as in the mystery plays. Beza's play is thus a striking example of Thomas Wilson's rhetorical values in action: the persuasive qualities of rhetoric make it a source of power, though Wilson had other targets than the devil in mind as the object of rhetorical domination. While *Abraham's Sacrifice* was not written for court performance, its deep genuflection to rhetorical skill parallels the elegant exchange of compliment and power in court productions.

Nicholas Udall's career manifests ambiguities that quite possibly point to courtly ambition as his primary motive. His reforming goal in *Ezekias* may have involved a certain degree of court posturing, for his close personal association with Mary Tudor and his continued activity in the office of the revels during her reign have been taken as evidence that he was a timeserver, able to set his sails according to the changing winds of politics and religion.[48] Certainly he would not have been alone if he did so: Sir John Cheke, who condemned the rising of 1549, and William Baldwin, who published *The Mirror for Magistrates*, were both adept at serving the interests of power, whatever its religious persuasion happened to be. They illustrate the extraordinary pressure that Tudor government was able to exert on those who committed themselves to its social escalator. Puttenham characteristically identifies a related form of courtly reversibility as a rhetorical figure, "*Paradiastole*, which therefore nothing improperly we call the *curry-favel*, as when we make the best of a bad thing, or turn a signification to the more plausible sense . . . moderating and abating the force of the matter by craft, and for a pleasing purpose, as appeareth by these verses of ours, teaching in what cases it may commendably be used by courtiers."[49] Puttenham's commendation of this rhetorical figure for courtiers is closely related to his maxim regarding monarchy: "Qui nescit dissimulare nescit regnare" (p. 186). Puttenham thus advocates the very thing that Peter Idley warns his son against in the mid-fifteenth century: "put aside al fals dissimulacion / And also fained countenance of this new fassion."[50] Like many of Puttenham's figures, *paradiastole* enacts what it describes: an English courtly reality with an elevated Greek name in effect makes the best of a bad thing, allowing a clever rhetorician to advocate what could hardly be advocated in any other terms. When the same courtly reality appears in Shakespearean drama, it usually does so in ambitious characters whose origin is in medieval dramatic tradition (like Richard III or Iago). In that tradition, the assessment of dissimulation is the opposite of Puttenham's.

After Elizabeth's accession, a socially demarcated pattern in biblical drama can be more clearly discerned. Most important, the mystery plays fell prey to official repression and had ceased almost entirely by about 1580. No doubt the iconoclasm of Elizabeth's government played an important part in this suppression, as Harold Gardiner and Glynne Wickham have pointed out.[51] But another, albeit unproveable motive for official opposition suggests itself in view of what was happening elsewhere in Elizabethan culture and its literary expression. This explanation concerns the subversive impression of both style and content in the old plays. They had been tolerated, after all, during the height of iconoclastic frenzy at midcentury, and their suppression coincides with the effective consolidation of Elizabethan power, the emergence of a confident English high style, and the sudden outpouring of courtesy books that enjoined familiarity with the gestures of ambition and privilege—from the anonymous *Institucion of a Gentleman* (1555) to Puttenham's *Arte of English Poesie* in 1589. To see the devil on stage dressed as a foppish courtier and offering advice about how to succeed in the courtly power struggle may well have disconcerted the elite for a number of complex reasons, not all of them theological. The courtly images of the mystery plays consistently debunk social striving and domination, and their style is more strongly influenced by Augustine's redefinition of rhetorical theory than by classical decorum. To the late sixteenth-century governing class, the plays must have seemed unbearably impertinent (at the very least they mingle kings and clowns indiscriminately), and their language must have appeared every bit as loose, hard, and obscure as Puttenham thought Langland's.

At first glance, the decline of the mystery plays seems to contradict the evidence concerning other kinds of popular biblical plays during Elizabeth's reign. For the latter increase dramatically in number: only two or three of the roughly twenty-five biblical plays that originate in this period can be identified with a boys' school or university; the rest have unknown auspices or can be identified either with the early Elizabethan popular canon or with one of the commercial acting companies after 1576.[52] To be sure, the small minority of elite biblical plays perpetuate the courtly adulation and neoclassical eloquence that characterize such plays before Elizabeth's accession. *Sapientia Solomonis*, for example, originally written by the German Lutheran Sixt Birck in 1540, was updated for a single lavish production by the boys of Westminster School in 1566, when it was performed in Latin before the queen on a state occasion: the visit of Princess Cecilia of Sweden.[53] The play flatteringly compares Elizabeth to Solomon by virtue of her wisdom, and Cecilia to Solomon's rich and brilliant visitor, the Queen of Sheba. Such plays manifest essentially the same dramaturgy of power as other courtly forms—royal processions, masques, tournaments, triumphs, disguisings. The growing prestige of classical myth as a vehicle for royal flattery may have made biblical compliments seem passé (they had been a prime feature of Edwardian compliment); if so, then the small number of biblical plays for elite auspices in this period may well complement the decline of the mystery plays.

The increasing number of biblical plays in the popular repertory during Elizabeth's reign almost certainly points to biblical drama's continuing affinity with residual political realism. It is important to note, first of all, that the increase occurs only after 1587: for almost twenty years prior to that date, as Ruth Blackburn notes, "we have no records of any native Biblical plays" (*Biblical Drama*, p. 155). This silence, then, corresponds to the small number of biblical plays for elite audiences and to the decline of the mystery plays. The evidence suggests, moreover, that the renewal of popular biblical plays has a social motive as well, for late Elizabethan biblical drama seems to be a stalking horse for social dissent. Though few such plays have actually survived, we know who wrote most of them, namely, the so-called university-wits—Robert Greene, Thomas Lodge, George Peele, and others. These men manifest what Anthony Esler has called "the aspiring mind of the Elizabethan younger generation" in a book bearing that phrase as its title.[54] Elizabeth's preference for crown servants of established reputation and her parsimonious contraction of court largesse meant that the path to preferment for younger hopefuls was effectively blocked. They could still enjoy the means to advancement: the university, the Inns of Court, the trappings of humanist education were all in place; but without the expected reward of living idly and without manual labor, the new generation could not so credibly bear the port, charge, and countenance of gentlemen, nor be called master. For to earn one's living by writing for the commercial theater looked altogether too much like *otium*: "But they that be governours," Elyot points out, "nothing do acquire by the said influence of knowledge for their own necessities" (*Governour*, pp. 6–7). Certainly the public stage was an unpromising route to advancement at court: despite the increasing prestige of the commercial theaters, Henry Peacham still stipulated, as late as 1622, that "whosoever labor for their livelihood and gain have no share at all in the nobility or gentry, as . . . stage-players," mountebanks, bearwards, and the like.[55] The inevitable consequence of disappointed social expectation was deep frustration. John Lyly eschewed the public theater to write exclusively for the elite, but even so his magniloquent mythical plays of hopeless sexual longing barely mask his social frustration, as G. K. Hunter has argued,[56] and the titanic frustration of Christopher Marlowe has become a commonplace, as the allusive title of Esler's book indicates. Marlowe despised the native popular style—"the jigging veins of rhyming mother wits"—and almost single-handedly created an effective high style for the popular stage. Yet his ambivalence about the power and prestige that were denied him underlies his demystifying assault on established power in all his plays.[57]

In this context, the revival of biblical drama by the university wits makes sense as a covert protest that deliberately adopted a residual form. Greene's first biblical play (now lost) was called *Job*, and though we know nothing about it, its title at the very least indicates a portrayal of patient suffering at the hands of inscrutable omnipotence. In other words, the play may well have been a characteristically self-pleading portrait of Robert Greene in a social system dominated by a seemingly omnipotent monarch who was certainly inscrutable. Greene's and Lodge's *Looking-Glass for London and England* is reminiscent of the social protest in Crowley's gospelling pamphlets: the prophet Jonah in their play recalls Crowley's affinity with the prophet Joel and puts their play into a long tradition of residual social protest that includes the mystery plays—by then suppressed. In much the same vein is Greene's prose pamphlet, *A Quip for an Upstart Courtier* (1594), which is a prose version of Francis Thynne's *Debate between Pride and Lowliness* (1570). Thynne's poem is in the old-fashioned mode of *Piers Plowman*: using the medieval dream vision and convention of clothes symbolism (the debate is between Cloth Breeches and Velvet Breeches), Thynne excoriates the pride of social privilege and extols the virtues of poverty and humility. As Greene's title suggests, his revival of this residual mode is not disinterested: he uses it as a means of oblique attack on the privilege he covets but cannot attain. Peele's *David and Bethsabe* is of unknown auspices (probably never performed), yet its image of royalty is in striking contrast to the apotheosis of Elizabeth in Peele's courtly *Arraignment of Paris*: David is lustful, tyrannical, and oppressive, like the powerful in the English mystery plays. But Peele also portrays the king in defeat and humiliation, lying prostrate while Simei reviles him and throws dirt on him, and the play finally suggests that David's true kingliness consists not in social elevation but in the wisdom he gains through suffering and repentance. Despite its aureate poetry, Peele's play thus revives what is essentially the residual dramaturgy of power in the mystery plays: their realism about exploitation and oppression, their recognition of spiritually ennobling humility, and their assimilation of true majesty to the paradoxical sublimity of Christ's impoverishment, defeat, and criminal's death. The humanizing and demystifying image of royalty in this play makes it an important transitional link between the mystery cycles and Shakespearean tragedy.

A brief survey of biblical drama cannot capture the subtlety and complexity of power relations in Tudor drama as a whole, but this is not the place to tell that story. Enough has been said to indicate that drama follows the pattern of Tudor culture in all forms of its expression: the centralization of power, especially under the effective administration of

Elizabeth, made the court increasingly the center of culture, and the result was a transformation of ideology that expressed itself, in part, in a socially loaded demarcation of stylistic levels. Social relations are produced in accordance with material productivity, Marx observes, "but we also produce *ideas, categories*, that is to say, the abstract ideal expressions of these same social relations. Thus the categories are no more eternal than the relations they express. They are historical and transitory products."[58] The demands of the Renaissance high style became increasingly refined and exclusive, until a political revolution at the end of the eighteenth century proved how historical and transitory the high style was, despite its claim to a metaphysical timelessness and perfection: the challenge to prevailing social relations also challenged the style that was their sign. But that story cannot be told here either, for it is time now to turn our attention to Shakespeare, a gifted young provincial who entered London when the Tudor high style was in the early flush of its full golden triumph.

CHAPTER 4 ❧ DECONSTRUCTIVE COMEDY

Shakespeare's response to the Tudor separation of styles is deeply ambivalent. On one hand, as his career ripened, he perfected what Marlowe had begun, producing a supple and evocative blank verse after a remarkably short time and creating a decorous stratification of style that mirrors the social standing of its speakers, with particularly brilliant effect in *Midsummer Night's Dream*. The only play Shakespeare wrote that contains no audibly distinguishable low-life characters at all is *Troilus and Cressida*, which is his purest expression of satire in the innovative humanist manner. Thersites rails in prose in that play, but for all his clownish ways, he is himself a Greek officer, and when Cressida converses with her servant, Alexander, they both discourse wittily, first in blank verse, then in prose, without making any social distinction between each other (1.2). In effect, *Troilus and Cressida* is thus Shakespeare's only play that deals exclusively with the elite, and that fact is an important indication that his response to the high style and its social implications is marked by deep reservations after all. For in spite of its style and privileged characters, *Troilus and Cressida* is a strikingly unflattering view of classical heroes who are obsessed with power and honor, both in battle and in bed. Similar qualifications of social privilege abound in all Shakespeare's plays, even in *Midsummer Night's Dream*, and may account as much as anything does for the decline of Shakespeare's reputation in the late seventeenth and eighteenth centuries and its sudden resurgence during the Romantic revolution. What I want to suggest in this chapter is that one of the consistent qualifications of socially differentiated style in Shakespeare's early comedies is their openness to vestiges of medieval dramaturgy. If the well-made comedy was a sign of power, then Shakespeare's early comedies deconstruct not only the well-structured play but the social assumptions that gave rise to the ruling idea of such a play in the first place.

This is not to say that Shakespeare was a reincarnation of John Ball. His early histories depict popular uprising in terms that would have pleased the author of the *Homily against Disobedience and Willful Rebellion*, and a credible case can be made that Shakespeare's early career in particular reflects quite serious social ambitions. No one would quar-

61

rel with Francis Meres's judgment, for example, if Meres had *The Comedy of Errors* in mind when he compared Shakespeare to Plautus, and *Titus Andronicus* in mind when he compared Shakespeare to Seneca. What is probably Shakespeare's first comedy aspires to perfect comic decorum, borrowing heavily from Plautus's *Menaechmi* and adopting the elegance and economy that characterize tight neoclassical form. The action takes place in one day; the scene is individable, in Polonius' phrase; and the action proceeds in a necessary or probable sequence of events—"both by Aristotle's precept and common reason"—from our discovery of Egeon's dilemma to its resolution in his family's reunion at the play's end. With such a play Sidney could have had no quarrel, and if Shakespeare had never written comedies of any other kind, he would almost certainly have won Sidney's approval, despite his undistinguished social background, lack of a university education, and ignoble means of material support. True, Shakespeare's village school education, complemented by the deep affinity with nobility and royalty in his plays, eventually led to the conclusion that the drama ascribed to him must not be his after all, and this judgment follows logically from the social assumptions that prevailed when Shakespeare was alive; but the particular containing strategy of simply denying works of genius to an upstart author did not gain favor until the nineteenth century, when enough time had elapsed, a sufficiently reactionary opinion was prevailing, and the Romantic mystique of authorship was strong enough to make such a strategy suddenly seem credible.

Shakespeare's decision to open his career on a flawless neoclassical note, then, was not merely an esthetic decision. In choosing Plautus as a model, he had to reject *Clyomon and Clamydes*, and his choice to do so was no less socially significant than Ascham's rejection of Malory or Puttenham's of Langland. We can see the same social significance in Shakespeare's attempts to win courtly patronage by dedicating his two narrative poems to the earl of Southampton. He also seems to have circulated his sonnets in manuscript, in the manner of a courtier, for Meres had seen the sonnets by 1598, or at least heard that they had circulated, and they were not printed until 1609. How close Shakespeare came to familiarity with the court is a matter of continuing debate, but we know he used the wealth he earned from the theater to buy a large prestigious house in his home town in 1597, and he almost certainly supported his father's application for a coat of arms, which was granted in 1599, thus making father and son both "gentlemen of the first head," as Sir Thomas Smith scathingly calls those whose social ambition took this particular form:

> If need be, a king of heralds shall also give him, for money, arms newly made and invented, [the title whereof shall pretend to have

been found by the said herald in perusing of] old registers, where his
ancestors in times past had been recorded to bear the same. Or if he
will do it more truly and in better faith, he will write that for the
merits of that man, and certain qualities which he doth see in him,
and noble acts which he hath done, by the authority which he hath
as king of heralds and arms, he giveth to him and his heirs these and
these arms, which being done I think he may be called a squire, for
he beareth ever after those arms. These men be called sometime in
scorn "gentlemen of the first head."[1]

If the herald in good faith saw merit and noble acts in John Shakespeare's
application, they are as likely as not to have been son William's narrative poems and sonnets, whose compendious, sententious, and delectable style indeed sorted well with nobility.

For Shakespeare's extraordinary linguistic skill was an important
means of social mobility in an age that placed such a high premium on
rhetorical ability. This ability allowed Shakespeare to bypass the acknowledged means of advancement (the universities and inns of court)
and still to entertain a realistic expectation of gaining considerable social privilege. It is little wonder, therefore, that Robert Greene should
refer to him spitefully as "an upstart crow beautified with our feathers"
when Shakespeare had likely written little more than the *Henry VI*
plays: to a frustrated and well established "rare wit" who had paid the
dues of a university education (even including a Cambridge M.A.) with
little visible reward, it must have been galling to see a "rude groom"
achieve recognition with no more than a grammar school education.[2]
Equally illuminating, on the other hand, is the career of Ben Jonson, who
was no provincial (he was the son of a London brickmaker) but who was
also like Shakespeare in his lack of a university education. Jonson's determination to succeed at court eventually paid off handsomely, thus
illustrating by default what Shakespeare almost certainly could have
done had he wanted to. Jonson's career at least makes it impossible to
conclude that Shakespeare stayed with the commercial theater because
social necessity denied him any other choice.

The stylistic counterpart to Jonson's successful ambition is his careful and rigorous cultivation of the neoclassical separation of styles and
his eventual attainment to the foremost rank among writers of court
drama in English. Jonson's reaction to Shakespeare's style—ambivalent
at best, censorious and patronizing at worst—is therefore a clue to
Shakespeare's reservations about the separation of styles and a complement to Shakespeare's modest social achievements when compared
with Jonson's, for stylistic ambiguity in this period is inevitably an ambiguity about social standing. We can see something of this ambiguity
even in *The Comedy of Errors*, for all its apparent neoclassical perfec-

tion. One of the changes Shakespeare makes in his classical source is the addition of the frame story—the separation and reunion of Egeon and Emelia. The change is arguably perfunctory and awkward, since Egeon's problems are mentioned only at the beginning and end of the play and ignored in between. Yet the frame adds a dimension, as it were, that supplies depth to the two-dimensional neoclassical comedy, and this dimension is deeply indebted to the popular dramatic tradition of the sixteenth century.

What the frame story adds to *The Comedy of Errors* can be schematized (see below) in a series of thematic oppositions—a structural

	FRAME STORY	MAIN STORY
Source	popular native drama	Plautus
Number of locations	many	one
Dominant location	the sea	the city
Length of time covered	untold years (Egeon's birth to the present)	less than one day
Manner of presentation	chronological and episodic	Aristotelian unity of action
Source of problems	external (natural & civil strife)	internal (human error)
Severity of problems	life-threatening, family-separating	wholly illusory
Solution of problems	recognition and self-knowledge	none
Dominant tone	tragi-comic	farcical

feature that also characterizes thematically richer plays, like *A Midsummer Night's Dream* and *The Winter's Tale*, but that operates in this play specifically to complicate the tidiness of the Plautine source. While the frame plot is decorously enclosed by the temporal and spatial restrictions of the neoclassical action, Egeon's story is reminiscent of the old-fashioned popular drama that had paid no attention to the unity of place—"where you shall have Asia of one side and Africa of the other, and so many other under-kingdoms that the player, when he cometh in, must ever begin with telling where he is, or else the tale will not be conceived."[3] Sidney's indulgent description of how the old romances handled dramatic time is a virtual synopsis of the story Egeon tells: "Now of time they are much more liberal, for ordinary it is that two young princes fall in love. After many traverses she is got with child, delivered of a fair boy; he is lost, groweth a man, falls in love, and is ready to get another child" (*Apology*, p. 197). Sidney opines that such ineptitude is absurd and inartistic, but most important, that it falls short of Italian dramatic perfection. His judgment, in other words, is esthetic and social at the same time, inextricably combining his response to dramatic structure with his response to Italy as a power to be emulated—just as one emulated it in the art of courtliness or rhetoric.[4]

Shakespeare's clear demarcation between the frame story and the Plautine story takes on evaluative weight when we consider the kind of comic problem and solution that each story embodies—and significantly, this implicit evaluation is the opposite of Sidney's. The frame story does more than expand the action imaginatively in time and space; it also creates problems for its characters that diminish the problems of the classic plot by comparison and italicize their artifice. Egeon and Emilia and their young twins are innocent victims of "the always wind-obeying deep," which impresses upon them "a doubtful warrant of immediate death" (1.1.63 and 68). The disruptive sea thus anticipates the civic disruption that later seizes Egeon—again a literally innocent victim—and imposes a death sentence on him. This double confrontation with apparently inevitable death lends a tragic quality to Egeon's story that is wholly lacking in the story of his sons: the play invites no laughter at all until Egeon has left the stage at the end of the first scene in a mood of despair: "Hopeless and helpless doth Egeon wend, / But to procrastinate his lifeless end" (1.1.157–58). The Plautine problems of the adult Antipholuses and Dromios are a contrast with their parents' problems in every respect, never deriving from anything objective and external to them (like the sea or civil strife) but always from their own imperception, delusion, and failure of self-recognition. Joel Altman has pointed out that the Plautine plot is a paradigm of "explorative" dramaturgy because all the characters are so egocentric that they create a static and socially monadic world: "Their errors, it would seem, are a metaphor of their essential egoism, and *the plot is a function of their characters.*"[5] While it is true that Egeon briefly contributes to the resulting chaos, he does so just moments before the entry of Emilia, who brings with her the solution to both the frame story (which has resumed with Egeon's entry) and the main plot. The overall impression therefore remains one of contrast between the two stories at the level of solution as well as problem, for the difficulty of the twins is apparently irresolvable—an ever more complex and endless farcical round of mutual accusation and misperception. The relatively more serious frame story centers in characters whose lives seem to have more weight, both because they have borne difficulties imposed from without, whose result is potentially tragic, and because the solution to all the problems emerges with these characters and only with them. Their plot too, then, is a function of their characters, if only in the sense that they are familiar long-sufferers who inhabit the kind of popular romantic plots from which their story derives.

65

In the context of this consistent distinction between the two stories in *The Comedy of Errors*, we can see unmistakable allusions to the archetypal medieval drama that historically underlay the romantic plot. The romantic pattern of separation, wandering, and reunion, as David Bevington points out, derived directly from the moral pattern of fall from grace, temporary domination of evil, and rediscovery of divine favor—the structure that enabled travelling actors to adapt the vast drama of salvation history to the exigencies of a small troupe.[6] What is therefore the oldest story in English drama permeates the language of the frame plot and contributes to its qualitative distinction from the newly fashionable classical action that it encloses. "My fall" is the play's first rhyme phrase, followed closely by "the doom of death": "Proceed, Solinus, to procure my fall, / And by the doom of death end woes and all" (1.1.1–2). "I am not partial to infringe our laws," the stern duke insists, identifying himself with harsh perpetrators of the "old law" in medieval dramatic renderings of the history of salvation (1.1.4). Those who have not been able to "redeem their lives" before the duke of Syracuse "have seal'd his rigorous statutes with their bloods" (1.1.8–9). The familiar romantic dilemma of shipwreck, global wandering, and years of familial separation is thus reinforced with vestiges of the ageless theological dilemma of the fall of humankind and the law of sin and death. Occurring exclusively in the frame story, these casual hints add texture to other differences between it and the Plautine story.

Archetypal drama is again implied in the play's conclusion, when the frame story is completed and the solution to the neoclassical story is introduced. Liberation from error and the threat of death are physically enacted when Emilia recognizes Egeon: "Whoever bound him, I will loose his bonds / And gain a husband by his liberty" (5.1.339–40). A few lines later, Solinus refuses Antipholus' offer of ransom money and gratuitously abrogates the harsh law that he had upheld as the play began: "It shall not need; thy father hath his life" (5.1.390). Emelia's subsequent comparison of the family's separation to the pangs of childbirth articulates the miraculous quality of their reunion: "After so long grief, such nativity" (5.1.406). The wonder of physical childbirth in these lines catches up one of the oldest of Christian metaphors ("Ye must be born again") and hints at the central event in all the cosmic dramas of salvation.

The Comedy of Errors, in short, is more of a hybrid than it appears to be at first, and the social implications of its style are therefore ambiguous. Its neoclassical plot and elegant economy represent an attempt to appropriate fashionable standards, and authorially such an attempt inevitably suggests a desire for the power and prestige that these standards represented—just as certainly as lower-class violation of Elizabethan sumptuary laws represented a desire for the status ascribed to upper-class clothing.[7] While this pursuit of status is most apparent in Shake-speare's earliest comedies (and is probably strongest in *The Comedy of Errors*), it is a strategy for social mobility and preservation that Shake-speare never entirely abandons. His most serious characters are invaria-bly those with the greatest social prestige, and the proportion of their numbers in his plays is roughly in inverse ratio to their real proportion in the society he belonged to—mute testimony to the importance he bestows on them. This inverse ratio, moreover, corresponds to the Eliz-abethan elite's view of their own importance, since they were vastly out-numbered by those who lacked their status. Conversely, in Shakespear-ean drama, characters who lack social privilege are not only outnumbered by their social betters (even in a play like *1 Henry IV*, which has an unusually high proportion of commoners), but are usually treated with a comic distance that invites the audience to respond to them indulgently—the slapstick beatings that the Dromios receive being a case in point. On the other hand, Shakespeare does not press this stratification as hard as he might, and he qualifies it dramaturgically in ways that soften and even reverse its social impact. The most effective image of renewed community in *The Comedy of Errors*, for example, is presented by the servant twins as the play ends. In contrast to "the en-mity and discord," "the rancorous outrage" with which the action be-gins and the classical plot compounds, the frame story concludes with the two Dromios walking amiably to a waiting feast: "We came into the world like brother and brother, / And now let's go hand in hand, not one before another."

Such an image defies the logic of Renaissance social hierarchy, which would reserve moral wisdom for the words and actions of those at the top. But the culminating friendship and cooperation of the two Dromios is a secular counterpart to the medieval dramaturgy of power, which insistently presents the dignity of the humble and their unex-pected capacity for cosmic and moral insight. Parallel examples appear in virtually every Shakespearean comedy, including the earliest, where the young playwright seems most intoxicated with the high style. In *Love's Labors Lost*, we laugh with the elite at the silly pageant of the Nine Worthies, but no careful auditor can dismiss the protest of the pro-vincial schoolmaster who produced the play for his social betters: "This is not generous, not gentle, not humble" (5.2.626). Holofernes may be pretentious and pedantic, but he cannot be blamed for the learned stan-dards he foolishly apes, since they were established by those he aims to please. Launce's parody of lovers parting (2.3) and the Petrarchan blazon (3.1) in *Two Gentlemen of Verona* similarly qualifies the courtly aspi-ration of Proteus: this silly servant accurately identifies the hollow pos-turing of his gentleman master. Bottom's "rare vision" in *Midsummer Night's Dream* is truer than the "cool reason" of Duke Theseus, because the rude mechanical has indeed experienced what the lofty courtier would feign deny to exist; and by the time we get to a wise fool like Lavatch, in *All's Well That Ends Well*, Shakespeare explicitly identifies the source of this particular social inversion: "I am for the house with the narrow gate," Lavatch cryptically remarks, "which I take to be too little for pomp to enter. Some that humble themselves may, but the many will be too chill and tender, and they'll be for the flow'ry way that leads to the broad gate and the great fire" (4.5.50–55). The seeming irrelevance of this allusion to Matt. 7:13–14 is clarified by the recognition that *All's Well* is the only Shakespearean play that depicts a principal romantic relationship between social unequals.[8]

Explicit allusions like Lavatch's are probably infrequent and obscure because the reality they point to was so travestied by its pervasive use as a device for enhancing prestige and effecting social containment: the Elizabethan elite, after all, were anything but irreligious. But at least one other such allusion appears in the comedies, specifically in *Much Ado About Nothing*. Dogberry is mostly a lovable ass, and inevitably we see ourselves as superior to him—especially *linguistically* superior. Yet he solves the problem of the play's main plot and wins unexpected recognition for doing so: "What your wisdoms could not discover, these shallow fools have brought to light" (5.1.227–29). It is tempting to read these lines in the context of the humanist tradition of "wise folly," exemplified in Erasmus' *Praise of Folly*. But the medieval dramatic analogue is much truer, because Erasmus' Folly is rhetorically sophisticated and delivers a skillful public oration, consistently employing the modesty *topos* (a rhetorical pose of humility) and concluding with a rapt neo-Platonic vision that compares favorably with the later vision at the end of Castiglione's *Courtier*.[9] In effect, Folly is the persona of a humanist distinguishing himself from the putative wisdom of medieval scholastic philosophy—with all that that implies socially. But Dogberry is a childish innocent—as innocent as a medieval shepherd identifying the cosmic significance of the birth of Christ—and the proper gloss on Borachio's comment about Dogberry is not humanist but biblical: "If any man among you seem to be wise in this world, let him be a fool that he may be wise. For the wisdom of this world is foolishness with God; for it is written, 'He catcheth the wise in their craftiness' " (1 Cor. 3:18–19).

One need not see Shakespeare as a crypto-Puritan to recognize that his drama includes elements of what might well be called a residual tradition, and that some of those elements come from the popular religious drama in the Middle Ages. The ambiguity of "humble" as a social term and also one that described a particular quality of mind and spirit was alive not only for Augustine but also for Shakespeare, and this linguistic ambiguity virtually ensures a subterranean religious dimension to a social critique that in any way values those who lack power and social privilege: "[God] hath showed strength with his arm; he hath scattered the proud in the imagination of their hearts. He hath put down the mighty from their seats, and exalted them of low degree. He hath filled the hungry with good things, and sent away the rich empty" (Luke 1:51–53). The other side of the medieval dramaturgy of power is what Augustine calls *libido dominandi*, as we noticed in chapter 2. This kind of desire is what animates medieval tyrants like Satan, Herod, and Pilate; and in the morality play it is what animates the Vice, who is a devil in the dramatic shorthand of personification allegory. Shakespeare's dramaturgical reservations about the high style include aspects of this "lust to dominate," in addition to an insistence on the dignity of the unprivileged. Not surprisingly, however, *libido dominandi* in Shakespearean drama takes a peculiarly Renaissance form, which reflects a contemporary shift in the sense of human self.

Perhaps the best way to characterize this new sense of self is in terms of social invulnerability, a conception that underlies much of what others have said about Renaissance selfhood and also helps to clarify its relationship to the changing dynamics of power. "Self-fashioning," for example, as Stephen Greenblatt observes, was a Renaissance innovation, whose best known expositer is Machiavelli.[10] Machiavelli's early republicanism, significantly influenced by the ideals of the old Roman republic, gave way to his admiration for signorial efficiency in the city states, with the result that he abandoned republican ideals and advocated centralized power, whose workings he described with memorable accuracy in *The Prince*. Crucial to Machiavelli's vision of centralized power is the ability to preserve oneself in an environment of constantly changing and challenging power relationships: "For Machiavelli, man is free insofar as he is able to adapt himself to changing circumstances, and he can adapt insofar as he can fashion his identity. The entire book [i.e., *The Prince*] is devoted to an exposition of the 'methods and rules' . . . which govern self-fashioning."[11] In other words, Machiavelli might be said to describe how one makes oneself socially invulnerable in the pursuit of power. The sort of Protean self Machiavelli describes, of course, may well pose a threat to personal integration, with the paradoxical result that the freedom essential to social invulnerability may produce an internal sense of imminent personal chaos over which one has no control—a process Shakespeare seems to be exploring in *Richard III* and even more subtly in *Macbeth*. Moreover, this is a self-reinforcing process: the more aggressively one seeks to guarantee social or political invulnerability, the more threatening the world appears to be, and the more fragile one's sense of internal security consequently becomes. Self-fashioning, as Greenblatt perceptively notes, "always involves some experience of threat, some effacement or undermining, some loss of self.

. . . Any achieved identity always contains within itself the signs of its own subversion or loss" (*Renaissance Self-Fashioning*, p. 9).

What was innovative is not what Machiavelli observed, since power had been sought and held no less before he wrote than it was thereafter. What is innovative in the Renaissance is that interest in the ideal of the invulnerable self became widespread among a new class whose upward mobility was closely tied to literacy at the same time that printing made the dissemination of such an ideal widely available to those who had power, as well as to those who had less power than they wanted.[12] In this process the illiterate were inarticulate because they lacked power—they are Wilson's "country fellows"—and they remain inarticulate to us because their illiteracy permitted them to leave no record of themselves. When we generalize about the fifteenth and sixteenth centuries, we are usually talking about the privileged minority whose literacy alone gave them considerable power and widened their scope for literary self-perpetuation and display. In other words, we are talking about those whose pursuit of power made them receptive to the new ideal of the invulnerable self.

Closely related to Machiavelli's *Realpolitik* as a strategy for achieving the same sense of self is the so-called courtesy tradition. Here were a set of guidelines, as Frank Whigham argues, that articulated the boundaries of privilege by prescribing how those who enjoyed it ought to behave if they wished to distinguish themselves from their would-be inferiors. What they created was a new idea of the self: identity began "to be a function of actions rather than of birth—to be achieved rather than ascribed."[13] The actions constituting this identity focused on the artful cultivation of apparent invulnerability in the scramble for prestige. One might even feign the opposite to achieve the desired effect, for "the profession of a very courtier," as we have seen Puttenham declaring, "is in plain terms cunningly to be able to dissemble."[14] This innovative social ideal—itself a product of and a response to new social mobility—helps to explain how attitudes toward "the new fashion" changed. Uniformly negative in the fifteenth century, as we noticed in chapter 2, attitudes are increasingly positive (like Puttenham's) or ambivalent in the sixteenth century. One could always decry excess, but the motive for doing so was no longer so clearly moralistic, since it was complicated now by the fierce competition that virtually everyone who was literate was involved in: moralism could be a powerful way of putting someone down. "Predatory self-deprecation" (as Whigham calls it), for example, is a recommended tactic of courtesy literature (*Ambition and Privilege*, pp. 102–12). A cunning exfoliation of the modesty *topos*, this tactic involves a public show of self-abasement whose aim is to win vocal protestation regarding one's superior status and thereby to compel acknowledgment of one's position in the social scale. "Is it not perchance more requisite," Puttenham asks rhetorically, "our courtly poet do dissemble not only his countenance and conceits, but also his ordinary actions of behavior, or the most part of them, whereby to win his purposes and good advantages . . . ?" (*Arte of Poesie*, pp. 299–300). In his gnomic anatomy of the seventeenth-century French court, La Rochefoucauld described the same strategy without Puttenham's particular rhetorical flourish: "Humility is often but the mask of submission, assumed in order to conquer: it is an artifice of pride, which stoops that it may rise the higher: and pride, which adopts a thousand forms, is never so well disguised nor so capable of deception as when it masquerades as humility."[15]

The sense of self that emerges from repetitive Renaissance courtesy books is thus essentially the same as that in Machiavelli. Cardinal Bembo's neo-Platonic vision at the end of *The Courtier* seems antipodal to Machiavelli's realism, but in fact the two are complementary, for both fed the appetite for power among an exclusive social elite. Pico's *Oration on the Dignity of Man* takes "man" in the same narrowly circumscribed sense as Castiglione: neither one dreams of dignifying manual laborers (they would have found Wordsworth as incomprehensible as Marx), because both aim to provide a high-minded rationale for the seemingly limitless upward movement that had suddenly become possible for literate humanists. The Protean self heroically imagined by Pico is a subtle emblem of power, connoting on one hand the heady possibilities of social transformation (as in Marlowe's *Tamburlaine*) and on the other hand, the infinite faces one was obliged to wear to maintain what one gained in a world of constantly shifting power relationships (as in Marlowe's *Jew of Malta*). The transformation of the Vice into Subtle or Volpone was well under way.

In the English court of the 1590s, the scramble to win individual purposes and good advantages became increasingly frantic and cynical, eventually issuing in Essex's violent bid for power just after the turn of the century.[16] Court striving was therefore increasingly risky, like contemporary voyages to the new world: one could win enormous benefits, but in the process one risked losses that were even more spectacular. The yoking of upward mobility and overseas adventuring appears not only in *The Merchant of Venice* (in the symbiotic relationship of Bassanio and Antonio) but in Donne's love poetry, indicating that contemporaries responded to the two undertakings as parallel risks. Because the environment of the court was so insecure, it became increasingly receptive to strategies for achieving apparent invulnerability, and inevitably those who had the most power seized the most spectacular strategies for themselves. Royal mythology in this period might well be summarized as a mythology of political invulnerability, as Elizabeth's personal motto, *Semper eadem*, suggests. The image of the chaste virgin that was at the center of Elizabethan royal mythology went far beyond biographical fact: it appropriated the Petrarchan image of the inviolate female, which offered infinite variations for expressions of queenly power in a court full of importunate males, all seeking to breach her defenses in the cunning guise of mythical suitors. Spenser's court allegory of Raleigh as the brokenhearted lover, Timias, is a poetic example of strategic self-deprecation—invulnerability masquerading as its opposite. Raleigh is portrayed as a loser in the hope of being recognized as a winner after all, as if nothing had ever happened: in Spenser's allegory, Raleigh assumes a mask of submission in order to conquer. The Erastian theory appropriated by both Elizabeth and James in varying degrees is the most ambitious tactic of this kind—immortality being only one of God's characteristics that could be borrowed to bestow a mythic (but nonetheless powerful) social invulnerability on a mortal monarch.

At a less exalted social level, personal invulnerability is also a key element in the late Elizabethan dramaturgy of power. Tamburlaine is the first of Marlowe's principals who quest after invulnerable selfhood only to discover that the nature of things makes their quest devastatingly hopeless in the end. Faustus's devilish pact is born of a wish to avoid with impunity the traditional morality play acknowledgment of human dependence, and the sequence of scenes that depict him in his ascendance—boxing the Pope's ears, coolly planting antlers on the forehead of a court rival—is a heady portrait of aspiring invulnerability. Whether the source of Faustus's destruction is divine or demonic or both is perhaps beside the point: what grips this learned courtier in the end is the ghastly exposure of his own utter vulnerability. Marlovian drama in effect projects a deeply felt personal and social dilemma onto a cosmic screen. While Marlowe does not lend himself readily to a philosophical label, other playwrights more clearly reflect an ideological inclination—frequently that of Stoicism, mediated importantly through Senecan tragedy. The Stoic ideal of *apathia* might well be described as an ancient philosophical attempt to maintain an internal invulnerability that matches what one is seeking externally. Not surprisingly, this ideal gained new vitality in the sixteenth-century cultural context, as did other aspects of the Roman past that had been fostered by the politics of centralized power in the ancient world. Chapman's Bussy initially reflects Pico's ideal of upward mutability, as does Marlowe's Tamburlaine, but Bussy dies like a Stoic sage—erect, leaning on his sword, utterly impervious to the last great change of his mortality.

For Jonson too, Stoicism is important, not only in *Sejanus* and *Catiline* where one expects it, but in his comedies, where a rich variety of characters make immortal fools of themselves principally because they lack the inner coherence of Stoic sagacity. Jonson's ideal of the "centered self" is consistent with his satiric exposure in his comedies of Protean characters like Volpone, who has deep affinities with the court striver Jonson compares to Proteus in *Cynthia's Revels*.

> With him there meets some subtle Proteus, one
> Can change and vary with all forms he sees;
> Be anything but honest, serves the time,
> Hovers between two factions, and explores
> The drifts of both, which (with cross face) he bears
> To the divided heads, and is received
> With mutual grace of either: one that dares
> Do deeds worthy the hurdle or the wheel,
> To be thought somebody, *and is, in sooth,*
> *Such as the satirist points truly forth,*
> That only to his crimes owes all his worth.[17]

Jonson's resistance to self-transformation is paradoxical for a man of the theater, as Jonas Barish points out, and Jonson's satiric treatment of the upwardly mobile seems to belie his own evident determination to succeed at court.[18] But these contradictions are consistent with the cultivation of Stoic invulnerability as a strategy for social and personal survival. One who valued the centered self must inevitably have responded to the theatrical self, as Barish calls it, with deep ambivalence and mistrust. Despite his brilliance in creating theatrical characters, Jonson's ambiguous rejection of them is consistent with his preference for court drama—and so, of course, is his own ambition for court favor. In his masques he lavished his awesome erudition on allegorical dramaturgy that centered in neo-Platonic images of royal immutability, thereby doing an important political favor both for the king and for himself. In this context, images of the Protean self were dismissed in the anti-masque, which was performed, with pointed social significance, by professional actors. Jonson's anticourtly satire belongs to an Elizabethan tradition that extends back at least as far as Spenser's *Mother Hubberd's Tale* in the 1570s. This tradition criticizes courtly behavior from within, not from without: it identifies excesses and abuses of an acknowledged courtly ideal as a means of ultimately vindicating the ideal itself.[19] Jonson's critique of self-fashioning in court competition is thus reconcilable with his own ambition, which expressed itself by a different means to achieving the same end.

To find a critique of the court that begins with genuinely anti-courtly assumptions, one must go to a culturally residual tradition, where one also finds a quite different conception of the self. For Jonson was not alone in mistrusting self-fashioning. More's lurid depiction of it in his portrait of Richard III may well be based on his own experience of the "new fashion," and if he indeed remembered *The City of God* in his expressed hesitation about public service (above, p. 19), then More exemplifies an early sixteenth-century connection between a residual sense of self and rejection of the new courtly ideal. We can find a later example of the same connection among the Puritans, who represent a residual tradition throughout this period. For the Puritans follow Augustine in promulgating what might well be called the vulnerable self, which we have also seen in the medieval dramaturgical tradition of *potentia humilitatis* (above, chapter 2). The central image of every passion play is not one of Stoic immutability but of an innocent poor man unjustly sentenced to torture and the death of a criminal. The self he displays is anything but invulnerable, and his friends are not the privileged but fishers and tax collectors. In the morality play, the vulnerable self has no inherent social and political ramifications, as it does in the mystery plays, but it is a key feature of dramatic structure. For without coming to the end of himself in repentance, Humanum Genus cannot discover divine mercy for himself, which is the culminating movement of every morality play. "He was of yowr nature and of yowr fragilité," Mercy tells Mankind, in recommending that he model himself on the example of Job.[20] "What is a man withowte mercy?" Mankind asks as he repents, acknowledging that his human wholeness consists only in dialogue with God (l. 835).

The precedent of Augustine is again important here. *The Confessions* are the classical prototype of what Stanley Fish calls the "self-consuming artifact," which became a major literary vehicle of seventeenth-century self-expression.[21] Rhetorically *The Confessions* are addressed to God, because they represent an act of self-discovery that is identical to Mankind's: Augustine fashions his identity only in acknowledging his "nature and fragility," as Mercy calls it, in dialogue with God. While his self is consumed in this process, however, it is also recreated, and *The Confessions* are meant to be overheard by a human audience as well, because they model the socially disinterested process of repentance on the part of a particular human being. To distinguish this process from cunning rhetorical self-display, Augustine recalls his boyhood skill in rhetorical declamation and rejects it, because his skill in imitating others hid him from himself (*Confessions* 1.17). The episode is important in distinguishing Augustine's self-conception from that of Stoicism, because what he advocates in rejecting declamatory self-fashioning is not the immutability and impermeability of the self but its brokenness before God, which begins in the recognition of self-deception—of one's ability to create effective disguises not only from others but from oneself. Augustine is thus arguably a precursor of what Paul Ricoeur has called "the school of suspicion" in the nineteenth century.[22]

Augustine's influence is pervasive and explicit in a popular early seventeenth-century book by the Puritan Daniel Dyke, *The Mystery of*

Selfe-Deceving, which can be said with some accuracy to be an extended explication of the vulnerable self:

> Ransack we therefore our own hearts, and finding any of the vizers of deceitfulness, let us take them off by repentance. This is the best uncasing of the hypocrite, namely, when he shall uncase himself, not when God shall uncase him by judging him, but when he shall uncase himself by judging and humbling himself, . . . not when God shall wash out thy paintings with the dashing tempests of his judgment, but when thy self shalt wash them out with the sweet dew of thy repenting and weeping eyes, being angry with thy self for former deceit. . . .[23]

Augustine's influence on Dyke unfortunately did not improve his style, for the English Puritan is repetitive and given to scholastic hairsplitting. Nonetheless, he often achieves genuine insight, and his references to contemporary social reality are evidence that in the seventeenth century, as in the Middle Ages, the ideal of the vulnerable self was particularly attractive to those on the margins of power and privilege. Whereas Puttenham commends decorous courtly dissembling, for example, Dyke condemns the dissembling of those who seek office or preferment as mere greediness and cruelty (p. 18, Cv). The best he can say for it is that it sometimes compels one to restrain one's other vices in the interest of satisfying one's ambition; in this regard, "policy" is more effective "sometimes than is grace in some that are truly religious" (p. 20, C2v). (Dyke might also be said to anticipate the school of suspicion.)[24] For him, idealist conceptions of the self (like Stoic *apathia*) are merely a sophisticated form of self-deception: "Many natural men there are whom God never renewed by his grace, in whom yet he so moderateth and bridleth many corruptions, as pride, lust, cruelty, etc. that they break not forth. Hence such men deceitfully imagine that they are framed of some purer mold, and are of a better nature and disposition" (pp. 41–42, D5–D5v).

As medieval dramatists had done long before, Dyke identifies true nobility with the vulnerable self, not with the courtly ambition that religious playwrights had ascribed to devils and Vices:

> Our ruffling and swashing cutters, with whom a word and a blow, a lie and a stab, think themselves of an heroical spirit, and in no hand would endure the imputation of pusillanimity, of baseness of mind and cowardice, yet the truth is, they are most base and vile cowards, slavishly yielding to their own vile affections, which to overcome and by repentance to be avenged of is a far greater argument of a noble and generous spirit than to pursue so eagerly the revenge of every petty injury. . . . (p. 41, D5)

Dyke is clearly aware of idealist apologies for upward mobility, such as Pico's *Oration on the Dignity of Man* or closer to home, Thomas Wilson's claim that the persuasive power of rhetoric makes one "half a god among men."[25] For "the rich worldling," Dyke maintains, is deceived about his felicity:

> The men of this world, whose bellies God filleth with the hid treasure of the earth, upon occasion of their outward prosperity, are quickly brought into this fool's paradise of thinking themselves to be special darlings of God; for if the godly themselves have oftentimes their eyes so dazzled with the outward glittering and flourishing estate of the wicked as thereupon they are ready to say of them, "the generation of God's children," which was once David's error for a time, how much more then, think we, will the wicked think so of themselves? (p. 51, E2)

In the history of English literature Dyke is a nonentity (Douglas Bush does not mention him in *The History of English Literature in the Early Seventeenth Century*), and even in the history of the vulnerable self, Dyke is much less readable, though frequently no less insightful, than Donne in the *Holy Sonnets* or Herbert in *The Temple*. But Dyke was a popular writer: *The Mystery of Selfe-Deceving* went through eleven editions between 1614 and 1642, and Dyke's treatise on repentance ran a close second, with six impressions between 1616 and 1635. The likelihood, in other words, is that many more people read popular writers like Dyke than the more difficult Donne and Herbert. The popularity of *Selfe-Deceving* in fact led to a French translation of it by Jean Vernueil in 1634, and this translation exerted considerable influence on La Rochefoucauld's trenchant secular maxims about human self-deception, based on observations of courtly behavior in France.[26] La Rochefoucauld's maxim on predatory self-deprecation (quoted above, p. 71) could easily have been abstracted from courtesy literature itself or the vocal anticourtly tradition in France, but a maxim like the following (number 358) is close to the spirit of Dyke and represents, in effect, a description of the vulnerable self: "Humility is the true touchstone of the Christian virtues: without it we retain all our faults, which are simply concealed through pride that would hide them from others, and often from ourselves."

That insights generated by an explicitly religious tradition of the vulnerable self could and did find secular expression in the seventeenth century is important in considering Shakespeare. For no other Elizabethan playwright is as sensitive and sympathetic to the vulnerability of even the most admirable of human beings, and none so insistently uses this vulnerability as a way of qualifying the claims of privilege. In Shakespearean comedy, as in the Tudor morality play, characters are repeatedly brought to the end of themselves as a function of achieving their comic end. Sometimes this process is explicitly related to its dramaturgical origin, as in *As You Like It*, when Duke Frederick is "converted / Both from his enterprise and from the world" by an "old religious man" (5.4.159–61), and Oliver describes his divided self:

> Twas I; but 'tis not I. I do not shame
> To tell you what I was, since my conversion
> So sweetly tastes, being the thing I am.
>   (4.3.136–38)

Often, however, Shakespeare does not present the vulnerable self in religious terms, especially when it comes to characters who are more central to our concern than Oliver and Duke Frederick. Although Rosalind is famous for her brilliant "counterfeiting," which Duke Frederick perversely but understandably (for an ambitious man) interprets as motivated by ambition, we love Rosalind not only for her theatrical self-fashioning but for her vulnerability, which convinces us that she is genuine. Her weary spirits in the forest (2.4) and her swooning when she sees the cloth stained with Orlando's blood (4.3) are not artful gestures but unintended revelations of her human limitations. Such moments have long been taken for prototypes of Romantic feeling—outbursts of the heart despite the head's best efforts at control—and Shakespeare's renewed popularity in the nineteenth century no doubt owes much to such a reading. But if we understand Rosalind as an exemplar of the vulnerable self, it is clear that for all her anticipation of the Romantics, the deepest affinities of her characterization are with the residual tradition of religious medieval drama.

Like Rosalind is Rosaline, in *Love's Labors Lost*, where the young Shakespeare adopts the highly fashionable mode of Lylyan court comedy, as he had aspired to neoclassical standards in *The Comedy of Errors*. The rhetorical virtuosity of this play indeed rivals the best of Lyly, and Shakespeare's understanding of Lyly's mode is evident in the play's focus on courtly character, artful posturing, and the dynamics of Petrarchan love.[27] The title itself glances at the frustrated sexual striving that animates so many of Lyly's comedies. Unlike any play by Lyly, however, *Love's Labors Lost* is a critique of the genre it exemplifies. We have already briefly noticed part of this critique in the unexpected (albeit momentary) dignity of its lower-class characters, which has no parallel in Lyly but for which one can find ubiquitous precedent in medieval religious drama. Shakespeare also dismantles the assumptions of court comedy in exposing his noble characters' use of clever language as a means of self-defense—in effect, a means of making themselves publicly invulnerable. This exposure is analogous to the implicit critique of Roman comedy in *The Comedy of Errors*, because it turns on a contrast between the artificial problems generated by the verbal (if not verbose) mannerism of courtly competition and the real problem of death that intrudes for the first time in act 5, scene 2. The bittersweet ending of *Love's Labors Lost* is specifically related to the demand made by the Princess after she hears of her father's death: that King Ferdinand and his noblemen spend a year tending the sick in order to discover whether they have a truer self than the demands of courtly self-exhibition have allowed them to cultivate and display. The Princess's mistrust of such self-fashioning is explicit ("Your oath I will not trust" [5.2.790]), as is her determination to discover her own true self in "a mourning house, / Raising the tears of lamentation / For the remembrance of my father's death" (5.2.804–6). Rosaline similarly requires Berowne to spend a year comparing the superficial "gibing spirit" that he has displayed heretofore with the reality of suffering and dying:

> Then, if sickly ears
> Deaf'd with the clamors of their own dear groans,
> Will hear your idle scorns, continue then,
> And I will have you and that fault withal;
> But if they will not, throw away that spirit,
> *And I shall find you empty of that fault,*
> *Right joyful of your reformation.*
> (5.2.859–65, my emphasis)

Among Shakespeare's early comedies, perhaps the most forthright qualification of privilege, the high style, and the invulnerable self is *The Two Gentlemen of Verona*. Here Shakespeare experiments with pastoral romance, still another model of the high style and high society in late sixteenth-century England.[28] Don Felix in Montemayor's *Diana*, however, becomes Proteus in *Two Gentlemen*, a change that signals a change of attitude toward the court in the transition from prose romance to Elizabethan drama. For Proteus personifies the theatrical self, a shape-changer, as his name implies, whose perfidious self-fashioning is explicitly undertaken for ambitious and ego-serving motives.[29] Proteus may thus be Shakespeare's first attempt to adapt the Vice to a contemporary social context. Proteus as a duplicitous Italian courtier enacts the sixteenth-century "new fashion," while his frequent soliloquies take the audience into his confidence in ways that link him dramaturgically to medieval tradition. Proteus appears to be merely immature as well, however, and this problem is treated in ways that are analogous to early Tudor morality plays like *Youth* and *Mundus et Infans*, for Proteus falls easy prey to wordly temptation as soon as he confronts it. His problem is stated at the outset by Valentine (1.1.1–8) and emphasized again by his father, Antonio, and his father's servant, Panthino, who thinks the problem would be solved by sending Proteus to court:

There shall he practice tilts and tournaments,
Hear sweet discourse, converse with noblemen,
And be in eye of every exercise
Worthy his youth and nobleness of birth.
  (1.3.30–33)

Panthino is seriously mistaken. What Proteus learns at court is what he
himself calls "three-fold perjury": abandoning Julia, betraying his friend
Valentine, and attempting to seduce Valentine's sweetheart Sylvia. The
soliloquy in which he admits all this is a vocal exercise in deliberate
self-deception:

I cannot leave to love, and yet I do;
But there I leave to love where I should love.
Julia I lose and Valentine I lose.
If I keep them, I needs must lose myself;
If I lose them, thus find I by their loss
For Valentine myself, for Julia Sylvia.
I to myself am dearer than a friend,
For love is still most precious in itself. . . .

. . . .

I cannot now prove constant to myself,
Without some treachery us'd to Valentine.
  (2.6.17–33)

The repetition of "I" and "myself" in these lines is a stylistic reflection
of Proteus' adolescent narcissism, and his ensuing attempt to make himself invulnerable in his pursuit of Sylvia adopts the rhetorical device that
Puttenham calls "paradiastole" or "*curry-favel*, as when we make the
best of a bad thing, or turn a signification to the more plausible sense."[30]
This is essentially the rhetorical strategy of the Vice, as Proteus makes
clear in his brief anticipation of Iago's and Edmund's tactics:[31] pretending to assist the duke in turning Sylvia against Valentine, Proteus suggests slandering Valentine in order to discredit him with Sylvia. The
duke responds exactly as Proteus wants him to, by urging that Proteus
should undertake the slander himself, since it would be more credible in
a friend than an enemy. But Proteus' overt response is to demure: " 'Tis
an ill office for a gentleman, / Especially against his very friend" (3.2.40–
41)—an answer that makes him appear to be conscience-stricken about
the very thing he has been manipulating the duke to request of him.
Self-fashioning and the quest for social invulnerability thus abet self-
deception.

  The conclusion of Proteus' career as a courtly Humanum Genus is
his sudden and inexplicable repentance, which makes *Two Gentlemen*

the first among Shakespeare's "comedies of forgiveness," as R. G. Hunter calls them:[32]

> My shame and guilt confounds me.
> Forgive me, Valentine. If hearty sorrow
> Be a sufficient ransom for offense,
> I tender't here. I do as truly suffer
> As e'er I did commit.
>
> (5.4.73–77)

Proteus asks forgiveness of his friend, not of God, but in doing so he is just as certainly compelled to reveal his vulnerability as are any of his morality play predecessors, and Valentine's response makes this dramaturgical precedent explicit:

> Then am I paid.
> And once again I do receive thee honest.
> Who by repentance is not satisfied
> Is nor of heaven nor earth, for these are pleas'd.
> By penitence th'Eternal's wrath's appeas'd.
>
> (5.4.77–81)

The man who forgives his perfidious but repentant friend so readily is significantly a "masterless man," as the sixteenth-century called such people—an outlaw living among outlaws, devoid of power or privilege. Yet he is morally superior to his social superiors at court, a motif that appears again as part of Shakespeare's critique of the court in later plays, especially *As You Like It*. There, as in *Two Gentlemen*, the motif goes beyond Shakespeare's elegant pastoral sources (which are themselves part of a genre attuned to ambition and privilege) and incorporates elements of a medieval anticourtly tradition that queries the implicit values of his sources, just as the vestiges of medieval drama in *The Comedy of Errors* implicitly challenge the esthetic and moral values of neoclassical comedy.

The *Two Gentlemen of Verona* is a youthful and problematic play, but some of its problems are perhaps less difficult when their tradition is recognized. A final example is Valentine's bizarre offer to give Sylvia to Proteus in reward for Proteus' repentance, even though Proteus had been on the point of raping Sylvia when Valentine intervened. The only explanation for Valentine's offer is the classical ideal of male friendship, known to the sixteenth century principally through Cicero's *De Amicitia* and celebrated in Shakespeare's elegant humanist source, the tale of Titus and Gisippus from Elyot's *Governour*. For by any other reckoning Valentine's action is pointless, mistaken, and indefensible: it betrays Valentine's own commitment to Sylvia; it reduces Sylvia to a commodity; it destroys the point of Julia's extraordinary fidelity to Proteus; and it rewards Proteus' lust rather than his repentance. The question, then, is whether the Ciceronian ideal is represented credibly enough in *Two Gentlemen* to make Valentine's offer sympathetic and understandable. Two factors suggest that it is not. First, declarations of friendship in this play are invariably betrayed by Proteus' perfidy. For him, they carry no more weight than any other idle word he speaks: "I to myself am dearer than a friend." His only gesture of true friendship in the play is his repentance, whose tradition is not Platonic or Ciceronian but Augustinian and medieval. Second, Valentine's high-minded idealism is undone by Julia's swooning, which closely parallels the later swoon of Rosalind in *As You Like It*. Julia's vulnerability, in other words, is the play's answer to Valentine's wrongheaded idealism—not only a literal answer, in that she swoons immediately in response to his offer to give Sylvia to Proteus, but also an answer in the broader sense of qualifying yet another high-minded classical ideal. For her swoon leads directly to her reconciliation with Proteus, whereas Valentine's offer to sacrifice Sylvia only reintroduces and compounds the dilemmas that Proteus' repentance had almost resolved.

Attending to Shakespeare's dramatic heritage thus suggests that the young playwright initially responds to the prestige of those literary forms and accompanying attitudes that were identified with social privilege. His sympathetic treatment of upper-class characters, his attention to neoclassical demands, his responsiveness to Italian novelle and fashionable court comedy, all point to an unmistakable aspiration to achieve what the ruling idea required of a socially ambitious playwright. Yet Shakespeare's romantic comedies cannot adequately be described merely as exercises in upward mobility. Repeatedly this provincial newcomer reveals a sensitivity to the popular dramatic tradition and its implicit attitudes—a sensitivity too keen and sympathetic to be dismissed as no more than caviar for the general. Rather, Shakespeare would seem to be drawing on popular dramaturgy from the outset as a means of implicitly qualifying the claims of power. In this regard, he is not only an appropriator of popular dramatic technique; he is a perpetrator of informed skepticism about power that had combined the political realism of Augustine and the subversiveness of folk tradition in medieval religious drama. The medieval playwrights' perception that evil masquerades in the guise of court gallantry is essentially continuous with Shakespeare's perception that human weakness in the likes of Proteus is exacerbated at court. This skepticism about power, as we shall see, becomes more pronounced in comedy as Shakespeare's recourse to medieval religious drama becomes more self-confident. In the meantime, however, let us turn to his history plays, where Elizabethan political relations are enacted more explicitly and where Shakespeare's dependence on medieval drama is rather different from that in his comedies.

CHAPTER 5 ✌ INVENTING SECULAR HISTORY: THE HENRY VI PLAYS

When Elizabethan playwrights turned to their own history, they had no classical models to guide them and therefore no ascribed social expectations to meet in shaping their material. If Shakespeare was the first in this field, as he may well have been, he had to find a pattern of his own. The anonymous popular play, *The Famous Victories of Henry V*, may have preceded the *Henry VI* plays, but if it did, Shakespeare eschewed it as a model, though he learned some important things from it, which he put to use when he wrote his own series of plays about Henry V several years later. *The Famous Victories* shapes history as if it were a moral comedy, taking the prince to be a young wastrel who has to learn to conquer himself morally before he can conquer France. This is good humanist state theory, ultimately traceable to Plato, and the play therefore implicitly espouses the social values that had defined Tudor privilege for several generations. The carnival-like atmosphere in which a prince strikes the lord chief justice and robs the king's receivers is severely rejected and curtailed in the prince's edifying career as king, so that *The Famous Victories*, for all its popular auspices, manifests a deep social affinity with the movement from antimasque to masque in Jonson's later court entertainments. From the outset, however, Shakespeare's history plays do something quite different. While they unquestionably enact Tudor social prejudice, they do not mystify power but examine empirically how it really works. Comparing a Shakespearean history play to *The Famous Victories* is a little like comparing Machiavelli's *Prince* to Erasmus' *Enchiridion*.

Early critics of Shakespeare's histories came to quite a different conclusion about them. Recognizing that Shakespeare had no classical models, they explained his procedure in terms of the putative view of history in the chronicles from which he drew his material.[1] This view was said to be providential and teleological: God had rewarded England with the Tudor regime because England had suffered enough during the Wars of the Roses, which had, in turn, been divine chastisement for Henry IV's usurpation of Richard II's throne. This "Tudor myth," as

E.M.W. Tillyard called it, not only explained the history plays' internal coherence; it also explained why they came into being in the first place. For they appear suddenly in the years following the Armada victory, and their assumed vindication of providential English history thus answered what was thought to be a widespread euphoria about the Armada victory as an act of God on England's behalf. What Shakespeare's histories were said to show, in other words, is that God had always been a special presence in English history. Shakespeare's histories might lack the privilege of classical precedent, but as versions of the Tudor myth they made up for that lack, manifesting the same kind of social aspiration that we find in explicit literary apologies for the regime, like Spenser's *Faerie Queene*.

The internal coherence and social appeal of this argument made it enormously influential, but it has been thoughtfully challenged in detail by almost every critic of the history plays over the last twenty years.[2] Even Shakespeare's chronicle source for the *Henry VI* plays, Edward Hall, is now recognized to be more pragmatic than Tillyard allowed in his construction of the Tudor myth.[3] The thesis about the history plays and the Armada also encounters difficulties, for the *Henry VI* plays seem an odd way to celebrate the greatness of the English past: though they are Shakespeare's first ventures into English history and were written immediately following the Armada, they are extraordinarily bleak. Why the young playwright would commemorate a great national victory with a penetrating and dispiriting analysis of how England lost her French possessions and collapsed into civil war is not clear. To explain that the *Henry VI* plays form a unit with *Richard III* and therefore depict the divine chastisement that necessarily preceded divine reward is to fall back on Tillyard's discredited providentialist thesis, repeating his error of imposing a spurious integrity on the first history plays Shakespeare wrote.

In fact, the bleakness of the *Henry VI* plays more accurately reflects the national mood in the time they were probably written than does the euphoric celebration of English triumph in *The Famous Victories*. To be sure, the immediate response in 1588 was enormous relief, but it was shortlived, as the reality of a costly, bloody, and enervating war of attrition sank in.[4] Even where the Armada itself was concerned, the government was not sure that a victory had been won at all—only that defeat had been avoided—and much mutual recrimination arose over the British fleet's failure to engage the Armada effectively in the Channel and to intercept and destroy its remaining ships later as they crossed the bay of Biscay.[5] Spain remained a very serious source of anxiety to England, despite the Armada misadventure, and Elizabeth's government was preoccupied with countering the Spanish threat throughout the rest of her reign. In 1589–90, when Shakespeare very likely composed the

Henry VI plays, Philip II was showing his hand with particular strength in France, where England had an expeditionary force under the command of Lord Willoughby (Wernham, pp. 131–80), and the French setting of *1 Henry VI* could hardly have been understood as anything else but a reflection of this concern. If any event from the recent past is recalled in these plays, it would be the fall of Calais in January 1558 rather than the Armada victory. A weak monarch, a divided council, insufficient support for English forces in France, the suspicion of treachery, fear that "the devil was raised up and become French"—all these factors are cited by Holinshed in the 1587 edition of the *Chronicles* (which Shakespeare consistently used), as he recounts how Calais fell, and the same factors appear in Shakespeare's account of how England lost her French possessions in the fifteenth century, including the devil rising up and becoming French in support of La Pucelle in *1 Henry VI*.[6] Sir Walter Mildmay, chancellor of the exchequer, cited Mary's misgovernment as the cause of Calais's loss in the Parliament of 1584–85: "a marvelous blow to this realm, and so is like to prove whensoever wars shall happen between us and the French."[7]

The bleakness of Shakespeare's early histories thus answers more credibly to their political realism than to their appropriating Elizabethan mystifications of power. "The fraud of England, not the force of France" is what destroys the achievement of Henry V in the *Henry VI* plays, and the process involves an analytical delineation of effective centralized power giving way to the chaos of civil war because of uncontrolled factionalism at court. The distinctively Tudor character of this process is evident in a number of ways, but most strikingly perhaps in its parallel with the English political transformation of the sixteenth century. The first stage of this transformation was the transfer of power from warrior to educated elite, as we noticed briefly in chapter 3, and this transformation is depicted, in effect, in *1 Henry VI*. Shakespeare focuses on successive public-spirited pillars of state in the first two plays, as critics have pointed out, and he shows the downfall of these characters resulting from intense competition for power at court.[8] The first of them is Talbot, a heroic warrior who is finally defeated by the French because York and Somerset are quarreling too bitterly to provide him with effective aid. Talbot admirably embodies the ideal of the aristocrat as warrior: he is fearsome in battle, loyal to the king, removed from divisive court politics (no mere court butterfly), and yet capable of handling himself effectively in a situation involving a duplicitous political power play at the castle of Auvergne (*1 Henry VI*, 2.3). (Shakespeare returned to this kind of character again in Hotspur of *1 Henry IV*, but from quite a different point of view.) After Talbot's death, English power passes to two characters: York, who is opportunistically waiting for the right moment to move in force against his own king, and Suffolk, a rhetorically gifted courtier whom we first meet as a student at the Inns of Court, boldly declaring that he has been "a truant in the law, / And never yet could frame my will to it, / And therefore frame the law unto my will" (2.4.7–9). In *1 Henry VI* we thus witness the transfer of power from successful and heroic warrior aristocrats (Henry V and Talbot) to mere opportunists and educated courtiers who sap the nation's strength while selfishly and sophistically pursuing their own interests. "Emulation" is a word used more than once in *1 Henry VI* to describe the kind of rivalry inspired by the likes of York and Suffolk (4.1.113 and 4.4.21), and "emulation" is a favorite contemporary word, as Frank Whigham points out, for describing the "coincidence of struggle and assimilation" that marked the peculiarities of upward mobility in Elizabethan society.[9]

In *2 Henry VI* no warrior of Talbot's stature remains, but a significant degree of power is still retained by a selfless courtier, Humphrey, duke of Gloucester, who in many respects represents the humanist ideal embodied for the sixteenth century in a man like Sir Thomas More. Like Talbot, Gloucester is not interested in his own power and reputation as ends in themselves but only as by-products of his exemplary service to king and country. His dismay at the loss of French territory in Suffolk's negotiation for Henry to marry Margaret of Anjou is thus contrasted with York's regret: Gloucester is alarmed at the blow to English dignity and the undercutting of past military achievement (*2 Henry VI*, 1.1.73–101), while York is sorry only that he will have less territory to call his own when he wrests the kingdom from Henry VI (1.1.212–36). Gloucester eventually succumbs to the weight of predatory opposition arranged against him. Putting their differences aside in a perverse determination to eliminate what seems to be the kingdom's one remaining good man, Gloucester's enemies frame him, compel the king to abandon him for political reasons, and finally hire assassins to kill him. Gloucester's fate is thus a simple outline of the sixteenth-century courtly ideal being undone by those who willfully abuse it, for all of Gloucester's enemies are interested only in enhancing their own political positions without appearing to do so. While Duke Humphrey commends legitimate public-spirited ambition (2.1.13–14), his enemies maliciously twist his commendation to undo him by accusing him of hypocrisy and dissimulation ("Who cannot steal a shape that means deceit?" [3.1.79]), thereby appearing to be public-spirited themselves as a way of disguising their own drive for power. Suffolk's rhetorical ability is a telling characteristic of these merely ambitious courtiers, since he repeatedly uses his persuasive power to frame the law to his will, as he puts it. His ability caricatures humanist rhetorical aims, as we have seen Thomas Wilson express them: "Such force hath the tongue and such is the power of eloquence and reason that most men are forced even to yield in that which most standeth against their will."[10] Suffolk is the one who provides the final argument for destroying Gloucester, pointing out that since Gloucester has been accused, he must be guilty, and if he is guilty he should be destroyed before he can do any harm! "For that is good deceit / Which mates him first that first intends deceit" (3.1.264–65).

After Gloucester's fall, what follows in *3 Henry VI* is a chaos of mere oppugnance—an uncontrolled struggle for power in which even family loyalties are sacrificed to political advantage. The king disinherits his son in a weak gesture of hopeless political compromise; Margaret separates from Henry in retaliation; Clarence abandons his brother, Edward IV, because of the king's foolish marriage, and then abandons his father-in-law, Warwick, in response to Richard of Gloucester's persuasive power. The resistance of Edward IV's brothers to the king's marriage with Elizabeth Grey has topical importance, as well as thematic significance, in its portrayal of the brothers' opposition as primarily social: they object to Edward's alliance with a woman of lower status than themselves. This social snobbery accurately renders the tension of upward mobility in Tudor society: those who were able to secure higher status for themselves (as the Yorkists do in this case) were concerned to preserve the exclusiveness of what they had gained by denying it to others who were seeking the same objective. A typical strategy of social preservation in such a situation was to abuse those who sought preferment as malapert assheads—exactly the strategy of Edward's brothers regarding the Greys.[11] The end of this process of petty but deadly squabbling is Richard's stunning soliloquy in *3 Henry VI*, 3.2.124–95, a declaration of allegiance to himself ("I am myself alone" [5.6.83]) that perfectly expresses the diabolical dissimulation and hypocrisy that courtly self-fashioning appeared to foster, even in the view of those who regarded courtesy as a worthy ideal, as virtually everyone did who acknowledged it as a ruling idea in the sixteenth century. Richard has dramatic affinities with the Vice of the morality play, but Shakespeare depicts him specifically as a courtier whose craving for power is closely involved with his pride in self-fashioning and his exemplification of Puttenham's principle that "the profession of a very courtier . . . is in plain terms cunningly to be able to dissemble":[12]

> Why, I can smile, and murder whiles I smile,
> And cry "Content" to that which grieves my heart,
> And wet my cheeks with artificial tears,
> And frame my face to all occasions.
> (3.2.182–85)

Richard might well take Puttenham's Latin tag as his motto: "Qui nescit dissimulare nescit regnare" (*Arte of English Poesie*, p. 186), for he is a master of the rhetorical figure we have encountered before, the one that Puttenham calls *paradiastole*, "as when we make the best of a bad thing, or turn a signification to the more plausible sense" (*Arte of English Poesie*, pp. 184–85). Richard's comparison of himself to Proteus (*3 Henry VI*, 3.2.192) is thus consistent with the way Shakespeare portrays the character Proteus in *Two Gentlemen of Verona*, which was written at about the same time. Indeed, Richard of Gloucester's chief precursor in these plays, the earl of Suffolk, debates with himself about whether or not to seduce Margaret of Anjou (*1 Henry VI*, 5.3.6off.) in terms that closely parallel Proteus' sophistical debate with himself about his pending disloyalty to Valentine and Julia (*Two Gentlemen*, 2.6). In both Proteus' case and Suffolk's, the eventual decision is predictably self-serving.

The claim put forward here that Shakespeare's early histories reproduce what we now recognize as the central processes of change in sixteenth-century English political life need not be regarded as willful anachronism, as if to suggest that Shakespeare had read Lawrence Stone. For what Stone recognized and exhaustively documented is what the sixteenth century recognized about itself, though obviously not in the conceptual terms of the modern social historian. Humanists recognized that they were competing for power with the landed aristocracy, as we noticed in chapter 3, and they were quite conscious of establishing new criteria (such as the "new learning") by which to define privilege so that they could compete more effectively. But the mystique of the old warrior aristocracy did not cease: if anything, it rose in the course of the sixteenth century, taking new life in the elaborate rituals of courtly chivalry and discovering new deadliness with the introduction of the rapier in midcentury.[13] For Castiglione the courtier is first and foremost an accomplished fighter, and Sidney begins the *Apology* with a brilliant analogy drawn from equestrian chivalry, the horse and rider being a potent symbol of humanist reason restraining the powerful beast it governs. What Shakespeare represents as a process of decline in the *Henry VI* plays, then, he probably understood in terms of comparative prestige—from warrior aristocrat, to public-spirited humanist courtier, to self-serving opportunist. In the *Henry VI* plays he rendered this comparison as a process because of his interest in creating what Edward Berry calls "patterns of decay"—from a stable commonwealth to one in chaos. In doing so, he inevitably presented a different picture of political change from the one we now see in the sixteenth century. True to Tudor practice, he always assumes that centralized power is the key to political stability: thus Henry VI's weakness is what allows the factions at his court to explode into civil war. We now understand the centralization of power, however, to be the catalyst for the changes Shakespeare depicts: only when the Tudor monarchs had gathered sufficient power in their own hands could they effectively neutralize the old aristrocracy, and they did so, in part, by creating new criteria for privilege and a new educated privileged class—Suffolk, in effect, to replace Talbot.

Given the absence of dramatic models for Shakespeare's historical analysis, the question naturally arises as to where he derived it. Machiavelli is a suggestive possibility, and Marlowe was shortly to flaunt this source openly in the prologue to *The Jew of Malta*, which enacts a political reality at least as bleak as *3 Henry VI*, though a good deal more comical. The implicit historical thesis of the *Henry VI* plays—that strong central leadership is essential to prevent an inevitable decline into political and social chaos—is derivable from Machiavelli and certainly anticipates Hobbes. But one cannot easily conclude that materialism is therefore emergent in Shakespeare's plays.[14] For one thing, Hobbes's kind of analysis was available to the sixteenth century in a work that was anything but materialist, namely, Augustine's *City of God*. Moreover, Augustine derived his outlook on secular history from his theological distinction between history and eschatology—the City of Humankind and the City of God. As we saw in chapter 1, the *saeculum* is defined not by the absence of God but by the inaccessibility of the divine plan and the consequent necessity to understand history tentatively "from below," rather than through the definitive means of divine revelation. The resulting secular analysis of power is what Augustine outlines in *The City of God*, and his analysis plays a part in the medieval dramatic attempt to assimilate the *saeculum* to sacred history, as we saw in chapter 2. If one wanted to understand secular history per se, then, one would have to do so empirically, and if one were a dramatist, one would require a different model from the only model for dramatizing history that Shakespeare had—that is, the mystery plays, which deal with sacred history.

At several points in the early histories, we can find evidence that Shakespeare arrived at his model by a process of contrasting secular dramatic history with its sacred prototype, in much the same way Augustine derived his sense of the *saeculum* from the Bible. This is not to say that Machiavelli played no part in Shakespeare's conception, but that as a dramatic model Machiavelli was little help, and we cannot clearly distinguish what might be Machiavelli's influence from a version of secular history that is fully compatible with Augustine. Distinct points of continuity with the medieval dramaturgy of power in the early histories thus coexist with a consistent pattern of departure from the mystery plays. The result is that when these plays recall medieval dramatic precedent, they almost invariably do so to emphasize how centralized power works in fact—or fails to work. Yet the history plays' continuity with medieval drama means that they can just as credibly be said to adhere to Augustine's notion of *libido dominandi* as to Machiavelli's, and the fact that they eliminate Augustine's answering feature of transcendent humility is precisely what makes them secular: they deal with the City of Humankind, not the City of God. Class relations are thus treated with considerable realism in the history plays, but without the symbolic import of class relations in medieval religious drama. The commoners' largest role is in 2 *Henry VI*, where they are extremely disruptive, but their rebellion is a direct consequence of the breakdown of central authority: York exploits Cade as an instrument of his opportunism, remarking with cynical satisfaction that Cade has learned his boldness and military prowess in crushing and deceiving Irish kerns (3.1.360–70). This remark incisively clarifies who the big fish are and who the little, without choosing morally between them, for it is clear that Cade's success is due to his ability to play York's opportunistic game with considerable skill. But Cade is not the only commoner in 2 *Henry VI*. The hardship of common people is presented sympathetically to the king (3.2.242–69), and the evil of enclosure is twice referred to (1.3.23 and 4.2.66). The play's most arrogant character is the earl of Suffolk, who is accused of enclosure (1.3.22–24) and attempts to preserve his life by pulling rank with the pirates who have captured him (4.1.121–29). But for once his rhetorical skill fails him, and he is summarily executed. Nothing in his life or death is inconsistent with the medieval dramatic conception of power as the lust to dominate. What is lacking in Suffolk's world is the cosmic context that would explain how *libido dominandi* relates to creative and redemptive providence.

That the history plays draw on medieval drama is hardly a new idea. The influence of the morality play has long been recognized, and Emrys Jones pointed out more than ten years ago that "a major obstacle to a close historical understanding of Shakespearian drama, and particularly the histories and tragedies, has been the failure to bring into relation with it the great body of dramatic writing known as the mystery plays."[15] Jones makes up for this failure in a number of ways, including a close analysis of Duke Humphrey's fall in 2 *Henry VI* against the background of medieval passion plays. In both cases, he points out, the action moves through four recognizable phases: first, concentration on the victim's enemies and their implacable malice; second, their well-coordinated conspiracy against their victim; third, their determination to proceed according to strict legality in order to disguise their dastardly intentions; fourth, their successful isolation of the victim from all sources of support and assistance in order to ensure his downfall (*Origins*, p. 52). Jones also notes that the two principal conspirators in Humphrey's case, Queen Margaret and Cardinal Beaufort, proceed very much as Caiaphas and Annas do in the passion plays—abetting one another's perverse instincts and inciting others to the same fever pitch of hatred that they feel themselves. Beaufort's clerical vestments even recall the biblical priests in medieval drama, who were typically costumed and titled as dignitaries of the medieval church.

Parallels such as these carry conviction because they involve long sequences of dramatic action and configurations of staging—a large conspiratorial group standing over against an isolated innocent man, for example, whom they proceed to judge and condemn. Nor is the fall of Humphrey the only such parallel from the mystery plays in Shakespeare's treatment of Henry VI's long reign, as we shall see. First, however, it is worth noting that in Humphrey's case the parallel illustrates how Shakespeare departs from his medieval model even as he draws on it for emotional impact. The fact that a churchman is involved in Humphrey's condemnation recalls the peculiar topicality in medieval religious drama that we noticed in chapter 2. The trial of Jesus in the mystery plays involves an archetypal confrontation between innocent humility and the lust to dominate, but the action proceeds neither as personification allegory nor as a simple recreation of events from the past: its archetypal quality consists in its appropriation of social and political reality from the world of its auditors. What they saw was theologically rich and profound: the same social institution that oppressed them was also at work in the destruction of Jesus—namely the dubious justice of fifteenth-century ecclesiastical courts. A similar kind of topicality operates in 2 *Henry VI*, but with a very different effect. What Elizabethan auditors saw was the destruction of an innocent man by the same kind of "factious emulation" that seemed to be threatening political stability in the 1590s. The scene is thus a dramaturgical palimpsest: it borrows emotional force from medieval passion plays, but its topical relevance is not fifteenth-century and theological but contemporary and secular.

This point can be illustrated in another way by considering the great oath that Warwick swears when he sees the newly strangled corpse of Duke Humphrey:

> As surely as my soul intends to live
> With that dread King that took our state upon him
> To free us from his Father's wrathful curse,
> I do believe that violent hands were laid
> Upon the life of this thrice-famed Duke.
> (2 *Henry VI*, 3.2.153–57)

This is indeed an extraordinary oath, as Suffolk immediately acknowledges with a guilty start: "A dreadful oath, sworn with a solemn tongue" (158). Warwick's oath adds resonance to the solemn sense of passion drama that the scene as a whole invokes, as Jones notes (*Origins*, p. 46). But this effect of Warwick's words is at odds with their function in the politics of the scene. For Warwick is a close ally of York and therefore ranged against Suffolk, who declared his support for Somerset when the rivalry between York and Somerset first boiled into open conflict in the quarrel of the roses (*1 Henry VI*, 2.4). Warwick's great oath therefore challenges Suffolk's high-handedness not in defense of Gloucester but as an epicircular side skirmish in the expanding rings of court competition that mark Henry VI's chaotic reign. For all the awful solemnity of Warwick's oath and its suggestion of pious candor, it is actually intended— and actually functions—as a weapon to disarm a court rival.

From the beginning, then, Shakespeare's secular history plays are strikingly innovative but not radically discontinuous with the only other dramatizations of human history he could have known—the mystery plays. Repeatedly Shakespeare borrows dramaturgically from these impressive theatrical treatments of the human past but always with the effect of analyzing the political process empirically rather than identifying the hand of God in the government of humankind. Augustine had pointed the way to this kind of analysis in his skeptical review of Roman history in *The City of God*—a history that revealed nothing more than an unremitting competition for power and wealth and not at all the awesome *fatum* that Virgil had found, nor the *justitia* that Cicero had maintained as the essential defining quality of *res publica*, nor even the process of decline from noble republican leadership to sordid *imperium* that Sallust and Livy had pointed out, because in Augustine's view Roman history had always been a tawdry struggle for domination, dressed up by poets, historians, and philosophers in terms of religious and philosophical idealism. While Augustine had higher hopes for political order under Christian leadership, he did not regard Christian and pagan social constructions as differently consitituted in essence, because the City of God was not identifiable with any human institution, including the church. As we noted in Chapter 1, while Augustine's thoroughgoing providentialism disallowed resistance to established power, his pessimistic understanding of power relations also disallowed idealization of the political process, in contrast to late medieval political theory and the standard practice of Renaissance princes. Their claim to providential authorization for what was a good deal less than perfect justice merely duplicated the classic Roman mystification of power that Augustine incisively identified and rejected. A careful analyst of the sixteenth-century political scene might well conclude that the Tudor penchant for assimilating English history to Roman imperial destiny deserved the same skepticism with which Augustine had surveyed the Roman exercise of power.

A providential habit of mind that is very close to the approach of contemporary state apologists in fact appears in a highly unsympathetic character in the *Henry VI* plays. This character is young Clifford, who undertakes a personal holy war in explicitly apocalyptic terms as he finds cosmic significance in his father's death at the battle of St. Albans:

> O, let the vile world end,
> And the premised flames of the last day

Knit earth and heaven together!
Now let the general trumpet blow his blast,
Particularities and petty sounds
To cease!
        (*2 Henry VI*, 5.2.40–45)

Clifford wreaks vengeance with learned humanist decorum, comparing himself to the avenging Fury of Senecan tragedy (*3 Henry VI*, 1.3.30–31), and murdering children as Medea did (cf. *2 Henry VI*, 5.2.57–59). Clifford's outlook is comparable to that of John Foxe, who interprets English history in the *Actes and Monuments* according to an apocalyptic pattern, finding the key to recent events in the design of salvation history as divinely revealed in the Bible and dramatically represented in the mystery plays. John Bale's interest in medieval dramatic forms derives from a similar impulse to bestow cosmic significance on Reformation history. What motivated this kind of providentialism was the early reformers' identification of religious reformation with Tudor power, so that English history was given sacred shape in the same way that the king was elevated to iconographic sainthood.[16]

By the end of the sixteenth century, however, the political situation was very different from the situation earlier in the century. Reformation had been institutionalized for more than three decades as a program of political containment, with a clearly defined demand for ameliorative reform now officially discredited and suppressed. Careers, fortunes, and political expectations were now deeply committed to preventing an erosion of the power base enjoyed for many years by the same privileged fraction of the population. Foxe printed Simon Fish's *Supplication of Beggars* whole and unexpurgated in the 1563 *Actes and Monuments*, though Fish's book had been so alarmingly radical when it was originally published in 1524 that Henry VIII made it first among forbidden books and Thomas More was moved to refute it in print.[17] Foxe liked Fish's book not only because it was anticlerical but because its combination of religious social critique and apocalyptic zeal seemed logical and compelling: with the end of the world in sight, it was appropriate to expect a brave new one that would eradicate injustice. The coexistence of radical expectation with admiration for royal power, however, was shortlived, given the Tudor conception of royal prerogative, and by the end of the century it was clear that the apocalypse had not arrived or seemed likely to displace the reality of Elizabethan politics as usual. The early histories' unusually patronizing attitude toward commoners is thus consistent with the moderate social ambition that we see signs of elsewhere in Shakespeare's early plays: despite his openness to archaic dramaturgy, he is committed to the existing hierarchy, not to a vision of social levelling from the past. In keeping with the soberer mood of the post-Armada years, Clifford's apocalyptic vengeance brings about no "promis'd end," as Kent calls it in *King Lear*, but only breeds more vengeance and hastens the decline into political chaos, intensifying the carnage rather than definitively ending it.

Clifford is a curious portrait of radical providentialism in action, and the ironic emptiness of his zeal illuminates David Kastan's description of Shakespeare's history plays as open-ended.[18] But this structural feature has more than philosophical and esthetic significance. Certainly, as Kastan argues, the history plays' episodic linearity and lack of closure distinguish them from the mystery plays, which manifest absolute closure in the divine acts of Creation and Last Judgment, and this kind of structural distinction indeed reflects a profound difference in the sense of history itself that the two kinds of historical drama enact—one sacred and providential, the other secular and governed exclusively by human action (or inaction, in the case of Henry VI). But Shakespeare's secular perspective on the English past emerged in a context of social and political change that influenced his sense of form as profoundly in his history plays as it did in comedy or tragedy. Shakespeare, in other words, did not achieve the same effect in borrowing medieval dramaturgy as Bale did, because the late Elizabethan political scene was different from what it had been earlier in the sixteenth century.

What we find in Shakespeare's debt to religious drama in the history plays, then, is a familiar insistence on human government as an endless contest for power but put now in a context that emphasizes contingency and human volition in the secular past rather than sacred direction in history. This point can be illustrated in a series of dramaturgical borrowings from the mystery plays in *3 Henry VI*, where the effect is the same as the parallel with the passion plays in the fall of Duke Humphrey: in every case the derivative dramaturgy heightens the emotional intensity of the incident while ultimately emphasizing its secular context. In the play's opening scene, for example, we witness the Yorkists' boldest bid for power: Richard of York's seizure of Henry VI's throne in Westminster Palace. The Yorkists have broken into this place by force, and their violence is strongly antipathetic. The clan's boldness is heightened by the reason for their gathering: to celebrate their first taste of victory at St. Albans. They are made repugnant by means of theatrically effective but literally impossible details as they display fresh battle trophies: dripping swords whose victims are mordantly identified, and the newly severed head of Somerset, gruesomely rolling about the floor while York and his youngest son address it mockingly:

RICHARD: Speak thou for me and tell them what I did.
YORK: Richard hath best deserv'd of all my sons.
    But is your Grace dead, my lord of Somerset?
    (1.1.16–18)

As a way of adding to the natural repugnance that this scene arouses, Shakespeare patterns it on the opening scene in all the extant mystery cycles: the fall of Lucifer. The pattern is most impressive in York's theatrical imitation of Lucifer's seating himself in God's throne, but as in the fall of Duke Humphrey, the scene involves a sequence of actions that surround this bold gesture. First, the rebel feigns a dissembling compliance with the superior he plans to challenge. In the Chester cycle, Lucifer and Lightborne (who later rebels as well) gracefully hymn God's praises along with the other angels until God leaves to "take my trace / And see this blesse in every tower"; then Lucifer suddenly makes his unexpected move.[19] This kind of dissembling typifies York above all other characters in the first two parts of *Henry VI*: "A day will come when York shall claim his own"; "Then, York, be still awhile, till time do serve."[20] Second, the rebel defiantly seats himself in the throne of his absent superior, and third, having occupied the throne, he lays confident claim to it on the basis of both right and might. Thus Lucifer in the Towneley play:

> If that ye will behold me right,
> This maistre longys to me.
>
> . . . .
>
> Agans my grete might
> May [no]thing stand ne be.[21]   *nor be*

York likewise occupies King Henry's throne with the intention "to take possession of my right" (*3 Henry VI*, 1.1.44), and his precaution in concealing soldiers throughout the palace clearly signals his belief that he can make good his right by power. "By words or blows here let us win our right," he urges (1.1.37). York's preparation to support his claim with a show of power exactly parallels Talbot's tactic at the castle of Auvergne when he concealed his soldiers to prevent a surprise capture (*1 Henry VI*, 2.3). But this parallel serves to show how badly the situation has disintegrated. Talbot had used the military precaution to prove that the substance of his heroic reputation was in his deeds, but York uses it to turn the balance of power in his favor as he challenges the very king whom Talbot had ceremoniously acknowledged with "submissive loyalty of heart" (*1 Henry VI*, 3.4.10). Fourth, a debate is held between the supporters of the rebel and those who support his superior. The long debate that rages between Yorkists and Lancastrians in the first scene of *3 Henry VI* has a structural analogue in the debate between the *Boni* and *Mali Angeli* regarding Lucifer's right to sit in God's throne. In all these respects, then, *3 Henry VI* begins like the cosmic history of salvation: we see a repugnant and dissembling usurper; he boldly occupies the empty throne of his rightful superior; he claims his right to do so; he is urged on by his lieutenants; he argues his case at length with those who believe he is acting wrongly. Though Shakespeare took the suggestion for this scene from the chronicles of Hall and Holinshed, he devised its staging entirely according to his own imagination, and it seems clear that his imagination turned to an impressive dramaturgical precedent in the mystery plays.

Though much happens in the opening scene of *3 Henry VI* to qualify the significance of the medieval analogue, it will be helpful to consider first another such analogue that appears at the end of the first act. Importantly this scene again involves the duke of York, but this time in his defeat rather than his triumph. Again a potent medieval precedent serves to emphasize and heighten our natural reaction, which this time is a feeling of surprise at the reversal of fortune in York's pitiable death. The gross inequity of several combatants against one, the deliberate mental torture of taunting him with the news of his young son's murder, the unqueenly cruelty of Margaret, York's pious frame of mind in death—all these factors weigh heavily against the Lancastrians in this incredibly savage scene. If the Yorkists have also earned our dislike by taunting a fallen enemy as the play opened, they at least waited until he was dead.

But the archetypal dramatic analogue of York's death contributes more than anything to our feeling that nothing in York's life became him like the leaving it. This analogue is suggested by a passing reference in Holinshed:

> Some write that the duke was taken alive, and in derision caused to stand upon a molehill, on whose head they put a garland instead of a crown, which they had fashioned and made of sedges or bulrushes; and having so crowned him with that garland, they kneeled down afore him (as the Jews did unto Christ) in scorn, saying to him: "Hail, king without rule! Hail, king without heritage! Hail, duke and prince without people or possessions!"[22]

Among several possible versions of how York died, this is the one that Shakespeare chose to dramatize (Hall makes no mention of it), and he could hardly have done so in ignorance of the well-developed medieval tradition depicting the buffeting and scourging of Christ. Like the fall of Lucifer, this event is found in all the extant mystery cycles, and its treatment produced some of the most powerful scenes in medieval drama. Their power derives largely from a juxtaposition of extraordinary brutality with an elaborately pretended game on the part of the soldiers who abuse Christ: "Bot more sorow thou hase / oure myrth is incresying" seems to be the principle behind their "jape."[23] The influence of this dramaturgical tradition is clear in Margaret's mockery of York:

CHAPTER 3

> I prithee, grieve, to make me merry, York.
> What, hath thy fiery heart so parch'd thine entrails
> That not a tear can fall for Rutland's death?
> Why art thou patient, man? Thou shouldst be mad;
> And I, to make thee mad, do mock thee thus.
> Stamp, rave, and fret, that I may sing and dance.
> Thou wouldst be fee'd, I see, to make me sport.
> York cannot speak, unless he wear a crown.
> A crown for York! And, lords, bow low to him.
> Hold you his hands, whilst I do set it on.
>   *Putting a paper crown on his head.*
>   (1.4.86–95)

If our natural sympathy is engaged for York in this horrible ordeal, our sympathy can only be heightened by the play's dramaturgical allusion to the archetypal innocent sufferer.

Whatever else can be said about York's medieval archetypes in 3 *Henry VI*, it is clear that they pose difficult questions for an interpretation that assumes the play's support for Tudor power. Thirty years ago the question of how to deal with the significance of the first scene would have been answered by the nature of the parallel itself. Assuming that Shakespeare's histories were staged versions of the Tudor homilies or mirrors of Elizabethan policy, interpretation tended to emphasize whatever orthodox elements it could find in the plays and to ignore the rest. Assuming, for instance, that the cosmic analogue of the first scene is designed to reinforce disapproval of willful disobedience and rebellion leaves one at a loss about how to interpret the Christlike death of the Luciferian rebel three scenes later. Only by denying the dominant emotional tone of the scene can it be seen as "savagely ironic," in that "every clashing analogy to the death of Christ" drives home the lesson that York is being repaid for a life that "has been evil in the highest degree."[24] For this irony is impossible to detect in the theater, where the effect of the scene is to evoke pity for York's suffering. Since the parallels with Christ's suffering intensify this pity, those parallels tend to make us forget York's evil, not to make us more aware of it.

A closely parallel emotional double bind in 3 *Henry VI* is created by another likely medieval allusion in the play: the slaughter of the innocents. Shortly before York's death we witness the murder of his twelve-year-old son, the earl of Rutland, whom Shakespeare portrays as an unarmed schoolboy. His murderer, young Clifford, incredibly claims to be avenging the death of his father, who was killed in fair fight at the battle of St. Albans. This grandiose excuse for attacking a child may owe something to the debased idea of heroism that characterizes Herod's soldiers in the medieval plays. In the Chester cycle, for instance, the Primus

Miles initially balks at Herod's command to slay the infants, until he discovers that the order concerns thousands of babies, not just one or two, for this news appeals to his warped sense of epic derring-do.[25] But if the scene in *3 Henry VI* does recall the slaughter of the innocents, it creates ambivalence in the play's auditors and a crux for orthodox interpretation, since the Yorkists repeat the same crime later when they murder Prince Edward (5.5). This time the scene includes a distraught mother, Queen Margaret, who was another feature of the medieval plays, as Shakespeare remembered when he had Henry V threaten the citizens of Harfleur that if they did not surrender they would see their

> naked infants spitted upon pikes,
> Whiles the mad mothers with their howls confus'd
> Do break the clouds, as did the wives of Jewry
> At Herod's bloody-hunting slaughtermen.
>   (*Henry V*, 3.3.38–41)

If Bethlehem innocents appear on both sides of the conflict in *3 Henry VI*, whom are we to execrate as Herod? When the slaughter of the innocents appears again in *Macbeth*, Shakespeare uses it effectively as part of a theme of outraged innocence that runs throughout the play ("'Macbeth does murder sleep,' the innocent sleep"), but in *3 Henry VI* he creates the equivalent of a child-murdering Macduff as well.

The kind of ambivalence created by these multiple allusions to medieval drama can be traced to a more contemporary dramaturgical model—the plays of Christopher Marlowe. The *Henry VI* plays were almost certainly written in the wake of Marlowe's startling success with *Tamburlaine*, and one of Marlowe's most effective techniques was the creation of a profound ambivalence about his characters that resembles what we have seen in *3 Henry VI*.[26] At the same time, for instance, that we admire Tamburlaine for his compelling rendition of the high style, his incredible daring, and his power to command, we fear him for his cruelty and bloodthirstiness. Again, no matter how decadent and hateful Bajazeth may be as ruler of the anti-Christian Turks, he inevitably wins our pity when Tamburlaine cages him like an animal until he and his wife despairingly kill themselves (in full view of the audience) by ramming their heads against the bars. The horror of their deaths is intensified, moreover, by the lengthy lament of Zenocrate, who pities them and fears for her savage husband's future when such deeds are part of his record. Marlowe's treatment of Bajazeth provides a dramatic pattern for Shakespeare's treatment of York: though both characters begin with our antipathy, our initial response to them is qualified by the suffering of their terrible deaths, and this suffering in turn qualifies our response to those who inflict it. This is not to say, however, that Marlovian dramaturgy has the same effect in *3 Henry VI* that it has in *Tamburlaine* or

The Jew of Malta. Marlowe demystifies the power he craves but cannot obtain, a not uncommon strategy of frustrated social ambition on the Elizabethan political scene. Gabriel Harvey is a parallel case, though he lacked the extraordinary rhetorical gifts that graced Marlowe. Harvey's obsessive cultivation of the signs of power coexists with his insistent debunking of them, a contradiction that was recognized and satirized by young aspirants like Nashe, whose rhetorical nimbleness made them hopeful that they had a chance of succeeding where the ponderous Harvey invariably failed.[27] Despite his borrowing of Marlowe's iconoclastic dramaturgy, Shakespeare's skepticism functions as political analysis rather than a projection of social striving. The Marlovian subversiveness of 3 *Henry VI* focuses attention not on the simultaneous desirability and hypocrisy of power but on human history as a process that invariably falls short of the archetypes that bestow definitive meaning in sacred history.

This point can be illustrated by returning to the scenes we have examined already—York's usurpation and his death—in order to examine their effect more carefully against the background of their archetypal analogues. Though York's bold occupation of King Henry's throne has a Luciferian clarity about it, that quality begins to blur long before York's death—indeed almost as soon as Henry comes on stage. What God had always done in Henry's situation was to hurl the usurper from the pageant's heaven to its hell mouth by merely reappearing: this was the true consequence of rebellion in the purity of its sacred pattern. But what Shakespeare gives us is different: the supposedly godlike King Henry is all too human to handle the situation effectively. He challenges York bravely enough at first, but as soon as the king's partisans take up the same line, Henry suddenly and inexplicably (one is tempted to say perversely) appeals to them to be patient. The impatient Clifford's answer comes just short of insolence as he tellingly contrasts the king with Henry V: "Patience is for poltroons, such as [York]. / He durst not sit there, had your father liv'd" (1.1.62–63). Clifford's manner exposes the king's lack of authority even further, and at the same time Clifford's retort introduces an undeniable reality about centralized power. For in his peremptory action against a nascent rebellion inspired by York's father (Richard, earl of Cambridge), Henry V had demonstrated—as he had in his French campaign—that the right to power is inextricably bound up with the ability to make that right good in fact. This ability is clearly lacking in his unfortunate son.[28]

The first scene's emphasis on human fallibility is echoed in the pitiable death of the king's rival, York, where the surprising archetype is the suffering of Christ. If the king is not God, it follows that his opponents are not devils but men, and this includes York. The pity we feel for him is for a human being under extreme duress, no matter how demonic he has been. The dramaturgical parallel with the suffering Christ is therefore appropriate and effective in offsetting a tendency to caricature York as a principle of evil in the play. Evil there is to be sure—even Henry's weakness has a part in it—but no one has a premium on it, and very few characters are utterly without redeeming human features. This is not to say that York exhibits the kind of saintliness that Henry does in his death in act 5, scene 6, but only to suggest that the human historical context is always emphasized in the play, no matter what may be put forward in the way of patterns from the drama of salvation history.

The subversive effect of treating York ambiguously in the first act of *3 Henry VI*, then, is to reduce the political process to human scale by contrasting it with its sacred archetypes. In the first scene York should fall as Lucifer did, but he does not, because Henry is not God even though he is God's representative on earth. The Elizabethan doctrine of the king's two bodies has long been recognized in *Richard II*, but in fact an imaginative equivalent of that doctrine seems to have informed Shakespeare's view of history from the beginning, and the *Henry VI* plays are best understood in light of the same contrast between sacred and secular order that informs *Richard II*.[29] Mystifying the office of the king as a representative of God on earth is designed to enhance the king's power by making him appear invulnerable, as we noticed in chapter 4; but if the king is politically inept, then mystifying his power only serves to emphasize the gap between ideal and reality, and that is precisely the effect of contrasting the archetypes of sacred history with the secular history of Henry VI, just as Richard II's continual evocations of sacral monarchy serve to emphasize his inability to measure up to them. Henry's inability to establish his right by credible command of the situation at Westminster Palace is matched by his ineffectual attempt to defend his legal right. Here again a comparison with the sacred archetype of Lucifer's fall is potent and devastating, especially considering that Shakespeare's source has no hint of a confrontation between York and Henry at this point: Hall reports that the compromise between York and the king was negotiated by Parliament, not by the king in person (Bullough, *Narrative Sources*, 3:175). The God of the pageant wagon mustered complex and sophisticated theological arguments from Augustine and Aquinas in his defeat of Lucifer.[30] God thus established the right to his throne beyond all possible doubt: in the face of such claims Lucifer could not hope to do anything more than run squeaking and gibbering to hell. King Henry, however, is victimized by the ambiguities of primogeniture, a principle of historical order that is irrelevant to the eternal order of the God he represents. "I am thy sovereign," he tells York, only to hear the instant retort: "I am thine" (1.1.76). Suddenly Henry is being accused of usurpation himself, and he is struck speechless by York's claim: "I know not what to say; my title's weak" (1.1.134). Even

Exeter, a Lancastrian partisan, begins to urge the justice of York's case: "His is the right, and therefore pardon me. . . . My conscience tells me he is lawful king" (1.1.148, 150). What follows is the desperate compromise in which Henry disinherits his son in order to retain the throne for his lifetime, a move not only ungodlike but politically suicidal, as Queen Margaret incisively points out (1.1.231–37). By the end of the first scene Henry has been abandoned by his wife, his son, and all of his followers except Exeter, who had candidly admitted his disbelief in the king's inheritance. The play's promising start, with its suggestion of a clear-cut moral opposition, has dissolved into the ambiguities and frustrations of power politics—a dissolution Shakespeare effectively heightens by inducing our ambivalence and uneasiness about the king and by evoking archetypal patterns that the king dispiritingly fails to enact.

The Marlovian techniques in the first scene of 3 *Henry VI* thus generate skepticism about the human capacity for fair and effective government, and skepticism of that kind is much older than the social changes of the sixteenth century. Augustine's formulation of the same skepticism (kingdoms as large-scale pirate bands) may have influenced Thomas More, as we saw in chapter 1. More's Hythlodaeus is so doubtful about the possibility of just and effective order in real kingdoms that he will have nothing to do with them, preferring to tell stories about the ideal commonwealths he has discovered on fantastic sea voyages. Hythlodaeus' interlocutor, persona More, is less dubious than his philosophical companion but only slightly: he argues that the philosopher should serve a real prince because "what you cannot turn to good you must make as little bad as you can."[31] This doubtful affirmation of limited political amelioration suggests that political order is neither static nor perfect but a continual struggle against entropy in public affairs. If Shakespeare's Henry VI had a little of More's wisdom, he would clearly be a better king, since he does not effectively resist the evil in his kingdom, much less promote anything good.[32] Henry is certainly not an evil man himself; on the contrary, he is pious and peace-loving, but his political ineptitude contributes disastrously to the kingdom's slide into civil war at a time when effective authority is required to maintain political equilibrium—as the fall of Duke Humphrey makes clear. Ironically, Henry formulates his own vision of perfection in pastoral terms (2.5.1–54), as if pastoral images bore no relation to the power politics he wishes to abjure. In fact, pastoralism was deeply implicated in the struggle for power, as Louis Montrose has pointed out,[33] and Henry's longing for a static life of regular and measured activity is qualified by our frustration at his indecision and inaction, a frustration voiced sympathetically by the queen and Clifford when they chided him from the battlefield (2.2.73–75). Margaret and Clifford are not generally sympathetic themselves, of course, but we cannot help feeling, as they do, that if

Henry shared York's sense of timing, he would not be standing apart from the battle meditating on time: he would be seizing it in the interest of preserving political stability by maintaining Lancaster's inherited dominance, as York is seizing time to unsettle the situation by promoting his own faction's interest. In short, Henry's pastoral vision, as Robert Ornstein points out, is artificial and conventional and serves to show how far out of touch he is with reality: if Henry "had had his wish to be a shepherd," as M. M. Reese remarks, "he would certainly have lost his sheep."[34]

The contrast between sacred paradigms and human action in the *Henry VI* plays can be highlighted by comparison with *Richard III*. For in this play an archetypal pattern is also invoked, but the entire action of the play conforms to it, in contrast to the three preceding plays that dissect the disintegration of centralized power during the reign of *Henry VI*. The archetypal pattern of *Richard III* is that of salvation history itself, in which a devilish spoiler destroys the order of an innocent beginning (the "glorious summer [of] this son of York" [1.1.2]), spreads his corrupt influence as far as he can, and is finally undone by the wiliness of his own machinations and the superior force of a God-sent deliverer. Richard's bid for power in this play becomes increasingly like the strategy of the morality play Vice, as Bernard Spivack has pointed out, and less like the machinations of real courtiers.[35] And the more Richard looks like the Vice, the closer he is assimilated to the archetypal role of Lucifer and the human tyrants who imitate Lucifer in the mystery plays, particularly in a context like the N-Town *Passion Play*, where Lucifer appears as a court gallant who offers advice about how to succeed in social competition. The sense of restored order and future promise that prevails at the end of *Richard III* is unlike anything that concludes the three history plays preceding it, and the promised marriage of Richmond and Elizabeth of York has affinities with comedy rather than history, for it introduces the conclusive sense of well-being and restored harmony that accompanies marriage (or the prospect of marriage) at the end of Shakespeare's comedies and romances. Though Shakespeare experimented widely with the conventions of Senecan tragedy in *Richard III*, the basic formal identity of this full-scale political romance was not suggested by the sensational dramaturgy of Seneca but by Hall's synopsis of the Tudor myth:

> But the old divided controversy between the forenamed families of Lancaster and York, by the union of matrimony celebrate and consummate between the high and mighty prince, King Henry the Seventh, and Lady Elizabeth, his most worthy queen (the one being indubitate heir of the house of Lancaster and the other of York), was suspended and appalled in the person of the most noble, puissant,

and mighty heir, King Henry the Eighth, and by him clearly buried and perpetually extinct. So that all men (more clearer than the sun) may apparently perceive that as by discord great things decay and fall to ruin, so the same by concord be revived and erected. (Bullough, *Narrative Sources*, 3:17)

What Hall describes are the characteristics of dramatic romance, not of the history play: the extinction of controversy, the miraculous emergence of concord from discord. Hall's analysis of Richmond's marriage is important for an understanding of *Richard III*, because Hall compares the marriage to the crucial event of salvation history:

By union of the Godhead to the manhood, man was joined to God, which before by the temptation of the subtle serpent was from him segregate and divided. By the union of the Catholic church and the outworn synagogue, not only the hard ceremonies and deadly pains of the Mosaical law were clearly abolished and made frustrate, but also Christian liberty is inferred and Christ's religion stablished and erected. By the union of man and woman in the holy sacrament of matrimony, the generation is blessed and the sin of the body clean extinct and put away. By the union of marriage, peace between realm and realm is exalted, and love between country and country is nourished. By conjunction of matrimony, malice is extinct, amity is embraced, and indissoluble alliance and consanguinity is procured. What profit, what comfort, what joy succeeded in the realm of England by the union of the forenamed two noble families, you shall apparently perceive by the sequel of this rude and unlearned history. (Bullough, *Narrative Sources*, 3:17)

Hall's own chronicle does not bear out the promise of this brave preface, and *Richard III* conforms to it only in formal retrospect, but insofar as Hall's preface affects *Richard III* at all, it is a different play from those that precede it. This difference was ignored by Tillyard in his anxiousness to draw Shakespeare's first history plays into a coherent tetralogy, and the difference still raises a question: if Shakespeare rejected archetypal models for the shape of human events in the *Henry VI* plays (and in the history plays that follow *Richard III*), why did he suddenly reverse himself and adopt the definitive model of salvation history in *Richard III*? The answer may well lie in what the Tudor myth idealized: the stability of centralized power. Providential explanations for Richmond's victory at Bosworth Field were an unchallenged commonplace, and Shakespeare shaped Richard III's reign in approximate accordance with this received opinion while exploring it thoughtfully in a variety of ways.[36] Moreover, Henry VII and his heirs had provided England with a period of unusual political equilibrium by the effective exercise of centralized power, which the *Henry VI* plays show in the process of unravelling. If political realism was unprepared to trace the hand of God in the interplay of power politics, it might nonetheless be ready to agree that the advent of a politically effective dynasty was something of a miracle.

Shakespeare's conforming of history to a sacred paradigm in *Richard III* illustrates by default the extraordinary new dramaturgy of power in the *Henry VI* plays. Idealizing centralized power was not the only way of responding to it, either in the fifth century or the sixteenth. On moral grounds, one could both defend power and emphasize its inherent limitations, as Augustine did (and as medieval drama did implicitly), or one could analyze it, as Machiavelli did in *The Prince* and Shakespeare did from the beginning in his history plays. Elizabethan political theorists were incurably abstract and consistently oblivious to the realities of secular power, as Wallace MacCaffrey notes,[37] and their limitations are understandable in view of the irresistible pressure on all intellectuals to defend a regime that had appropriated the age's most compelling myths of invulnerability. Machiavelli's political realism was called atheism because he did not sacralize the state, and any Elizabethan theorist who followed Machiavelli would have been thought of in the same way. That is why Shakespeare's choice to show centralized power in the process of collapse is so striking, especially given his evident commitment to the existing political system and social scale. Like Jacobean tragedians who displace courtly intrigue onto decadent Italy, Shakespeare displaces the contemporary political scene onto the fifteenth century. His Henry VI is not a heroic model of timeless perfection but a willful, foolish man with bad political judgment and an inability to command respect, and he appears in a series of plays that emphasize the process of history, not its static sacral archetypes. This is about as far from *The Faerie Queene* as one can get in Elizabethan literature, for it aims to do precisely the opposite of Spenser's great epic: not to turn history into compelling myth but to observe the process of human history without recourse to myth of any kind.

CHAPTER 6 ❧ THE ELIZABETHAN HAL

Shakespeare did not abandon his critical interest in Elizabethan power when he dramatized the reigns of the three kings preceding Henry VI; if anything, he made it clearer. The topicality of one these plays, *Richard II*, seems to have been recognized at once, not only by the censor, who prudently refused to permit publication of the deposition scene, but by the followers of the earl of Essex, who daringly commissioned a revival of the play on the eve of Essex's rebellion, and by the queen herself, who ominously claimed to know that she "was" Richard II.[1] This is not to say that the play would have had precisely the same impact when it was first written that it had in 1601, but merely that Shakespeare's practice of displacing contemporary power relations onto the past—begun in the *Henry VI* plays—continued with the mature histories. Also consistent with Shakespeare's early attempts in this vein is his insistent and demystifying contrast between sacred and secular history, and here again his recourse to medieval dramatic precedent is a powerful means to achieving that contrast.

Let us begin with the way the later histories deal with church and state, for the Tudors profoundly altered this relationship, and their effect on it is what Shakespeare's plays enact, rather than the pre-Reformation reality. In Henry VIII's bid to consolidate power in his own hands, one of his most effective moves was to make himself supreme head of the church, for by doing so he vastly reduced a major source of independent power in the kingdom and made religion for the first time a responsive instrument of royal policy. We noticed in chapter 3 that one consequence of this move was virtually to eliminate the church as a source of articulate social criticism. Henry's policy was innovative and strange enough that its ramifications in law and political relations took a long time to work out. Many of them were still unclear when Elizabeth revived essentially the same policy in the settlement of 1559, but thirty-five years later definite patterns had established themselves, and these are what appear in the Lancastrian history plays. Henry V's church, for example, is effectively without pope and cardinals: the highest cleric we see is the archbishop of Canterbury. The phrase "holy church" (*Henry V*, 1.1.23) is consistent with Elizabethan usage. The king is virtually unchallenged as the governor of a unified national state whose political and ecclesiastical destiny is focused in himself, "the mirror of all Christian kings" (2.Pro.6), one of the Elizabethan poets' favorite images for their sovereign. Canterbury's allusion to the belief that "miracles are ceas'd" (1.1.67) is a Protestant anachronism. Henry's fleeting allusion to the Te Deum and Non Nobis (4.8.122) may strike a modern ear as medieval, but in fact the two psalms he alludes to were only one psalm in the Vulgate, whereas they appear separately, with the Latin names the king uses, in the Elizabethan Book of Common Prayer. Retaining such "papistical" details as Latin titles was offensive to Elizabethan Puritans, but the queen insisted on using them, for her taste was conservative in matters of ritual.[2]

The *Henry IV* plays are consistent with *Henry V* in depicting a church that is substantially, though not obtrusively Elizabethan, and these plays therefore contrast with *King John*, the *Henry VI* plays, and *Henry VIII*, all of which are more clearly pre-Reformation in their church polity. Yet even in the non-Lancastrian plays, an Elizabethan perspective is evident in varying degrees of opposition to an independent church. When Wolsey, the most famous among Tudor ecclesiastical statesmen, appears in a Shakespearean play, he is a monster, an unambiguous threat to the emergence of rightful power in the king rather than the church.[3] The only other cardinals in Shakespearean drama (Beaufort in *1* and *2 Henry VI* and Pandulph in *King John*) similarly threaten the kingdom, the best efforts of right-minded citizens, and the authority of the monarchy. Such depictions need not be dismissed as unreflective Protestant bias, since they belong to a consistent Shakespearean pattern of dealing with the Elizabethan present as if it were the past.

Relations between church and crown come into unusually clear Elizabethan focus in the first scene of *Henry V*, where two high churchmen try to arrive at a strategy for dealing with the monarchy. Shakespeare follows Holinshed closely in this scene, but the point at issue is the royal seizure of ecclesiastical land, and this had been a central issue in church/state relations since the dissolution of the monasteries; more important, it was still a matter of urgent concern to the episcopacy in the 1590s. Radical reformers had long advocated the legal appropriation (or "alienation") of church land in the interest of social justice, but they were astonished and disappointed after the dissolution, when they discovered that new prince was but old priest writ large, and the poor were as badly off as ever. They had reckoned without the pressure of upward mobility in the Tudor consolidation of power, for Henry used church land to reward loyal supporters, and their appetite was hard to satisfy. (Suffolk in *2 Henry VI* is contemporary in this regard, too, for he is accused by commoners of enclosing land, a practice often followed by the upwardly mobile who acquired ecclesiastical land from the crown in the sixteenth century.) The transfer of church property to secular ownership had been one of the principal reasons for Mary Tudor's inability to undo the work of her father as much as she had wished to, for that transfer had created an irreversible vested interest in Protestant policy.

Under Elizabeth, the elaborate system of patronage centering in the queen depended on her ability to award gifts to her courtiers, and when she came to the most valued gifts, i.e., those in real estate, she obviously preferred to bestow ecclesiastical lands rather than surrender crown capital, on the principle that other people's property is easier to give away than one's own.[4] The church therefore remained the object of unrelenting predation where its temporal lands were concerned. Matthew Parker, the first Elizabethan archbishop of Canterbury, protested the alienation of church lands before his consecration, and he was still concerned with the same problem on his deathbed: his last act was the drafting of a letter to the queen on this subject.[5] That was in 1575, and by the 1590s the queen had actually been compelled to come to the bishops' aid in curbing the more blatant imposition of her courtiers. Their increasing legal sophistication had opened up new lucrative avenues to ecclesiastical property, particularly the so-called concealments, or lands that had escaped appropriation at the time of the dissolution.[6] Private individuals were licensed to search out such lands so they could be added to the crown's rent rolls for eventual dispensation to deserving patrons. So serious were the resulting legal problems for the episcopate that legislation was twice passed in parliament to restrict the practice: once in 1593 and again in 1597–98. John Whitgift, the last Elizabethan archbishop of Canterbury, was himself the object of concealment suits, which he protested to Burghley in 1578 when he was bishop of Worcester. Canterbury's problem was apparently still unresolved in the 1590s, judging from a two-page list of "inconveniences ensuing upon the passing of lands as concealed belonging to churches" that Whitgift sent to Burghley some time before the latter's retirement.[7]

The archbishop of Canterbury, of course, is one of the two churchmen who are concerned about the loss of church land in the first scene of *Henry V*. The other is the bishop of Ely, whose Elizabethan successor was, if anything, more famously embattled on the issue of church lands than his superior. Until February, 1599, Elizabeth had appointed only one man, Richard Cox, to the bishopric of Ely, and he had been the most vociferous of all the bishops on this issue. He spent twenty-three years in the episcopate fighting successive legal battles to avoid depredation at the hands of Elizabeth's courtiers, among them Sir Christopher Hatton, one of the queen's favorites, whom she admitted to the privy council in 1577 and made lord chancellor ten years later. "For Christ Jesus' sake," Cox implored the queen, "be ye a most pious nurse, favorer and defender of your clergy in this wicked and atheistical age!"[8] When

Shakespeare wrote *Henry V*, the see of Ely had been vacant for eighteen years—ever since Cox had died in 1581—and Elizabeth's inordinate delay in appointing his successor was probably in revenge for Cox's outspoken resistance to the attempted alienation of temporal lands belonging to Ely, for the bill of 1559 permitted the queen to take advantage of a bishop's death by exchanging spiritualities of relatively little profit for wealthy temporal lands as long as the see remained vacant.[9]

Shakespeare's focus on the bishops in *Henry V* is usually regarded as satirical, particularly given his subsequent treatment of their support for the war in France. The undeniable topicality of the first scene, however, points beyond satire to the dynamics of Tudor monarchy. For the alienation of church lands was central to Elizabethan royal supremacy, which in turn was a matter of effective power, as it had been for Henry VIII, and that kind of power is the consistent focus of Shakespeare's history plays, as we noticed in the case of the *Henry VI* plays in the preceding chapter. Effective power was the motive behind the parliamentary bill of 1559 permitting the queen to disendow ecclesiastical property, for the bill was part of her attempt to reassert royal control over the church after her sister's partial undoing of the Henrician reformation.[10] In other words, royal expropriation of church land was not prompted simply by greed—though greed was certainly not absent from the process—but by Elizabeth's perception of her need to gain control of political affairs. If she was, as she carefully phrased it, "supreme governor" of the church, then she had at her disposal the framework for controlling the church as a political force, and one means of making her control actually work was to lay claim to church property. As Archbishop Whitgift incisively remarked, in a letter to the bishop of Ely, "The temporalty seek to make the clergy beggars that we may depend upon them."[11]

Elizabeth's canny focus on effective power explains why, in the course of her reign, her attitude toward the episcopacy underwent an apparent change. If the bill of 1559 was designed to put the church in its place vis-à-vis the crown, so was Elizabeth's choice not to appoint fresh faces from the clergy to her first privy council. It was, in fact, decidedly pro-Protestant, but it excluded powerful clerics like those who had served in the councils of her grandfather and father, and their exclusion signalled secular control of the church without openly declaring it.[12] Later, however, when Puritan resistance to episcopacy increased, Elizabeth began to give the bishops more support. Not only did she move to restrict the seizure of ecclesiastical property, but in 1586 she also appointed Archbishop Whitgift to the privy council. This was a reversal of means only, not of political ends, for her actions both in opposition to the bishops and in support of them were direct expressions of the crown's supremacy, since Puritan opposition to episcopacy began to challenge Elizabeth's initiative in religious policy more seriously than episcopacy itself had done hitherto.

Inevitably the assertion of royal prerogative produced political deals of the sort that appear in *Henry V*, and just as inevitably their outcome favored the crown, as does the outcome of *Henry V*. If the particular trade-off in that play has no actual Elizabethan parallel, the issue itself was certainly familiar, and more important, the mere fact of such political dealing between church and crown was quintessentially Elizabethan. (Historically, the bill mentioned in *Henry V* 1.1 was actually introduced by Lollard sympathizers during the reign of Henry IV; it was strongly resisted and quickly quashed for its heretical implications.[13] In other words, the original bill was attended by none of the politicking Shakespeare depicts, and though he follows Holinshed closely in rendering the scene, its appeal to him may well have been its familiarity.) One small example of episcopal maneuvering is worth noting because it came close to Shakespeare. Late in his life, Archbishop Parker created six scholarships to Corpus Christi College, Cambridge, for poor students from his own see of Canterbury. One of the first students to win a Parker scholarship was Christopher Marlowe, the son of a Canterbury shoemaker. Parker's action in creating these scholarships conforms to a pattern of defensive action taken by Elizabethan bishops to justify their temporal incomes, on the argument that if a leader of Christian pastors was to provide an example of charity to other clergy, as his place required, then he had to have the means to be charitable. This argument and the actions to accompany it, such as the Parker scholarships, were often cited by Elizabethan bishops in opposition to royal expropriation of church lands.[14]

Henry V's resemblance to the only monarch Shakespeare had ever known at the time he wrote his history plays goes much deeper than parallels in church polity, but such resemblances always elucidate the exercise of centralized power. From the time Henry V first appears as a prince in *1 Henry IV*, he is incurably theatrical, and his theatricality is inseparable from his pursuit of power, a link that should identify him with Richard III but in fact shows how far Shakespeare had come in this vein since he wrote the early histories. Stephen Greenblatt has pointed out how closely theatricality and power were identified in Renaissance culture, and as we noticed in chapter 4, this is true not only in the self-fashioning advocated by a realist like Machiavelli but in the directions for courtly behavior put forward by putative idealists like Castiglione and Puttenham, who were much influenced by Italian neo-Platonism and thoroughly understood its utility in self-enhancement. Shakespeare's creation of an ambitious courtier like Richard III illustrates how readily medieval dramatic tradition could be adapted to the new cultural reality. Indeed, it would be more accurate to speak in terms of a continuous popular tradition that produces characters like the N-Town Satan in the fifteenth century, the Vice in the early sixteenth, and Richard III in the late sixteenth—always from the same perspective on the "new fashion."[15] Richard is related dramaturgically to the N-Town Satan and also to Satan's duplicity, arrogance, and ambition (above, p. 101).

Yet for all the usefulness of medieval dramatic tradition in rendering Tudor power, Shakespeare does something quite different with Henry V as prince and king from what he had done with Richard III. To put it succinctly, Henry is no longer self-evident, and he is therefore much harder to understand. Richard III's motives, like those of the Vice or of the courtly N-Town Lucifer, are always divulged to us, even though they are concealed from others. Richard's innermost self is therefore transparent, and the moral reality he admits to violating is clear. His debate with himself before the battle of Bosworth (5.3.176–206) belongs to psychomachic tradition, as does Proteus' debate with himself in *Two Gentlemen*, 2.6, and the aim of that tradition is precisely to clarify the lines of moral conflict. Other ambitious characters in the early histories work the same way Richard does: Suffolk, Winchester, York, all tell us what they are up to, and we watch in ambivalent fascination as they show off to us godlike auditors the impudent pranks they dare not show those in their own imagined world. This dramatic strategy in the early histories is one of the ways that Shakespeare preserves the sense of a positive courtly ideal, for only those who are morally duplicitous in seeking power thus bare their gleeful guilty souls before us. Talbot and Humphrey Duke of Gloucester, on the other hand, carry on in moral single-mindedness, without a hint of difference between action and intention.

In contrast to the transparency of Richard III and those like him is the opacity of Henry V, who however is no less theatrical. Henry V therefore renders much more compellingly the kind of theatricality that was evident everywhere on the Elizabethan political scene: his relative opacity is Shakespeare's consummate version of theatrical invulnerability cultivated in the interest of position and power. "Cunningly to be able to dissemble" required a credible representation of what one pretended to be, and credibility is shattered by asides that reveal the duplicitous self behind the dissembling, however effective such things may be in the theater. When Elizabeth was a princess, she found herself in a position where she had to dissemble convincingly to preserve her life— to make herself literally invulnerable—to say nothing of preserving her hope for power. Ironically, this position vis-à-vis her sister, Mary Tudor, was exactly the same position that Mary Stuart would be in vis-à-vis Elizabeth herself thirty years later: a serious contender for the throne, whose religious sympathy made her the natural focus of widespread political opposition. Given Elizabeth's situation in 1553, her sister justifiably regarded her with deep suspicion, and Mary's insistence that Elizabeth publicly declare her allegiance to Catholicism was not motivated so much by disinterested concern for her sister's soul as by Mary's anxiousness to deal a body blow to the opposition by depriving them of a leader—as Elizabeth would do later by executing Mary Stuart. This is where Princess Elizabeth had to dissemble, and her skill in doing so gave her good reason to mistrust Mary Stuart later. Elizabeth chose the Feast of the Nativity of the Virgin Mary as the day on which to take her first public mass.[16] The theatricality of this choice is striking: it reveals an unsurpassed ability to conjoin private action (religious commitment) with public show; it seemed to express exemplary Catholic piety; and it flattered Mary decorously by emphasizing the saint for whom she was named—the Queen of Heaven, at that. Given Elizabeth's subsequent history, this event seems remarkably pragmatic, if not cynical. Yet Elizabeth cannot have allowed any suggestion of its pragmatism to escape for Mary to see it that way, or to be able to prove it if she did see it. Referring to Elizabeth's conversion, the French ambassador wrote his king: "Everyone believes that she is acting rather from fear of danger and peril from those around her than from real devotion,"[17] but mere suspicion was not enough to impugn Elizabeth's action. The gesture itself was opaque, creating a sufficient truth about Elizabeth to enable her personal and political survival.

"In pompous ceremonies a secret of government doth much consist," noted an observer of Queen Elizabeth's court, and the observation underscores the queen's ability to rule by means of compelling illusions like her Catholic conversion in 1553.[18] This ability was an open secret of political success that Jonson would recognize and exploit in the masques he wrote for Elizabeth's successor. But Shakespeare seems to have recognized it earlier, and to have made plays—not masques—that enact it. His preparation for creating a king with Elizabeth's kind of theatrical opacity is evident in *Richard II*. The most theatrical character in this play is King Richard himself, but in talking about his role-playing to the whole world he makes his act inseparable from his identity as king: his kingly role, in the full sense of the word, is to do thus. By swift turns he takes on the roles of Phaeton and Christ (3.3 and 4.1), and his intention in doing so is to shape his auditors' response to the king's dilemma—not to dissemble his motives in the interest of power, as Shakespeare's earlier political actors had done. Who Richard is apart from these roles we do not know, and as a man in pursuit of power he is therefore much harder to assess morally than Richard III. Only after his deposition do we begin to see a personality separating itself from the public role, and then only in the solitude of his prison in Pomfret Castle. At this point, shorn of his power and his audience, Richard discovers his vulnerablity, and the discovery is accompanied by "thoughts divine" that identify its tradition, "As thus, 'Come, little ones,' and then again, / 'It is as hard to come as for a camel / To thread the postern of a small needle's eye' " (5.5.12–17). What Richard discovers in his destitution is also true to medieval tradition, as here he achieves more human dignity than he had ever possessed in the inflated versions of himself as king. He is still indelibly theatrical ("Thus play I in one person many people"), but with power no longer his object, his playing is disinterested and allows him to see the truth about himself:

> But whate'er I be,
> Nor I, nor any man that but man is
> With nothing shall be pleas'd, till he be eas'd
> With being nothing.
> (5.5.38–41)

Like Shakespeare's comic heroes, Richard discovers himself in coming to the end of himself. However, in this play self-discovery is not the climactic focus of the action but a small eddy of solitary activity that emphasizes how difficult such discoveries are in the pursuit of power. Richard's story is no comedy but part of a history, and Richard is an idle captive, another's Jack of the clock, while time "runs posting on in Bolingbroke's proud joy" at the apex of power.

Bolingbroke, on the other hand, is a different case again: a truly opaque self, like his son. Never revealing a transparent dissembling self, like the power seekers of the early histories, and never discovering himself outside the pursuit of power, Bolingbroke is to all appearances a single-minded character like Talbot or Duke Humphrey, and he certainly seems to want the world to think of him that way. Yet his repeated declaration that he has returned to England merely to reclaim his stolen duchy is impossible to reconcile with the timing of his return, the size of the force he brings, or what he does after landing. Words and actions do not say the same thing, either in this case or in many others, as when Henry IV wishes he were rid of "this living fear" and then punishes Pierce of Exton for murdering Richard. In contrast to Richard, Bolingbroke appears to be untheatrical, and he indeed lacks his opponent's way with words and grand gestures. Yet Bolingbroke would seem to understand no less well than Richard III the maxim from Puttenham's *Arte* that we have encountered before as a quintessential expression of self-fashioning and power: "Qui nescit dissimulare nescit regnare."[19]

Shakespeare's invention of the opaque self achieves its best expression in Henry V, whose cultivation of invulnerability in the quest for power is distinctly Elizabethan, like his government's relationship with the church. Henry V's theatricality, like Elizabeth's, is invariably designed to acquire and maintain political advantage, yet the advantage is always a matter of inference, because action and intention are ostensibly the same, as they are with Henry IV. As a heroic exemplar of courtly expectations, Henry far surpasses Talbot of *1 Henry VI*; indeed he is explicitly compared to the earl of Essex (*Henry V*, 5.Pro.30–32), who was by far the most impressive courtier of the late 1590s. Yet the later histories are ambiguous about a positive standard of courtliness, unlike the *Henry VI* plays, because they create no qualitative distinction between disinterested state servants (like Talbot and Duke Humphrey) and those who quest for power. Every character can now be rendered in relation to that quest, because no revelation of ulterior motive is required; this is the utility of the opaque self, and it is a signal gain over the early history plays in enabling a realistic enactment of contemporary power relations. One is tempted to surmise that at about the time Shakespeare wrote *Richard II*, he recognized the inherent orientation of courtesy to power and invented the opaque self as a means of conveying that orientation on the stage.

Admittedly, Henry V's occasional soliloquies would appear to be exceptions to his opacity—as in Prince Hal's soliloquy in *1 Henry IV*, 1.2., where he reveals his motive for consorting with tavern haunters and commoners. This soliloquy is more subtle than a mere updating of Richard III's Vicelike revelatory asides, however. Its primary function is to make Hal look just the opposite of Richard III—not a bad man pretending to be good but a good man pretending to be bad. For Hal's soliloquy signals Shakespeare's departure from the tradition of *The Famous Victories of Henry V*, in which the madcap prince indeed surrenders to the unyoked humor of tavern idleness. Shakespeare's prince must reassure us that he is not really wasting his time: he is only pretending to be a profligate in order to look all the better by comparison when his sudden reformation takes place later on. But Hal's transparency is disingenuous. His strategy inescapably involves power because he is going to be king. As he frankly points out later, "When I am King of England I shall command all the good lads in Eastcheap" (2.4.13–14). Since Hal is going to inherit power, no matter what he does, he is quite different from Richard III, but he is identical to Richard in being concerned from the outset that his power be effective, or to put it another way, that he have no effective rivals. The virtue he claims is therefore indistinguishable from *virtù*. He appropriates moral language ("loose behavior," "reformation"), but what he is really talking about is the skill of the courtier, whose very profession, as Puttenham says, "is in plain terms cunningly to be able to dissemble."[20] A similar opacity characterizes Henry V's soliloquy before Agincourt (*Henry V*, 4.1.227–81). Apparently a demystifying meditation on the distinction between kingly office and mortal king, this soliloquy actually reveals very little, if anything, about the king's self—or if it does, it shows a self absorbed in the office. Humility is inevitable, and therefore not difficult, when one faces the kind of military odds Henry does in this case—and we must not forget that Henry got himself into his present predicament by his own political ambition: he invaded France, not vice versa. To put it bluntly, this soliloquy reveals no more than that the king is cast back on his own resources out of political necessity. The interrupted soliloquy continues with a prayer in which Henry begs God to forget Henry IV's usurpation of Richard II's throne— a pragmatic request under the circumstances, because the evidence for God's "remembering" will be Henry's defeat, and that is what Henry is trying to forestall by reminding God of the chantries he has funded "to pardon blood" (4.1.297). Unlike Lear's recognition of the disparity between "ceremonious affection" and the king's mortality, Henry V's meditation on ceremony is opportunistic, even if the king himself does not appear to see it that way at the time he says it. His self-deception comes closest to the surface when he construes his lot as harder than a peasant's (4.1.263–81). Only a king preoccupied with problems of his own making could convince himself that peasants always sleep soundly with their bellies full and are therefore happier than kings. Lear in his destitution discovers something quite different.

Hal therefore remains opaque, even in soliloquy, and the question inevitably arises whether an identity apart from the one he shows us even exists. In common sense terms, of course, it obviously does not: we know nothing more of his character than what is enacted before us. But the fact that the question arises at all says something about Hal's ambiguity, and it is a politically significant question because it also arises in connection with theatrical public figures in real life, thus bearing directly on the Elizabethan psychology of pursuing power. In the late 1590s, no power seeker apart from the queen herself was more remarkable than the earl of Essex, and although the late histories were completed before his death (indeed before the failure of his Irish expedition), the manner of Essex's fall and death illustrates how perfectly Shakespeare renders the ambiguities of theatrical opacity in contemporary politics.

Essex was already highly controversial at the time Shakespeare praised him in *Henry V*. He was enormously popular, and he courted popularity carefully and skillfully: in 1601, when he attempted a coup d'état, he depended for his success on an uprising of the London populace, and he was sure it would happen because he had prepared for it so deliberately. But not everyone was convinced. Essex had bitter enemies, and one of them, Everard Guilpin, published a satire of Essex in 1598 that might easily describe Shakespeare's Richard III:

Who would not think him perfect courtesy?
Or the honeysuckle of humility?
The devil he is as soon: he is the devil,

Brightly accoustred to be-mist his evil:
Like a swart rutter's hose his puff thoughts swell,
With yeasty ambition: *Signior Machiavel*
Taught him this mumming trick, with courtesy
T'entrench himself with popularity,
And for a writhen face, and body's move,
Be barricadoed in the people's love.[21]

Criticism like Guilpin's was easy enough to dismiss as the baying of a Blatant Beast, as Spenser does in *The Faerie Queene*, but the Beast principally haunts Calidore, the Knight of Courtesy, and Spenser's recognition that courtesy somehow attracted calumny is not so far from Guilpin's critique. Guilpin does not interpret courtesy as a disembodied moral virtue, as Ray Heffner did fifty years ago in reading Calidore as a topical allegory of Essex;[22] Guilpin sees courtesy as involved with ambition and duplicity in the pursuit of power, for courtesy is taught by "*Signior Machiavel.*" Guilpin's response to this new fashion, in other words, is identical to Peter Idley's response to the "dissimulacion" and "fained countenance" of "new fassion" in the fifteenth century (above, chapter 2).

Essex as the "honeysuckle of humility" is remarkably like Hal, who "sounds the very base string of humility" in consorting with loggerheads and tavern drawers, and Hal would appear to have modelled himself on his father:

And then I stole all courtesy from heaven,
And dress'd myself in such humility
That I did pluck allegiance from men's hearts.
    (*I Henry IV*, 3.2.50–52)

The humility thus publicly exhibited is intensely self-interested. A nearly contemporary description of it appears in La Rochefoucauld's maxim 254, which we noticed in chapter 4 in the context of courtesy and the cultivation of invulnerable selfhood: "Humility is often but the mask of submission, assumed in order to conquer: it is an artifice of pride, which stoops that it may rise the higher ["My reformation, glitt'ring o'er my fault / Shall show more goodly and attract more eyes"]: and pride, which adopts a thousand forms, is never so well disguised nor so capable of deception as when it masquerades as humility."[23] "Judge of me," Essex charged those who were assigned to try him after his failed coup, "as a good Christian, and as one that never sought to exceed the degree of a subject. . . . I thank God I am far from atheism; I doubt not by God's grace to die a Christian."[24] This is part of his spirited defense, which consisted chiefly in attacking his accusers and asserting his entire blamelessness. When his attack on Robert Cecil (whom Essex believed to be absent) became too blatant, Cecil burst out of concealment and heatedly denied Essex's charges, ending with a pious thrust: "You have a wolf's head in a sheep's garment, in appearance humble and religious, but in disposition ambitious and aspiring. . . . I beseech God to forgive you this open wrong done unto me, as I do openly pronounce that I forgive you from the bottom of my heart" (Harrison, pp. 308–10). Essex was too accustomed to the rhetoric of courtly competition to let this pass: he knew full well that to accept another's forgiveness was to acknowledge the need for it, i.e., to admit guilt. Hence the deadly counterthrust of his ferociously humble retort, which conceded absolutely nothing: "And I, Mr. Secretary, do clearly and freely forgive you with all my soul; because I mean to die in charity with all men."

By modern standards, of course, Essex's trial was a witch-hunt—not designed to discern the truth but to wring a confession from him. Sir Edward Coke exclaimed quite without irony at one point that the way the truth had emerged was miraculous, since all the witnesses agreed "without either rack or torture to any of them" (Harrison, p. 304). The point is not whether justice was done but how it was perceived to be done. Essex's gamecock defense left the council deeply worried, because as long as Essex denied his guilt, many were ready to believe his countercharge that he had been framed by his enemies. Essex's opacity, in other words, was dangerously ambiguous and could make the government vulnerable from beyond his grave. His personal priest, Abdias Ashton, was therefore sent to him to try to extract a confession of treason. Ashton was successful in doing so, but Essex's confession leaves him as opaque as Hal's soliloquy leaves the prince in *1 Henry IV*, 1.2, for the impression is inescapable that Essex used even his confession as he used his "forgiveness" of Robert Cecil: to get in one more blow in his own interest. What creates this impression is the extraordinary theatricality of Essex's pious admission of guilt. He wrote a four-page confession, which consists largely of incriminating charges against his fellow conspirators. Even his sister, Penelope Rich, does not escape: "I must accuse one who is most nearest to me," Essex said, "my sister who did continually urge me on with telling me how all my friends and followers thought me a coward, and that I had lost all my valor. She must be looked to, for she hath a proud spirit" (Harrison, p. 319). Nothing publicly approves one's own humility more than the public reproving of another's pride. Essex was glad to "confess" even his sister's adulterous affair with Lord Mountjoy, which had no bearing whatever on his own treason.

The question in all of this is the question that Hal's opacity also raises: is the dissimulator aware of his dissimulation, or has the habit of cultivating theatrical invulnerability become so ingrained that no self exists, in effect, apart from it? In a play written shortly after *Henry V*,

Shakespeare portrays an ambitious power-grabber in the process of trying to define a true self apart from his public posture. Contemplating the possibility of repentance, Claudius recognizes that he would have to surrender what his charade has won him if his prayer for forgiveness is to be sincere. "In the corrupted currents of this world," he acknowledges, "the wicked thing itself / Buys out the law." Self-fashioning before God, however, is another matter:

> But 'tis not so above.
> There is no shuffling, there the action lies
> In his true nature, and we ourselves compell'd,
> Even to the teeth and forehead of our faults,
> To give in evidence.
>   (*Hamlet*, 3.3.56–64)

Essex would appear to be involved in the kind of charade Claudius describes, judging from his behavior just before his death. As Beach Langston has pointed out, "Essex died according to the book," that is, his repentance and death conformed to conventional expectations regarding the art of dying.[25] But to say that Essex's end was conventional is not to dismiss it as trite. In conforming to convention, he resorted to rhetorically powerful gestures, becoming deeply moving to those who watched him—and he made certain that he was always highly visible. The night before his execution he opened his window and addressed his guards: "My good friends, pray for me, and tomorrow you shall see in me a strong God in a weak man; I have nothing left but that which I must pay the Queen in the morning" (Langston, "Art of Dying," pp. 127–28). This sentiment would not be known had the guards not reported it, and they could not have reported it had Essex not made certain that they heard it. As he approached the scaffold next day, he prayed aloud, and after pardoning the executioner he again prayed aloud. The ax fell in the midst of Essex's loud recitation of Psalm 51, a prayer of personal penitence: "Have mercy upon me, O God, according to thy loving kindness: according to the multitude of thy compassions put away mine iniquities." Such a death was *designed* to be construed in just the way Langston construes it: as "humble, pious, brave. . . . [T]he final impression on the audience on that cold morning must have been one of the power of God's grace in the prisoner" (Langston, p. 111). The result was that Essex became more popular in his death than he had ever been in life: his memory was instantly beatified, and a spate of ballads and popular sermons began to commemorate his pious death. It is hard to believe that this event was totally unforeseen by a man who had lived his whole life in the cultivation of popularity. "His chief care evidently was, as he had ever lived popularly, to leave a good opinion in the people's minds now at parting," wrote John Chamberlain after witnessing

Essex's execution (quoted by Langston, p. 121). What the council feared would happen without Essex's confession thus came about because of it. Essex used the public show even of personal vulnerability to make himself invulnerable and to deal his enemies a telling blow after the ax had silenced him forever.

The topical point of this comparison between Hal and Essex is not that Hal somehow represents Essex. He does not. What Henry V enacts are the realities of Tudor power, and those realities are best known to us (as they were to Shakespeare) in those who were most powerful—in the queen, Essex, Raleigh.[26] In fact, the ambiguity of Elizabeth's conversion to Catholicism is a close parallel to Essex's exemplary death and Hal's tavern haunting. If Mary had lived as long as Elizabeth and had reigned as successfully, the pragmatism of Elizabeth's conversion might still be impossible to detect, since she would have been compelled to remain Catholic for the same reason she converted to Catholicism in the first place. In that case, would her original decision have appeared to be merely pragmatic—even to herself? W. P. Haugaard, who has studied Elizabeth's book of private devotions, concludes that in creating the prayers she used daily by herself she had an eye to what others who read them would make of her.[27] Behind her devotions, in other words, lay essentially the same impulse that lay behind Essex's artful death. This is not to say that Elizabeth was merely opportunistic, for her Protestant convictions seem to have been deeply held. The influence of her father, Anne Boleyn, Catherine Parr, and her education would all have inclined her in that direction, and she put up with a great deal of personal and political tribulation to maintain a consistent, moderately Protestant policy. Yet the control that Protestantism gave her over the church was a signal political advantage in an age when political rivalry more often than not took religious form. If the trade-off for her advantage was a necessary concession of power to Parliament, the long-range implications of that concession were not easy to predict in the early years of her reign, and she proved adept at minimizing them when they finally emerged as an inevitable result of her religious policy.[28] Shakespeare, at any rate, had more than one model for the Elizabethan Hal.

Shakespeare gives us no opportunity to witness a Henrician self-display in death, like that of Essex, but in *1* and *2 Henry IV* the Prince seizes on another conventional model of the self to his political advantage: the morality play. Continuity with medieval drama in these plays has usually been discussed as if Shakespeare were using such a model, but to speak of Hal's doing so is really more to the point.[29] The difference can be clarified by recurring briefly to Duke Humphrey in *2 Henry VI*. There, as we noticed, the playwright uses the full dramaturgical spectrum from the passion plays to heighten the emotional intensity of a character's death and at the same time to accentuate its secular context. The one who models the good duke on Christ is not Humphrey himself, in other words, but the playwright. When Richard II compares himself to the betrayed Christ, however (*Richard II*, 4.1.170ff.), the situation is quite different, as Emrys Jones remarks: "The effect is to draw our attention to his bold and startling figure of speech, and, far from making us see Richard as another Christ, we are perhaps surprised into noticing the differences between them—*Richard is, among other things, a man who finds such comparisons appropriate.*"[30] Richard and Hal are alike in this respect: each is created as the kind of character who finds theatrical comparisons appropriate, and in Hal's case the most appropriate and consistent comparison he reaches for is the failing and miraculously restored hero of the morality play—Youth, Lusty Juventus, Infans. No other myth so perfectly creates the impression about himself that he wishes to create: a young man mired in loose behavior who undergoes an astonishing reformation. Hal's use of this myth exactly parallels Essex's use of the art of dying.

But more potent parallels than Essex were available as well, for Queen Elizabeth herself handled myths of her own power in a manner that parallels Hal's recourse to morality tradition. As J. E. Neale has pointed out, when Elizabeth came to the throne her gender and marriageability put her in the same politically vulnerable position her sister had been in five years before—a position Mary had not handled well; and in due time Elizabeth was also confronted with the example of another queen, Mary Stuart, who failed politically because her personal attachments and antipathies created chaos in the importunate male hierarchy she had to control in order to rule effectively.[31] Elizabeth eventually learned to resolve the almost impossible difficulties of Tudor queenship by converting the vulnerability of her gender into a myth of political invulnerability. Her early flirtation with Leicester may well have been an affair of the heart, but when her instinct for political survival ruled out marriage with Leicester, she did not abandon him; she transformed her romance with him into a formality that became the model for her successful relationship with all her courtiers and ultimately with the entire nation. Her public claim to be married to her kingdom, symbolized by the ring she wore, is justly famous, for it epitomizes her ability to turn her personal circumstances to public advantage. Sonnets to Celia, Diana, and Phoebe are expressions of the stylized romance between Elizabeth and her courtiers, whose support she needed and whose hyperbolic adoration was a ritual acknowledgment of her power.[32] Like her religion, Elizabeth's personal relationships thus became peculiarly private and public at once, as they were made to serve the interests of crown policy.

Elizabeth's politic myth of vulnerable gender thus parallels Prince Hal's myth of a vulnerable *human genus*, and the model for Hal's rela-

tion with his tavern companions is the queen's relation with her courtiers. In the late 1590s the most striking and best known of Elizabeth's
courtly relationships involved the earl of Essex, who fortuitously bore
the same first name as Leicester. On Essex's lips too was the language of
romantic devotion, as in this letter of 1591, written when he was returning from France, after Elizabeth peremptorily recalled him:

> At my return I will humbly beseech your Maj. that no cause but a
> great action of your own may draw me out of your sight, for the two
> windows of your privy chamber shall be the poles of my sphere,
> where, as long as your Maj. will please to have me, I am fixed and
> unmoveable. When your Maj. thinks that heaven too good for me, I
> will not fall like a star, but be consumed like a vapor by the same
> sun that drew me up to such a height. While your Maj. gives me
> leave to say I love you, my fortune is as my affection, unmatchable.
> If ever you deny me that liberty, you may end my life, but never
> shake my constancy, for were the sweetness of your nature turned
> into the greatest bitterness that could be, it is not in your power, as
> great a Queen as you are, to make me love you less. Therefore, for
> the honor of your sex, shew yourself constant in kindness, for all
> your other virtues are confessed to be perfect.[33]

The neo-Platonic imagery and the intimacy and devotion of Essex's language parallel the strategy of the sonnets and court entertainments that
mythically celebrated Elizabeth's virginity. The intense struggle for
power is both concealed and revealed in such ritual acknowledgments,
which take the prime feature of the queen's political vulnerability and
use it paradoxically to enhance her inviolate strength.

As the reigning monarch was doing at the time the Lancastrian
plays were written, Prince Hal not only uses a myth of vulnerability
himself but encourages others to do so as well. Poins is the first to abuse
Falstaff in language that suggests a personification allegory of gluttony
(*1 Henry IV*, 1.2.110–14), but he is not the last, and no one does it more
insistently and effectively than Hal in the play ex tempore: "Thou art
violently carried away from grace. There is a devil haunts thee in the
likeness of an old fat man . . . that reverend Vice, that grey iniquity"
(2.4.441–48). From the time we first see Hal and Falstaff together, the
Prince needles Falstaff in this manner, using him as a sparring partner
with whom he practices his political invulnerability, for the flow of jo-
vial abuse is always from prince to knight, and the joke, as Poins recognizes, is to exercise Falstaff's literally incredible ability to deflect Hal's
well-aimed thrusts: "The virtue of this jest will be the incomprehensible
lies that this same fat rogue will tell us when we meet at supper"
(1.2.180–82). The fact, however, that these jokes are made at the expense of a rogue by a man who will some day be king makes quite clear

that those who are indeed politically vulnerable are those who lack power, for all the prince's public myth of spiritual vulnerability. As in 2 *Henry VI*, we quickly realize in 2 *Henry IV* that the apparent dace is really a pike looking for daces in his own turn, as Falstaff exploits Mistress Quickly, Justice Shallow, and several country fellows who lack the means to bribe a recruiting officer. But the one person who suffers no exploitation at all is the one who attempts to secure his power by a myth of vulnerability: "You follow the young Prince up and down like his ill angel" says the lord chief justice to Falstaff (2 *Henry IV*, 1.2.162–63), thus indicating the extent of Hal's success in political mythmaking.

What such myths do to personal relationships is what the myth of romantic attachment did to Elizabeth's relationships with her courtiers: it makes them static, formal, externalized, readily identifying the users in the rituals of state that at once express and contain the enormous tensions of power. This is why King Henry uses such language again in banishing Falstaff, when he calls him the tutor and the feeder of his riots. Whatever the truth about their relationship, the most important thing for Hal is that it be defined in the categories of morality drama, because those conventions are such effective conveyors of the broad generalizations about his supposed moral development that Hal wishes his people to believe about him as he proceeds in securing his power. Essex counted on his theatrical death to display a strong God in a weak man, and Hal counts on the same inference being drawn from his coronation, when he repeats the myth of a vicious Falstaff and a gullible prince. His success appears in a summary of this myth at the beginning of *Henry V*—repeated by the man who had crowned him:

> The courses of his youth promis'd it not.
> The breath no sooner left his father's body
> But that his wildness, mortified in him,
> Seem'd to die; yea, at that very moment
> Consideration, like an angel, came
> And whipp'd the offending Adam out of him,
> Leaving his body as a paradise
> T'envelope and contain celestial spirits.
> Never was such a sudden scholar made;
> Never came reformation in a flood,
> With such a heady currance, scouring faults;
> Nor never Hydra-headed willfulness
> So soon did lose his seat, and all at once,
> As in this king.
>
> (1.1.24–37)

But Ely would appear to have a more realistic political sense than Canterbury, for his alternative explanation for Hal's sudden change describes what really happened:

> The strawberry grows underneath the nettle,
> And wholesome berries thrive and ripen best
> Neighbor'd by fruit of baser quality;
> And so the Prince obscur'd his contemplation
> Under the veil of wildness, which, no doubt,
> Grew like the summer grass, fastest by night,
> Unseen, yet crescive in his faculty.
>   (1.1.60–66)

Hal's morality play myth about himself convinces not only those in his own play world; it has also convinced subsequent interpreters of the plays. Yet Hal's relationship to Falstaff may well owe less to the morality play than to a much more recent stage tradition whose social and political context helps to explain what goes on between the prince and the fat knight. This tradition is actually one man, Richard Tarlton, who had played Derick the clown in *The Famous Victories of Henry V* and who would therefore appear to be a plausible stage inspiration for Falstaff the clown in Shakespeare's plays about Henry V.[34] To speak of Tarlton as a tradition is not a misnomer, for he became a living legend, and in retrospect he epitomizes the first phase of the permanent commercial theater in England.[35]

From what little we know about Tarlton, a portrait emerges that illuminates Falstaff more fully and subtly than the Vice tradition does. Admittedly, information about Tarlton is derived principally from just two sources, both of which contain a considerable quantity of apocryphal matter: what contemporaries said of him and sundry writings attributed to him.[36] But historical reliability is not the point of the parallels between Tarlton and Falstaff: what matters is Tarlton's reputation in the 1590s. For one thing, Tarlton was most famous for extemporal wit, which is also what delights Falstaff's auditors. Most of the witticisms in *Tarlton's Jests* are stories of clever retorts, frequently spoken in rhyme to the astonishment of those who hear them. Even more to the point, Tarlton's "court-witty jests" almost invariably make light of his social betters, in contrast to his "sound city jests" and his "pretty country jests," in which he as often as not comes off second best, as Falstaff does in *The Merry Wives of Windsor*. Given Tarlton's lower-class origin (he is identified variously as a swineherd and a water carrier),[37] his impertinence at court clearly subverts aristocratic decorum, and the only thing that makes its subversiveness permissible is its irresistible laughability. In other words, Tarlton is like Falstaff in putting risible intelligence to work as a means to compel social acceptance for himself in situations where he would not have it otherwise.

Consider, for example, the social dynamics of the following jest:

> It chanced that in the midst of a play, after long expectation for Tarlton, being much desired of the people, at length he came forth, where, at his entrance, one in the gallery pointed his finger at him, saying to a friend that had never seen him, "That is he." Tarlton, to make sport at the least occasion given him and seeing the man point with the finger, he in love again held up two fingers. The captious fellow, jealous of his wife, for he was married and because a player did it, took the matter more heinously and asked him why he made horns at him. "No," quoth Tarlton, "they be fingers.
>
>> For there is no man, which in love to me,
>> Lends me one finger, but he shall have three."
>
> "No, no," says the fellow, "you gave me the horns!" "True," says Tarlton, "for my fingers are tipped with nails, which are like horns, and I must make a show of that which you are sure of." This matter grew so, that the more he meddled, the more it was for his disgrace, wherefore the standers-by counselled him to depart, both he and his horns, lest his cause grew [*sic*] desperate. So the poor fellow, plucking his hat over his eyes, went his ways. (Halliwell, *Jests*, pp. 14–15)

The social status of Tarlton's butt in this incident is specified with the phrase "in the gallery," and his consciousness of his status is signalled in the explanatory phrase, "because a player did it." This superior self-conception is what the jest pinpoints and derides, and the social disparity between the interlocutors is what gives the incident its breathtaking quality: by means of his wit, a lower-class actor literally drives his social superior out of the theater.

Like all means to social advancement, however, wittiness courts failure as well as success, and this was as true for Tarlton as it is for Falstaff. Nungezer records an incident when Tarlton was "universally applauded by all" at court for his forthright political jabs at Raleigh and Leicester, but the queen "was so offended that she forbade Tarlton and all her jesters from coming near her table, being inwardly displeased with this impudent and unreasonable liberty" (Halliwell, *Jests*, pp. xxi–xxx). As Falstaff discovers to his undoing, the power of wit can always be cancelled by the displeasure of power. Hal in fact never allows himself to be discomfited by Falstaff as the playgoer in the gallery is discomfited in Tarlton's jest; the prince's repeated allusions to the gallows, to banishment, and to his own status serve as constant reminders of the disparity in power between himself and Falstaff and effectively contain the potential subversiveness of Falstaff's wit. The prince's jest in robbing the robbers at Gadshill does more than supply a good laugh at Falstaff's expense; in effect, it ensures that the prince's patrimony remains intact, since the stolen money is returned to the king's exchequer. The jest is therefore an emblem of the relationship between Hal and Falstaff: the prince uses the stalking-horse of companionship to make himself invulnerable to the potential thrust of Falstaff's court-witty jests, and when the warlike Harry becomes himself, his displeasure with the fat knight's impudent and unreasonable liberty results in Falstaff's banishment.

The disparity of power between Hal and Falstaff is what principally makes Tarlton a more persuasive model for Falstaff than the Vice. In social terms, as we have seen, Shakespeare's updating of archaic personification allegory on the stage is consistent with medieval practice: those who are power-hungry act according to the "new fashion" of dissembling, hypocrisy, and cunning, just as the Vice did before them. Without doubt, Falstaff is upwardly mobile, like Tarlton, but Falstaff is no cunningly ambitious dissembler, and his "temptation" of Hal is far more complex than the pattern of a cony-catching urbanite or courtier with an ingenu. Moreover, his peculiar vulnerability has no precedent in Vice-tradition, but it precisely reproduces the social vulnerability of a court fool like Tarlton.

Recognizing the difference between Falstaff and the Vice enables a more precise sense of social history in the early English theater. In Weimann's argument about the theater and popular culture, Falstaff is important evidence that the clown is a secular outgrowth of the Vice. But this argument reckons without the social satirical function of devils and Vices in religious drama. As enactments of *libido dominandi*, they are variant dramatic means of satirizing the "new fashion," as we noticed in chapter 2. Falstaff and Tarlton, however, are alike in still another respect: both are products of sixteenth-century social change in England. Far from satirizing the new fashion, they are its beneficiaries. Without it, Tarlton would not have had the kind of attention he achieved at court, where he persuaded Sir Philip Sidney to be his son's godfather and made the queen laugh till her sides ached.[38] No actor before him had aspired to authorship or been accorded such high social status, and it is impossible to imagine an actor winning this kind of approbation fifty years earlier, when Vice comedy held the popular stage—a very different kind of comedy from Tarlton's. At the same time, however, as Weimann points out, Tarlton was a product of native popular decorum, before the rise of neoclassical sensibility decried the companioning of kings and clowns. As Andrew Gurr incisively notes, Tarlton died in the same year that Marlowe effectively proclaimed the stage clown's death knell in the opening lines of *Tamburlaine*, where he declares that the theater would have no more to do with "jigging veins of rhyming mother wits / And such conceits as clownage keeps in pay."[39] Hamlet's concern that the clown not play more than his part would also appear to recall Tarlton, and the prince's severe opinion may have less to do with Shakespeare's view than with an aristocratic assessment of popular stage clowning. In retrospect, the banishment of Falstaff by the king may well capture something of the changing social conditions in Elizabethan stage history.

As king, Hal continues to exploit the morality play myth about his immaturity (as in his response to the French ambassador), but *Henry V* tends to favor myths that are heroic and godlike—no more "modest stillness and humility" but "the action of the tiger" (3.1.3–5). The power of these myths is undeniable, giving *Henry V* a quality like that of the late movement in *The Famous Victories of Henry V*, when we see a king who is fully in control of himself also asserting his control over France. But *Henry V* is not as far removed from its immediate predecessors as its apparent similarity with *The Famous Victories* might suggest. For the focus in this play is still on the real functions of power, specifically on the way myths of invulnerability are pressed into political service. Shakespeare exploits two literary conventions to convey the heroic invulnerability of the king. The first is Renaissance epic, which took its principal inspiration from the Roman imperial epic, Virgil's *Aeneid*.[40] Elizabethan church polity is relevant again here, for defense of the Elizabethan arrangement between crown and church was sought in the precedent of Constantine and the eastern emperors, who were held to represent a true imperial tradition that Henry VIII had revived.[41] Yet another route to the prestige of centralized Roman power was thus opened up by the Tudors, and the implications of their claim to inherit Roman imperial destiny were broad and complex, touching everything from the imagery of the queen's portraits to literary reconstructions of continuity between the mythical past of Rome and Britain. The imperial theme can therefore be seen as part of the foundation of the Elizabethan national epic, Spenser's *Faerie Queene*, which does for England what Virgil had done for Rome: at the center of both poems stands a deified mortal who denies personal desire in the interest of national destiny. Shakespeare's familiarity with this tradition is suggested in his allusion to "our gracious Empress" (5.Pro.30), and his choice of epic devices in *Henry V* follows the Renaissance convention that the epic poet should choose a heroic character from the past to praise the reigning monarch, as Virgil chose Aeneas' story to praise Augustus.

The second literary tradition that operates to enhance Henry V's image is that of romantic comedy, which is also used as political myth, but in rather a different way.[42] The result of the king's setting out to create a heroic myth about himself is a comic story, in the technical Aristotelian sense that the problems faced by the hero at the outset are resolved by the end. *Henry V* is unique among the histories in taking this kind of shape, and it is also unique in its focus on a single central character. The effect of this generic borrowing is to render a persuasive portrait of centralized power in operation, for the problems Henry confronts and resolves are those of effective centralized power. (In this, too, he is quintessentially Elizabethan.) That is why the king is so public about establishing his claim to France at the beginning of the play; in effect, he extends the definition of his kingdom to include France as well, so that an essentially foreign war can be interpreted as a problem in maintaining domestic tranquility. Like Queen Elizabeth, Henry V turns his marital destiny into state myth when he courts Katherine. Here the play's resemblance to romantic comedy is most striking, but power is inextricable from this romance, as it was from Elizabeth's, since Henry's courtship issues in a marriage that seals the peace between England and France—or in Henry's terms, it restores order to a vastly enlarged kingdom, with himself firmly in charge. The device of using marriage to represent harmony on many levels is familiar from Shakespeare's romantic comedies, as is the complementary imagery of fertility and renewal of nature that enters *Henry V* in Burgundy's speech on the world's best garden (5.2.25ff.). But in *Henry V* there is no hint of the hero's coming to the end of himself in order to achieve the end of his comedy, as Shakespeare's comic principals typically do, because the king did all that (or appeared to) as a young man, and myths of vulnerability do not suit conquering heroes and successful suitors who are "plain soldiers."

The persuasive power of this comic structure is undeniable, especially in combination with Henry's heroic success in France, but like everything about *Henry V*, it is fraught with ambiguity, and the play is perhaps most Elizabethan in its ability to create an ideal political image (as it does in its epic evocations and its comic structure) that at the same time becomes the measure of human fallibility. Elizabeth, after all, was uncannily successful in maintaining control of her kingdom while remaining popular and projecting a royal myth of almost unprecedented idealism. But despite all this, the political reality required uncommon cunning, duplicity, repression, ruthlessness, and an espionage system that at some point seems to have hired Shakespeare's fellow playwright, Christopher Marlowe.[43] Moreover, the political climate became particularly unhappy as the 1590s progressed and a new generation of ambitious courtiers, epitomized by Essex, made their weight felt. The reality of the Elizabethan political scene is therefore as difficult to describe definitively as the optical illusion invoked by Norman Rabkin to describe *Henry V*.[44] The illusion is neither a rabbit nor a duck; it is both, depending on how one looks at it. To ponder the idealist mystifications of Elizabethan power is to apprehend a reality that seems to belong to a different world from Burghley's lists of pros and cons in varying courses of political action or Walsingham's machinations to uncover the plotting of Mary Stuart. Yet the machinations and the myth belong to the same

political scene. But Rabkin's illusion breaks down for *Henry V* in the
same way that it breaks down for Elizabeth. For while no evaluative distinction can be made between a rabbit and a duck, the royal myth embodied an imaginative vision that stirred the soul, even while the diurnal reality of secular politics created fear, mistrust, cynicism, and
despair. The timeless myth thus accentuated the failure of diurnal reality, even when myth was compelled into political service, as it was by
Elizabeth and Shakespeare's Henry V. Generically the ambiguous affinity of *Henry V* with romantic comedy therefore suggests that history,
even at its best, is a spoiled comedy.

A pertinent example of how the comic vision is spoiled in *Henry V*
is the king's interpretation of his French campaign as a religious crusade.
From Canterbury's speculation about the young king's religious conversion to Henry's claim that God fought at Agincourt, this stirring invocation of divine sanction is heard repeatedly in the play. Imaginatively
its appeal is irresistible, giving substance to what the Chorus calls the
mirror of all Christian kings and therefore contributing effectively to the
potent myth surrounding the monarch. Politically, however, the king's
crusade is another instance of Hal as Elizabethan tactician, skillfully
pressing religion into the service of secular policy. Moreover, this crusade conforms exactly to what sixteenth-century epic poets frequently
deplored, namely, the waste of European energy in internecine warfare
between Christian princes while the Turkish menace remained un-
checked. In the early 1590s, Lord Burghley himself drew up "instructions for a league with France," including a hope for peace that would
allow European armies to be turned against the Turks.[45]

In his equivocal attempt to order his kingdom, Henry V thus
achieves no more than his father, for Henry IV had repeatedly declared
his intention to undertake a crusade to the Holy Land but was continually denied his intention because of trouble within his own borders.
Historically Henry Bolingbroke achieved an international reputation as
a crusader before he fell out with Richard II, but Shakespeare ignores all
that, giving us an impression of a king so preoccupied with securing his
own dominance that he is unable to undertake a quest whose motive is
comparatively timeless and disinterested. This impression is reinforced
by the contrast between Bolingbroke and his old rival, the duke of Nor-
folk, who was banished at the same time as Bolingbroke but who ended
his life very differently:

> Many a time hath banish'd Norfolk fought
> For Jesu Christ in glorious Christian field,
> Streaming the ensign of the Christian cross
> Against black pagans, Turks, and Saracens;
> And, toil'd with works of war, retir'd himself

> To Italy, and there at Venice gave
> His body to that pleasant country's earth,
> And his pure soul unto his captain Christ,
> Under whose colors he had fought so long.
>   (*Richard II*, 4.1.83–101)

In *Henry V* the contrast between a crusade to the Holy Land—symbolically the pursuit of a timeless goal—and the diminished timely task of secular politics is made with devastating dramatic irony in King Henry's jocular courtship of Katherine:

> Shall not thou and I, between Saint Denis and Saint George, compound a boy, half French, half English, that shall go to Constaninople and take the Turk by the beard? Shall we not? What say'st thou, my fair flower-de-luce? (5.2.207–11)

At the height of Henry's success and power, the old dream of his father still haunts him, and the fleeting nature of his own achievement is underscored by a glance at the disastrous reign of his son, Henry VI, who not only did not go to Constantinople but who lost everything his father had gained in France and finally lost his own kingdom. *Henry V* thus signals its essential affinity with the open-ended, time-bound continuum of secular history, even at the moment when its comic vision most nearly approaches perfect closure.

In short, despite its affinity with epic and romantic comedy, *Henry V* remains a characteristic Shakespearean history play. Its lack of closure is emphasized in the epilogue, which actually names Henry VI and reminds us of the dynamics of power in managing a state, "which oft our stage hath shown" (ep. 13). Like the *Henry VI* plays, *Henry V* also shows us the process of state-managing, and if that process is remarkably like stage-managing, the reason is not necessarily that Shakespeare was Romantically preoccupied with his own art; it may be that the history plays enact the history Shakespeare knew, in which power was handled theatrically by people who had thoroughly absorbed the humanist lesson that in plain terms the very profession of a courtier is "cunningly to be able to dissemble." As enactments of Elizabethan power, the later histories achieve more than the *Henry VI* plays and *Richard III* by rendering no distinction between even the most courteous of Christian kings and those who dissemble in the quest for power. In *1 Henry VI*, Henry V is a heroic memory on whom a chivalric warrior of the old school like Talbot models himself, in contrast to modern scheming opportunists like Suffolk. In *Henry V*, on the other hand, the heroic king is exactly like the chivalric heroes Shakespeare really knew: utterly opaque in his ability to charge his single-minded quest for political dominance with the compelling vision of a sacral ideal.

CHAPTER 7 ❧ POWER AND ARCHAIC DRAMATURGY IN ALL'S WELL THAT ENDS WELL

Two comedies that Shakespeare wrote after *Henry V* show the clear impression of what he had done in the history plays. These two are *All's Well That Ends Well* and *Measure for Measure*, both of which have been recognized as "problem plays" since F. S. Boas called them that in the late nineteenth century.[1] To a large extent, their problems can be understood as an experiment in the dramaturgy of power. On one hand, Shakespeare more explicitly—one is tempted to say, more confidently—recalls the traditions of popular medieval religious drama in these two plays than he had done in any comedy to date, and the consequence is a stronger critique of socially exclusive assumptions than we find in the romantic comedies. Helena's class difference with Bertram is a striking example: Shakespeare marries what Polixenes calls "a bark of baser kind" to "bud of nobler race" (*Winter's Tale*, 4.4.94–95), thus defying received social opinion more clearly than he does in any other marital relationship he dramatizes. Moreover, Helena's association with transcendent virtue recalls the medieval dramatic habit of blessing the dispossessed with a vindicating prophetic vision of cosmic justice. On the other hand, the problem comedies are like the history plays in exploring the ambiguities of applying archetypal models to real human situations. What happens, they seem to ask, when the humble are the powerful?

The central difficulty of these plays is anticipated in *The Merchant of Venice*, a romantic comedy from the mid 1590s that has not traditionally been thought of as a problem play at all.[2] Portia is a figure with undoubted power, yet she enunciates the play's definitive moral insights, and she uses her power to try to coerce a socially marginalized character into a higher state of moral awareness. Portia is granted the full power of the Venetian court in her conflict with Shylock, whom she attempts to persuade to a vision of Christian mercy:

> Though justice be thy plea, consider this,
> That in the course of justice, none of us

Should see salvation. We do pray for mercy,
And that same prayer doth teach us all to render
The deeds of mercy.
(4.1.196–200)

This is one of Shakespeare's two explicit allusions to the Christian doctrine of the atonement (the other allusion is in *Measure for Measure*), but it is followed in *The Merchant of Venice* by Portia's forcible constraint of Shylock to accept Christianity anyway when her attempt to persuade him fails. To be sure, Shylock is a figure of oppressive power in a drama with an archetypal structure: like the powerful Jews who pursue a remarkably un-Semitic Jesus to death in medieval drama, Shylock vindictively determines to encompass the death of an innocent Christian. Yet Shylock's intended victim is rich and socially respected, and Shylock suffers socially at the hands of Christians, being spurned and spat upon like Christ himself. The "old law" of strict justice and the "new law" of Christian mercy are undoubtedly at issue in *The Merchant of Venice*, but the conflict between them is darkened by the realities of power.[3] Portia's courtroom thus contrasts strikingly with the social realism of trial scenes in medieval drama, where contemporary abuses of ecclesiastical law are the means of undoing powerless peasants like Jesus or his parents, and the prosecutors unwittingly defeat themselves in pursuing their oppressive ways. In *The Merchant of Venice*, the one who unwittingly undoes himself is a social outcast to begin with: his reward for boldly attempting to invoke the power of the Venetian state against a citizen is to have the full weight of Venetian law fall on him in the end.

One might conclude that *The Merchant of Venice* reflects a deep ambivalence about power on Shakespeare's own part; certainly such conclusions are being drawn with increasing frequency by those who write about the problem comedies and attempt to stage them.[4] Close attention to the dramaturgy of power that Shakespeare inherited, however, suggests that he was experimenting with it in these plays. Indeed, Portia, Helena, Duke Vincentio, and Duke Prospero from *The Tempest* all share characteristics of what might be called the benign trickster, a central feature of the medieval dramaturgy of power. For a deceptive redeemer is precisely what medieval dramatic tradition saw in the peasant/king it celebrated, who is socially marginal but cosmically vindicated. An important common element of both theology and drama in this case may well be the Trickster of popular folklore, as Kathleen Ashley has argued; certainly the influence of the Trickster in theology appears to have brought the doctrine of God the deceiver into disfavor with scholastic thinkers in the late Middle Ages.[5] The idea of the atonement as a divine deception is the oldest Christian explanation for the incarnation and passion of Christ: from as early as the second century, theologians argued that in order to undo Satan's power over humankind, God adopted human disguise and endured the limitations of human social deprivation, thus using the trick of Satan's serpentine incarnation to overcome Satan's tyranny. Patristic teaching was unanimous in endorsing this idea, and Gregory of Nyssa explains it with particular pungency:

> Two persons may both mix poison with food, one with the design of taking life, the other with the design of saving that life . . . and in no way does the manner of the cure adopted spoil the aim and purpose of the benefit intended; for although a mixture of poison with the food may be effected by both of these persons alike, yet looking at their intention we are indignant with the one and approve the other; so in this instance, by the reasonable rule of justice, he who practised deception receives in return that very treatment, the seeds of which he had himself sown of his own free will.[6]

Many points in Gregory's exposition help to account for its popular appeal and also suggest the procedure of Shakespeare's benign tricksters: borrowing the tactics of the enemy to undo the enemy, using deception and disguise to fulfill a loving purpose, appearing to lose in order to win. A trickster who figures importantly in Jewish tradition is the wily Jacob, who deceived his brother out of his birthright and thereby became God's choice as the national progenitor (Gen. 27). Jacob is not prominent in English medieval drama (only the Towneley cycle includes him), but the medieval interpretation of Jacob and Esau as the church supplanting the synagogue (or the new law fulfilling the old) makes Jacob a figure of Christ and is consistent with what Shakespeare does with Portia in *The Merchant of Venice*, where Jacob is frequently mentioned in symbolically important ways.[7]

While Jacob is not central to medieval religious drama, God the deceiver undoubtedly is.[8] Divine deception is fundamental, for example, to the well-known Towneley *Second Shepherds' Play*, where it is a key element in relating Mak's story to the story of the Nativity. The secret theft of a sheep by Mak, who at first significantly pretends to be a nobleman, is discovered because of the socially oppressed shepherds' charitable desire to present a gift to Mak's "baby," just as Satan, the prince of this world, is undone by the charitable gift of God's son. At the end of the play, Primus Pastor presents another gift, this time to the Christ child, whom he addresses paradoxically as a king:

> Haill, comly and clene, haill, yong child!
> Haill, maker, as I meyne, of a madyn so milde!
> Thou has waryd, I weyne, the warlo so wilde;   *cursed / ween / warlock*
> The fals giler of teyn, no goys he begilde.[9]   *malevolent beguiler*

In the Towneley *Herod the Great*, Nuntius describes the "worthy wonderly" Herod as 'Secouthly sory; / For a boy that is borne herby / Standys he abast" (23–25), and Herod later raves indignantly at the trick that has been played on him: "Hard I never sich a trant [trick], that a knafe so sleght [base] / Shuld com like a sant and refe me my right" (235–36). Here, as in the *Second Shepherds' Play*, the point is that God deceived the proud and overthrew them by coming humbly in human form. V. A. Kolve relates this idea to the wrestling match in the *First Shepherds' Play*, where the young and untried shepherd unexpectedly defeats his powerful and experienced opponent.[10] This dramatic precedent of using power to defeat power in the incarnation provides an illuminating context for Shakespeare's benign tricksters.

The difference in Shakespeare's problem comedies—and where power is concerned, these include *The Merchant of Venice* and *The Tempest*—is that they make the trickster a figure of political power, rather than the reverse. The trickster of popular tradition resorts to clever but dubious measures in order to offset disadvantages of size, power, gender, or social standing, and this folk conception made the classic doctrine of the atonement particularly attractive to the popular drama of the Middle Ages. As Ashley points out, the real trickster in medieval religious tradition is not the devil but Christ: "The ambiguities attributed to the trickster in folk mythologies more clearly belong to Christ the trickster, who cunningly mediates between divine and human in his Incarnation and proves himself the Arch-trickster" ("Guiler Beguiled," pp. 131–32). Some of the apocryphal treatments of Jesus' life so enthusiastically adopted characteristics of the trickster that they made their hero cruel and vengeful, as in the gospel of Thomas's account of the child Jesus killing a playmate with a curse after the child threw a stone at him.[11] Such interpretations failed to gain canonical status because they were theologically incompatible with the atonement as an act of divine love. But early Christian thought was captivated by the folk justice and homely realism of divine deception as an explanation for the atonement, and these qualities kept the older idea alive in popular art and drama when Anselm and Abelard attempted to replace it with a more intellectually coherent idea of the atonement as a human satisfaction of divine justice. In the sixteenth century, in conscious opposition to scholastic theology, Luther gave the classical doctrine new life and profundity, using it as part of his exposition of the *Deus absconditus*: "*Deus revelatus* is always at the same time *Deus absconditus*; the God who reveals Himself and delivers humankind is also present, hidden, in the lowliest and most despised. This is God's 'deceit' " (Aulén, *Christus Victor*, pp. 126–27). The applicability of this description to *The Second Shepherds' Play* suggests the indebtedness of both popular medieval art and Lutheran theology to certain strains of patristic thought.

To make the trickster politically powerful, however, as Shakespeare does in *The Merchant of Venice*, *All's Well That Ends Well*, *Measure for Measure*, and *The Tempest*, inverts the traditional idea and introduces a degree of specifically Renaissance realism. For coercive deceivers were the common stock of Renaissance drama and politics, and nothing pleased them more than the humanist (ultimately Platonic) idea that their dissimulation was both benign and godlike. Once again Puttenham's declaration is relevant: "Qui nescit dissimulare nescit regnare." Bacon agrees. In a striking passage from *The Advancement of Learning*, he adduces an explicit parallel between divine and monarchical inscrutability as he explains the insignia of Pan, one of the court allegorists' favorite choices for representing James I:

> The sheephook also representing empire contains a noble metaphor, alluding to the mixture of straight and crooked in the ways of nature. And this rod or staff is crooked principally in the upper part, because all the works of Divine Providence in the world are mostly brought about in a mysterious and circuitous manner, so that while one thing appears to be doing another is doing really; as the selling of Joseph into Egypt, and the like. Moreover, in all wise human governments, those who sit at the helm can introduce and insinuate what they desire for the good of the people more successfully by pretexts and indirect ways than directly. Nay (which perchance may seem strange), even in mere natural things you may deceive nature sooner than force her; so ineffectual and self-impeding are all things which are done directly; whereas on the other hand the indirect and insinuating way proceeds smoothly and gains its end.[12]

Bacon makes dissimulating coercion a principle of the cosmos—of nature and divine nature alike—and thus makes it irresistible indeed, especially to a monarch who aspired to absolute power.

In medieval drama, God appears as an outcast of human society in order to undo the apparently invincible tyranny of Satan over the human race, but tricksters who are in positions of power to begin with may be difficult to distinguish from political schemers who wish to appear benign in order to preserve their positions with popular support: in effect, such schemers kill their playmates with coercion, if not with a curse. Stephen Greenblatt thus meditates provocatively on Marlowe's Tamburlaine and Spenser's Prince Arthur as alter egos: "Tamburlaine is the face Arthur shows to his enemies or, alternatively, Arthur's is the face Tamburlaine shows to his followers."[13] If any character in Elizabethan drama is constructed with this Janus-face of power, that character is surely Shakespeare's Henry V, who has no counterpart in medieval drama, for he is more realistic and subtle than anything made possible by the medieval dramaturgy of power. Yet the benign tricksters of the problem comedies share many of Henry V's characteristics, among them a passion for disguise and a remarkable opacity of character.

What finally distinguishes these benign tricksters from Henry V is their comic context and the extent to which it borrows positively from the medieval dramaturgy of power, as we shall see. While gaining and preserving effective power is Henry V's sole purpose, power is incidental—though certainly not irrelevant—to Portia, Helena, Vincentio, and Prospero. Insofar as they have recourse to power, they do so in the interest of achieving something better, yet their power inevitably creates ambiguities, and these constitute Shakespeare's ultimate critique of power in a comic context: the best that one hopes to achieve in public life may be contaminated by coercion and inconsistency. Portia's vengeance violates her own high ideal of mercy, but mercy remains preferable to vengeance, and Portia remains a surer bet to enact mercy—however imperfectly—than Shylock. "The web of our life is of a mingled yarn, good and ill together," says the First Lord in *All's Well*, "our virtues would be proud if our faults whipp'd them not, and our crimes would despair if they were not cherish'd by our virtues" (4.3.70–73). This sober and unflattering appraisal of human fallibility seems to be characteristic of the problem comedies, and it distinguishes them definitively from the flattering vision of virtue and power in court masques.

In *All's Well*, Shakespeare borrows a technique for qualifying social privilege that he had consistently used in the history plays, namely, the detailing of how power really works in a political context. The French king arguably plays a role that is analogous to that of comic "blocking" characters, but he is much more politically sophisticated than any such character in the romantic comedies, and he departs from his predecessors in his attempt to further Helena's romantic quest rather than hinder it. What makes him like Duke Solinus or Duke Frederick—or even Shylock—is his quickness to impose extraordinary penalties on those who are subject to his power. Helena and Bertram are both exposed to this kind of threat: she will be executed if her cure fails (2.1.185–86), and he will be ruined if he refuses to marry Helena (2.3.157–66). Referring to parallels in folk motifs and the play's sources does not alter the fact that these threats are made in all seriousness and that they are part of our experience of the king in the play. When R. G. Hunter compares the king's tirade against Bertram to Queen Elizabeth's temper tantrums, he makes clear that more than literary context needs to be considered.[14] At the end of the play, when the king offers to pay Diana's dowry for any husband she chooses, the impression is inescapable that we are still dealing with the same kind of character, since his offer repeats the one he made to Helena earlier, when it yielded a troubled sequence of events issuing from the king's "producing" his power.

The political world over which the French king presides is also more fully realized and more ambiguous than that of any earlier comedy. The war involving the young French nobility in *All's Well* is introduced with remarkable fidelity to Renaissance political reality: the king officially denies Florence's request for aid because of a weightier request from "our dearest friend" Austria not to support Florence. Having said this, however, the king nonetheless permits his young nobles to go to Italy to fight on whichever side they choose, because the war may "serve / A nursery to our gentry, who are sick for breathing and exploit" (1.2.15–17). Presumably this nursery could set the French nobility against each other, a policy that would seem to be cynical enough. In the event, however, we see French noblemen fighting only for Florence, in direct defiance of what the king had promised Austria. The duplicity of this policy is suggested by the First Lord's declaration to the Florentine duke about his purpose in having come from France:

> Holy seems the quarrel
> Upon your Grace's part; black and fearful
> On the opposer.
> (3.1.4–6)

The conjunction of such pious declarations with *Realpolitik* belongs to the world of *Henry V*, and it appears in a comic context for the first time in *All's Well*.

The hypocritical Parolles and the viciously class-conscious Bertram would appear to be the natural appurtenances of such a court, and even the honor Bertram supposedly wins in Italy needs to be considered in its political context, especially given the king's charge to his departing noblemen: "see that you come / Not to woo honor, but to wed it, when / The bravest questant shrinks" (2.1.14–16), for this is the rhetoric the First Lord uses in speaking to the Duke of Florence. "Tell [Bertram] that his sword can never win / The honor that he loses" by consorting with Parolles, the countess charges the two French lords (3.2.92–93). Both Parolles' vapid ambition and his humiliating exposure are modelled on the Jonsonian court gull, as many critics have pointed out, and the reason would appear to be that Jonsonian satire better represents the dynamics of late Elizabethan courtliness than any other comic mode Shakespeare had at his disposal. Shakespeare's implicit tribute to Jonson in *All's Well* is therefore another example of the play's unusual political realism in a comic context. Frank Whigham points out that Castiglione contrasts the courtly virtue *sprezzatura* with *affettazione*, and the contrast is illuminating for Parolles:

> Two forms of attack on affectation can be distinguished. One sort of affectation is deceitful: the familiar false claim to a virtue or capacity one does not have. Exposure of this real absence devastates the claim. But another kind of attack reveals a knowledge or skill as being exercised only with strain; this is a matter of trying too hard. Here the issue is not overt deceit but the stylistic virtue of self-man-

agement. The problem is not the substantive skill but the "social character" of the person.[15]

Both kinds of *affettazione* are evident in Parolles. His pretense to honesty and courage is devastated by its exposure in Florence, and the strain of his efforts to be courtly is manifest whenever he meets someone who recognizes it, like Helena, Lafew, or Lavatch. This kind of strain is what Lavatch parodies in his satiric attempt to use one phrase, "O Lord, sir!" as a response to all questions and comments (2.2). Ostensibly designed as a linguistic form of Protean self-defense—"a barber's chair that fits all buttocks"—this noncommital phrase inevitably outlives its usefulness and traps its user verbally, as Parolles is later trapped in fact while pursuing a "very plausive invention" (4.1.26) like Lavatch's. "I see things may serve long, but not serve ever," as Lavatch pointedly remarks (2.2.55).

Bertram's class-consciousness is the most extraordinary and complex example of social realism in *All's Well*. The unusual sensitivity to social rank in the sixteenth century was due to the perceived possibility of change, particularly change for the better. No one was keener to maintain the exclusivity of privileged status than those who had just attained it, and the implicit function of courtesy literature, as Whigham argues, was to define signs of status that were supposed to prevent the dilution of rank, though the publication of such definitions in fact made them more accessible to those who coveted higher status. Marriage across classes was especially frowned upon because it posed such an obvious threat to ascribed status. John Ferne thus condemns exactly the situation that prevails in *All's Well*, 2.3, when the king orders his ward to marry a woman of lower status:

> if the lord who hath the tuition and guard of the body and lands of his pupil and tenant within age, being a gentleman and holding by the noble service of knighthood (as at the beginning of that service they were all gentlemen, either of blood or coat-armor that held lands by the same service) shall marry the same pupil (not yet of discretion to like) unto the daughter of any of the foresaid persons . . . be they yeomen, merchants, burgesses, or bondmen, and although the woman be formed of a most excellent proportion of body, her years tender, her beauty fresh, her portion rich, and her heritage very ample, yet for all this, here is a disparagement, and it is the unequal coupling in yoke of the clean ox and the unclean ass, an injury not only done to the person of the young gentleman but eke a dishonor to the whole house from which he is descended, and that upon this reason in that nobility should not be joined with ignobility, so that the issue of their kinsman, descended as it were of Abraham and Hagar should seem but half noble, nay but half a man,

monstrous in kind and degenerated from the rest of his family, and hereby the house suffereth a lamentable diminution and rebatement of her nobleness even in that line which ought to be the chiefest honor to the same.[16]

In Ferne's analysis of such situations, the onus falls on the guardian—who in *All's Well* is the king—because he compels his ward to diminish their mutual nobleness. Ferne's point therefore complements Howard Cole's argument that according to the expectations of Elizabethan wardship the king in *All's Well* legally abuses his position by compelling Bertram into "disparagement" and the miseries of an enforced marriage.[17]

Given this conjunction of social and legal perspectives in the king's enforcement of Helena's choice, it is clear that one can pity Bertram only by appealing to standards of class distinction that the play everywhere challenges. One such challenge, as Muriel Bradbrook has pointed out, would appear to be the humanist "question 'Wherein lies true honour and nobility?' " a question that "was older than the new and fantastic codes of honour, or the new ideas of what constituted a gentleman"— the kind of ideas, in other words, that appear in *The Blazon of Gentry*.[18] The answer to this humanist question, of course, is that true nobility is virtue, and Bradbrook rightly points to *Fulgens and Lucrece* and *Gentleness and Nobility* as earlier dramatic treatments of the idea. But the humanist commonplace is problematic in *All's Well*. Late sixteenth-century courtesy theory indeed came later than humanism, yet far from being discontinuous with humanism, as we saw in chapter 3, it was a natural product of the social conditions in which humanism initially flourished. Courtesy theorists, in fact, tirelessly expounded the humanist commonplace about virtue and nobility. John Ferne, for example, describes the social hierarchy as rigidly static and genetically defined, as we have just seen, yet he devotes several pages to the proposition that true nobility lies in virtue (pp. 14–21; sigs. Bvii^v–Ciii). The promulgation of this apparent contradiction points to complexities of sixteenth-century social change that we have encountered before. The assertion that nobility was based on virtue justified upward mobility and self-servingly flattered the already privileged with a high-minded moral assessment of their worth. The simultaneous insistence on rigid hierarchy was necessary, however, to preserve the sense that what one gained was worth achieving and not open to every malapert asshead who wanted it. Early humanist plays like *Fulgens and Lucrece* emphasize the principle of moral mobility because the humanist struggle with the old aristocracy was just beginning.[19] As M. E. Moeslein remarks, in his edition of Henry Medwall's plays, John Tiptoft very likely translated Buonaccorso's *De vera nobilitate* (the basis of *Fulgens and Lucrece*) for self-serving reasons, because Tiptoft was one of Henry VII's "new men."[20] By the late sixteenth century, however, the situation had changed considerably. Humanist standards of privilege had become part of the power structure, and the spate of courtesy literature published during Elizabeth's reign reflects the tensions and ambiguities of a social system that seemed to offer open opportunity to those capable of intellectual labor, yet in fact was fiercely competitive and all but closed.

What the king says to Bertram about honor and virtue is not therefore a qualification of the play's emphasis on political and social realism but actually constitutes another facet of that realism. To combine an appeal to virtue with the threat of absolute ruin is not morally consistent or psychologically perceptive, but it is a realistic enactment of the kind of power wielded by Renaissance monarchs. The king's tirade is the scene's second ostentatious display of male power (Bertram's rejection of Helena is the first), and it is no more appropriate than its predecessor, since the most it can do is to produce the sham acquiescence that Bertram, as the king's ward, is immediately compelled to offer (2.3.167–73). Since this kind of acquiescence is not a satisfactory romantic resolution, the king's apparent gesture in Helena's behalf is closer to the obstacles thrown up by previous comic blocking characters than it appears to be at first: his display of power against Bertram has the effect of removing Bertram from Helena in the profoundest possible way, for like the Pauline law, the king's order can publicly constrain, but it cannot make the heart comply. Bertram might have chosen to endure financial and social ruin in order to remain unmarried to Helena, and such a choice might have made another promising story, given Helena's unswerving devotion, but it is not the story Shakespeare chose to write in this play.

The strongest qualification of class consciousness in *All's Well* is Helena herself, not only because she initiates a cross-class marriage but because she belongs to literary and dramatic traditions whose origin and appeal are popular rather than privileged. What Helena brings with her is not the humanist equation of virtue and nobility enunciated by the king but the medieval conception that true nobleness is humility, an idea whose origin is very different from that of the humanist commonplace. Equating virtue with nobility is a classical idea and probably Platonic in origin; certainly it is epitomized in Plato's memorable image of the philosopher king. If true goodness is true knowledge, as Plato argues, then only those capable of the highest knowledge can be truly virtuous, and in a well-ordered society those who possess that knowledge will naturally govern those who do not. The noble, in short, are the wise and virtuous: kingly status depends on the wisdom and virtue of those who possess it. Thomas More's version of this doctrine appears in that remarkable passage in *Utopia* where he enunciates a system of social mobility based on intellectual labor and achievement.[21] For both Plato and More the sure sign of a disordered society is that the virtuous are not the noble. For More, this disorder explains the peripatetic life of Hyth-lodaeus; for Plato, it explains the death of Socrates, a noble mind over-thrown by a society that refused the direction (in effect, the ennobling governance) of a wise and virtuous man.

The idea of equating nobleness with Christian humility is patristic in origin, taking its impetus from reflections on martyrdom in a strati-fied society. In Prudentius' story of the martyr Saint Romanus, the mar-tyr declares:

> Far be it from me that the blood of my parents or the law of the senate-chamber should make me noble; it is Christ's noble teaching that ennobles men. If you examine into the first origin of our birth by constructing a family tree, it is from the mouth of God our Father that our existence begins. Whosoever serves him is the true noble-man; he who will not submit to the Father turns out to be de-based.[22]

Another expression of the same idea is Augustine's conception of *poten-tia humilitatis*, which is pervasively encoded in the power relations of medieval religious drama, as we saw in chapter 2. The deaths of Socrates and Christ epitomize the difference between Augustine's idea and the classical conception of virtue that he rejected and that achieved prestige again in the sixteenth century. For Augustine, the death of Christ equates goodness with humility, not with Platonic wisdom, which can-not encompass the humanity and mortality of a god. Augustine makes this point frequently, but perhaps his most forthright statement of it is in *The City of God* 10.29, where he chides "the Platonists" for their failure to acknowledge the incarnation and passion of Christ:

> You refuse to recognize the incarnation of the unchanging Son of God, which brings us salvation, so that we can arrive at those real-ities in which we believe, and which we can in some small measure comprehend. ... The grace of God could not be commended in a way more likely to evoke a grateful response, than the way by which the only Son of God, while remaining unchangeably in his own proper being, clothed himself in humanity and gave to humankind the spirit of his love by the mediation of a man. ... And because he has implanted in our nature the desire for blessedness and immor-tality he has now taken on himself mortality, while continuing in his blessedness, so that he might confer on us what our hearts de-sire; and by his sufferings he has taught us to make light of what we dread. But humility was the necessary condition for submission to this truth; and it is no easy task to persuade the proud necks of you philosophers to accept this yoke. ... Then what basis is there for your notion that escape from any kind of body is an essential con-

dition for our happiness, a notion that makes you feel that you have rational justification for your rejection of Christianity? The only reason, I repeat, is that Christ is humble, and you are proud.[23]

Platonic "pride" here is precisely the ennobling knowledge that the Athenians rejected in Socrates. The direction of Augustine's thought in this passage is diametrical to Plato's and inimical to the later humanist derivatives of Platonic wisdom that were used as the ideological underpinning of Tudor privilege. For Augustine's point is that the humility of God in becoming human reached its perfection in Christ's identification with the humble in his death. Since Christ was king of kings, it follows that true nobility involves an appropriation of Christ's humility:

> He who stood before the judge, he who was struck in the face, he who was scourged, he who was spat upon, he who was crowned with thorns, he who was covered with blows, he who was hanged on a tree, he who while hanging on the tree was mocked, he who died on a cross, he who was pierced with a lance, he who was buried: the same is risen. Let earthly powers rage as they may: what can they avail against the King of kingdoms, the Lord of all kings, the Creator of all worlds?[24]

Augustine's argument is an important formative factor in the passion sequences of the mystery plays, because they enact the climax of Christ's paradoxical kingship. The rhetoric of social disdain that appears in Bertram's rejection of Helena is first established in English drama by the likes of Caiaphas, Annas, and Pilate in their rejection of Christ. In effect, they respond to him exactly as John Ferne's interlocutors respond to peasants—as if he were a threat to their power and privilege. "Where was thy sire at bord when he met with thy dame?" asks the Towneley Caiaphas,

> What, nawder bowted ne spurd, and a lord of name?
> Speke on in a torde, the dwill gif the shame, *devil / thee*
> Sir Sybré!
> Perdé, if thou were a king,
> Yet might thou be riding.
> Fi on the, fundling!
> Thou lifys bot by brybré.

> Lad, I am a prelate, a lord in degré.
> Sittys in min astate, as thou may se,
> Knightys on me to wate in diverse degré.
> I may thole the abate, and knele on thy kne *allow you to*
> In my present. *humble yourself / presence*
>
> (*The Buffeting*, 146–57)

In socially rejecting Christ, Caiaphas ironically demonstrates the failure of his own nobility, despite his insistence on established social hierarchy ("a lord in degré," "min astate," "in diverse degré"), because he fails to recognize the equation of kingship and humility that Christ represents. The same irony appears elsewhere in the mystery plays, but particularly in sequences dealing with the torture and execution of Christ. In the York *Death and Burial*, such socially abusive terms as "faitour," "brothell," "warlou," "harlott," and "caitiff" are used of Christ and occasionally of his followers, who are commoners.[25] In the Chester *Trial*, the vocabulary is similar ("babelavaunt," "fameland freare," "freyke," "scalward"), and the irony is profound when Jesus is mockingly dressed as a king and introduced by Pilate to his tormentors: "Lordinges, here you may se / Your king all in his royaltie."[26] At this moment of his greatest degradation, Jesus is in fact in his full royalty, as the Chester author makes clear in the dialogue between Pilate and Jesus that precedes Pilate's announcement (257–90).

In contrast to the abuse heaped on Jesus by false noblemen is the language of social elevation used by those who recognize the transcendent humility he embodies. In the York *Death and Burial*, Mary, Longinus, and Nichodemus all refer to Jesus as "jente," "jentill," or "judged unjente." In the Towneley *Harrowing of Hell*, Belzabub echoes the worldly scorn of Jesus' persecutors, "That lad that thou callys Lord in lede / He had never harbor, housse, ne hall" (138–39), but King David recognizes that the one who was crucified is the conqueror of hell:

> Nay, with him may ye not fight,
> For he is king and conqueroure,
> And of so mekill might
> And stif in every stoure.
> Of him commys all this light
> That shinys in this bowre.
> He is ful fers in fight,
> Worthy to win honoure.
>   (128–35)

King David also Jesus refers to his humble followers as "fre" (noble) when he tells Satan that they no longer belong to hell (309). As Rosemary Woolf has pointed out, devotional poets developed a familiar metaphor of Christ as a medieval knight, and this metaphor appears in the passion plays too, though ironically put in the mouths of Christ's persecutors.[27] "In faith, sir, sen ye callyd you a king," says Primus Tortor mockingly as he nails Christ to the cross in the Towneley *Crucifixion*,

> You must prufe a worthy thing
>   That falles unto the were;   *war*

> Ye must just in tornamente; *joust*
> Bot ye sitt fast, els be ye shentt,
>   Els downe I shall you bere.
>   (89–94)

Like Pilate presenting Christ in royal robes to his persecutors, Primus Tortor ironically says more than he realizes.

The idea that humility is true nobleness appears not only in the mystery plays; it is pervasive in medieval religious drama. In liturgical drama, it appears as early as the twelfth century in the Fleury *Slaughter of the Innocents*. Here already is the ranting worldling, Herod, lacking in emotional self-control and raging against the white-stoled innocents, who process serenely after the *agnus Dei*, "the hallowed lamb slain for us / ... The splendor of the Father, the splendor of the Virgin Birth."[28] After their slaughter, the innocents rise from a prone position in a figure of Christ's resurrection, and echoing the Easter liturgy they praise the soldiership of Christ, apocalyptic commander of the martyrs: "O Christ, O youth skilled in the greatest wars, how great an army do you gather for the Father" (54). In this play, as in the later vernacular passion plays, the action can hardly be understood apart from its enactment of transcendent humility.

The same affirmation also appears in the English saint's play. John Velz has discussed the Digby *Mary Magdalene* as a study in comparative sovereignty, and when viewed in this way the king who comes off most nobly is the one who dies on the cross in the course of the action, not those who boast about their power and lineage, such as the Emperor, Herod, Pilate, Cyrus, or the King of Marseilles.[29] The three Marys, "arayid as chast women with signs of the Passon printyd upon ther brest," acknowledge Christ's victory over devilish power in choral union:

> Heylle, gloriows crosse! thou barist that Lord on hye
> Which by thy migth deddist lowly bowe don, *might*
> Mannys sowle to bye from all thraldam,
> That evermore in peyne shold a-be.
> By record of Davit, with mild stevyn, *voice*
> *Domine, inclina caelos tuos, et descende!*[30]

In the Digby *Conversion of St. Paul*, Saulus's seventy-line sermon on humility is the play's climax, where Saulus accounts for his own transformation from boastful and destructive worldling and admonishes his auditors at the same time:

> So owr Saviour shewith us exampls of meknes,
> Thorow grace of his goodnes mekly us groundys.
> Tr[e]wly it will us save fro the sinnes sekenes,

For Pride and his progeny mekenes confoundys.
Quanto major es, tanto humilia te in omnibus:
The gretter thou art, the lower loke thu be.
Bere the[e] never the hyer for thy degré.[31]

This variation on the medieval dramaturgy of power helps to explain why *All's Well* has been understood by many critics as a secular miracle play. Helena describes her social status as "humble" no fewer than three times (1.3.153; 2.1.197; 2.3.83), and she brings with her a power that defies belief—"the rarest argument of wonder that hath shot out in our latter times" (2.3.7–8). Helena's power, moreover, is benign and restorative, healing the king's disease and eventually winning Bertram's heart against all social expectation, as the king's coercive power could never do. In urging the king to make trial of her claim to be able to cure him, Helena expressly acknowledges that she is a mediatrix of divine power (2.1.149–54), and in view of Augustine's argument that the Christian reversal of social rank is modelled in the incarnation of Christ, it is noteworthy that three allusions to the incarnation in *All's Well* are all associated with Helena's love for Bertram. The first is in Helena's apostrophe to her absent husband, after she has received his letter of rejection: "My being here it is that holds thee hence. / Shall I stay here to do't? No, no, although / The air of paradise did fan the house / And angels offic'd all" (3.2.122–25). This is one of those luminous comments that ties Helena to the redemptive figures of medieval religious drama. Still another is in Helena's subsequent letter to the countess: "Ambitious love hath so in me offended / That barefoot plod I the cold ground upon" (3.4.5–6). The countess, who consistently thinks like Helena, makes a third such allusion after reading Helena's letter: "What angel shall / Bless this unworthy husband? He cannot thrive, / Unless her prayers, whom heaven delights to hear / And loves to grant, reprieve him from the wrath / Of greatest justice" (3.4.25–29).

The distinctive virtue that Helena represents is recognized by others than the countess. Lavatch, for example, who has a keen eye for courtly foibles, identifies the devil with the court—as the N-Town *Passion Play 1* does—and then elliptically states a biblical paradox like those in Richard II's "thoughts divine": "But, sure, he [i.e., the devil] is the prince of the world; let his nobility remain in's court. I am for the house with the narrow gate, which I take to be too little for pomp to enter. Some that humble themselves may, but the many will be too chill and tender, and they'll be for the flow'ry way that leads to the broad gate and the great fire" (4.5.49–55). As we noticed in chapter 4, Lavatch is paraphrasing Matt. 7:13–14, one of the many biblical sayings that inspired Augustine's distinction between Christian and Platonic conceptions of virtue. Curiously, Lavatch's identification of the devil with the court is one opinion the bitter clown shares with Parolles, who urges Bertram to ape the models of court fashion more closely: "and though the devil lead the measure, such are to be followed" (2.1.55–56).

As a qualification of Tudor social expectation, what Helena is in herself is complemented by what she does for Bertram. We noticed that legally and socially he identifies himself strongly with the kind of privilege that was endorsed in late sixteenth-century courtesy theory. In doing so, he follows a very different social standard from that of his parents. The old count's social attitude is described approvingly by the king in a context where he is not being coercive:

> Who were below him
> He us'd as creatures of another place,
> And bow'd his eminent top to their low ranks,
> Making them proud of his humility,
> In their poor praise he humbl'd. Such a man
> Might be a copy to these younger times,
> Which, follow'd well, would demonstrate them now
> But goers backward.
>   (1.2.41–48)

The fact that both the king and Bertram are goers backward from what the king professes to admire does not negate its validity or its importance. The king is not describing predatory self-deprecation: the old count did not pretend to be humble in order to compel others to assert his true worth. Rather, he treated those who were socially inferior to him without regard to rank, and "he made the humble proud of the fact that he was humbling his own eminence in praising them."[32]

The old count's behavior is not merely an idealized reminiscence in *All's Well*, because we see it in action in his wife. Given the formidable social barriers to Helena's love for Bertram, Helena's reluctance to admit her love to the countess in 1.3 is as understandable as the countess's response is unexpected. What we expect—and what Helena expects—is the kind of response Posthumus gets from Cymbeline (though Cymbeline lacks the countess's social justification for what he does), but the countess does not react by the book, or at least not by any sixteenth-century book prescribing social responses in such a situation. The model for her loving response to Helena is her dead husband, as described by the king: she literally uses one below her as a creature of another place, refusing to allow Helena's social inferiority to make any difference. "I say, I am your mother, / And put you in the catalogue of those / That were enwombed mine" (1.3.139–41). In effect, the countess models the social paradox of medieval drama, enacting true nobleness in humbling herself to love one who is hierarchically inferior. The extraordinary empathy between these two women is one of the difficulties that stand in the way of construing *All's Well* as a darkly satirical comedy, for the countess incurs no obligation to Helena (unlike the king) and has nothing to gain by supporting her except an unusually gifted daughter-in-law.

Bertram's mother seems from the outset to be concerned that her son will be a goer backward from his parents' standard, judging by her advice to him as he first takes his leave:

> Be thou blest, Bertram, and succeed thy father
> In manners, as in shape! Thy blood and virtue
> Contend for empire in thee, and thy goodness
> Share with thy birthright.
>
> (1.1.61–64)

In the countess's psychomachic conception of Bertram, the kind of virtue that she hopes will contend with his blood is what the countess demonstrates later with Helena, and it is therefore distinct from the king's problematic iteration of the humanist commonplace about virtue and nobility. Bertram does not gain real *virtus* (which encompasses heroic manhood as well as ethical insight and action) until he comes to the end of himself and acknowledges Helena as his wife, both in name and substance (5.3.306). His capitulation closely parallels that of Proteus in *Two Gentlemen of Verona*, whom Bertram also resembles in his determined attempt to maintain a Protean front of courtly invulnerability. In effect, Bertram is compelled to agree with Lavatch, a commoner who often comments clairvoyantly about the court: "I see things may serve long, but not serve ever."

That Bertram's capitulation involves his psychological and sexual self-conception rather than his relationship to God does not deny its continuity with medieval dramaturgy or its contrast to the kind of courtly identity represented in a power broker like the king. Bertram is Helena's husband, after all, and his identification with her as his wife appropriately involves sexuality as well as less tangible qualities like the ability to ask forgiveness.[33] His early refusal to consummate their marriage makes it literally sterile and therefore participates symbolically in the death wish represented in the king's despair about his disease and in Helena's early despair about her class difference with Bertram: "The hind that would be mated by the lion / Must die for love" (1.1.93–94). Although Bertram goes to Italy to win military honor, all we actually see him involved in there is the exposure of Parolles' folly and of his own, though he does not know he is involved in the latter until the play's final scene. Both these incidents play a part in the eventual redemption of his *virtus*. Parolles' exposure opens Bertram's eyes to courtly pretension in a man he had foolishly adopted as his mentor; and Bertram's night with Helena humbles and ennobles him at once, in a way that he only recognizes for the first time at the end of the play, when he literally recognizes his *virtus* in her: she is pregnant by him and his ring is on her finger. Florence is therefore a place of conversion for Bertram, as John Velz calls it: a place where profound psychic changes occur that make this place distinct from his place of origin.[34] In this respect, too, Bertram is like Proteus, whose sudden change occurs in the forest, apart from the corrupting court. The rings that Bertram and Helena exchange in Florence are visible tokens of the change in Bertram: his ring is associated with the honor of his father's house (4.2.42–45), which he symbolically bestows on Helena without knowing it; hers is the "token to the future [of] past deeds" (4.2.64)—a symbol, like Helena's pregnancy, of Bertram's delayed-action conversion.

Helena's popular origin, both in folklore and medieval dramaturgy, makes her Shakespeare's most forthright qualification to date of the high style and its implicit social assumptions.[35] Her literal social status in the dramatic action is symbolic of the traditions she represents in *All's Well.* The political and social realism surrounding the court thus complements the dramaturgical archaism surrounding Helena as an implicit challenge to received standards of esthetic and social decorum. She does not belong to the court, yet she wins spontaneous approbation there for the life-giving power with which she redeems the sterility that coercive power and a rigid class system have produced. Far from diluting Bertram's rank, as courtesy theory would maintain, she morally ennobles it by preserving it from itself and its own worst inclinations. Shakespeare returns to this kind of ennobling again in *The Winter's Tale*, when Polixenes defends vegetative crossbreeding:

> Yet nature is made better by no mean
> But nature makes that mean. So, over that art
> Which you say adds to nature, is an art
> That nature makes. You see, sweet maid, we marry
> A gentler scion to the wildest stock,
> And make conceive a bark of baser kind
> By bud of nobler race. This is an art
> Which does mend nature, change it rather, but
> The art itself is nature.
>   (4.4.89–97)

Like the king in *All's Well*, Polixenes fails to apply to his own situation (i.e., to Florizel) what he advocates in general, but in neither play does that failure obviate the truth of what the king says. In *All's Well*, as in *The Winter's Tale*, when the gentle scion of the high style and its social implications is married to the wildest stock of folklore and medieval religious drama, the product is not monstrous in kind, as Ferne would maintain, but an art that mends nature, without ceasing to be natural and without failing to be art.

All's Well is problematic, however, in ways that *The Winter's Tale* is not, as most critics have indicated by their hesitation to endorse the earlier play as a satisfactory comedy: despite its title, it does not seem to end well, after all. The principal problem, I have suggested, is Helena's recourse to power as a benign trickster. That she is tricky no one attempts to deny, either in the play or in commentary on it. "This deceit so lawful" is how the Florentine widow describes the bed trick, and Diana's opinion of it succinctly describes the essential principle of the classic doctrine of the atonement: "In this disguise, I think't no sin / To cozen him that would unjustly win" (4.2.75–76). Ambrose's explanation of this doctrine helps to clarify its relation to the archaic Christian affirmation of nobility as humbleness, for Ambrose rings repeated rhetorical changes on the phrase "the prince of this world" as he emphasizes the divine use of guile:

> It is for no small reason that the virginity of Mary beguiled the prince of this world, who when he saw her espoused to a man, could not have supposed the birth suspicious. That the purpose of this plan was to beguile the prince of this world is made clear by the words of the Lord himself, when the apostles were told to keep silent about Christ, when the healed were forbidden to brag of the cure, when the demons were enjoined not to speak of the Son of God. To beguile, as I said, the prince of this world, the apostle too declared to be the purpose of this plan, saying: "But we speak the wisdom of God hidden in a mystery, which none of the princes of this world knew; for had they known it, they would never have crucified the Lord of Glory"; that is to say, they would never have brought it about that I should be redeemed by the death of the Lord. He beguiled therefore for us, he beguiled that he should conquer, he beguiled the devil when he was tempted, when he was questioned, when he was called the Son of God, so that at no point did he confess his proper divinity. But yet more he beguiled the prince of this world: for though the devil sometimes had doubts, as when he said, "If you are the Son of God, cast yourself down," assuredly, too late he recognised him and departed from him.[36]

Langland makes the same point in *Piers Plowman*, when he has Christ "of his gentrice . . . joust" disguised in the armor of Piers, that is, fight the devil in the disguise of human form. The humble appearance of God incarnate deceived Satan, in response to Satan's deception of Adam and Eve:

> Thow, Lucifer, in liknesse of a luther addere   *deceitful, treacherous*
> Getest bi gile tho that God lovede;
> And I, in liknesse of a leode, that Lord am of hevene,   *human being*

Graciousliche thi gile have quyt: go gile ayein gile!
And as Adam and alle thorugh a tree deyden,   *died*
Adam and alle thorugh a tree shul turne to lyve,
And gile is bigiled and in his gile fallen.[37]

A close parallel to Langland's formulation appears in Christ's words at the beginning of the York *Harrowing of Hell* (which is closely followed by the Towneley adaptor):

The feende thame wanne with trayne,   *plot, device*
Thurgh frewte of erthely foode;
I have thame getyn agayne,
Thurgh bying with my bloode.
   (9–12)

In her assault on privileged assumptions, Helena's recourse to dissimulation is an important part of her redeeming love for Bertram: disguising herself, as it were, in the body of Diana, she undoes her proud husband at the same time that she fulfills his harsh demands. This parallel with medieval dramaturgy is part of a congeries of related parallels that surround Helena: humility as true nobleness, the weak overthrowing the strong, the appropriation of cosmic power by the socially oppressed—"greatest grace lending grace," as Helena puts it (2.1.160).

Yet Helena's recourse to power in her redemption of Bertram creates difficulties that do not appear in a parallel situation, as when Rosalind disguises herself to court Orlando. Bertrand Evans perceptively notes that Helena deceives *us* in ways that Rosalind never does, but he does not add that what makes this opacity most troubling in Helena is that she allies herself with coercive power rather than being victimized by it, like Rosalind.[38] Helena's strategy to win Bertram's heart involves the king from the moment of its inception: "The King's disease—my project may deceive me, / But my intents are fix'd and will not leave me" (1.1.227–28). Helena conceives this plan knowing that Bertram is the king's ward as a result of old Rosillion's death, and the countess approves the plan before Helena carries it out (2.1.225ff.). Helena's humbleness thus ambiguously allies itself at the outset with the same power from which it redeems Bertram in the end. Some have tried to avoid this difficulty by suggesting that Helena is a character who learns by her mistakes, like Bertram, and that her first mistake is to ally herself with the king.[39] The problem with this view is that Helena never acknowledges that she has made a mistake, despite the fact that she has an opportunity to do so in soliloquy (3.2.99–129). She does register her solicitude for Bertram's involvement in the Italian wars, and she blames herself for putting him there, but while these sentiments demonstrate her selfless devotion to Bertram, they give no hint that she regards her alliance with the king as inconsistent, let alone erroneous. If Shakespeare wanted us to see Helena as coming to a recognition like Bertram's—that things may serve long, but not serve ever—he would surely not have made her totally opaque where that change was concerned.

Moreover, Helena does not abjure the power of the king after the crisis in the French court. The ring that begins to unravel Bertram's falsehood in the end was given to Helena by the king, "and when I gave it Helen," the king tells Bertram, "I bade her, if her fortunes ever stood / Necessitied to help, that by this token / I would relieve her" (5.3.82–86). To be sure, Helena does not offer this ring in an open appeal to the king's support: the king recognizes it by chance on Bertram's finger. Yet Helena placed it on Bertram's finger during the time she was in bed with him, and she could hardly have done so without foreseeing some such outcome as occurs in the play's last scene. Indeed, she bestows it on Bertram with a clear indication that she not only foresees but intends the outcome, as Diana tells Bertram before the bed trick occurs:

> And on your finger in the night I'll put
> Another ring, that what in time proceeds
> May token to the future our past deeds.
> (4.2.61–63)

Helena's readiness to avail herself of the king's power a second time raises serious questions about how much she regards her first recourse to his power as a mistake. Moreover, while one might possibly construe her soliloquy in 3.2 as an admission of failure, she makes no admission of any kind at the end of the play. One's belief that she has matured along with her immature husband can be no more than an unsupported inference, for while Bertram's repentance is brief enough, Helena's (if it occurs at all) is entirely implicit.

Helena's wiliness and her unsettling alliance with the apex of power have also led to the inference that far from changing for the better, she deliberately employs dissimulation from the beginning in order to advance herself socially.[40] In this view, her humility is no more than self-serving pity to hide her ambition. She is therefore distinct from Parolles only in being able to play his game much more successfully than he does. She is like him in her ambition; she is unlike him in gaining court favor through coercion and dissimulation without getting caught. Richard A. Levin goes so far as to argue that Helena attempts to bribe Parolles into helping her early in the play, but failing to do so she suborns the countess's steward, uses her sexual power to dominate Lafew and the king, plans every move she makes in Florence, successfully bribes one of the French lords, and through him masterminds the exposure of Parolles, whom she regards as a rival. To his credit, Levin acknowledges that *All's Well* is "almost like a Rorschach test" in revealing our predispositions about it, but Levin is remarkably quick to draw unsupported inferences from *All's Well*, and he draws many more such inferences than do those who understand Helena as a woman who learns from her mistakes.

A more balanced view of Helena is surely truer to the play's complex sense of human life as a web with mingled yarn. Parolles as a flashy social climber is an apt foil to Helena, and an important index to the difference between them is Lavatch's response to each. While Lavatch is quick to sense Helena's erotic motive for going to court (1.3.1–88), he later uses the language of biblical paradox, as we noticed, in a comment that seems to refer specifically to Helena's class difference with Bertram (4.9.49–55); and at the same time Lavatch reserves some of his least ambiguous and most vitriolic remarks for Parolles late in the play (5.2.126). Helena's love for a man of higher social class than hers is undeniable; because of it she uses phrases like "th'ambition in my love" (1.1.92) and "ambitious love" (3.4.5). But a difference must surely be acknowledged between her loving Bertram, who is incidentally in a higher social class, and her loving a higher social class whose nearest representative happens to be Bertram. Her love is literally ambitious, but she is unlike Parolles in that ambition is not her love. If it were, she would be quick, when Bertram rejects her, to choose any of the other noblemen at court who have declared their happiness to be chosen by her (2.3.77–98). But she takes neither this alternative—seemingly irresistible to a socially ambitious schemer—nor the alternative that she considers at the outset: subsiding into the passivity expected of her by others and apparently even by herself (1.1.81–100). To condemn her chosen course requires credible explanation of a cogent alternative for her to reject, but given her love for Bertram she would appear not to have much of an alternative, and her love is what paradoxically produces the play's principal redemptive movement.

Since W. W. Lawrence pointed out folk parallels to Helena more than fifty years ago, the idea of appealing to popular art in *All's Well* has fallen into disfavor. Certainly Lawrence claimed too much. Recognizing popular elements in *All's Well* does not solve the play's ambiguities, as he argued, but only heightens them. Helena as a Clever Wench and Helena as a benign trickster clearly have a great deal in common, but since Helena is not divine, her trickiness lacks the peculiar sanction of archetypal stories and is therefore humanly complex and difficult. The social and political complexity of her world should work to the same social end she does as a vestige of popular dramaturgy, but in fact that complexity only makes her loving cleverness hard to distinguish from the courtly dissimulation she ostensibly opposes and redeems, at least in Bertram. Her popular semi-divine origin helps to explain why she does not appear to make mistakes and learn from them, but her ready appropriation of the king's power is too ambiguous to be resolved by claiming that she is using power to overcome power. Indeed, where power is concerned, it is hard not to feel that the trickster has followed Portia's example and effectively killed her playmate with a curse.

Yet Helena cannot be reduced to the proportions of a Machiavellian politician. No matter how ambiguously she is involved with power and ambition, she seeks neither for itself. Not only is she morally distinguished from Parolles, but in a more subtle way she is distinguished from the king, whose moral sense, unlike hers, is tied specifically to Renaissance conceptions of social privilege. Helena's vision is more gracious than the king's, and she shares it with the countess, who articulates it in terms that recall the paradoxical power of humility in popular religious drama. These two women therefore stand at the apex of a hierarchy of moral insight that parallels similar hierarchies in the romantic comedies. Helena is not identifiable with Parolles, any more than Rosalind is with Audrey, or Oberon with Bottom. Helena derives from a dramatic tradition where miracle and redemption are not the stuff of dreams but daily show heavenly effects in earthly actors. That she is humanly fallible does not eliminate her continuity with this tradition, however much her power reminds us that in a less than perfect world, our virtues would be proud if our faults whipped them not.

CHAPTER 8 ❧ STYLE, GOODNESS, AND POWER IN *MEASURE FOR MEASURE*

The title of *Measure for Measure* has long been recognized as an allusion to the eschatalogical discourse of the Gospels, and its application to Angelo is clear: "Judge not, that ye be not judged. For with what judgement ye judge, ye shall be judged, and with what measure ye mette it shall be measured to you again" (Matt. 7:1–2; cf. Mark 4:24 and Luke 6:36–38). In *Measure for Measure*, the duke echoes Jesus' idea when he meditates gnomically on Angelo's hypocrisy: "Shame to him whose cruel striking / Kills for faults of his own liking" (3.2.260–61). Angelo judges Claudio guilty of death for the same deed Angelo secretly commits. Recently, however, interpreters of *Measure for Measure*—both critically and in performance—have begun to emphasize the ironic applicability of the play's high moral standard to the duke himself. Interpretation of this play thus increasingly suggests parallels with a pattern noticed some time ago in *The Merchant of Venice*: a figure who vindictively abuses his legal power (Shylock, Angelo) is caught by another powerful figure (Portia, the duke), whose subsequent pursuit of the law raises troubling questions about her or his own moral consistency. To make this problem clear in performances of *Measure for Measure*, the duke is frequently shown in extraneous dumb shows, fantasizing sadistically, or salaciously recalling his seduction of the boy who sings for Mariana at the moated grange. By the same token, Isabella's rejection of the duke's proposal at the end of *Measure for Measure* has become a theatrical commonplace, elucidated by Jonathan Goldberg's identification of the duke with Angelo: "The Duke's wooing of Isabella, even though he offers marriage, seems at least as much an assault upon her integrity as Angelo's proposition."[1]

This kind of interpretation may be extreme, but it is not fatuous or unfounded. The ambiguities surrounding Helena because of her recourse to power in *All's Well* are *ipso facto* intensified for the duke in *Measure for Measure* because he possesses what is, in effect, absolute power to begin with. "He who the sword of heaven will bear / Should be as holy as severe" (3.2.254–55) is an unambiguous statement about the duke's expectations concerning those who wield power, and it is a statement that must therefore be applied to him as well, just as Portia's statements about mercy must be the standard for her own actions as well as Shylock's. In the background of the duke's rigorous moral expectations are not only the Gospels but the medieval dramaturgy of power, which *Measure for Measure* invokes more richly even than *All's Well*. Against this background, the duke's relative inconsistency becomes apparent, for he advocates a standard that had been modelled by God incarnate in religious drama but that serves in *Measure for Measure* as a standard of human fallibility.

The duke's relationship with Lucio is a good example of how Shakespeare hedges authority about with something quite other than divinity. Lucio and the duke have a great deal to do with each other in the course of the play, and until the very end the pattern of their relationship consistently works to the duke's discomfort. In 3.2 and 4.3, Lucio slanders the duke when the duke cannot retaliate because of the necessity to preserve his strategic friar's disguise, and while Lucio is certainly preparing his own comeuppance in these lines, the immediate effect is to make a rather severe authority look helpless in the face of very funny insults. The same effect reappears even in the climactic judgment scene at the end of the play, when Lucio repeatedly interrupts the duke, clearly irritating him and throwing him off balance. The joker in these scenes undoubtedly engages our comic sympathy, and the effect is akin to the topsy-turvy world of carnival.

Lucio's irreverent influence is not finally definitive, but the fact that it appears at all in *Measure for Measure* makes Shakespeare's play very different from his source play, George Whetstone's *Promos and Cassandra*, especially considering that in Whetstone's dedicatory epistle, Shakespeare would have read one of the most forthright Elizabethan rejections of popular dramaturgy, defined specifically in terms of social status. In a letter that explicitly seeks powerful patronage, Whetstone pointedly remarks that the grave senators of ancient Rome approved the drama because they won morality from it as the bee sucks honey from weeds. In contrast, Whetstone condemns the drama of modern Italy, France, and Spain for its lasciviousness, but his heaviest censure falls on the English:

> The Englishman in this quality is most vain, indiscreet, and out of order: he first grounds his works on impossibilities, then in three hours runs he through the world, marries, gets children, makes children men, men to conquer kingdoms, murder monsters, and bringeth gods from heaven and fetcheth devils from hell. And that which is worst, their ground is not so unperfect as their working indiscreet, not weighing so the people laugh, though they laugh them (for their

follies) to scorn. Many times, to make mirth, they make a clown companion with a king; in their grave counsels they allow the advice of fools; yea, they use one order of speech for all persons—a gross indecorum, for a crow will ill counterfeit the nightingale's sweet voice. Even so, affected speech doth misbecome a clown. For to work a comedy kindly, grave old men should instruct; young men should show the imperfections of youth; strumpets should be lascivious; boys, unhappy; and clowns should speak disorderly, entermingling all these actions in such sorts as the grave matter may instruct, and the pleasant delight, for without this change, the attention would be small and the liking less.[2]

Whetstone appears to move illogically in this passage from moral censure to stylistic critique, but the coherence of his argument is quite evident when it is considered in the context of the Tudor assumption we have encountered frequently in the preceding pages—the assumption that virtue is distributed in proportion to social standing, with those at the top being most fully endowed. For on this assumption, the esthetic deficiency of popular dramatic romance is also a moral deficiency simply because romance *is* popular, and the indecorum of companioning a king with a clown is perhaps the most serious moral failing because it is such an obvious social indiscretion. In keeping with this assumption, Whetstone decorously separates his own play into discrete scenes of comic lowlife and scenes containing the "grave matter" of the upper class story: the latter instruct, while the former delight. Whetstone is concerned that even this literal-minded interpretation of classical dictates may be offensive, however, for he admits that he himself may not have avoided the "learned censure" of his patron in *Promos and Cassandra*. The dedicatory epistle of Whetstone's play thus contains all the hallmarks of the high style as a sign of privilege: strict separation of style on social principles, tacit association of high social status with virtue, an obsequious plea for upper class approval, abusive rejection of the lower classes and their art, and an implicit endorsement of rigid social distinctions that coexists paradoxically with an attempt on the dedicator's part to improve his own social status by gaining privileged patronage.[3]

While Shakespeare undoubtedly followed Whetstone's lead in introducing lower-class elements into the Italianate story that both he and Whetstone inherited, he pointedly eschewed Whetstone's strict social separation of styles and subjects, preferring instead the popular—and ultimately medieval—model of mingling kings and clowns freely. Given Whetstone's remarks, Shakespeare could hardly have made this change without being aware of its social implications. Indeed, he appears to flout Whetstone's assumptions deliberately in the peculiar relationship of Lucio and the duke. By Whetstone's standards, what Lucio does to the duke is more than indiscreet: it is a moral scandal. If G. K. Hunter is right in tracing the inspiration for the final scene in *Measure for Measure* to Guarinian tragicomedy, then the joke on Whetstone is doubled: not only does the scene allow a clown to mock a king, but it follows the lascivious Italian drama in creating a complex mood that hovers uncertainly between the serious and the comic.[4]

As in other plays, Shakespeare's preference for popular dramaturgy in *Measure for Measure* is not merely a stylistic choice: it is a social and moral choice as well. The benign trickster as an all-powerful duke is very different from the peasant Jesus, whose very humility—spiritual and social alike—is the essence of his divine deceit and the undoing of his privileged and arrogant oppressors. But Shakespeare retains enough of the archaic dramaturgy to ensure that the duke, for all his power, cannot possibly be mistaken for the godlike icon of the court masque: Lucio sees to that. The Erastian principles of Jacobean kingship were spelled out explicitly in terms of power by the king himself:

> Kings are justly called Gods, for that they exercise a manner or resemblance of divine power upon the earth. For if you will consider the attributes of God, you shall see how they agree in the person of a king. God hath power to create or destroy, to make or unmake at his pleasure, to give life or send death, to judge all and to be judged nor accomptable to none, to raise low things and to make high things low at his pleasure, and to God are both soul and body due. And the like power have Kings: they make and unmake their subjects, they have power of raising and casting down, of life and of death, judges over all their subjects and in all cases, and yet accomptable to God only. They have power to exalt low things and abase high things and make of their subjects like men at the chess, a pawn to take a bishop or a knight, and to cry up or down any of their subjects, as they do their money.[5]

The king's echo of the Magnificat ("He has put down the mighty from their seats, and exalted them of low degree" [Luke 1:52]) is ironic from any perspective but his own, and it indicates the profound difference between power in religious drama and Jacobean monarchical theory. This difference makes Shakespeare's debt to his predecessors particularly vivid, for King James's claims cannot find compatible expression in a figure as limited and fallible as the duke, particularly when he is the consistent object of derision from a character as funny as Lucio.

This is not to say that Lucio deserves carnivalesque apotheosis. For he is like Falstaff not only in being rejected by the ruler he had slandered earlier but also in callously exploiting those with less power than he has. He reveals his feckless dealing with Kate Keepdown in the process of needling the duke (4.3.169–72; cf. 3.2.194–96), who uses this information later to improve Kate's situation by forcing Lucio to marry her (5.1.514ff.). This is not gentle justice on the duke's part, but to pity Lucio for being subjected to it is to overlook the material improvement it represents for Kate, who is like Mariana in her victimization by a faithless male. More cruel still is Lucio's refusal to offer bail for Pompey Bum, when Pompey is arrested for procuring. Lucio's cruelty consists not so much in the refusal itself as in his manner: "No, indeed, I will not, Pompey, it is not the wear. I will pray, Pompey, to increase your bondage. If you take it not patiently, why, your mettle is the more" (3.2.72–76). Lacing mockery with moralism, Lucio has no compunction about identifying with oppressive power when he feels like it.

Lucio in fact has an important precedent in a vicious character from the mystery plays called Raise Slander, whose context helps to clarify Shakespeare's debt to the medieval dramaturgy of power in *Measure for Measure*. Raise Slander is *primus detractor* in the N-Town *Trial of Mary and Joseph*: *secundus detractor* is called "Bakbytere." Both are paid witnesses in a corrupt ecclesiastical court that is convened to try Joseph and Mary on charges of fornication because she is pregnant without being married. Raise Slander accuses Mary and Joseph falsely, as Lucio slanders the duke, and Raise Slander is also like Lucio in turning his quick tongue on the presiding bishop, Abyachar, accusing him late in the trial of partiality toward the defendants. Abyachar responds by compelling the slanderer to drink the "botel of godys vengeauns," a potion designed to test the innocence of the accused.[6] The result is unfortunate for Raise Slander: he suffers the consequences of the guilty, unlike Joseph and Mary, who have imbibed unharmed. Raise Slander, in short, is a "guiler beguiled," like many other characters in medieval drama, especially in the N-Town cycle,[7] and his treatment exemplifies the medieval dramaturgy of power. He victimizes innocents cruelly, abusing the small authority accorded to him by the court, and he is finally undone to his surprise by "godys vengeauns," which functions as a hidden vindicator of his victims: the divine trickster thus identifies mysteriously with the oppressed, even when he is not present. The social realism of the trial scene serves as a satire of contemporary legal abuses, at the same time that it leaves no doubt on whose side God stands in the ecclesiastical courts' exploitation of the powerless.

This important medieval precedent to Lucio is part of a pattern in all the extant English religious plays that deal with sexual conduct, as *Measure for Measure* does. Muriel Bradbrook remarked almost fifty years ago that *Measure for Measure* resembles "the late medieval Morality. It might be named The Contention between Justice and Mercy, or False Authority unmasked by Truth and Humility."[8] She correctly implies that no morality play of this name is known, but the plays focusing on sexual conduct—whether mystery, morality, or miracle plays—all have parallels with the contention between mercy and justice, or false authority and humility, in *Measure for Measure*. This contention appears most schematically, perhaps, in cycle pageants on the woman taken in adultery, extant from Chester, N-Town, and York. A related subject, the repentance of Mary Magdalene, appears in two of the cycles, though its most suggestive treatment is in the N-Town *Passion Play 1*. Mary Magdalene is also the subject of one of the few surviving miracle plays in English, the Digby *Mary Magdalene*, where the playwright again proceeds in a manner that is consistent with the tradition in the mystery plays and also anticipates *Measure for Measure*. So consistent, in fact, is dramatic treatment of Mary Magdalene as a repentant prostitute that a mid-sixteenth-century Protestant morality play, Lewis Wager's *Life and Repentance of Mary Magdalene*, offers another parallel to Shakespeare's play, despite Wager's strident anti-Catholicism. Finally, the only other plays in the mystery cycles that deal with sexual transgression, that is, the plays of Mary and Joseph, again produce the contrasts Bradbrook describes, as we have just briefly noticed in the N-Town *Trial of Mary and Joseph*.

This medieval tradition requires attention, for it is suggested from the outset in *Measure for Measure*, when "the properties of government" are focused on the question of executing laws pertaining specifically and, in effect, exclusively to sexual behavior. This focus, moreover, is treated in terms of the most inclusive of several common features about sexual transgression in medieval religious drama, namely, a contrast between "old law" and "new." We have seen this contrast briefly before in *The Merchant of Venice*, where justice and mercy are again central issues, and Portia explicitly alludes to the passion of Christ (as Isabella does in *Measure for Measure*, 2.2.77–79) as a model for human action, especially in judging others. The racial opposition of Jew and Christian is eliminated in the later play, and the Pauline collocation of the "old law" (i.e., the law of Moses) and the "old man" or "the flesh" ("which is corrupt through deceivable lusts")[9] appears instead, suggesting that Shakespeare's "Viennese" law may be as theological in its inspiration as it is political or sociological. Pompey's shrewd comment about gelding and splaying all the youth of the city (*Measure for Measure*, 2.1.229–30) is a keen observation not only about the difficulties of law enforcement but about what Paul calls "the law of sin which is in my members" (Rom. 7:23), that is, the human bent for concupiscence, or what Shakespeare repeatedly calls "scope" in *Measure for Measure*, as opposed to "restraint."[10] When Pompey's "law" shows up in Angelo, who advocates harsh legal measures to suppress it in others, the classic theological conflation is evident: the "old law" (strict conformity to codes of external behavior) has become one with the "old man" (the human failure to do what we know we ought to do). This is the only Shakespearean play in which such a conflation appears.

In Angelo, the properties of government are clearly tyrannous, and the outlines of his tyranny are distinctly medieval. True, he is not a boasting tyrant like Herod or Pharaoh, and far from seeking power he explicitly tries to avoid it when the duke suddenly thrusts it on him (1.1.48–51). Nor does Angelo manifest any jealousy of Escalus, whom the duke regards as better able to rule than Angelo (1.1.3–14) and appoints to an ambiguous power-sharing position with Angelo. Moreover, Angelo surrenders his power to the duke at the end of the play without any evident hesitation, an act seemingly inconsistent with a man who is eager to acquire power and retain it. But if *libido dominandi* is not apparent in Angelo where his superiors are concerned, it is all too clear in his dealings with those who have less power than he does, and the principle of his tyranny is explicitly identified by the duke:

> He doth with holy abstinence subdue
> That in himself which he spurs on his pow'r
> To qualify in others. Were he meal'd with that
> Which he corrects, then were he tyrannous;
> But this being so, he's just.
>   (4.2.81–85)

The duke says this to the unwitting provost in the full knowledge that the reverse is true: Angelo *is* tainted with what he corrects, and he is therefore tyrannous. The modern recognition that sexuality and power are closely related is particularly illuminating where Angelo and Isabella are concerned. The way he treats her is, in effect, a rape, since it is based on his total personal domination of her, is designed to humiliate and misuse her, and is closely associated in his mind with the cruelty he inflicts on her in the violence of her brother's execution. The almost clinical accuracy of his own sexual repression is thus mirrored in his perverse repression of those who are subject to his power.[11] In short, Angelo's expressed obsequiousness to the duke ("always obedient to your Grace's will, / I come to know your pleasure" [1.1.26–27]) is not inconsistent with Angelo's lust to dominate: on the contrary, the coexistence of his anxiousness to please those more powerful than he is with his abuse of those less powerful accurately renders the working of an authoritarian personality and may well hold the mirror up to Elizabethan nature, given the dynamics of social struggle in a rigidly stratified society. We have noticed an attitude something like Angelo's in the dedicatory epistle of Whetstone's *Promos and Cassandra*.

In keeping with the medieval contrast between the lust to dominate and the power of humility is the contrast between Angelo's tyrannical power and Isabella's extraordinary power to forgive. To be sure, her power is also sexual, as Lucio recognizes—and if anyone is in a position to recognize the power of female sexuality, Lucio is surely the man:

> LUCIO: Assay the pow'r you have.
> ISABELLA: My power? Alas, I doubt—
> LUCIO: Our doubts are traitors,
>> And makes us lose the good we oft might win,
>> By fearing to attempt. Go to Lord Angelo,
>> And let him learn to know, when maidens sue,
>> Men give like gods, but when they weep and kneel,
>> All their petitions are as freely theirs
>> As they themselves would owe them.
> (1.4.76–83)

As events turn out, Lucio is right, of course: Angelo's "sense grows" with Isabella's passionate appeal for Claudio's life, though Lucio seems not to have guessed the perverse direction that Angelo's sexuality would take. Isabella's sexual power, however, is capable of arousing more than male response. As Arthur Kirsch points out, her appeal for Angelo's life at the end of the play is made possible, in part, by her own recognition of her sexual power: "I partly think / A due sincerity govern'd his ideas, / Till he did look on me" (5.1.450–52). Isabella's second appeal for a man's life is thus charged with as much passion as her first appeal, but in the second case she understands her passion much more clearly, and she directs it to forgiving a man whom she has every right to hate. Her passion thus suffuses her charity, as she enacts the Gospel's admonition to "love your enemies . . . do good to them that hate you, and pray for them which hurt you and persecute you" (Matt. 5:44).

This contrast between Angelo's tyrannical power and Isabella's power to forgive precisely reproduces the dramaturgy of power in medieval plays about sexual conduct. In the N-Town *Joseph's Return*, the conflation of "old law" and "old man" animates Joseph, as it does Shakespeare's Angelo. "Ya, ya," exclaims Joseph disbelievingly, when he sees his young wife pregnant,

>> all olde men to me take tent
> And weddyth no wyff, in no kynnys wyse,   *wed / by any means*
> That is a yonge wench, be my assent,   *by my advice*
> Ffor doute and drede and swych servyse.
> (49–52)

A brilliant adaptation of the literary marriage between "January" and "May" thus conflates the fabliau "old man," traditionally impotent, lustful, overbearing, and insanely jealous of his young wife, with the Pauline "old man," who cannot see the miracle of God's grace, though it is standing before him in the Virgin Mary, because of his "carnal" blindness.[12] At the same time, the "old man" also resorts to the harsh rigor of the "old law":

Ffor this synne that thou hast do,
I the forsake and from thee go,
Ffor onys evyr and ay.
     (59–61)

Joseph's rejection of the pregnant virgin thus enacts the Jewish rejection of Christ, bringer of the "new law." A few lines later Joseph explicitly evokes the law of Moses:

To the bussop I wole it telle,
That he the law may here do,
With stonys here to qwelle.
     (95–97)

His obsessive pursuit of this "ve[n]geabyl dede" (line 99) accords with the argument of Justicia in the allegorical debate of the Four Daughters of God that immediately precedes this play: "Man offendyd hym that is endles, / Therfore his endles punchement may nevyr sees" (*Parliament of Heaven*, 92–93). In keeping with this parallel between the two pageants, Joseph's believing response to the angel, his sudden ability to see that the fullness of time has come, and his plea for mercy to the Virgin, all reenact the reconciliation of the Four Daughters of God, who present a heavenly expression of divine charity in the preceding pageant. Paralleling the model of Mercy, who offers a reconciling kiss to her sisters in the allegorical pageant, Mary invites her husband to kiss her, thus richly infusing the paradigmatic reconciliation of Mercy and Justice with human tenderness:

Nay, lett be my fete! Not tho[se] ye take:
My mowthe ye may kys iwys,
And welcom on to me.
     (186–88)

Since this comic resolution of a timeless human dilemma is achieved by grace, charity, and human forgiveness, the little pageant of Joseph's doubt offers a structural as well as a thematic analogue to *Measure for Measure*.[13]

We noticed earlier that Raise Slander in the N-Town *Trial of Mary and Joseph* anticipates Lucio in *Measure for Measure*. Here again, the playwright dichotomizes characters theologically, treating Raise Slander thematically as the old law, in opposition to the new law of grace and mercy that Mary is literally pregnant with. Raise Slander and Backbiter signal their destructive alliance in an ostentatious kiss (19–20) that parodies the kiss of the Four Daughters and of Joseph and Mary, for like

Lucio, the paid slanderers are mockers of order, human and divine. The ending of the trial pageant, moreover, is one of merciful reconciliation, like the ending of *Joseph's Return*. After suffering the effects of "godys vengeauns," Raise Slander pleads for mercy from Mary: "Mercy, good Mary, I do me repent / Of my cursyd and ffals langage" (333–34), and Mary replies in the spirit of the new law: "Now God Lord in hevyn omnipotent / Of his gret mercy your sekness aswage" (335–36). Loving her enemies, she does good to the slanderer who misused and tried to ruin her, thus providing a dramaturgical precedent to the charity of Isabella.

The contention between justice and mercy, the old law and the new, is treated again in one of the most impressive medieval anticipations of *Measure for Measure*: the N-Town *Woman Taken in Adultery*. In this pageant, a forty-line prologue, spoken by Jesus himself, is addressed to the audience as an appeal based on the new law. The principles he enunciates are the same as those recited gnomically by Shakespeare's duke, in a verse form that is also used by old Gower in *Pericles* to suggest the popular and the archaic:

> He who the sword of heaven will bear
> Should be as holy as severe;
> Pattern in himself to know,
> Grace to stand, and virtue go;
> *More nor less to others paying*
> *Than by self-offenses weighing.*
> Shame to him whose cruel striking
> Kills for faults of his own liking!
>   (*Measure for Measure*, 3.2.254–61, my emphasis)

The duke's idea is the same one we noticed earlier in his definition of Angelo's tyranny (4.2.81–85), and the idea also appears in Jesus' prologue to *The Woman Taken in Adultery*:

> Uppon thi neybore be not vengabyl,
> Ageyn the law if he offende.
> *Lyke as he is thou art unstabyl:*
> *Thyn owyn frelté evyr thou attende.*
> Ever more thy neybore helpe to amende,
> Even as thou woldyst he shulde the.
> Ageyn hym wrath if thou accende,
> The same in happ wyll falle on the.
>
> Eche man to othyr be mercyable,
> And mercy he shall have at nede.
>   (25–34, my emphasis)

The last four lines quoted here are in fact another version of the idea on which the title of *Measure for Measure* is based.[14]

As a dramaturgical forebear of Shakespeare's play, *The Woman Taken in Adultery* is no less illuminating in its action than in its thematic parallels. In the medieval play, Scriba (representing the "scribes" of John 8:3) and Phariseaus agree that Jesus is a threat to their law:

> Alas! Alas! Our lawe is lorn!
> A fals ypocryte, Jhesu be name,
> That of a sheppherdis dowtyr was born,
> Wyl breke oure lawe and make it lame.
>   (41–43)

The familiar medieval motif involving social scorn of Jesus is evident in these lines. His enemies set out to "beguile" him (line 120), as the detractors set out to beguile his parents in *The Trial of Mary and Joseph*, but the ploy in this pageant is to force him to judge either against the law of Moses or against his own law, that is, the law of mercy:

> Ffor Moyses doth bydde in oure lawe
> That every advowterere we shulde quelle,
> And thitt with stonys thei shulde be slawe.
> Ageyn Moyses if that he drawe
> That synful woman with grace to helpe,
> He shal nevyr skape out of oure awe,
> But he shal dye lyke a dogge whelpe.
>   (106–10)

In the following scene, a woman is literally taken in adultery, and the exuberant realism of her angry young lover running out of the brothel with his shoes untied and breeches falling down marks a stylistic trait of medieval drama that is consistent with the realistic portrayal of the Elizabethan underworld in *Measure for Measure*. Given the medieval conception of humbleness as nobility that we noticed in chapter 7, the kingship of Jesus is paradoxically inextricable from his social standing as a peasant, whose full reality must therefore be dramatically rendered: this king cannot be separated socially from clowns, because he is one of them.

Like Shakespeare's Angelo, too, is the Accusator's harsh refusal of the woman's plea for mercy and his threat of death for sexual offense:

> Aske us no mercy; it shal not be.
> We shul so ordeyn ffor thi lott
> That thou shalt dye for thin advowtrye.
>   (157–59)

Accusator and his fellows are also like Angelo and old Joseph in combining adherence to the old law with bondage to the "old man": the playwright interprets Jesus' writing in the dust as a revelation of his enemies' secret lust, so that their stealing away is motivated by fear of shameful exposure. They realize, as Angelo does, that power divine has looked upon their passes (*Measure for Measure*, 5.1.374–75). Here again the guilers are beguiled, this time in a manner that directly parallels the exposure of Angelo as well as his particular weakness.

In medieval religious plays about sexual conduct, the nature of true sovereignty (or what Shakespeare calls "the properties of government") is explicitly addressed when the playwrights turn to the subject of Mary Magdalene. The conflict between the old and new laws is also present in the Magdalene plays, chiefly in the emphasis on Christ's mercy and forgiveness of her. But she has no accusators or detractors, as do the Virgin Mary and the woman taken in adultery, and the old law is hardly alluded to, while the "old man" has a muted representative only in Simon's or Judas's complaint that Mary wasted her ointment in wiping Christ's feet with it—obvious evidence of their worldly or "carnal" myopia. Only in Lewis Wager's *Life and Repentance of Mary Magdalene* does the opposition of new and old law have a dominant place in an early English play about Magdalene, and Wager treats this opposition essentially as earlier dramatists had treated it in *The Woman Taken in Adultery*, despite his effort to promote Protestant propangada.[15] In the Digby miracle play of Mary Magdalene, on the other hand, the properties of sovereignty are again a major concern, even more than in the cycle plays.[16]

The exegetical tradition associating true sovereignty with the story of Mary Magdalene need not be detailed here, but the essential argument is familiar: her repentance is evidence of Jesus' kingship, for his power to heal her derives from and expresses his grace, humility, and mercy, which transcend and destroy the power of death, hell, and Satan that are manifest in Mary before her repentance. This notion of Jesus' kingship is closely related to the new law: he might be said to rule, as king, according to the new law rather than the old. The dramatists' distinction between Mary Magdalene and the woman taken in adultery is therefore a difference of emphasis, not of substance. In an understated way, the Chester author in fact introduces the theme of Christ's sovereignty into the story of the woman taken in adultery as well, by pairing her story with the temptation of Christ, where the power of Satan's "soverayntie . . . and principallitye" is broken in his eventual recognition that the man Jesus is also the divine son of God.[17] When the *Primus* and *Secundus Phariseus* then proceed to "tempt" Jesus with the dilemma of the woman taken in adultery (222), they are ignorantly repeating the error of Satan in his temptation of Christ, and the woman's confession of Christ's divinity is a redemptive triumph of his sovereignty that echoes the defeated acknowledgment of Satan earlier in the play:

Hethenforth filth will I flee,
And serve thee in good faye.
For Godhead full in thee I see
That knowes worke that doe wee.
I honour thee, kneelinge one my knee,
And so will I doe aye.
    (Pagina 12, ll. 275–80)

The way toward this interpretation of the woman taken in adultery is pointed by Augustine's comment, which is alluded to in the Chester cycle's version of the story (lines 285–87):

What, then, is the meaning of "tempting Him that they might accuse Him"? We understand, brethren, that a wonderful gentleness shown out pre-eminently in the Lord. They observed that He was very meek, very gentle: for of Him it had been previously foretold, "Gird Thy sword upon Thy thigh, O most Mighty; in Thy splendor and beauty urge on, march on prosperously, and reign, because of truth, and meekness, and righteousness" [Ps. 45:3–4]. Accordingly, as a teacher, He brought truth; as a deliverer, He brought gentleness; as a protector, He brought righteousness. That he was to reign on account of these things, the prophet had by the Holy Spirit foretold.[18]

Augustine's exegesis of the adulterous woman's story indicates a common theological understanding of how Jesus responded to her and Mary Magdalene. The power of Jesus as king—his "sword" and the sign of his reign—is meekness and gentleness, which he exhibits toward penitent transgressors of the old law. That this understanding of Jesus' kingship influences the Chester story of Mary Magdalene is evident in Philippus' opening acknowledgment of Christ's power in raising Lazarus and healing Simon through "pittye" and "grace" (Pagina 12, ll. 13–16): the power of Satan has been broken in these two miracles, as it will be again in this play in the repentance and forgiveness of Mary Magdalene. Accordingly, in asking for Jesus' mercy and forgiveness, Mary not only addresses him as "lord of leale" and "my heale" (41–42), but also as "my comfort and my kinge" (129), a term not used for Christ in other plays about sexual transgression.

In the N-Town play this treatment of Jesus' kingship achieves its richest development. Here, in the face of biblical precedent, Mary Magdalene's repentance has been transposed to the Last Supper, so that it is actually a part of the passion play and serves to illuminate the humble kingship epitomized by Jesus' torture and death. As in Chester's Pagina 12 (dealing with the temptation and the woman taken in adultery), this play opens with the boasting of "Lord Lucifer" about his power over humankind. Lucifer's only concern is a man who poses a threat to Lucifer's "grett domynacion" (45) by "hese werkys ful grettly mervellys" (36), and Lucifer therefore intends to "arere new Engynes of malycious conspiracy" (50) in order to destroy Christ once and for all. Here is the N-Town cycle's paradigm of the "guiler beguiled," for even as Lucifer plots boastfully, his plan to destroy Christ through Judas's betrayal actually outlines the greatest of Christ's "werkys mervellys": the definitive triumph over Satan and death in the resurrection and the harrowing of hell. In the context of this imminent triumph, the playwright introduces Mary Magdalene as an exemplum of Christ's marvelous works and proof of his sovereignty, for she enacts the vulnerable self that Christ himself models later in the same play, in his trial and execution. The social foil of Christ's humble kingship is thus the magnificent court gallant who appears as Lucifer at the beginning of the play, boasting about his rich clothing and describing techniques of courtly competition. Like the Chester Magdalene, Mary in the N-Town *Passion* not only pleads for mercy but addresses Christ as "kynge of grace" (483), and his casting out of the seven devils enacts three earlier predictions about the breaking of Satan's power: "And the prynce of the wer[l]d is cast owth" (182 and 297) and "Confusyon on to the fynd Sathan" (305). Since this triumph is associated with the "tyme of mercy" (179 and 294), Mary's grateful acknowledgment effectively states the passion play's soteriological center: "Now I am brought from the fendys brace / In thi grett mercy closyd and sh[u]tt" (505–6).

The multiple parallels between *Measure for Measure* and medieval plays about sexual transgression indicate more than a context of archaic ideas: they indicate the vitality of dramaturgical continuity. Except for *Troilus and Cressida*, no other Shakespearean play is so preoccupied with erotic ambiguities, and no other play treats those ambiguities so clearly in the medieval dramatic tradition of the new and old law. Contemporary legal measures designed to control sexual activity are not irrelevant to *Measure for Measure*, but they are not its primary impetus, nor are they the primary context for interpretation: for that, we must look to the popular dramatic tradition that Shakespeare chose in deliberate contrast to Whetstone. Particularly illuminating in this tradition is the idea of sovereignty that is assumed in medieval plays about sexual transgression. The law by which Christ "reigns" is the new law of mercy, and it confronts a vindictive and repressive attitude that anticipates as closely as anything does in medieval culture the dynamics of power and sexuality as described by Foucault.[19] The reappearance of this "old law" in Angelo's treatment of Isabella is one of the most striking features in Shakespeare's appropriation of medieval dramaturgy.

Yet for all the illumination that continuity provides, it cannot be definitive, and the contrasts it reveals are as important as comparisons.

Perhaps the most significant contrast is the one we noticed at the outset: the ultimate beguiler in *Measure for Measure* is the duke, whose power is ambiguously political and therefore contrasts importantly with the dispossessed trickster who champions the new law of mercy in medieval drama. The duke also prefers mercy, but he repeatedly insists that social problems are exacerbated by the failure of law enforcement:

> We have strict statutes and most biting laws,
> The needful bits and curbs to headstrong weeds,
> Which for this fourteen years we have let slip,
> Even like an o'ergrown lion in a cave
> That goes not out to prey. Now, as fond fathers,
> Having bound up the threat'ning twigs of birch,
> Only to stick it in their children's sight
> For terror, not to use, in time the rod
> Becomes more mock'd than fear'd; so our decrees,
> Dead to infliction, to themselves are dead,
> And liberty plucks justice by the nose;
> The baby beats the nurse, and quite athwart
> Goes all decorum.
>   (1.3.19–31)

The duke links images of predation and terrifying patriarchal punishment with social order, and he appears to believe what he says, because he offers it in confidence to Friar Thomas, when explaining his decision to leave his place to Angelo and go about disguised. Moreover, the duke repeats the same idea to Pompey (3.2.33–34), to Lucio (3.2.98), and again to everyone late in the play just before he publicly throws off his disguise:

> I have seen corruption boil and bubble
> Till it o'errun the stew; laws for all faults,
> But faults so countenanc'd, that the strong statutes
> Stand like the forfeits in a barber's shop,
> As much in mock as mark.
>   (5.1.323–27)

Like Portia, the duke champions the new law of mercy and yet uses strict legality to undo offenders, compelling Angelo and Lucio into legal marriages that they had willfully evaded. The folk justice of his proceeding in the last act is clear, but the duke's power and his appeal to the law make his procedure very different from that of his divine predecessor in medieval drama, who champions the oppressed without recourse to power and coercion himself.

The duke's ambiguity is reinforced by Angelo's reiteration of the duke's opinion about law enforcement and social order:

> We must not make a scarecrow of the law,
> Setting it up to fear the birds of prey,
> And let it keep one shape, till custom make it
> Their perch and not their terror.
> (2.1.1–4)

But the duke's role as a dispenser of justice is also complicated by two links with contemporary politics. The first of these is King James's opinion in *Basilikon Doron* that strict law enforcement at the beginning of a reign is the key to public order:

> For if otherwise ye kyth [display] your clemency at the first, the offences would soon come to such heaps and the contempt of you grow so great, that when ye would fall to punish, the number of them to be punished would exceed the innocent, and ye would be troubled to resolve whom-at to begin, and against your nature would be compelled then to wrack many whom the chastisement of few in the beginning might have preserved.[20]

Among many putative Jacobean parallels with *Measure for Measure*, this one is the most credible, particularly since it refers specifically to James's own experience.[21] Whether the parallel flatters James or not depends on how one sees the duke. If one perceives him as a godlike and benign deceiver, then one can well understand why King James liked the play when he saw it at court and wanted to see it again, because its portrait of power exposing corruption and correcting moral turpitude is just how James liked to see himself and in fact did see himself flatteringly mirrored in the Platonic allegory of court masques. But if one recognizes the duke's differences from his divine predecessor on the popular stage, the portrait of power in *Measure for Measure* is not so reassuring to the powerful. We can only guess at James's reasons for liking the play, but its suggestion that those with power may be fallible and inconsistent is one reason that can be pretty firmly ruled out.

The second connection between the duke and contemporary politics also qualifies his godlike aspect. Norman Holland noticed thirty years ago that the duke's decision to put a surrogate authority in charge of law enforcement has a close parallel in Innocent Gentillet's *Anti-Machiavel* (1602), where the practice is alluded to three times and is followed by no less a political schemer than Cesare Borgia.[22] Given the demonic reputation of Machiavelli in Renaissance England, this connection with the duke would appear to be less than flattering; at the very least, it negates the claim that the duke's power is spiritual and has nothing to do with Renaissance political reality. Holland rightly sums up with a challenge: "interpretations of *Measure for Measure* that treat the Duke as a symbol of divine grace or the like must take into account his probable descent from Cesare Borgia" ("The Duke and the Prince," p. 20).

In short, while the duke undoubtedly shares with the medieval Christ some functions of divine sovereignty, he is far from godlike and seems an ambiguous example at best of the Renaissance commonplace that the king represents God on earth; indeed, in this respect, he is like Shakespeare's English kings. Given his human limitations, his procedure is unavoidably political, rendering him indistinguishable from a Renaissance prince in his rivalry with Angelo. The duke eventually exposes Angelo's hypocrisy by eavesdropping and role-playing, not by the high mystery of incarnation or the cool omniscience that enables Jesus to write in the dust the sins of those who have accused the woman taken in adultery. Isabella borrows Gregory of Nyssa's imagery of the atonement (above, p. 130) in her confidence that the duke's dissimulation in the last scene is "a physic / That's bitter to sweet end" (4.6.7–8), but her confidence in this benign trickster is fraught with difficulties that do not beset Mary Magdalene's confidence in the "grett mercy" of Christ. As for Angelo's nasty surprise for the duke in 4.2—when the order comes through for Claudio's execution despite the bed trick—no medieval dramatic treatment of divine sovereignty parallels the scrambling the duke is subsequently forced to undertake. The shattering of his calm assurance that Angelo will pardon Claudio is an event that is simply unimaginable for the medieval Christ, and the difference between the two is yet another device to heighten the many limitations of Shakespeare's character.

Yet these limitations are not enough to justify a reductive equation of the duke with Angelo or Lucio. The duke's ambiguity is inherent in his power and does not need to be staged by means of dumb shows that depict his supposedly insatiable sexual appetite. All we know directly about his love life is that he tells Friar Thomas he is invulnerable: "Believe not that the dribbling dart of love / Can pierce a complete bosom" (1.3.2–3), and yet he asks Isabella to marry him in the play's closing lines. From this contradiction one can infer that the duke seems to learn something about himself in the course of the play, as Angelo and Isabella do—though he never admits as much, any more than Helena does in *All's Well*. Escalus says that the duke, "above all other strifes, contended especially to know himself" (3.2.227–28), and self-knowledge heads the duke's list of desirable characteristics in those who govern (3.2.256). The duke's awareness of the need for self-examination is in keeping with the medieval tradition he belongs to, as we have seen, and the pattern of his apparent self-discovery brought about by love is a very old one that typically applies to the untried. Benedick similarly has a hard heart and loves none at the beginning of *Much Ado about Nothing* (1.1.121–22), and like the duke he also falls in love.

Indirect evidence of something much more sinister in the duke's erotic experience comes from Lucio, who damagingly ascribes the duke's preference for mercy to his "feeling for the sport" (3.2.116–17). Despite the disguised duke's indignant protest, this is a claim Lucio will not relinquish: the duke was a drunkard; he had intercourse with "your beggar of fifty"; "he would mouth with a beggar, though she smelt brown bread and garlic." The weight of these extraordinary allegations is increased by their being intermingled with equally pungent comments about Angelo that invariably ring true: "Some report a sea-maid spawn'd him; some, that he was begot between two stock-fishes. But it is certain that when he makes water his urine is congeal'd ice; that I know to be true" (3.2.105–8). Lucio's charges are the principal basis for staging the duke as a more seriously disturbed neurotic than Angelo, but these charges need to be considered carefully before they are given so much credence. The duke's alleged misuse of destitute women ("your beggar of fifty") is a fantasy of exploitative power that in fact characterizes the behavior of Lucio himself. He is first introduced as a man who loves to joke with other men about his experiences with prostitutes (1.2). Mistress Overdone's arrest is a consequence of Lucio's gratuitously reporting her activities to the authorities (3.2.193–94)—a whimsical and cruel display of his power over her. We noticed earlier that Lucio abandons Kate Keepdown after making her pregnant, abusively referring to her thereafter as a "rotten medlar" (4.3.172) and a "punk" (5.1.527). While Lucio is anything but sexually repressed, he is the play's prime example of unlimited scope inevitably becoming restraint: his self-indulgent freedom is exercised at the expense of his own health (1.2) and to the detriment of the women he abuses, who are the slavelike victims of his insatiable predation.

To see the duke himself as a predator of this kind is not only to credit Lucio's dubious report but to assume that everything overtly neurotic about Angelo (including Lucio's assessment of him) is covertly true of the duke. We have abundant evidence in Angelo's soliloquies and behavior that what Lucio says about him is true; we have no evidence, aside from Lucio's charges, that "the fantastical duke of dark corners" is a hypocritical philanderer. That he believes in and practices coercive power there can be no doubt, but that he abuses his power in sexual exploitation is alleged by only one man, who is compulsively exploitative himself. Indeed, Lucio's exploitative scope is what the duke seeks to restrain in giving Lucio his comic comeuppance at the play's end and compelling him to marry Kate. This coercive solution is clearly imperfect for either spouse in the newly made pair, but its imperfection distances it from the duke and Isabella in a way that is not radically distinct from other comic hierarchies—Rosalind's and Orlando's distance from Touchstone and Audrey, for instance, or Viola's and Orsino's from Sir

Toby Belch and Maria. The duke in fact would appear to be the opposite of what Lucio alleges: far from abusing his power in scretly exploiting women, he uses it to restore a measure of justice to Kate and Mariana, who have been exploited in varying ways by Lucio and Angelo.

A fair assessment of the duke apart from his ambiguous power suggests a character modelled on familiar comic lines. Both Rosalind, for example, and the duke adopt disguise; in their disguise they deceive the one they love, though that was not the intent of their disguise at first; both learn more about themselves in this process; both assist their less mature sweethearts to a richer understanding of themselves and of what a loving relationship entails; and both thus initiate and grow into a loving relationship while remaining incognito. Helena and Bertram move through a very similar process in *All's Well*, and loving trickery in fact consistently characterizes Shakespeare's comedies, appearing in principals as diverse as Julia, Petruchio (where certain problems of power are again evident), Don Pedro, and Viola, as well as Rosalind. Varying degrees of self-confidence distinguish these tricksters from one another, but none has the political power of the duke, who is therefore troubling in ways that are not characteristic of his forerunners in the romantic comedies.

Power also distinguishes the duke from medieval tradition, as we have seen. The Gospels' caution that God judges human beings as they judge each other is the basis of the realized eschatology in medieval religious plays about sexual behavior, where Jesus exposes the limitations of vindictive and repressive judgment. This kind of exposure is the duke's aim in his dealing with Angelo: "Hence shall we see, / If power change purpose, what our seemers be" (1.3.53–54). Unlike his counterpart in popular drama, however, the duke is not divine but all too human. Isabella's passionate rhetoric about fallible authority is directed at Angelo, but its truth is no less important for the duke:

> but man, proud man,
> Dress'd in a little brief authority,
> Most ignorant of what he's most assur'd,
> His glassy essence, like an angry ape,
> Plays such fantastic tricks before high heaven
> As makes the angels weep; who, with our spleens,
> Would all themselves laugh mortal.
> (2.2.121–27)

Like the First Lord's remark in *All's Well*, about the web of our life being a mingled yarn, Isabella's description of authority is demystifying and creates a troubling, complex view of human existence. Isabella has not experienced the meaning of what she says when she says it, but having done so, she emerges stronger and more mature by the end of the play.

So, implicitly, does the duke—a good man made better, though hardly perfect, by what he learns. This very shortfall of perfection and a demonstrated ability to change and grow is what distances the duke, as it distances Shakespeare's drama, from the static idealized images of eternal perfection that were the ultimate logic of the high style and its celebration of power in Jacobean court drama.

CHAPTER 9 ?? *TRAGEDY: NOBLE WEAKNESS*

Apart from the history plays, for which no classical dramatic precedent existed, the young Shakespeare consistently turned to Roman drama for what he seemed to regard as acceptable models. In comedy, as Francis Meres noted, Shakespeare imitated Plautus, and in what was thought of as the much more demanding form of tragedy, he imitated Seneca.[1] To be sure, the influence of Seneca has been exaggerated, and few would venture to discuss it any longer as J. W. Cunliffe did in the late nineteenth century—as a tissue of quotations and motifs transplanted directly from Senecan tragedy into *Titus Andronicus, Richard III, Hamlet,* or *Macbeth*.[2] What were once taken to be distinctively Senecan traits in Elizabethan drama are now recognized to have precedents in the popular native tradition as well: ranting tyrants, heightened rhetoric, bloody spectacle, slaughtered children, revenge. Nonetheless, Senecan influence on Shakespeare is a reality, and it can best be recognized, perhaps, in the way he responds to the relative social prestige of literary models. When looked at this way, what he does in tragedy is closely analogous to what he does in comedy: starting under the heavy influence of prevailing social assumptions about the well-made play, he eventually turns increasingly to the native popular tradition as his tragic style matures. The result is the distinctive tragic effect that Shakespeare derives from the collapse of profoundest hope: meaning and coherence are ultimately lost when they appear to be capable of enduring the worst.

Shakespeare only arrived at this sense of tragedy after experimenting with the fashionable form of Stoic revenge tragedy, whose tragic effect is quite different. Conceived in social terms, "Senecan" influence needs to be broadened to the set of attitudes that Katharine Maus calls "the Roman frame of mind"; for a distinct ideological stance can be identified as "Roman" for the Elizabethans, and this stance has important social implications that associate it specifically with tragedy.[3] Jonson's tragedies, *Sejanus* and *Catiline*, for example, are not normally thought of as Senecan, yet they become most intelligible when considered as attempts on Jonson's part to produce tragedy with a coherent set of commitments in mind that he learned from Roman moral philosophers—including Seneca, but not confined to him. Jonson was attracted to the Romans for the same reason that the young Shakespeare turned to them in *Titus Andronicus*—because their way of dealing with Roman imperial reality was so compatible with prevailing strategies for confronting the unsettling courtly world of the late sixteenth and early seventeenth centuries. The same set of social circumstances that produced the high style thus produced the fascination with Senecan tragedy as well.

For tragedy, as everyone knew in the Renaissance, is a "high" genre: it deals properly with great persons in a high or lofty style. "Poets Tragical," Puttenham specifies, "meddled not with so base matters" as poets comic, "for they set forth the doleful falls of unfortunate and inflicted princes."[4] Sidney calls tragedy "high and excellent" in dealing with "the greatest wounds," i.e., those of kings; moreover, tragedy stirs "the affects of admiration and commiseration, teaching the uncertainty of this world and upon how weak foundations guilden roofs are builded."[5] Both critics associate instability and uncertainty with social privilege, and they do so for other reasons than the medieval commonplace that tragedy depicts the misfortune of the highly placed—"the fall of princes." For humanist and courtier alike, social advancement was highly competitive, heavily dependent on favor at the top, and therefore risky in the extreme. No one knew better than Sidney how completely fortune governed the court, for he never gained the preferment he continually sought and keenly desired. The ancient Stoic ideal of *apathia* had been cultivated in a very similar atmosphere in imperial Rome—the Rome of Livy, Suetonius, Seneca, and Tacitus—and it was therefore attractive to English courtiers in the late sixteenth century, as it was to Italian humanists and courtiers who were often their models. "To thine own self be true," is Polonius' debased version of *apathia* in the uncertain and deadly world of the Danish court, governed by a ruthless power-seeker and populated with social hopefuls like Rosencrantz and Guildenstern, who assume that the heir apparent is motivated by simple ambition because they are themselves. For intrepid self-reliance appeared to be the one sure defense against the vicissitudes of success and failure in an atmosphere where success could bring enormous material and social rewards but with absolutely no guarantee. In such an atmosphere, Horatio—"more an antique Roman than a Dane"—is Hamlet's most trustworthy companion, because Horatio cultivates a studious indifference to the very rewards that he is paradoxically committed to winning by his active presence at court and especially by his friendship with Prince Hamlet. In historical terms, Horatio might well be described as a Senecan character—like the historical Seneca himself, that is, who moralized continuously about the importance of caring nothing for the kind of spectacular benefits he reaped in the imperial service. The risks of that service are apparent in his obedience to Nero's order that he kill himself—the ultimate proof of his truth to himself and of his sagacious indifference to what he won or lost.

Senecan tragedy, by the same token, can be taken as a study in Horatio's kind of noble invulnerability when it is stretched to the breaking point. What Sidney calls "the uncertainty of this world" produces a crucible of unimaginable infliction in which the suffering and shattering of the Stoic soul stirs "the affects of admiration and commiseration." The rhetorical purpose of Senecan tragedy, in short, is to create these affects for true nobility—not merely for social standing but for the virtue of heroic self-reliance, which can only be depicted in those of high social status because of the Renaissance assumption (with potent Roman precedent) that virtue is distributed in proportion to social privilege. Considered in this light, the suffering of Hieronimo in Kyd's *Spanish Tragedy* makes sense, and the young Shakespeare's goal in *Titus Andronicus* becomes intelligible. Like Lord Talbot in *1 Henry VI*, Titus is recognizably Elizabethan: a nostalgically idealized warrior aristocrat who is undone by pragmatic, self-serving, and power-seeking outsiders and upstarts. Unlike Talbot, however, who is destroyed by court factionalism while fighting bravely in France, Titus comes home as a conquering hero and confronts the corrupt court directly—and disastrously. His responses to duress, including his insane revenge, amount to an Elizabethan understanding of heroic Roman self-reliance, which the play attempts consistently to heighten and render admirable.

Consider, for example, the unusual number of young people deliberately slaughtered by Titus or at his behest: Alarbus, Mutius, and Lavinia. This kind of activity distinguishes Titus from all of Shakespeare's other tragic heroes except Macbeth, though even Macbeth is not shown in the act of killing his own children, as Titus is, and the effect of destroying young people is entirely different in *Titus* and *Macbeth*. For Titus, the gesture recapitulates innumerable stories of stoical Roman warriors whose heroic self-possession extends to their abrogation of the filial relationship—the most powerful of human relationships, in the Roman view, and therefore the most likely to erode intrepid resistance to emotional investments in anything outside the self.[6] Titus's dutiful son, Lucius, proposes the ritual slaughter of Alarbus, emphasizing the religious piety of the deed and using heightened language that actually breaks into Latin at one point (1.1.99–104). Tamora's objection to her son's destruction, on the other hand, betrays her ignoble lack of self-possession in its passionate excess (1.1.107–23)—an expression of emotional dependence that a noble Roman woman like Lavinia never permits herself, no matter how extreme her suffering. Titus's action is usually condemned for its inherent barbarity and for its consequences—the vengeful chain of events that follows it. But the episode does not call for liberal humanitarian judgment: its function is to highlight Titus's virtuously imperturbable resistance to emotional appeal when he is faced with patriotic religious obligation. Indeed, Shakespeare may well have had the archetypal Roman hero Aeneas in mind, who also has a strong Stoic coloring and who sacrifices Latin prisoners of war during the truce in Italy.[7] Moreover, the consequences of Titus's deed are irrelevant by Roman moral reckoning, for the Stoic sage performs virtuous deeds without regard to what might follow from them: to do anything else would admit an ulterior motive—a desire for something apart from the deed itself—and would therefore compromise the deed as a witness to one's immovable self-consistency. To blame Titus for what he suffers as a result of ordering Alarbus' death is equivalent to blaming Seneca for following Nero's order to kill himself. Even if the consequences are inherent in the deed, it must nonetheless be performed without regard to what will follow.

The pattern of Alarbus' death is repeated even more admirably a few lines later, when Titus stabs his own son, Mutius, for opposing Lavinia's marriage with Saturninus. Again, Titus's action needs to be considered in light of his Stoic characterization and without considering the events that follow, motivated as they are by passion and self-seeking treachery on the part of Titus's enemies. Having heroically denied his desire in turning down the proffered reward of the imperial title, Titus wishes to seal his loyalty to Saturninus by offering Lavinia to him as his bride. Mutius' resistance to this move therefore denies his father's integrity; Lavinia, in contrast, agrees with her father's decision, "sith true nobility / Warrants these words in princely courtesy" (1.1.275–76). Alone among Titus's family, Lavinia consistently understands and supports her father's heroic rectitude, and she is fittingly rewarded with death at his hands—the third time Titus is responsible for destroying a young person. This time he explains his action before committing it, citing the precedent of Virginius, who slew his daughter Virginia to preserve what he took to be her moral integrity—and, by implication, his own (5.3.36–38). Lavinia's death thus belongs to the pattern of Alarbus' and Mutius': all die at Titus's behest and as evidence of his refusal to compromise his commitment to heroic invulnerability through virtuous action. Gordon Braden's comment regarding the Senecan Medea's slaughter of her children is very much to the point: "The devastation of emotional ties is an unanswerable gain of power and control, political authority reclaimed as radical self-possession."[8] The Vicelike Aaron, in contrast, manifests a filial commitment that makes him a weak foil to Titus, since Aaron seeks desperately to preserve his son simply because he is "mine own" (4.2.107), and not because of a greater commitment that might, under certain circumstances, also lead him to abrogate the lesser. By almost any reckoning, Aaron's attitude to his son is morally superior to Titus's, but the Stoic perspective inverts priorities in a case like this and consistently distinguishes Titus and Aaron from one another as prototypes, respectively, of Stoic virtue and pragmatic vice in a deeply troubled political world.

Viewing Titus as an Elizabethan aristocratic ideal in Roman dress also helps to explain how his mad revenge against Tamora enhances his admirable nobility. As Lawrence Stone points out, a fresh outlook on personal revenge arose among the upper classes in the sixteenth century, as part of the multifaceted process of centralizing power.[9] Regional warlords became increasingly subservient to the monarchy as they were shorn of standing armies and massive fortifications, but their deeply ingrained habit of exercising power in the form of violent coercion did not change overnight, and one stage of its transformation was the replacement of the private army with the personal quarrel. Manuals of courtesy frequently offer precise and detailed instructions about how such quarrels should be conducted—a point Touchstone recognizes and deliciously satirizes in the last act of *As You Like It* (5.4.43–106). Titus does not, of course, wreak vengeance by a courtesy book, but his insane scheme enacts fantasies of revenge garnered from another source that was more prestigious than any handbook of courtly behavior: Ovid's *Metamorphoses*, to which Shakespeare turned for inspiration in his two courtly narrative poems, written at about the same time he wrote his first tragedy. Titus's revenge thus answers sixteenth-century expectations regarding offended nobility: "I will have my revenge," declares the Duke of Cornwall in *King Lear* (3.5.1), and he invokes the same privilege later in different words: "Our power / Shall do a court'sy to our wrath, which men / May blame, but not control" (3.7.26–28). The madness that produces Titus's revenge is no less a sign of high social dignity than is the revenge itself. His precedent is Senecan heroic *furor*, ultimately nurtured, as Braden argues, by the very success of world-conquering Rome: imperial derangement (the model for Senecan madness) "is in great part the derangement of the classical competitive ethos with nowhere to go—having survived, in a sense, its own culmination" (*Renaissance Tragedy*, p. 14). The competitiveness and ambition that kept Stoic sages close to the center of Roman power produced the spiritual complement to imperial aggression—the retreat into unyielding self-consistency: "Stoicism is in this regard but the inner form of imperialism, an extrapolation of classical selfhood into a new phase of completeness" (Braden, *Renaissance Tragedy*, p. 23). Titus Andronicus, world conqueror and Stoic sage alike, thus borrows potent classical precedent both for his steely intrepidity and his explosion into vengeful insanity. As a dramatic character, he is a striking culmination of the English fascination with Senecan tragedy that begins with a flurry of translations at midcentury. It is surely worth notice that this fascination coincides with the rise of effective centralized power, the dominance of humanist courtiers, and the emergence of a powerful high style. While the conventions of Senecan tragedy are exemplified ambiguously in *Titus*, its inner consistency with the Stoic drama of imperial Rome is essential to understanding it as Shakespeare's first attempt in the tragic vein.

The Ovidian style of *Titus Andronicus* has been condemned as vigorously as anything in the play, but here again the aim of rendering nobility admirable illuminates Shakespeare's procedure. In a now classic essay on *Titus*, Eugene Waith speculates that Shakespeare, like Ovid, "was more interested here in portraying the extraordinary pitch of emotion to which a person may be raised by the most violent outrage."[10] Waith notices Sidney's criterion of admiration for tragic suffering and relates it in *Titus* to the amoral grandeur of the characters he explores in his later book, *The Herculean Hero*. Moral neutrality, however, is hardly the point of Stoic endurance; on the contrary, the Stoic sage aims to scale heights of virtue that other mortals leave unchallenged, and this moral goal is what Shakespeare's Ovidian style enhances in *Titus Andronicus* by enhancing the noble character that exhibits it. Ovid was no Stoic, and he was eschewed as a literary model by those, like Ben Jonson, who steeped themselves in Roman moralist thought. But few Renaissance poets attained the discrimination of such judgments, and Ovid had been adapted to Renaissance Senecan drama as early as 1429, in Gregorio Correr's *Progne*, an imitation of the first neo-Senecan tragedy, Mussato's *Ecerinus* (1315).[11] As the title of Correr's play indicates, it draws on the same story in Ovid's *Metamorphoses* that Shakespeare uses in his account of Lavinia's rape and mutilation. (The story is explicitly identified in *Titus*, 4.1, when Lavinia sees her nephew reading it and frantically points it out as the clue to her own suffering.) In England the prestige of this precedent to *Titus* was firmly established in 1566, when a version of *Progne* was performed before Queen Elizabeth at Oxford. Given the weight of such precedents—in addition to Shakespeare's own Ovidian narrative poems, written for exclusively courtly consumption— there can be little doubt that Shakespeare conceived the ornate Ovidian style of *Titus* as a decorous complement to the titanic suffering of his first tragic hero. The success of his undertaking is dubious in retrospect, of course, but its aim can almost certainly be identified as an attempt to create admiration of the socially privileged after the high fashion of antique Rome.

Shakespeare may well have been doubtful of the result himself, for he never repeated the experiment. *Romeo and Juliet* takes modern Italy as its *mise-en-scène*, and the tragic conception in that play has nothing to do with Stoic virtue. In *3 Henry VI*, the declaration "I am myself alone" is potentially a statement of Stoic self-reliance, but the character who says it is Richard, duke of Gloucester, and it is the play's most ominous expression of self-serving pragmatism in an insatiable quest for power. Whereas *Titus* dramatizes the Senecan hero and the Vicelike Aaron as mortal opponents, *Richard III* is a striking early attempt to qualify Senecan characterization with the native dramatic tradition, for Richard himself has deep affinities with the Vice, while his ambition, intrepidity, and self-denial (his repression of sexual desire, for example, in the interest of ambition) all caricature the Stoic sage. Like Jonson's Tiberius in *Sejanus*, Richard is diabolically hypocritical, and though his primary hyprocrisy is explicitly Christian ("I thank my God for my humility" [*Richard III*, 2.1.73]), he nonetheless appropriates enough Stoic qualities to suggest that he is posing in the high-minded Senecan mode as well.

By the time Shakespeare returned to a Roman subject, he had left the ideal of the invulnerable Stoic hero behind, and with it the idea that tragedy is designed to arouse admiration for noble suffering. Even Brutus in *Julius Caesar* and Octavius in *Antony and Cleopatra* are far from admirable, though they represent the best in Shakespeare that republican and imperial Rome produced. Brutus is an idealist after the old republican pattern, but his noble Stoicism blinds him to his own ambition and makes him politically inept, consistently producing the opposite of what he hopes to achieve. In his case, unlike Titus's, the consequences of his actions are presented as serious judgments of him, and the judgments are invariably negative. As for Octavius, his Stoic intrepidity is played off against the passionate vacillation of Antony, but Octavius' consistency is laced with opportunism, duplicity, and exploitative ambition, and Antony in his "Roman thought" is always less appealing than in his vulnerability, his dependence on Cleopatra, and his ignominious death, when he bungles his attempt at Stoic suicide. The epithet "noble" and its derivatives are applied three times to Octavius, but they occur some thirty times in relation to Antony and Cleopatra, and her death is associated with a paradoxical nobility that inverts social categories and leads to her identifying herself with "the maid that milks / And does the meanest chares" (4.15.74–75), as well as to her recognition that so "poor an instrument [as the clown who brings her the asp] / May do a noble deed" (5.2.236–37).

Such a recognition is inconceivable for Titus, even though a clown is instrumental in Titus's noble revenge (*Titus*, 4.3 and 4.4). But we have seen Cleopatra's vision of social inversion before in Lavatch's comment about "the house with the narrow gate, which I take to be too little for pomp to enter" (*All's Well*, 4.5.50–52). Though Lavatch alludes to Matthew 7:13–14, his idea illuminates Helena as a culmination of transcendent humility in medieval drama, where true nobility is nearly always associated with social as well as spiritual humbleness (above, chapter 7). Shakespeare's increasing openness to medieval dramaturgy in comedy would seem to have a parallel in the difference between *Titus* and the later tragedies. The young Shakespeare's keen sensitivity to Tudor social stratification is suggested by his treatment of privileged subjects in a high style that is designed to elicit admiration and commiseration for noble suffering. The political realism of *Titus* is not an exception to this sensitivity, since the refusal to idealize the political process is essential to idealizing the Stoic hero, who grounds himself in his own virtue amid "the uncertainty of this world."[12] Political realism in *Titus*, in other words, is closely analogous to the political realism in Jonson's tragedies, where it is the logical inverse of political idealism in the Jonsonian masque.[13] This kind of idealism, however, never appears in Shakespearean drama (indeed, where political skepticism is concerned, *Titus* has a good deal in common with the early histories), and in the later tragedies Shakespeare combines political skepticism with a quite un-Stoic sense of human selfhood as vulnerable, dependent, and paradoxically ennobled in the discovery of its limitations. (Such a combination in *Richard II* is what gives that play a distinctively tragic quality, though it is subordinated to the sense of historical process by Richard's struggle with Bolingbroke and Bolingbroke's ambiguous success.)

Mature Shakespearean tragedy might therefore be justly said to respond to Augustinian imperatives more fully than anything Shakespeare had written earlier. For Augustine not only opposes the Ciceronian idealization of political order as defined by justice; he also opposes the Stoic conception of virtuous perfectibility and self-reliance. This is not to say, with Roy Battenhouse, that the premises of Shakespearean tragedy are Christian and specifically Augustinian.[14] Rather, the suggestion here is that the Augustinian roots of medieval dramaturgy bear fruit in Shakespearean tragedy, which can therefore be said with some justice to look to the past for its inspiration as well as to the Renaissance present.

Critical support for this argument appears from an unlikely quarter in the late seventeenth century, in the criticism of Thomas Rymer, the rigorous neoclassicist who reflects on drama from before the Restoration. Rymer is usually identified with a narrow-minded and bitter denunciation of Shakespeare for failing to adhere to the rules of drama as conceived by neoclassical criticism. Bitter and denunciatory Rymer indeed is, but he is witness to much more than Shakespeare's infraction of the so-called unities: he accurately identifies Shakespeare's medieval inspiration and condemns it specifically for its failure to observe social decorum. Though Rymer shows no familiarity with actual medieval drama (his only specific reference is to a French edict against popular drama in 1541),[15] he is perceptive about the relation between its social auspices and its dramaturgy, neither of which he countenances. "Illiterate fellows" is a phrase Rymer likes to combine with a list of menial occupations—carpenters, weavers, bum-bailiffs, cobblers—in describing those who staged biblical drama in the Middle Ages (*Works*, pp. 113,

144, 169). This is a formulation that follows sixteenth-century humanism in asserting the privileged status of literacy and rejecting manual
labor as ignoble for the learned. In modelling his tragedies on the drama
of such people, Rymer claims, Shakespeare fails to achieve a satisfactory
high style, "and it is then no wonder that we find so much farce and
apocryphal matter in his tragedies, thereby unhallowing the theater, pro-
faning the name of tragedy" (*Works*, p. 145). For Rymer, decorous style
is inconceivable apart from social stratification.[16] He thus condemns the
quarrel of Brutus and Cassius in *Julius Ceasar* as making fools of such
noble men. "But there is no other cloth in [Shakespeare's] wardrobe.
Everyone must be content to wear a fool's coat who comes to be dressed
by him. . . . Shakespeare's genius lay for comedy and humor" (*Works*, p.
169). Rymer tolerates Shakespeare as a comic dramatist, because comedy is a "low" genre, dealing with the kind of low people who staged the
mystery plays. In tragedy, on the other hand, Shakespeare "appears quite
out of his element: his brains are turned, he raves and rambles, without
any coherence, any spark of reason or rule to control him or set bounds
to his frenzy. His imagination was still running after his masters, the
cobblers and parish clerks and Old Testament strollers" (*Works*, p. 169).
Rymer's conception of tragic stature is predictably Stoic: Othello has
nothing about him "that comports with the condition of a general, or
indeed of a man, unless the killing of himself to avoid a death the law
was about to inflict upon him." But where the essence of Othello is concerned, "love and jealousy," these "are no part of a soldier's character,
unless for comedy" (*Works*, p. 134).

This is intemperate criticism, but it is not imperceptive. Rymer is
right that Shakespeare does not meet neoclassical criteria for the well-
made tragedy; he is right that Shakespeare does not observe social decorum in tragedy; and he is right that the model for Shakespeare's failure
in both respects is medieval drama. Brutus and Cassius are indeed fallible in the way Rymer says they are, and Othello is potentially Shakespeare's most perfect Stoic hero—until he falls in love with Desdemona,
for which Rymer condemns him. Then the long cultivated reserve that
has seen Othello through several decades of outstanding soldiership is
breached for the first time, and only then does he begin his career as a
Shakespearean tragic hero. What makes him admirable are precisely the
characteristics he takes on when he falls in love (that development, as
Rymer observes, that is "no part of a soldier's character"): his vulnerability, his dependence on something outside himself, his deep emotional
investment in a person utterly unlike him—a white, upper-class, Venetian woman—who calls up out of the depths of Othello's being a commitment quite different from the military comradeship he had known
among others, like Cassio and Iago, who offer him the like-mindedness
of Stoic *amicitia* but in doing so can show him no more than a lesser

version of himself. Othello's love, in short, is exactly what the Stoic sage eschews, and he eschews it because he believes it is bound to betray and disappoint the one who invests in it, as Othello comes to believe it is betraying him. Othello's discovery of his utter insufficiency—first euphorically in his love, then in his inability to handle his dreadful emotional torment, and finally in his recognition, too late, of his terrible mistake about Desdemona—such a discovery is "Augustinian" in the same way that Titus's noble self-reliance and heroic madness are "Stoic," and the dramaturgical model for Othello's self-discovery is medieval (above, chapter 4), as the model for Titus's endurance is Senecan. This is not to say that Othello's discovery is redemptive; Shakespeare's tragic effect is more complex than that. Othello's love redeems him, in Shakespeare's version of tragedy, from the immobility, passivity, and self-truncating inwardness of Stoic perfection; but Othello's redemption is also the final cause of his damnation—the very thing without which he would not cry in agony:

> When we shall meet at compt,
> This look of thine will hurl my soul from heaven,
> And fiends will snatch at it. . . .
>
> . . . .
>
> Whip me, ye devils,
> From the possession of this heavenly sight!
> Blow me about in winds! Roast me in sulphur!
> Wash me in steep-down gulfs of liquid fire!
> O Desdemon! Dead, Desdemon! Dead! Oh! Oh!
> (*Othello,* 5.2.282–90)

In *Othello* Shakespeare thus achieves the characteristic effect of his mature tragedies: the very thing we most hope for (Othello's redemptive love) is not only destroyed but becomes the means of destruction.

Rymer's criticism of *Othello* has a parallel in what Nahum Tate did to *King Lear* at about the same time Rymer was writing *A Short View of Tragedy.* Tate's dedicatory epistle to his revision is much more temperate than Rymer's criticism, but his critical assumptions are the same as Rymer's, and they correspond quite closely to the assumptions of George Whetstone in the dedicatory epistle to *Promos and Cassandra* (above, pp. 152–53). Tate claims to have made art out of the nature he found in Shakespeare—"a heap of jewels, unstrung and unpolished," is his metaphor, "dazzling in their disorder."[17] Part of the disorder lay in the social and stylistic indecorum of the original: Tate says his hardest task was to make "the chiefest persons speak something like their character, on matter whereof I had no ground in my author" (p. 1). Maynard Mack's careful comparison concludes that Tate sentimentalized Shakespeare,[18] but Tate's preface suggests a motive to preserve what he took to be the dignity of noble characters, and though the result is sentimental by modern standards (the concluding marriage of Edgar and Cordelia being the most striking example), that result needs to be assessed in light of what Tate claims he was trying to do. Writing for exclusively privileged auditors, he was responsive to their wish for a decorous image of social privilege: heroically enduring persons treated magniloquently (speaking "something like their character"), so as to demarcate them from the ignoble. Rymer's comment that "everyone must be content to wear a fool's coat who comes to be dressed by [Shakespeare]" clarifies both Tate's elimination of the fool and his restrained treatment of Lear's degradation and death. Tate's *Lear* thus takes its place with the lachrymose drama that was becoming popular at about the same time and that also grows out of the impulse to heighten high character, after the attempt to achieve the same goal in heroic drama had run its course.[19]

Unlike Rymer, Tate says nothing about medieval dramatic influence on Shakespeare, but the changes Tate makes are nonetheless designed to eradicate the mixed style in *King Lear* that Shakespeare inherited from his predecessors. One of the most striking effects of that style is to demystify the image of the king, in keeping with the medieval dramatic habit of interpreting nobility as humbleness and social elevation as overweening arrogance. This effect has been noticed and emphasized by recent critics who view Shakespearean tragedy as informed by emergent materialism. Shakespearean tragedy is thus seen as part of the preparation for the revolution of 1642, which is itself a dim anticipation of 1789 and 1917. Franco Moretti states this case most succinctly. The historical "task" of tragedy, he argues, "was precisely the destruction of the fundamental paradigm of the dominant culture. Tragedy disentitled the absolute monarch to all ethical and rational legitimation. Having deconsecrated the king, it thus made it possible to decapitate him."[20] Moretti is partly right: in deconsecrating nobility, Shakespearean tragedy indeed resists the dominant cultural paradigm, as we have just seen in the case of *Othello*. But Moretti may well be right for the wrong reason. The demystifying effect of Shakespearean tragedy is not necessarily a sign of nascent materialism: it is just as likely a thoughtful product of popular dramaturgy whose inspiration is ultimately Augustinian and biblical. Shakespeare's radicalism, like that of his predecessors, may have as much to do with residual Christian realism as it does with nineteenth-century materialism.

If anyone can be said to have provided a late-sixteenth-century precedent for the execution of Charles I, it would be the pragmatic Elizabeth I, who executed Charles's grandmother, Mary Stuart. The deconsecrating effects of killing a monarch were clearly recognized in relation to Mary's death even before it occurred in 1587, when Shakespeare was twenty-three years old and some thirteen years away from writing *Ham-*

let, the first of his mature tragedies. Mary's son, the future James I of England, wrote to Elizabeth, to warn her of the dire consequences of regicide:

> What law of God can permit that justice shall strike upon them whom he has appointed supreme dispensatories of the same under Him; whom he hath called Gods and therefore subjected to the censure of none in earth; whose anointing by God cannot be defiled by man unrevenged by the author thereof; who being supreme and immediate lieutenant of God in heaven cannot therefore be judged by their equals in earth?[21]

James here defines for himself—and incidentally for Elizabeth—a mythical invulnerability that he craved but hardly enjoyed as ruler of a politically chaotic nation where power was far from effectively centralized. In defiance of James's warning, Elizabeth executed Mary anyway, thus opening a large hole in the ideological armor of monarchy.[22] Her motive was almost certainly pragmatic, as a contemporary document in the hand of Burleigh's scribe suggests, where the political pros and cons of executing Mary are spelled out in meticulous detail.[23] Despite James's high-minded warning, Burleigh considers the Scots king's reaction to his mother's execution in purely political terms—how Mary's death will affect James's position vis-à-vis the English throne. This kind of pragmatism is what finally led to the execution of James's son, Charles I, though the later regicide was explicitly defended not on pragmatic grounds but in the Christian humanist terms of Milton's *Tenure of Kings and Magistrates*. If Shakespearean tragedy anticipates anything in relation to the execution of Charles I, it is Milton's kind of argument, which draws heavily on Saint Augustine.[24]

The medieval demystification of kingship in *King Lear* is acknowledged by Maynard Mack, who points to a fourteenth-century metrical romance, *King Robert of Sicily*, as an analogue to Lear's ennoblement through suffering and humiliation.[25] The paradigm this narrative represents is essentially the same paradigm that appears in the mystery plays; indeed, records of plays on the subject of King Robert appear in Lincoln for the midfifteenth century and in Chester for the early sixteenth, though neither play is extant.[26] In the verse narrative, King Robert boasts—as all tyrants do in medieval drama—that his power is unmatched by anyone else in the world. When he hears the Magnificat in church, he denies that God's might is sufficient to "make heyghe lowe / And lowe heighe."[27] God therefore sends an angel to impersonate the king, "for my fol [fool] I wole him make / Forte [until] he the nome of kyng forsake" (119–20). The angelic impersonation succeeds, and Robert is rejected by everyone as an imposter and a mad man. In an illuminating reversal of Odysseus' encounter with a beggar, the unrecognized

King Robert loses a vicious fist fight with his own gatekeeper and is brought bleeding and muddy before the angel, who denies Robert's claim to be king:

> "Thou art my fol," seide the angel,
> Thou schal be schoren, everichdel,
> Lych a fool, a fool to be.
> Wher is now thi dignité?
>   (153–56)

In his desperation, Robert eventually realizes he is like Holofernes, Nebuchadnezzar, and the rebellious angels,

> And in twynklyng of an eiye
> God binom heore maystrie   *took away / mastery*
> So hath he myn, for my gult.   *guilt*
>   (343–45)

Acknowledging his limitations, Robert repents and asks God for mercy, so that when the angel later asks him who he is, Robert replies:

> Sire, a fol; that wot I wel,
> And more then fol; yif hit may be;
> Kep I non other dignité.
>   (390–92)

Rymer's comment about social privilege in Shakespearean tragedy is worth recalling here: "Everyone must be content to wear a fool's coat who comes to be dressed by him."

King Robert of Sicily is a particularly illuminating parallel to *King Lear*, because the medieval narrative belongs to a different discourse about power from the New Historicist contrast between putative Christian idealism and emergent materialism. The Erastian claims made by James I are undeniably idealist: the king models himself on God in order to assert a natural hierarchy that justifies the monarch's position. Opposition to this claim, however, need not be materialist; it can be theological. For Christians as well as Marxists have criticized the claims of absolutist idealism, which makes God a projection of punitive authority—a myth shared by ruler and ruled alike in order to maintain the ruler's power. Jonathan Dollimore has shown that this skeptical reinterpretation of absolutist claims was already being articulated in the sixteenth century,[28] and Milton certainly articulates it later in the seventeenth century. But as we saw in chapter 1, Augustine had long since questioned the claim that Roman emperors—including Christian emperors—have the sort of status that James I repeatedly appropriated. This ancient theological critique of power is also enacted in medieval drama (above, chapter 2), and it is this critique that illuminates *King Lear*.

The retrojection of nineteenth-century attitudes onto *King Lear* is explicit in a recent essay by Stephen Greenblatt.[29] He cites a biography of Francis Wayland, a nineteenth-century American Baptist minister, who successfully made his fifteen-month-old son obedient by strategically withholding food and affection until the infant was willing to accept both at his father's hands in a compliant manner. Greenblatt suggests that Wayland is like Lear, and the minister's son is like Lear's daughters, who are coerced into expressions of endearment in order to win their father's possessions from his hand. God is a powerful fantasy that Wayland creates in his own mind and in his son's in order to justify the otherwise unendurable torture of an infant, just as God is a myth of absolute power created in the mind of ruler and ruled to justify political repression and conserve existing power relations.

Greenblatt's analysis of power is incisive, as always, and the parallel he cites is illuminating, but it falsifies the dramaturgy of power in *King Lear*. For Lear's story (like that of the medieval *King Robert*) is premised on the fact that absolutist claims are false: both kings find themselves in a cosmos that can "make heyghe lowe / And lowe heighe." What both stories imagine is the cosmic circumscription of power, not the idealization or defense of it. In this regard, *King Robert* is identical to the mystery plays, which also make the Magnificat a central structural feature. In the medieval story, God cannot be taken as a projection of the king's absolutist fantasy, for God is the agent that reduces the king to nothing and makes him aware of his human limitations. To be sure, King Robert's God is punitive, even using the tactics of Francis Wayland: when the impersonating angel orders Robert to eat with the dogs, the king refuses until his hunger drives him to compliance, "And whon hit nolde non othur be, / He eet with houndes gret plenté" (205–6). But this is not a father dealing with his child or a king dealing with his subject, and it does not fit the categories of New Historicist discourse. The story undeniably projects punitive parenting onto God's relation with the king, but this projection can hardly be understood as a justification of the king's power: imagining the king's relation to God as that of wayward child to corrective parent is very different from imagining it, in the manner of James I, as a privileging of absolute power. Lilian Hornstein in fact traces the motif of the Abased King (of which *King Robert* is an example) to the narratives of ancient Israel, where the experience of an enslaved and insignificant people informs their understanding of God as a limiter of oppressive human power.[30] The theology of ancient Israel is thus preserved in the theological politics of Augustine and in its radicalizing effect on medieval religious drama.

The impact of the medieval dramaturgy of power can be seen even in early sixteenth-century courtly drama where neoclassical prestige is beginning to make an impact. In John Skelton's *Magnificence*, for example, the classical virtue of the play's title derives from Aristotle, who explains it in a way that closely parallels the Platonic and Stoic identification of virtue with nobility, while at the same time explicitly excluding the poor and socially deprived. Aristotle argues that magnificence involves public spending but must be more than mere generosity, for it must be philanthropic spending on a grand scale, and the result must be

> worth the expense and the expense worth the result or even exceed the result. A magnificent man will spend amounts of this kind because it is noble to do so; for this motive is common to all the virtues. . . . But . . . we must also take account of who the agent is and what his resources are, for the expenditure must be in keeping with that and must be suited not only to the result achieved but also to the spender. That is why a poor man is unlikely to be magnificent; for he does not have the means for a suitable expenditure of large sums. If he tries to spend large sums, he is a fool; for he spends more than he can afford or ought to spend, whereas virtuous spending is right spending. But such expenditure is suited to persons who have the requisite means either by dint of their own effort or from their ancestors or their connections. It is suited to persons of high birth and reputation, and so forth, since all these qualities carry greatness and prestige.[31]

Skelton has often been thought to misunderstand magnificence, because his portrayal bears little resemblance to the classical virtue. It is possible, on the contrary, that living close to the court of Henry VIII he understood magnificence all too well and depicted it the way he did as an implicit critique of the "new fashion," with its appetite for self-serving classical virtue. Given the socially exclusive conception of magnificence, it inevitably became identified with Renaissance court entertainment, as Ben Jonson points out: "the most royal princes and greatest persons, who are commonly the personators of these actions [i.e., masques, are] studious of riches and magnificence in the outward celebration or show, which rightly becomes them."[32]

But in the early sixteenth century, the drama was far from the humanist sophistication it achieved in Jonson's hands, and Skelton, whose radical instincts are also rooted deep in the past, models his hero on the drama he knows best. While Magnificence lacks nothing in high birth, reputation, or prestige, as Aristotle specifies, he only becomes truly magnificent after a degrading submission to Crafty Conveyance, Courtly Abusion, Folly, Adversity, Poverty, and the like. He only achieves the perfection of the virtue he represents, in other words, after suffering the humiliating and punitive effects of degradation and defeat, in the manner of King Robert of Sicily.

Lear's story follows a similar pattern. As the play begins, the king completely identifies himself with "my power, / Preeminence, and all the large effects / That troop with majesty" (1.1.130–32). His sense of his power is convincingly grand and much more terrifying than the magniloquent claims to power made by medieval tyrants, even though Lear's rhetoric is more temperate than theirs from the outset: this king is no bombastic clown. Yet his determination to destroy innocents is no less firm than Herod's and is portrayed in a light that makes him look more like Herod than Titus—no Stoic hero destroying his children but a willfull tyrant who cannot brook the slightest threat to his authority:

> Hear me, recreant, on thine allegiance, hear me!
> That thou has sought to make us break our vows,
> Which we durst never yet, and with strain'd pride
> To come betwixt our sentence and our power,
> Which nor our nature nor our place can bear,
> Our potency make good, take thy reward.
> (1.1.168–73)

Lear's habit of exercising power is so deeply ingrained that he frequently breaks out in the same terrifying vein even after he has dispensed with the substance of his power—as in his treatment of Oswald (1.4.79–83), his curses on his daughters (1.4.272–98; 2.4.160–66), and his defiance of the elements (3.2.1–24). Indeed, anger and revenge are his motives for disdaining his daughters, abjuring all roofs, and deliberately encountering necessity's sharp pinch (2.4.207–10). "At your choice, sir" Goneril remarks (2.4.216)—cruelly, to be sure, in view of what follows, but accurately enough in view of her father's arrogant exercise of power.

The humbling of this arrogance is one of the play's most pitiable and most discussed movements, but its medieval precedent is not always acknowledged or understood. Since *King Lear* includes no God and no impersonating angel, it has seemed obvious to some that the play is a tract against Providence, drawing on a vein of Renaissance skepticism but hardly on medieval religious drama.[33] But this is an oversimplification. The play need not be addressing the question of Providence at all to reproduce an essentially medieval pattern in Lear's degradation. Rymer would have called the play medieval without hesitation, even though its denial of poetic justice (a term Rymer coined) would have been enough, in his mind, to have made it a denial of Providence.[34] The point is that Lear discovers how limited he actually is, coming to identify fully with the beggar whose impoverishment makes him cry out, "Is man no more than this? . . . Thou art the thing itself; unaccommodated man is no more but such a poor, bare, forked animal as thou art" (3.4.101–7). The king comes to the end of himself in making this discovery: he is shorn of his power, his dignity, and his seemingly invulnerable self-reliance.[35] This is indeed a deconsecration of majesty and an assault on Stoic self-conceptions. But it has potent dramaturgical precedent in centuries of popular drama whose central images involved making the high low and the low high. The defeat of Lucifer, the exile of Cain, the destruction of Pharaoh, the conversion of Octavian, the death of Herod, the tricking of Pilate, the abasement of King Robert, all involve essentially the same movement that we see in *Lear*: the powerful are reminded by the example of their own humiliation that they are no better than fools.

The medieval precedent to the circumscription of Lear's power has a complement in the ennobling of the humble. Unlike Faustus, who dies in tortured recognition of his vulnerability, Lear is not merely degraded: he gains far greater dignity in his humiliation than he had known in the grandeur of his power. King Robert, Octavian, and Magnificence all parallel this movement in King Lear, but the medieval dramatic archetype is the torture and execution of the peasant Jesus, which paradoxically renders him kinglike (above, chapter 7). Lear is every inch a king when he smells strongest of mortality, and his ability to acknowledge that he is a very foolish fond old man is a measure of almost superhuman capacity—not for power but for self-recognition and moral change. Though he and Henry V share a common recognition of the disparity between ceremony and the king's mortality, Lear's recognition is borne in upon him by his destitution, which convinces him of his identity with the destitute, in contrast to Henry V's inference that the king's lot is harder than that of peasants (*Henry V*, 4.1.263–81). Lear's discovery of himself is an experience that never occurs in the opaque life of Henry V, but Lear is taught by a fool that he is "an O without a figure," and he might well therefore affirm the hard won wisdom of Richard II:

> But whate'er I be,
> Nor I, nor any man that but man is,
> With nothing shall be pleas'd, till he be eas'd
> With being nothing.
> (*Richard II*, 5.5.38–41)

Lear's extraordinary achievement in self-knowledge, coupled with his reunion with Cordelia, is what gives him the buoyant sense of invulnerability with which he welcomes imprisonment at the beginning of 5.3. Dollimore is certainly right that this change in Lear—anticipated by his empathy with "poor naked wretches" (3.4.28)—is not socially ameliorative: "Insofar as Lear identifies with suffering it is at the point when he is powerless to do anything about it" (p. 192). But such a critique is beside the point—like blaming Stoic heroes for the consequences of their high-minded actions. Lear's self-discovery involves the abasing and ennobling of a king, not of Everyman, but insofar as it reit-

erates the medieval pattern, it points to the king's essential humanity—
his identification with beggars, madmen, and fools. This is not "the decentering of man," as Dollimore calls it; it is the decentering of social
arrogance and the consequent recentering of humankind. Dryden later
created a hero who is described admiringly as "eccentric," but Alaman-
zor is an attempt to meet the criteria for high-minded heroism that Rymer and Tate had in mind: Almanzor decenters nobility, in effect, by
taking it out of the human orbit and making it superhuman, as Lear
attempts to do in the easy grandeur of his power.[36] But Lear eventually
becomes heroic on another model altogether, one that requires the privileged to acknowledge their limitations and their essential identity with
the disenfranchised. Both models mystify social relations, and neither
satisfies the ethical demands of modern liberal humanitarianism, but to
recognize these limitations in *King Lear* is to recognize the play's essential continuity with medieval religious drama, and to deplore that continuity is to join Rymer in deploring what the play is.

Though Lear is not humbled by a punitive God, he is confronted by
people and circumstances that defeat him past all his expectations, and
he is assisted to a truly ennobling conception of himself by a fool and a
misused woman who is repeatedly associated with redemptive power.
Unlike Helena and Isabella, Cordelia is not identified with coercive
power in her quest to preserve her father: even the army she brings to
England is defeated. But Cordelia is like the heroines of the problem
plays in her sturdy resistance to male importunity and in her unfath-
omable capacity to forgive. Her response, "No cause, no cause" (4.7.77),
to Lear's assertion that she has cause to do him wrong is one of Shakespeare's most compelling expressions of charity, eloquent in its brevity.
"Thou hast one daughter," says an anonymous gentleman to the insane
king, "Who redeems nature from the general curse / Which twain have
brought her to" (4.1.207). This commendation, with its explicit theological allusion, is all the more impressive for having its source in a choric
onlooker, who is not himself a beneficiary of what he sees in Cordelia.
"Nothing almost sees miracles but misery," observes Kent, as he exam-
ines Cordelia's letter regarding the planned French offensive. In his el-
liptical description, she is "seeking to give losses their remedies"
(2.2.168–73). This kind of redemptive power operates effectively in
Lear, as it often does in Shakespeare, as a secular analogue to literal divine grace in religious drama. Skeptical opinion confirms this effect by
default, finding Cordelia no less embarrassing than Tate found the Fool:
Edward Bond eliminates her from his *Lear*, and Dollimore dismisses her
for her social ineffectiveness.[37] Whether in the seventeenth century or
the twentieth, revisers and critics with a sufficiently well-defined point
of view can often illuminate a text as much by what they reject as by
what they approve.

To recognize Cordelia as redemptive is not, however, to deny the tragic effect of *King Lear* or make it a romance. This has been the tendency of theologizing critics like J. F. Danby and G. Wilson Knight, and it has been perpetuated in a nontheological form by what Dollimore calls "humanist" criticism, whose instinct is to find something in *King Lear* that makes the play's unbearable conclusion somehow bearable.[38] That Cordelia is lovingly redemptive there can be no doubt, nor that Lear undergoes an extraordinary transformation: in many respects, *Lear* is Shakespeare's most powerful comedy of forgiveness. Yet Cordelia's destruction and Lear's tortured death ("He hates him / That would upon the rack of this tough world / Stretch him out longer" [5.3.317–19]) are the imaginative equivalents to hanging the angel in *King Robert of Sicily* and having King Robert die in agonized disillusionment. This is the ending that Samuel Johnson could not bring himself to reread and to which he preferred Tate's ending—not because Johnson was a sentimentalist but because he could hardly endure the imaginative experience of tragic realism that the end of *King Lear* entails. The peculiar power of Shakespeare's mature tragedies, as Howard Felperin observes, is essentially antiromantic: it derives not from consolation but from the experience of irredeemable loss.[39] This power, however, is in proportion to the shattered hope from which it derives. The picture of Lear's reconciliation with Cordelia at the beginning of 5.3 ("When thou dost ask me blessing, I'll kneel down, / And ask of thee forgiveness") is the necessary prelude to the old king's real tragedy, when he enters with his dead daughter in his arms, voicing his terrible invocation: "Howl, howl, howl! O, you are men of stones!" (5.3.261). The play's tragic impact derives from and depends upon transcendent hope in the same way that Shakespearean tragedy itself derives from and depends upon the transcendent drama of salvation history: only from within the confidence of faith can its destruction in secular tragic realism be fully felt.

The medieval dramaturgy of power is perpetuated in *King Lear* not only in what Octavius calls "noble weakness" (*Antony and Cleopatra*, 5.2.343) but in the play's archaic response to the "new fashion." *Lear* is the only Shakespearean tragedy with a fully developed double plot—a manifest violation of the Aristotelian recommendation regarding unity of action. The subplot's most spectacular character is Edmund, whose complicity with Lear's daughters reenacts a pattern Shakespeare had explored in his first tragedy, *Titus Andronicus*, where the old chivalric order confronts—and is eventually defeated by—an ambitious new pragmatism. This is the pattern of social change in the sixteenth century, as Rosalie Colie has pointed out in the case of *King Lear*.[40] Shakespeare's interest in this pattern is evident in the early histories as well, where it appears in the defeat of both Talbot in *1 Henry VI* and Gloucester in *2 Henry VI*. *Lear* recalls many features of the *Henry VI* plays: centralized power crumbling and giving way to civil war, familial quarreling, Machiavellian scheming. Indeed, Humphrey, duke of Gloucester may well be the inspiration for his namesake in the subplot of *King Lear*, whose story derives from Sidney's *Arcadia* but whose rank and title are the products of Shakespeare's imagination. Both Gloucesters are isolated and loyal supporters of a passing chivalric order; both are viciously framed and tried in a travesty of justice by cunning and power-seeking enemies; both are betrayed by close relatives who are also anxious for power; both endure terrible physical suffering—one in death, the other in being tortured; both are succeeded in their titles by Vicelike social aspirants and political schemers (the future Richard III and Edmund, respectively). Emrys Jones's argument that the earlier Gloucester's decline and demise are modeled on the passion plays is another reminder of how deeply Shakespeare's tragic conception is influenced by his medieval predecessors, as Rymer noticed three hundred years ago.[41]

That Edmund's duplicity and dissimulation are specifically designed to serve his ambition is evident from the moment he first reveals his thoughts, in Vicelike fashion, to the audience: "Legitimate Edgar, I must have your land. . . . Edmund the base / Shall top th'legitimate" (1.2.16–21).[42] Edmund's illegitimacy inevitably complicates his ambition, grounding it in motives born of marginalization and powerlessness. The primary force of his social handicap, however, is not to make him pitiable or sympathetic but to identify him with overweening power for its own sake, no matter what his motive may be. This emphasis is produced by his own cynicism and Edgar's lack of guile: if the legitimate brother were an oppressor (like Oliver in *As You Like It*), we would respond very differently to Edmund. As it is, Edmund identifies himself with archaic power-seekers, like the N-Town Lucifer, who sets "[nought] by precept nor by comawndement,"[43] anticipating Edmund's scorn for "the plague of custom . . . the curiosity of nations." Edmund's cruelty, ruthlessness, and "proper" appearance (1.1.18) all associate him with oppressive courtly power, which is also enacted by the N-Town Lucifer and by innumerable other medieval devils and Vices whose original motive is *libido dominandi*. To be sure, Edmund is an updated version of this motive in action. His passion for land, for example, is peculiarly Tudor, for the economic, political, and social advantages of land ownership all increased in the sixteenth century: "The medieval idea that land was held ultimately from God as a trust only, not to be used selfishly or exploited ruthlessly, was coming under heavy strain."[44] Henry VIII's dispersing of monastic real estate to his courtiers was a primary factor in this revaluation, and the subsequent quest for land remained intense among courtiers throughout the century, as we noticed in chapter 6. But while Edmund's acquisitiveness takes a contemporary form, he enacts an identification of evil with social ambition and competitive aggression that originates in religious drama of the fifteenth century: the sophisticated complications of power-seeking that we find in the later history plays are abandoned in *Lear* in favor of a simpler archaic mode that heightens the contrast between evil and good, giving additional potency to the play's redemptive symbols.

Edmund's theatricality is a characteristic of his viciousness that he shares with Richard III, Iago, and the medieval Vice, but that may well have originated in actual observation of social change in the fifteenth century—a new competitiveness that we have seen Peter Idley identifying as "fals dissimulacion / And . . . fained countenance."[45] The staginess of Edmund's plot against his brother is suggested by Edmund's own remark when Edgar suddenly appears: "and pat he comes, like the catastrophe of the old comedy: my cue is villainous melancholy" (1.2.137–38). Edmund's kinship with the Vice may indicate that he has affinities with popular tradition, as Robert Weimann and Walter Cohen have argued: in that case, his theatricality is part of a dramaturgical tradition whose origin is in subversive folk theater.[46] Edmund's "Figurenposition," as Weimann calls it, is close to the audience: he addresses the audience directly, takes it into his confidence, and stands psychologically with the oppressed in his illegitimacy and opposition to established power—both the king's and his father's. In Edmund's case, however, as in the case of the Vice itself, the actual social use of dramatic tradition needs to be considered, as well as one possible origin of that tradition. Edmund's cruelty is identical to that of Cornwall, who is a duke: indeed, Cornwall's torture of Gloucester is made possible only by Edmund's betrayal of his father. Edmund's position of power over against his tortured elderly parent makes Edmund's oppressed background all but irrelevant to the present situation. Dollimore cannily suggests that Edmund represents a "revolutionary (emergent) insight . . . folded back into a dominant ideology" (*Radical Tragedy*, p. 201), which is a sophisticated way of saying that the powerless often misuse power if and when they finally attain it. But Shakespeare's emphasis is on that misuse and on the suffering of its victims. Whatever their motive, the naked power craved by Edmund and Lear's daughters is crueller and more bloodthirsty than Lear's tyranny in the play's opening scenes. Edmund's cynical theatricality would appear to have more in common with sixteenth-century "self-fashioning," as Stephen Greenblatt calls it, than with popular tradition: the assertive self-promotion of Edmund certainly fits Greenblatt's picture of Protean Renaissance courtiers.[47] In this regard, as in his passion for real estate, Edmund is a contemporary version of the social reality that originally animated medieval devils and Vices.

Edmund's exercise of power in the "new fashion" is thus a foil to Lear's neo-Augustinian discovery of his foolish pride: "Take physic, pomp; / Expose thyself to feel what wretches feel" (3.4.33–34). Lear learns empathy with the powerless at the same time that Edmund schools himself in treachery and torture while questing for power. It is therefore fitting that the destiny of these two characters should come together in the end, and that Edmund should be the cause of Lear's final unspeakable suffering. This conjunction is like the oppression of the peasant Christ by the dandified courtly Lucifer in medieval drama: in neither case is the oppressor identifiable as oppressed. Yet in *Lear* the conjunction of destructive power and enduring powerlessness serves the purpose of tragic realism, not of redemptive suffering. Edmund's death-bed repentance ("Some good I mean to do, / Despite of mine own na-ture" [5.3.247–48]) is too little and too late—still another redemptive hope that does not survive in the end. Edgar's well-meaning restoration of justice in his trial by combat with Edmund has the same effect, since the elaborate neomedieval pageantry—including heralds, ritual chal-lenges, and disputes about social worth—takes place at precisely the same time that Edmund's order is being carried out by the opportunistic officer who hangs Cordelia. In Edmund's plot everything begins to right itself hopefully at the same time that Lear's plot takes a turn into irre-versible despair.

Again, however, the impact of that tragic turn depends on our irre-sistible hope that the play's redemptive symbols will be vindicated, and the evocative power of those symbols derives from dramaturgical models that had long since fallen from favor when Shakespeare wrote *King Lear*. The old king, physically frail and psychologically devastated, is no Stoically ennobled hero, just as the play in which he appears lacks the tidiness and economy of the neoclassical unities that Sidney, and Rymer after him, regarded as prerequisites of tragic art. If anyone quali-fies as a Stoic hero in this play, it is surely the imperturbable Edgar, whose intrepidity and fortitude remain unshaken through the most har-rowing experiences and finally seem to make him the logical successor to Lear, though it is hard to see that he has Lear's capacity for self-rec-ognition and change. Like his brother, in fact, Edgar would appear to be a foil to Lear, for in Edgar's wily dissimulation as mad Tom, his noble endurance, his chivalric rectitude, and his rapid rise from earl's son to heir apparent, Edmund's half brother is the benign face of the new fash-ion. To him and to Edmund the old order gives way, as the archaism that animates Lear's tragedy itself was giving way to customs implanted by innovative patterns of prestige and social change.

To argue that Shakespeare derived his tragic effect by default from archaic sources is to deny neither its modernity nor its distinctive power. Repeatedly the mature tragedies suggest peculiarly modern di-lemmas: the corrosive doubt of *Hamlet*, the destructive mistrust and alienation of Othello, Macbeth's poignant insistence on his freedom to choose a self-destroying course of action—all these rehearse familiar modern agonies yet are played out against a background of cosmic collapse that accompanies the human loss, and to ignore the larger loss is to rob the lesser of its significance. Horatio invokes flights of angels to sing Hamlet to his rest, but the only visitant from beyond the grave in *Hamlet* is profoundly ambiguous, and Hamlet's trust in providence is followed by a treacherous death that parallels his father's. Othello, as we noticed, discovers Desdemona's redemptive fidelity only after he has destroyed her himself, when the discovery washes him in steep-down gulfs of liquid fire. Macbeth's confidence in a redemptive alternative that he repeatedly rejects is reduced to Malcolm's politic summary: "this dead butcher." The lees of life that Macbeth felt he was reduced to are all that we are left with as well. "He hates him," Kent retorts, in the face of Edgar's optimism ("Look up, my lord") "that would upon the rack of this tough life stretch him out longer." Kent's lines are powerful and terrifying, but their power is in proportion to the hope that was born in Lear's reconciliation with his daughter. We depend "upon symbols and symbol systems," Clifford Geertz remarks, "with a dependence so great as to be decisive for our creatural viability and, as a result, our sensitivity to even the remotest indication that they may prove unable to cope with one or another aspect of experience raises within us the gravest sort of anxiety."[48] This is the anxiety that Samuel Johnson felt in response to *King Lear*, and our continuing to feel something like the play's extraordinary tragic power is revealed in efforts to deny it by reducing the play to a tract in skepticism. For reductive readings are no less an attempt to escape the anxiety Geertz describes than are romantic readings: reducers escape by denying the redemptive symbols (like Lear's self-discovery and Cordelia's forgiveness) that collapse in the face of the play's ending. But this escape is bought at the price of denying the play's tragic power, which depends on the symbols that "prove unable to cope." Either we acknowledge the symbols—and the tragedy with them—or we deny the symbols and reduce Shakespearean tragedy to something like absurdist theater. While both forms deal heavily in irony, the cosmic scope of redemptive symbols in tragedy make it quite distinct from its modern counterpart. To borrow Eliot's phrase, Shakespearean tragedy ends with an apocalyptic bang, but we will hear only a whimper if we set out to deny what makes the plays apocalyptic in the first place.

CHAPTER 10   RULING TASTE AND
THE LATE PLAYS

While the plays that follow the tragedies and conclude Shakespeare's career seem to belong to a different world from the tragedies, the differences do not eradicate some fundamental social continuities. The romances still observe Renaissance social decorum, bestowing the most serious roles on the social elite and depicting them in greater numbers than their inferiors, in defiance of Jacobean social reality. In contrast to the tragedies, redemptive symbols in the late plays are vindicated, and hard won self-knowledge is cherished by cosmic hope. Yet the spiritually ennobling process we witness in the romances is largely confined to the upper classes, as if they alone are capable of moral regeneration. The two gentlemen who resort to the brothel in Mytilene are converted to virtue by their encounter with Mariana, but Pander, Boult, and Bawd remain unchanged, regretting only that Mariana is reducing their trade (*Pericles*, 4.5.1–9 and 4.6.1–11). The transient rogue Autolychus in *The Winter's Tale* is similarly unimpressed by either the romantic affection of Perdita and Florizel or the reunion of Perdita and the penitent Leontes, which moves Autolychus' social betters to exclamations of wonder and incredulity (5.2).

Yet the late plays' continuity with the rest of Shakespeare's work includes qualifications of privilege, as well as conformity with social expectation. "Princes are / A model which heaven makes like to itself," declares King Simonides in *Pericles* (2.2.10–11), in a summary of Jacobean state theory. But neither constancy nor perfection (the ostensible qualities of heaven) actually characterizes princes in these plays. Antiochus is irredeemably wicked; Cymbeline, hopelessly weak; Leontes, a jealous tyrant; and Prospero, a benign trickster. Moreover, while the lower social orders are seldom directly involved in actions that are fraught with redemptive symbolism, we invariably encounter shepherds, servants, sailors, and the like whose actions exhibit greater moral awareness than the actions of many who are their social betters. The first scene of *The Tempest* is a particularly striking example, where the sailors' commitment to doing a difficult job well in a critical situation makes them a good deal more admirable than the fussy and worried noblemen who persistently mar their labor. Shakespeare's double means of qualifying received social wisdom in the late plays is consistent with his practice in the romantic comedies (above, chapter 4), and if anything distinguishes the romances in this regard from Shakespeare's earlier ventures into comedy, it is an even more explicit reliance in the later plays on the "old tales" of medieval religious drama.

That Shakespeare should revert to archaic dramaturgy in the first decade of the reign of James I is more noteworthy than his doing so as a young playwright in the early 1590s. For not only had the outdated style of the old plays receded further into the past by 1608–11, but the social processes that made that style outdated in the first place had accelerated and defined themselves more clearly with the accession of the new king. Any playwright with serious social pretensions eschewed what Jonson calls "moldy tales" in favor of modes that were more responsive to the ruling taste.[1] Jonson himself devoted most of his energy to the court masque, which he perfected over the next two decades, creating for himself a position from which he could offer the royal family serious moral advice and thus implicitly make himself their equal, if not their better, by the humanist maxim that virtue is the true nobility. Even those like Middleton, Webster, or Tourneur who took a jaundiced view of court life may have been more responsive to reigning fashion than Shakespeare— at least in his recourse to medieval dramaturgy—since the comparatively decadent tone of James's court was easily observable by everyone who had anything to do with it, and to focus on it in dramas of ostensible Italian decadence was therefore to respond to the "new fashion" with an ambivalent fascination that goes back to the sixteenth century. In a world of keen social striving, condemnation of decadent privilege can be profoundly ambiguous, as we have seen before: one can as easily be coveting what one is socially denied as rejecting what one morally disapproves.[2]

In any case, Shakespeare's interest in archaic dramaturgy flies in the face of the Jacobean penchant for "correct" standards in drama. This penchant develops a similar Elizabethan concern at the same time that it looks forward to the exact taste of Augustan England. Before the end of Elizabeth's reign, learning had been firmly established as a criterion of social privilege, as we saw in chapter 3, and this criterion was confirmed and strengthened in 1603 by the accession of a king who fancied himself a profound scholar. If the king valued learning as one of his chief attributes, then the association of learning with power was hardly contestable, especially since the king devoted much of his intellectual energy to establishing the grounds for his own power as absolute. To a playwright as learned as Jonson, the accession of James must have seemed like the promotion of a powerful kindred spirit, and Jonson wasted no time in exhibiting his own scholarly expertise to the king, for he lavished his learning on two of the triumphal arches for James's royal entry into London in March 1604.[3] The arcane mysteries of these arches were visible to everyone but designed to be accessible only to the understanding of a few—or better yet, of one—on the principle of rhetorical exclusivity established in the ancient world. "For a poem full of obscure allusions can from its nature only win the approbation of the few," asserts Cicero; "an oration meant for the general public must aim to win the assent of the throng."[4] Cicero's stipulation is echoed in Jonson's description of his decorous designs for the triumphal arches:

> Neither was it becoming, or could it stand with the dignity of these shows (after the most miserable and desperate shift of the puppets) to require a truch-man, or (with the ignorant painter) one to write, *This is a dog*, or, *This is a hare*: but so to be presented, as upon the view, they might, without cloud or obscurity, declare themselves to the sharp and learned. And for the multitude, no doubt but their grounded judgments did gaze, said it was fine, and were satisfied.[5]

"Grounded" judgments are incapable of ascent—either intellectual or social: the adjective is related to Hamlet's condescending term "groundlings" (*Hamlet*, 3.2.11), used to describe those who paid the smallest entry fee at contemporary public theaters and who therefore stood throughout the performance. Hamlet's opinion might well be Jonson's— that groundlings "are capable of nothing but inexplicable dumb-shows and noise." In short, Jonson's principle of rhetorical exclusiveness is pointedly social as well.

What was true for James's royal entry became even truer for the court masques, which were hidden from the gaze of the multitude within the confines of the Whitehall Banqueting House and were designed, like Jonson's triumphal arches, for the learned apprehension of a few. Though Jonson eventually became the most brilliant and favored author of masques, he was not alone in aspiring to excellence in this form, and he was not alone either in perceiving it as defined in large part by its social exclusivity. Samuel Daniel writes of his masque, *Tethys Festival*, performed at Whitehall on 5 June 1610: "in all these shows this is to be noted, that there were none of inferior sort mixed amongst these great personages of state and honor, as usually there have been, but all was performed by themselves with a due reservation of their dignity."[6] Years later, in *Neptune's Triumph* (1624), Jonson included a satirical discussion of courtly dramaturgy as part of the masque itself: in the antimasque, a Whitehall cook berates an author of masques for imagining that poetry and cookery are distinct:

> Seduced poet, I do say to thee,
> A boiler, range, and dresser were the fountains

Of all the knowledge in the universe,
And that's the kitchen, where a master-cook—
Thou dost not know the man, nor canst thou know him
Till thou hast served some years in that deep school
That's both the nurse and mother of the arts,
And hear'st him read, interpret and demonstrate!
A master-cook! why he is the man of men for a professor![7]

This is not Jonson laughing good-naturedly at himself; it is a represented fact, as far as Jonson is concerned, about the ignorance of manual laborers: their access to the sacred well of Helicon does them no good but only incites them to profane the mysteries they cannot comprehend. Sir John Harrington had made the same argument more than thirty years earlier, in his defense of the allegory in Ariosto's *Orlando Furioso*:

It sufficeth me therefore to note this, that the men of greatest learning and highest wit in the ancient times did of purpose conceal these deep mysteries of learning, and, as it were, cover them with the veil of fables and verse for sundry causes. One cause was that they might not be rashly abused by profane wits, in whom science is corrupted, like good wine in a bad vessel.[8]

Jacobean continuity with the ruling taste created by the Tudors was not accidental: it was a deliberate strategy of a Scots king in appropriating as much as he could of the prestige amassed by the English dynasty that he succeeded. At the time Shakespeare was writing the romances (1608–11), a large part of James's strategy was focused in his oldest son, Prince Henry, who was nine at the time of his father's accession and was created Prince of Wales in 1610, when he was sixteen. The late plays' unusual interest in royal family relations may have something to do with the novel accession of a king with a family, as David Bergeron suggests,[9] but Shakespeare's late plays enact more than family relations; they also enact the royal family's relation to power, a subject much on the mind of James I, whose first book, *Basilikon Doron*, belongs to the humanist tradition of the *speculum principibus* but has the added importance of being written by a king for his own son. James's lesson was not lost on Henry, whose precociously established power base and strong-willed independence had already begun to create tensions between himself and his father when the prince unexpectedly took ill and died in November, 1612, almost a year after Shakespeare had finished *The Tempest*.

The symbols of Prince Henry's power have survived in a revealing collection of courtly artifacts. Henry is the subject, for example, of the first deliberate equestrian portrait of an English royal personage, painted in about 1610 probably by Robert Peake.[10] The significance of this portrait is that the equestrian pose had been reserved for the emperor alone in Roman art and had been consciously revived by Italian Renaissance princes as a means of appropriating the prestige of ancient Roman power.[11] Henry thus updated the Tudor practice of drawing on Roman prestige wherever possible, as James had done earlier in entering London through a series of Roman triumphal arches. Like his equestrian portrait, Henry's sponsorship of the Virginia Company should also be read in light of his keen interest in the symbols of Roman imperial ambition. William Crashaw's sermon, preached before Henry and the leaders of the company in 1609, alludes to the Romans as civilizers: "for the time was when we were savage and uncivil and worshipped the devil as now [the Virginians] do; then God sent some [i.e., the Romans] to make us civil."[12] The pending expedition, Crashaw concludes, should do the same favor for the Virginians. The king's and prince's interest in the expedition shows them to be "new Constantines or Charles the Great: for by the attempting and achieving of this great work of the heathens' conversion, let their highnesses be assured, the ages to come will style them by the glorious names of James the Great and Great Henry" (sig. I2). This sermon, published in 1610, should probably be considered as part of the context of *The Tempest*, given Crashaw's emphasis on powerful European civilizers and the devil-worshipping natives they undertake to enlighten.[13]

Among the extant symbols of Prince Henry's power are Jonson's texts and Inigo Jones's drawings for two court entertainments, *Prince Henry's Barriers* (1610) and *Oberon, The Prince of Fairy* (1611), in which the Stuart attempt to capitalize on the Tudors' efficient centralization of power is clear. The basic procedure of both entertainments is simple and essentially the same: a prologue describing or depicting the decay of chivalry is followed by the "discovery" of Prince Henry and his knights, with the implication that they will restore chivalry to its antique glory. In both cases, the heavily Spenserian atmosphere deliberately recalls heroic themes in the celebration of Elizabethan power: Henry's restoration of contemporary decay looks back to the high moral tone of a court presided over by a virgin queen, whose strength was her virtue. But Jones's drawings indicate that the evocations go far beyond the previous reign: they go back to Rome. The stage set depicting the Fallen House of Chivalry in the *Barriers* is modelled on Roman ruins, and Oberon's Palace in *Oberon* is strikingly Palladian and modern, with its windows designed after examples in Serlio's *Architettura*, the last word in Baroque neoclassical design.[14] As Graham Parry points out, chivalry did not have medieval connotations for the Renaissance, but Roman: "To Elizabethan historians . . . chivalry first flourished in these islands among the Britons, and the British line of kings from Brutus to Arthur was contemporary with the age of Rome."[15] Among Inigo Jones's drawings for Oberon's costume are several studies of Roman imperial dress, including a *corona triumphalis* of bay leaves.[16] These drawings are complemented by one of Henry's last portraits, painted by Isaac Oliver, a miniature depicting the Prince in profile, "unequivocally presented as a Roman emperor."[17]

The pastoralism of *Oberon*, with its satyrs, silvans, and Silenus, presents a pacific picture but is no less a myth of power than are other Roman allusions in this masque. "Renaissance pastoral takes the court as its cynosure," Louis Montrose argues, because aristocratic shepherds in a courtly setting enact the upward mobility that was key to the centralization of power.[18] In *Oberon*, Prince Henry is praised as the transcendent source of natural plenty:

> Satyrs, he doth fill with grace
> Every season, every place;
> Beauty dwells but in his face:
> He's the height of all our race.
>
> . . . .
>
> He is lovelier than in May
> In the spring, and there can stay
> As little as he can decay.[19]

Royal power over nature is a constant theme in Jacobean adulation of the monarchy. One of the triumphal arches in James's entry was the Rustic Arch, where the king was lauded by Vertumnus, god of gardens, as the restorer of the kingdom's prosperity, just as Henry is praised in the *Barriers* and *Oberon* as the restorer of chivalry. In Jonson's *Vision of Delight* (1617), James is again praised in similar terms:

> Behold a king
> Whose presence maketh this perpetual spring,
> The glories of which spring grow in that bower,
> And are the marks and beauties of his power.[20]

The Vision of Delight was a New Year's masque, like *Oberon*, so the miracle of spring in winter was a compliment not only to James but to his master of masque machinery, Inigo Jones, who wrought stage miracles by means of the king's favor and munificence. Both Jonson and Jones were the sons of commoners—a brickmaker and a cloth-worker, respectively—so their responsiveness to pastoral and the neo-Platonic myth of plenitude as metaphors of court life was not socially disinterested: the bounty that flowed from the king to them was returned to him in the form of court masques that celebrated his magnificence. It is little wonder that Jones adopted a tone of orthodox adulation on a rare occasion of voicing his opinion in print: "In Heroic Virtue is figured the King's majesty, who therein transcends as far the common man as they are above beasts, he truly being the prototype to all the kingdom under his monarchy of religion, justice, and all the virtues joined together."[21] Jones echoes the sentiments in a speech by King James that we noticed earlier in chapter 8—a speech to both houses of Parliment in 1610, when they were assembled in the Banqueting House of Whitehall to hear the king declaim on majesty:

> Kings are justly called Gods, for that they exercise a manner of resemblance of divine power upon the earth. For if you will consider the attributes of God, you shall see how they agree in the person of a king. God hath power to create or destroy, to make or unmake at his pleasure, to give life or send death, to judge all and to be judged nor accountable to none, to raise low things and to make high things low at his pleasure, and to God are both soul and body due. And the like power have kings: they make and unmake their subjects, they have power of raising and casting down, of life and of death, judges over all their subjects and in all cases, and yet accomptable to God only. They have power to exalt low things and abase high things and make of their subjects like men at the chess, a pawn to take a bishop or knight, and to cry up or down any of their subjects, as they do their money.[22]

Not everyone was as ready to echo the king as Jones was, however, and not everyone who had doubts about the king's claim was as fatuous or menial as the cook in *Neptune's Triumph*. Sir John More heard James's speech and remarked that "the most strictly religious could have wished *that His Highness would have been more sparing in using the name of God and comparing the Deity with princes' sovereignty*."[23] In a letter to Prince Henry's tutor, Bishop Joseph Hall cites flattery and treachery as the two chief mischiefs of the court, and his thoughts about flattery can easily be construed as including court dramaturgy. "It had been better for many great ones not to have been than to have been in their conceits more than men," Hall asserts, and he almost certainly uses "conceits," as Jerry Williamson points out, in the archaic sense of "concepts," including imaginative concepts, which would encompass the symbols of power so compellingly displayed in court masques.[24] "Who can but wonder," Hall continues,

> that reads of some not unwise princes, so bewitched with the enchantments of their parasites that they have thought themselves gods immortal, and have suffered themselves so styled, so addressed? Neither temples, nor statues, nor sacrifices have seemed too much glory to the greatness of their self-love.

If Hall alludes circumspectly to the grandiose claims of Stuart court drama, others were much less inclined to pull their punches. "What think'st thou of a masque: will it be well?" asks Lysippus in Beaumont's and Fletcher's *Maid's Tragedy* (performed by the King's Men at some time between 1608 and 1611). "Yes," Strato replies,

> they must commend their King, and speak in praise
> Of the assembly, bless the bride and bridegroom
> In person of some god. They're tied to rules
> Of flattery.[25]

Shakespeare was therefore not alone in qualifying privilege, as he does in the romances, but he was virtually unique in qualifying it by deliberately evoking an archaic dramatic tradition that had conceived of kings as human beings, not gods. To be sure, the ideological motive behind that tradition shows up in other places, as in John Donne's funeral sermon for James I, preached at Denmark House in April 1625, shortly before the king's burial:

> And when you shall find that hand that had signed to one of you a patent for title, to another for pension, to another for pardon, to another for dispensation, dead; that hand that settled possessions by his seal in the keeper, and rectified honors by the sword in his marshall, and distributed relief to the poor in his almoner, and health to the diseased by his immediate touch, dead; that hand that balanced his own three kingdoms so equally, so that none of them complained of one another nor of him, and carried the keys of all the Christian world, and locked up and let out armies in their due season, dead; how poor, how faint, how pale, how momentany [*sic*], how transitory, how empty, how frivolous, how dead things must you necessarily think titles, and possessions, and favors, and all, when you see that hand, which was the hand of destiny, of Christian destiny, of the Almighy God, lie dead![26]

What Donne's sermon shares with Shakespeare's romances is the assumption that kings are mortal and their power is contingent—an unavoidably demystifying assumption in the context of Stuart court adulation. The N-Town *Death of Herod* is a specific medieval dramatic forebear to Donne's sermon, which has a more immediate precursor in Richard II's meditation on royal mortality (*Richard II*, 3.2.160–77). No matter how commonplace this idea might be, it is important to notice its Christian provenance, for it reminds us once again that a residual theological critique of power coexisted throughout this period with a dominant political idealism that expropriated religious language—as it attempted to expropriate everything else—in its own behalf. Indeed, the irrepressible prophetic strain in Christian tradition may have contributed to the increasing royal preference (under both Elizabeth and James) for Roman imperial symbols in place of the religious iconography that predominates in the midsixteenth century. Even Prince Henry's strong

Protestant sympathies expressed themselves in the fashionable imperial images, as we have seen, which give little direct clue to his specific religious convictions. The residual prophetic strain shows itself again, of course, in the open opposition to royal absolutism that bursts forth in 1642.

While Shakespeare is no Puritan radical, his affinity with a very old tradition of Christian resistance to overweening power is evident in his recourse to medieval dramaturgy, even in *The Tempest*, which is the most receptive of all the romances to courtly fashion.[27] At its center is a regal figure, whose power, at the time we see him, is directly dependent on his scholarly expertise. That expertise, moreover, enables Prospero literally to do what court masques like *The Vision of Delight* symbolically claimed that the king and prince could do—namely, control the natural elements. Indeed, Prospero's situation at the beginning of *The Tempest* is a vision of retributive delight: possessed of unchallenged and almost unlimited power, he has been able to put his enemies entirely at his mercy with little risk to himself. To construe Prospero's situation as a flattering tribute to Jacobean royal power is almost inevitable, given the masque's standard depiction of the royal presence banishing whatever elements happened to be troubling it. Shakespeare's sensitivity to ruling taste is evident in his careful attention to the neoclassical unities and in the masque Prospero produces for the wedding of Ferdinand and Miranda. In its context, the masque's celebration of the natural plenitude that accompanies virtuous restraint is topical, since Prospero has expressed his concern that Ferdinand not break Miranda's "virgin-knot before / All sanctimonious ceremonies may / With full and holy rite be minist'red" (4.1.15–17). In other words, Prospero's masque reflects the royal mind back to itself in precisely the manner of the real Jacobean masques that Shakespeare had certainly heard of, possibly performed in, and probably read.

Yet *The Tempest* is not tied to rules of flattery, no matter how richly it evokes the dynamics of courtly spectacle, and perhaps its chief qualification of power is its enactment of human limitations in the powerful. Even Prospero's masque, as Ernest Gilman argues, serves the purpose of challenging the assumptions on which the Jacobean masque was based: while ideally reflecting the timeless truths in Prospero's mind, the masque's unexpected collapse also reveals his mental perturbation and imbeddedness in time, and the sudden move from ideal aristocratic vision to the blundering antics of commoners who threaten aristocratic power is a move that reverses the masque's pattern of beginning with a grotesque lower-class antimasque, which is then banished and negated by the unfolding vision of an ideal political order.[28]

Another way of describing what Gilman points to in *The Tempest* is to say that Prospero discovers his vulnerability, which is a central feature of characterization that Shakespeare's early comedies share with medieval drama, as we noticed in chapter 4. R. G. Hunter's discussion of *The Tempest* as a "comedy of forgiveness" focuses on Alonso as chief among the "men of sin" (3.3.53): Alonso undergoes an ordeal that compels him to recognize his human fallibility, after the manner of Humanum Genus in the morality play.[29] But Alonso is not alone in making this discovery: Prospero makes it as well, even though he is himself the one who creates Alonso's healing ordeal. Prospero admits to Miranda that he discovered his political vulnerability when he neglected his responsibility and thereby "awaked an evil nature" in Antonio, who created an independent power base and seized Milan for his own (1.2.66–132). But a lesson in political vulnerability can easily incite one merely to be more wary and try harder the next time, and *The Tempest* suggests that Prospero drew precisely this conclusion. To be sure, from the outset he seems to aim at something more than the immediate destruction of his enemies, or he would not have made certain that all on the ship survived the tempest (1.2.217), but exactly what he does aim at is not clear: even after the banishment of the masque and Prospero's moving speech in recognition of human limitation ("We are such stuff / As dreams are made on, and our little life / Is rounded with a sleep" [4.1.156])—even after this moment, Prospero orders the punishment of Caliban, Stephano, and Trinculo, and remarks: "At this hour / Lie at my mercy all mine enemies" (4.1.264–65). This moment culminates Prospero's pursuit of invulnerable power ("Now does my project gather to a head" [5.1.1]), and his decision to proceed mercifully appears to be made only thereafter, in the course of his conversation with Ariel:

> ARIEL: Your charm so strongly works 'em
>   That if you now beheld them, your affections
>   Would become tender.
> PROSPERO:
>   Dost thou think so, spirit?
> ARIEL: Mine would, sir, were I human.
> PROSPERO:
>   And mine shall.
>
> (5.1.17–20)

Though we may surmise that Prospero had this intention in mind from the beginning, he certainly never says as much, and all we actually see him doing is aimed to enhance his political invulnerability—including his control of nature, his working through invisible intermediaries, and his acquired skill in preventing others from lifting their weapons.

This is not to say that Prospero is an evil man—any more than Duke Vincentio is in *Measure for Measure*—but that even a good man may have something to learn, particularly about himself. Like Vincentio,

Prospero is a political trickster, concealing his power and manipulating appearances so as to keep his enemies off balance. Prospero is unlike Vincentio, however, in that we actually hear Prospero (a royal figure, if ever there was one) admitting a serious political mistake, we see him very nearly make another such mistake (when he banishes the masque), and we also see him apparently coming to a recognition that something may be required of the powerful aside from the affliction of their enemies, namely, the recognition of human limitations and the need to be merciful. True, with Prospero as with Vincentio, Shakespeare gives us a trickster who is very different from the powerless and socially despised deceiver who is God incarnate in medieval drama. But as a royal trickster, Prospero is by far the most successful qualification of Renaissance power among Shakespeare's four experiments in this vein (Portia, Helena, Vincentio, and Prospero). For in addition to admitting and demonstrating his ability to learn and change, Prospero explicitly *renounces* his means to power at the moment when they have rendered him least vulnerable (5.1.33–57). Since he appears to do this in recogniton of his own frailty ("This thing of darkness I / Acknowledge mine," he says later of Caliban [5.1.278–79]), his renunciation enacts the point that Donne was later to make boldly in his funeral sermon for James I:

> Christ . . . *is like thee in everything*, but not absolutely, for *sin* is *excepted*; but in this glass now (*the body of our royal but dead master and sovereign*) we cannot, we do not, except sin. Not only the greatest man is subject to *natural infirmities* (Christ himself was so), but the holiest man is subject to *original and actual sin*, as thou art, and so a fit glass for thee, to see thyself in.[30]

Unlike the court masque, *The Tempest* does not climax in an epiphany of royal power; it ends in a royal figure's recognition of his human weakness, his decision to take the part of nobler reason 'gainst his fury, and his determination to discard the props of power and come out from behind them. More clearly than earlier plays of this sort, in other words, *The Tempest* suggests that to be morally credible, authority most be humble as well as powerful.

In comparison to what Shakespeare does with Prospero, other qualifications of power in *The Tempest* are relatively unimportant, but they serve nonetheless to clarify how Shakespeare turned to the medieval dramaturgy of power in his late plays. At the opposite end of the social scale from Prospero is Caliban, the universally despised native of the desert isle. Caliban can hardly be said to enact *potentia humilitatis*, for he is rebellious, sullen, and vengeful. But like many lower-class characters in medieval drama and in Shakespeare's romantic comedies, Caliban is graced with unexpected dignity (as in his lyric appreciation of the island's beauty and profusion), and more important, he eventually demonstrates a characteristic in common with Prospero and Alonso: the ability to come to the end of himself in acquiring moral wisdom:

> I'll be wise hereafter,
> And seek for grace. What a thrice-double ass
> Was I to take this drunkard for a god
> And worship this dull fool!
> (5.1.298–301)

No "grounded" character, in Jonson's phrase, Caliban is thus embraced within human society by the play's most important criterion for belonging to it. To be sure, Caliban's repentance is offensive to liberal humanitarian sentiment, for his moral insight does nothing to ameliorate his social situation: he is still Prospero's slave, only now more willing than before. To see this as the play's definitive moral stroke against Prospero, however, is to render meaningless the wisdom Prospero has acquired and to ignore the dignified humanity that Prospero and Caliban come to share. The point is not that Shakespeare sows the seeds of imperial exploitation in *The Tempest*, but that he implicitly denies the Renaissance assumption that virtue is reserved for those at the top of the social scale.

As qualifications of Jacobean ruling taste, what Prospero and Caliban have in common is complemented by what is shared between Stephano and Antonio. For the first two are paradoxically humbled and ennobled by a growing awareness of their limitations and the acquiring of wisdom, while the second two put themselves beyond the human pale by their grounded resistance to moral improvement of any kind. The fact that Antonio is brother to a duke also negates the Renaissance tendency to associate virtue with nobility, for Antonio's viciousness is what he shares with a drunken butler. In the first place, both are willfully myopic about the extraordinary beauty of the island on which they have been shipwrecked. Antonio sneers at Adrian's and Gonzalo's exclamations of wonder (2.1), and Stephano has an interest only in wine, no matter where he finds himself, or in what circumstances: the same butt of sack on which he escaped the shipwreck (2.2.120–22) is the source of his constant inebriation on the island. Caliban's intense longing for the island's beauty thus makes him naturally superior to Antonio and Stephano, even though he falls ready prey to the latter's alcohol in a distressing enactment of European corruption in the New World. Second, Stephano and Antonio are instinctive exploiters of what they find in their new environment. Stephano sees economic profit in Caliban the minute he perceives that this "monster of the isle" is a creature with language, and his purpose in making Caliban drunk is to capture him and present him to a European emperor—presumably in exchange for court preferment (2.2.68–79). Trinculo's thoughts run in the same vein, with more pointed significance for a Jacobean audience:

Were I in England now, as once I was, and had but this fish painted, not a holiday fool there but would give a piece of silver. There would this beast make a man; any strange beast there makes a man. When they will not give a doit to relieve a lame beggar, they will lay out ten to see a dead Indian. (2.2.28–33)

What occurs to a butler and a jester also occurs immediately to Prospero's brother when he first sees Caliban. In response to Sebastian's question whether "money will buy" the three clowns in their stolen apparel, Antonio calculatingly replies: "Very like. One of them / Is a plain fish, and no doubt marketable" (5.1.268–69). These are Antonio's last words in the play, and they therefore indicate that he, not Caliban, is one whose nature "any print of goodness [will] not take, / Being capable of all ill" (1.2.354–55). His cold estimate of Caliban's marketability is a foil to Prospero's treatment of the islander, for Prospero's first instinct was kindly and well intended (1.2.334–50). Whatever retrospective ambiguities may haunt Prospero's response to Caliban, they always need to be considered in conjunction with Antonio's response.

Third, Antonio and Stephano are alike in their common *libido dominandi*, the principal characteristic of tyrants great and small in the mystery plays (above, chapter 2). The absurdity of Antonio's lust for power is manifest in his tempting Sebastian to join him in assassinating Alonso at the first opportunity after their arrival on the island (2.1.197ff.). Even in the desperate exigency of being shipwrecked, Antonio's sense of mutual support is so deficient that he can think of nothing but his own political advantage among a community of six castaways. In this characteristic, too, Antonio contrasts with his brother, who is capable of renouncing his power when it is at its height. But Antonio has a kindred soul in Stephano, who quickly thinks of inheriting the island (2.2.173), though as far as he knows, it has only five inhabitants: Caliban, Trinculo, Prospero, Miranda, and himself. With a little information and encouragement from Caliban, Stephano quickly sinks to Antonio's level, planning an assassination attempt on the lord of the island: "Monster, I will kill this man. His daughter and I will be king and queen—save our Graces!—and Trinculo and thyself shall be viceroys" (3.2.107–9).

In sum, while Shakespeare's debt to the medieval dramatic heritage in *The Tempest* is general, it is also distinctive and definitive. A king and duke, like Shakespeare's tragic heroes, are most noble when their human fragility is most apparent, and the dramatic model for this paradox is not the royal apotheosis of the court masque but the afflicted peasant in medieval passion plays, who, like Lear, is every inch a king when he smells strongest of mortality. The same model, moreover, applies to the strange case of Caliban, a subhuman monster despised by everyone, who is yet surprisingly ennobled, as his social superiors are, by his repentance. "An heroical spirit," Daniel Dyke maintains, consists not in "a word and a blow, a lie and a stab" but in repentance, which "is a far greater argument of a noble and generous spirit than to pursue so eagerly the revenge of every petty injury."[31] If this concept of heroism is a characteristic of Shakespeare's romances that looks forward to Milton, it is not because Shakespeare was a radical Puritan but because Milton schooled himself in the same theological tradition that gave rise to the archaic dramaturgy Shakespeare turned to as a means of qualifying Jacobean social privilege in his late plays.

While a general contrast between that archaic heritage and courtly expectation appears in *The Tempest*, a more specific contrast is evident in *The Winter's Tale*. To be sure, in this play too Shakespeare shows a keen awareness of what was socially most acceptable. Commoners are outnumbered almost two to one by their social betters and are cast in exclusively comic roles. Perdita's apparent exception to this generalization is a classic illustration of why pastoral conventions gained such a wide appeal in the Renaissance, for she embodies a fantasy of upward mobility: concealing true nobility, unknown to her, beneath lower-class social restrictions until her identity is discovered, she is suddenly elevated to her deserving status and marriage with a prince. Shakespeare treats the social dimensions of pastoral explicitly with wry good humor in the comic promotion of Perdita's adoptive father and brother, who are inordinately proud to be suddenly gentlemen born and to shed their first gentlemenlike tears when the king recognizes them as his in-laws (5.2.128–75). These are precisely the malapert assheads whose social advancement was so distressing to those with long-established privilege, as well as to those whose more recently won prestige was threatened with dilution by the arrival of newcomers. The expectations of sophisticated taste are also met in *The Winter's Tale* in the masquelike statue scene (5.3), with its allusions to a contemporary Italian artist and use of stage spectacle to produce a sense of wonder in the beholder.[32] The drawing of a curtain to reveal a hidden mystery and Paulina's command, "Music, awake her; strike!" (5.3.98) are strongly reminiscent of techniques in court entertainment. Music was used very similarly, for example, in Dekker's pageant called "Nova Felix Arabia" on one of the triumphal arches celebrating James's royal entry:

> But a strange and heavenly music suddenly striking through their ears, which causing a wildness and quick motion in their looks, drew them to light upon the glorious presence of the King, they were suddenly thereby daunted and sunk down.[33]

Yet in spite of an undeniable openness to courtly fashion in *The Winter's Tale*, the play also embraces elements of popular dramaturgy whose very presence negates the neoclassical separation of styles on which the socially exclusive assumptions of the ruling fashion were based. A good example of deliberate indecorum in this play is the treatment of royalty. Thomas Rymer's objections to the indecorous representation of Shakespearean tragic heroes (above, chapter 9) applies with equal force to the romances—and for the same reason: because in the latc plays Shakespeare again turns to medieval religious drama for inspiration. Compare the stage image of the pregnant Hermione with Rymer's fulminations against Shakespeare's treatment of a Roman matron:

> [Shakespeare's] brains are turned, he raves and rambles without any coherence, any spark of reason, or any rule to control him or set bounds to his frenzy. His imagination was still running after his masters, the cobblers and parish clerks and Old Testament strollers. So he might make bold with Portia as they had done with the Virgin Mary, who, in a church acting their play called *The Incarnation*, had usually the *Ave Mary* mumbled over to a straddling wench (for the Blessed Virgin), straw-hatted, blue-aproned, big-bellied, with her Immaculate Conception up to her chin.[34]

Rymer is scandalized by Shakespeare's stage mistreatment of upper-class women: to him, it is not merely a social and artistic lapse but a moral failure that requires his scathing rhetoric and can only be compared to the blasphemous treatment of holy women in popular medieval drama.

Rymer's assertion about medieval stage analogues in Shakespeare is worth considering where the pregnant Hermione is concerned, for some of the pageants that include the Virgin Mary indeed offer instructive parallels to *The Winter's Tale*. The pageants involving Joseph's doubt about his pregnant fiancée are a case in point. Joseph's suspicion is sexual, like Leontes', though Joseph has more warrant for his misgiving than Leontes, because Mary is pregnant without Joseph's having done anything about it. Gail Gibson has studied the figure of jealous Joseph and has traced it to the fourteenth century and the reaction to nominalism and Wycliffite skepticism about the mysteries of faith.[35] Mary's suspicious husband, in other words, became popular at about the same time that the mystery plays were first being staged, and for much the same reason: as the plays were designed to encourage faith in God's mighty acts, Joseph was depicted as an exemplar of wayward doubt about the greatest act of all, the incarnation. His resemblance to Leontes therefore goes beyond sexual jealousy and includes the epistemological issues that pervade *The Winter's Tale*, from Leontes' total conviction about the reliability of his "knowledge" to Paulina's declaration that he needs to awake his faith. Even in the brief Coventry play of Joseph's doubt, Joseph adopts a tone of superior worldly knowledge about the inevitable activity of young women with aged husbands:

> Huse-bond, in feythe! and that acold!
> A! Weylle-awey, Josoff, as thow are olde!
> Lyke a fole now ma I stand
> And truse.[36]   *trust*

This attitude parallels Leontes' unshakeable generalizations about open gates, the bawdy planet, and the condition he shares with the steer, the heifer, and the calf.[37] Both jealous husbands also generalize from their own situation to that of the audience in passages of direct audience address:

> JOSEPH: All olde men, insampull take be me—
> How I am be-gylid here may you see!—
> To wed soo yong a chyld.[38]

> LEONTES: There have been,
> Or I am much deceiv'd, cuckolds ere now;
> And many a man there is, even at this present,
> Now while I speak this, holds his wife by th'arm,
> That little thinks she has been sluic'd in's absence
> And his pond fish'd by his next neighbor, by
> Sir Smile, his neighbor.
> (1.2.190–96)

Joseph's reductive empiricism views a miracle with an overactive fabliau imagination and makes it an act of gross infidelity: Gibson points to an iconographical tradition of Joseph's doubt that shows him touching his wife's pregnant womb, a gesture analogous to that of doubting Thomas.[39] Leontes is not confronted with a miracle, but he is like Joseph in his "eagerness to snatch at proofs," as Coleridge puts it, his "grossness of conception, and a disposition to degrade the object of it. Sensual fancies and images."[40]

Though Joseph is no tyrant, his mistrust of Mary and her pregnancy makes him, in effect, an enemy of God, which is the condition of every tyrant in the mystery plays. Joseph's abuse of Mary is thus theologically analogous to the oppression of the suffering poor, who are the friends of God in the old drama: "Deposethe myghty oute of place / And mylde allso he hansed hasse," as the Chester author renders the Magnificat.[41] This configuration of oppressive power and innocent suffering is ubiquitous in the mystery plays, taking its impetus from the passion sequence, which bequeathes significance to other instances of it, including Joseph's oppression of Mary—however mild that instance may be in comparison with the passion itself. In Shakespeare's late plays, the same configuration appears frequently, and while it does not take its significance from the passion, it does perpetuate a stage tradition that originates in the suffering of Christ and all that it implies socially, especially in comparison with changing conceptions of power in the Renaissance.

Leontes' reenactment of this pattern thus identifies him dramaturgically with tyrants like Herod and Pharaoh, a point that is reinforced by the recurrence of the word "innocent" in the scenes of Hermione's suffering, reaching a climax in her trial.

> My third comfort,
> Starr'd most unluckily, is from my breast,
> The innocent milk in it most innocent mouth,
> Hal'd out to murder.
> (3.2.98–101)

Like Herod, Leontes is a slaughterer of innocents, and a stage pattern from Herod's slaughter in the mystery plays in fact appears in *The Winter's Tale* when Paulina enters with the infant Perdita in her arms and boldly confronts the raging Leontes (2.3). In several of the cycles (including the Coventry fragments), the mothers of Herod's intended victims verbally abuse, and sometimes even attack, the soldiers who are trying to destroy the babies in their arms. Critics have noticed the strange mixture of violent farce and horrific inhumanity in Paulina's braving of Leontes.[42] What has gone unremarked is the dramaturgical precedent this effect has in medieval depictions of the slaughter of the innocents.

Leontes' tyranny looks back not only to medieval drama but to Shakespeare's mature tragedies. Leontes' assault on innocents has none of the Stoic rectitude about it that characterizes Titus but instead recalls Macbeth, for both Leontes and Macbeth achieve the same result in their assault on innocent sufferers: they destroy their own innocence in the process.[43] "What we chang'd / Was innocence for innocence," asserts Polixenes, of his boyhood friendship with Leontes (1.2.68–69). Nothing threatens this friendship until Leontes is seized with the insane jealousy that provokes his abuse of Hermione. Then follows alienation, sleeplessness, and despair, the condition of Macbeth, as well as the condition of a tyrant like Cain in the old plays, when he cuts himself off from the source of life and love, the "great bond" of human community:

> Nor night nor day no rest. It is but weakness
> To bear the matter thus, mere weakness. If
> The cause were not in being—part o'th' cause,
> She th' adultress; for the harlot king
> Is quite beyond mine arm, out of the blank
> And level of my brain, plot-proof; but she
> I can hook to me—say that she were gone,
> Given to the fire, a moi'ty of my rest
> Might come to me again.
> (2.3.1–9)

This is the suffering and rationalization of Macbeth: his agony at having scorched the snake, not killed it, his fear of being merely weak in not being more ruthless, his determination to kill again, and his unrelieved insomnia: " 'Sleep no more! / Macbeth does murder sleep.' The innocent sleep." Macbeth's dusty death is Leontes' winter's tale, and both have a dramatic heritage in the alienation of Cain and the despairing death of Herod.

Leontes' tryanny and sexual jealousy conflate two traditions of Herod that Shakespeare could have known, one popular and the other elite. The medieval ranter and persecutor of innocents was still widely reputed in the early seventeenth century, and Shakespeare may actually have seen him in Coventry as a child, but another Herod story had been published for the first time in English only ten years before Shakespeare wrote *The Winter's Tale*. Thomas Lodge's translation of Josephus' *Of The Antiquitie of the Jews* (1602) includes the story of Herod and his wife Mariamne, which had received numerous dramatic treatments on the continent in the sixteenth century, most of them in the Senecan vein.[44] Two contemporary English plays show the influence of this story, though neither seems to have been staged. The first is Elizabeth Carey's *Tragedy of Mariam* (ca. 1604; published 1613), and the second is *The Second Maiden's Tragedy*, which is almost exactly contemporary with *The Winter's Tale* (i.e., 1610–11). Moreover, though the bulk of the latter play is probably by Middleton, Eric Rasmussen has recently discovered evidence that parts of it may be by Shakespeare.[45] Mariamne's story is relevant to Hermione's in that it deals with Herod's morbid sexual suspicion of his wife (with no basis in fact), his eventual trial of her and order for her execution, and his profound remorse after her death. These elements are common to *Othello* too, of course, and the Mariamne story has been compared with Shakespeare's tragedy of sexual jealousy, but not with his romance on the same theme.[46] The possible presence of this distinctively Renaissance Herod tradition in *The Winter's Tale* may be another instance, among many in that play, of Shakespeare's deliberately combining two traditions from different kinds of sources that had quite different social implications.

Leontes' tale finally has more than a winter (unlike Herod's, Othello's, or Macbeth's), and Leontes' resemblance to Joseph extends to the transformation of doubt into faith. In both cases, this transformation depends on a child that is rejected *in utero* and unexpectedly restores its father's well being. The paradox of the child redeeming the father is at the heart of all the plays of Joseph's doubt, and it reappears in another form in *The Winter's Tale* when Perdita's escape to Sicily with Florizel becomes the means of her father's reconciliation with Polixenes and Hermione. The medieval precedent is almost certainly at work here, because the pregnant Hermione is consistent with Shakespeare's stage use of pregnant women as symbols of comic hope. In *Measure for Measure*, Juliet is sullied by Angelo's harsh pursuit of the "old law," though he cannot meet its standards himself. When she appears in the last scene of the play, however, her baby has been transformed by the subsequent action from a symbol of public shame to a symbol of new life and reconciliation.[47] In *All's Well That Ends Well*, Helena's pregnancy has the same kind of ambiguity: from one perspective, it is a product of Bertram's blind lust, which is the play's analogue to Claudio's "too much liberty," Leontes' "bawdy planet," and Joseph's "Frensche gyse." Viewed another way, however, Helena's pregnancy is a miracle that awakens her husband's faith, as Leontes' faith is awakened by a theatrical miracle at the end of *The Winter's Tale*, and Joseph's is awakened by the angel. In *Pericles*, Thaisa appears in dumb show, pregnant with Mariana (3.Cho.s.d.), again presaging a father's redemption by a child still enwombed. Both Mary and Hermione courageously endure harsh suspicion, and reconciliation is effected in both cases not only by a once rejected child but by the fathers' repentance and their serene wives' readiness to forgive.

Where power is concerned, archaic dramaturgy in *The Winter's Tale* has the same effect that it has in *The Tempest*, where it qualifies the assumptions underlying Renaissance social privilege. We have just seen an example in Rymer's strictures about Portia, for they apply equally to Hermione, who is even closer to the medieval models that Rymer saw as the corrupters of Shakespeare's imagination. Leontes as a Humanum Genus figure has been discussed by R. G. Hunter,[48] and the dramatic pattern in this case (as in Prospero's and Alonso's) has nothing to do with the Jacobean court and everything to do with plays like *King Robert of Sicily* (above, chapter 9), whose kingdom Shakespeare in fact has Leontes inherit, thus departing from Greene's *Pandosto*, where the sexually paranoid king rules Bohemia. Insofar as Leontes' rage is associated with the likes of Herod or Joseph, it creates a very different effect from the rage of a character like Arbaces in Beaumont and Fletcher's *A King and No King*, produced by the King's Men in the same year as *The Winter's Tale*. For Arbaces' grandiloquent transport is traceable to Senecan tragedy and late classical oratorical declamation, whose aims were to enhance the heroic proportions of the actor or speaker who represented a royal or mythical figure.[49] The representation of royalty in Fletcherian tragicomedy, in other words, is designed to magnify the royal image, whereas Leontes' rage has just the opposite effect: his kingly dignity is debased, he becomes a common *jalou* (hence the importance of his continuity with Joseph the carpenter and his fabliau associations), and Leontes only regains a semblance of nobility in the act of admitting his failure:

> I have too much believ'd mine own suspicion.
> Beseech you, tenderly apply to her

Some remedies for life. Apollo, pardon
My great profaneness 'gainst thine oracle!
    (3.2.151–54)

Ultimately Leontes thus humbles himself before a cosmic and benefi-
cent source of power, as King Robert does, and the effect is not to enhance the royal image itself but to dignify it with its proportionate place
and to humanize the man who bears it, as the old king is humanized by
the recognition of his mortality in *King Lear.*

While no commoner achieves the insight of Leontes in *The Winter's
Tale,* the commons as a whole come wonderfully to life in the great
sheepshearing festival (4.4). This literal mingling of kings and clowns is
Shakespeare's answer to Sidney's stricture about social decorum in
drama, a stricture that looks forward to Rymer. In Mopsa and Dorcas,
Autolycus and the unnamed clown, Shakespeare perpetuates the pastoral realism of medieval drama, not the pastoral artifice of neoclassical
tradition that became an elegant symbol of courtly striving in the Renaissance. Here again Shakespeare departs from Fletcher, who had recently tried unsuccessfully to correct the pastoral image on the popular
stage in *The Faithful Shepherdess* (1608–9). Fletcher followed the new
model for tragicomedy established by Guarini, and he discovered that
vulgar taste was disappointed to encounter something so unfamiliar:

> It is a pastoral tragicomedy, which the people seeing when it was
> played, having ever had a singular gift in defining, concluded to be a
> play of country hired shepherds, in gray cloaks, with curtal dogs in
> strings, sometimes laughing together, and sometimes killing one
> another; and missing Whitsun ales, cream, wassail, and morris
> dances, began to be angry.[50]

Shakespeare bows to neoclassical pastoral expectation in the elevation
of Perdita, as we have seen, but he makes her fully naturalized in her
peasant setting. "Methinks I play as I have seen them do / In Whitsun
pastorals," she says (4.4.133–34), thus alluding to precisely the kind of
thing a popular audience expected to see and quite possibly responding
to Fletcher's critique of that audience at the same time.

Fletcher's interest in Guarini cannot accurately be described as a
product of neoclassical taste, since Guarini had been condemned in Italy
by neo-Aristotelian critics,[51] but Fletcher's preoccupation may well have
been motivated by the same social development that produced neoclassicism in the first place, namely, the centralization of power. For the
courts of Renaissance princes became centers of culture and learning as
they became centers of power, and the resulting fascination with symbols of power was not always perfectly consistent—including, as it did,
both the neoclassical separation of styles on social principles and also

the new tragicomedy from Italy. What they had in common was a strict demarcation between the magniloquent prince and illiterate fellows. Even so outspoken a classicist as Jonson placed tragicomedy (not tragedy) at the apex of the genres on the title page of his 1616 *Works*, and his finest achievements were his masques—a spectacular, exclusively courtly form, of distinctly Renaissance provenance, whose end was to italicize royal power. Jonson's impatience with archaic dramaturgy in Shakespeare thus looks foward to Rymer in its perception of formal imperfection as a moral lapse:

> If there be never a servant-monster [in *Bartholomew Fair*], who can help it? he says; nor a nest of antics? He is loath to make nature afraid in his plays, like those that beget Tales, Tempests, and such like drolleries, to mix his head with other men's heels, let the concupiscence of jigs and dances reign as strong as it will amongst you.[52]

Jonson's concern here is not concupiscence itself (that is the province of Zeal-of-the-Land Busy in his own play), but the failure to distinguish vulgar dancing dramaturgically from morally ennobling action, as Jonson always did himself in the masque, where vicious and disordered action is portrayed in the opening antimasque and then banished by the royal symbolism of the masque itself. The antimasque of *Oberon, The Fairy Prince* thus includes a chorus of satyrs who initially make "antic action and gestures" but are transformed by the epiphany of Prince Henry.[53] The same actors who played satyrs in *Oberon* in January 1611, may also have appeared in *The Winter's Tale* a few months later, where "a dance of twelve Satyrs" takes place during the sheepshearing festival, "one three of whom," as the servant says, "by their own report, sir, hath danced before the king" (4.4.337–38).[54] Whether the actors were the same or not, the dramaturgy is certainly different, for in *The Winter's Tale* the satyrs dance before the king incognito at a peasant festival. Jonson's complaint about Shakespeare's concupiscent dances is thus another version of Sidney's complaint about mingling kings and clowns: when the royal image is presented theatrically, it should be enhanced, so as to elevate it morally—to create a theatrical version of the monarch's Platonic Idea. To mix that image confusedly with popular jigs and dances, as Shakespeare does in *The Winter's Tale*, is thus an ethical as well as a dramaturgical lapse. Jonson correctly perceived Shakespeare's violation of courtly social decorum in the theater, and he regarded such a lapse, in effect, as a profanation, as Whetstone had done earlier (above, chapter 8) and as Rymer was to do some seventy years later.

Archaic dramaturgy distinguishes *The Winter's Tale* from contemporaneous drama not only in its explicit treatment of social class but also in the quality of dramatic illusion it produces. Barbara Mowat has pointed out that the romances are markedly more "presentational" than the histories or tragedies: audience-directed soliloquies, obtrusive entrance announcements, and doggerel exits are revived in these plays, and all serve to create an audience detachment that is reminiscent of medieval drama. "Had Shakespeare produced his Romances early in his career, we could, in fact, easily explain their curiously nondramatic quality in terms of a medieval romance-play heritage not yet out-grown."[55] We noticed a specific example in Joseph's and Leontes' turning to us who watch them and including us in their own (supposed) condition as duped cuckolds. Such a gesture interrupts our imaginative identification with the play and creates a moment of detachment from it, as we are compelled to think of ourselves and our condition in the world outside the theater.

The political implications of dramatic illusion were first pointed out by Bertolt Brecht, who deliberately eschewed the proscenium arch tradition and revived something like the open staging of Renaissance popular drama in order to achieve what he called an "alienation effect," or pronounced dramatic detachment.[56] Brecht's aim was explicitly political, designed to compel an audience into recognition of power relations and class exploitation. Brecht's dramaturgy therefore anticipates recent critical developments like the New Historicism, and productions of Shakespeare in the English-speaking world are beginning to respond to the self-conscious model Brecht put forward in his own drama almost half a century ago.[57] These movements are salutary in raising consciousness about tacit conservative commitments—critical, theatrical, and political alike. But Shakespeare's peculiar political attachments are easy to misread, as we noticed in chapters 1 and 2, especially if they are construed against a background of medieval religious drama that is also misread. Shakespeare's difference from court drama is real, but it is not the same as the difference, say, between Brecht and fascist propaganda, as careful attention to the quality of Renaissance dramatic illusion makes clear.

On the one hand, the dramatic engagement demanded of an audience reaches a height of uncritical intensity in the court masque, where brilliant and cunning illusions were specifically designed to overwhelm and awe its exclusive auditors, though they were not much inclined to skepticism about what they saw anyway because their own social privilege depended on it so heavily. At certain moments in *The Winter's Tale*, something like this kind of intense engagement is created, only to be qualified in ways that point directly to what Mowat calls Shakespeares's "medieval romance-play heritage." As an example, consider Perdita in her role as queen of the sheepshearing feast (4.4). A number of things about her are reminiscent of the masque. First, she wears the allegorical costume of a goddess, a point that is mentioned by Prince Florizel, who can be expected to understand such mysteries, decorously enough, because he is a prince:

> These your unusual weeds to each part of you
> Does give a life; no shepherdess, but Flora
> Peering in April's front.
>   (4.4.1–5)

In thus costuming Perdita, Shakespeare may have recalled the published account of Lord Hay's masque (1607), which opened with "Flora, the queen of flowers, attired in a changeable taffeta gown, with a large veil embroidered with flowers, a crown of flowers, and white buskins painted with flowers."[58] The reminisence is made more likely by the fact that Flora proceeded to strew flowers about the stage—a detail that Shakespeare includes but that has no precedent in Greene's *Pandosto*. Second, and more important, Perdita's costume is an allegorical expression of her nature, as the costumes of royalty properly are in the masque. "Let the suits of the masquers be graceful, and such as become the person when the vizards are off," Bacon specifies.[59] Prince Henry's imperial weeds are a case in point, but a closer parallel to Perdita is Queen Anne's costume in *The Masque of Queens* (1609). For the queen wore a headdress that incorporated a celestial sphere, signifying her cosmic role as Bell-Anna, Queen of the Ocean, whose royal mind was a reflection of cosmic divinity.[60] By the same token, Perdita costumed as Flora, goddess of spring, is revealed symbolically as the principle of rejuvenation that she essentially is—the princess who is Leontes' sole heir and therefore his sole hope for the future. If the red blood reigns in the winter's pale in this play, it does so because of Perdita's return to Sicily and the resulting reconciliation of Leontes, Polixenes, and Hermione. Perdita as a masquelike Flora thus complements Perdita as the child who redeems its father in medieval drama.

Yet Perdita's costume does not work exactly like Queen Anne's, because the two ultimately function, as illusion, in opposite ways. Our engagement with the masque's illusion must be absolute, because that illusion serves the purpose of revealing the royal nature. That is why the illusion is heightened by elaborate symbolic costume, music, dance, and Vitruvian machinery: we approach Pan because we are enabled to approach Proteus in the illusions of the masque. But for Perdita the opposite occurs: the more we think about her as Flora, the more detached we become from the play's illusion. Florizel may announce her role accurately, but neither he nor she is aware of that fact: ironically, the princess does not herself know what her costume reveals about her as princess because she does not even know she *is* a princess. The intelligence that bestows Florizel's knowledge on him is not his own but the playwright's, and the more we think about Perdita as Flora, the more aware we become of the play as a play. If we recognize Perdita's costume as an emblem of her royal nature, in the manner of the masque, we are brought up short by the realization that she is not really a princess either, in the same way Queen Anne was a queen: "Perdita" is a boy playing a princess who thinks she is a shepherdess playing a goddess, and even though her costume suggests divinity, her link with cosmic power is not through Platonic symbol but through her unselfconscious humility and her "real" identity as a shepherdess, in the manner of the mystery plays. "The gods themselves," as Florizel tells her in explaining his own costume, "humbling their deities to love, have taken / The shapes of beasts upon them" (4.4.25–27).

The same detachment recurs when Perdita distributes flowers to those who have assembled for the pastoral feast. Here again, the scene becomes quasi-allegorical, intensifying Perdita's identification with Flora and decorously associating various flowers emblematically with those on whom Perdita bestows them.[61] But there are unexpected limits to this one-to-one correspondence, as Perdita admits: she lacks the flowers of spring—daffodils, violets, primroses, oxlips, the crown imperial, and lilies. This is a curious omission, given the fact that everything about the scene points to its having a springtime setting: Flora, goddess of spring, the sheepshearing, the allusion to Whitsuntide. Yet Perdita has only the flowers of middle summer and what she calls "flowers of winter," i.e., evergreens—rosemary and rue. The omission of spring flowers is so emphatic and so odd that we cannot help wondering about it, but the explanation is not in *Pandosto*, and it takes us in the opposite direction from allegory and emblem: it takes us in the direction of the theatrical limitations of a bare stage and therefore interrupts our imaginative identification with the stage illusion. Perdita lacks spring flowers because Shakespeare's acting company lacked them: the playing season began after the spring was over, when the weather was sufficiently warm and clement to permit outdoor performance. Perdita also lacks the flowers of autumn for the same reason, though Shakespeare covers this lack by attributing to her a niceness about hybrids and thereby introducing her conversation with Polixienes about nature and art. The flowers we actually see on stage, then (at least if we accept natural limitations), are summer flowers and evergreens—the first being seasonal and the latter available the year round. This is literally an art that nature makes—the art that Polixenes defends—and it is the opposite of the illusionistic art of the masque, which could make spring in the midst of winter.[62] Our awareness of the playwright's limitations ultimately issues in an enhanced appreciation of his ability to make a virtue out of theatrical necessity—a virtue both artistic and ideological.

The peculiar detachment of medieval dramaturgy clarifies more than the difference between Shakespearean romance and the court

masque: it also adds new insight to the much discussed distinction between the late plays and Fletcherian tragicomedy.[63] This may seem an
odd claim, on the face of it, because the plays of Beaumont and Fletcher
capitalize on elegant moments of esthetic detachment, whereas self-conscious esthetic distance of any kind is virtually nonexistent in medieval
drama: in that respect, the detachment from stage illusion in the romances is not archaic at all but strikingly innovative and even modern.
Yet with tragicomedy, too, as with the court masque, Shakespeare's revival of medieval dramaturgy provides a corrective to first impressions.

By the time Shakespeare wrote *The Winter's Tale*, Beaumont and
Fletcher had produced two tragicomedies: *Philaster*, in 1609, and *A King
and No King*, in 1611. Both were acted by the King's Men, so there is
little doubt that Shakespeare knew them, and he probably knew the theory behind them, announced somewhat self-importantly in Fletcher's
preface to *The Faithful Shepherdess*, printed no later than 1610. We have
already noticed that Shakespeare's depiction of shepherds deviates from
the social assumptions underlying Fletcher's theory, despite the fact that
Fletcher's star was rising quickly, and the dramatic form he introduced
to the English commercial stage would remain the most popular and
influential form of the seventeenth century. While very little in *The
Winter's Tale* specifically recalls Fletcher's plays, it shares with them a
number of dramaturgical features besides self-conscious esthetic detachment—such features as sudden and unexpected turns of plot, emotion-
ally charged dialogue, Protean characterization (especially evident in
Leontes), and tableaux-like scenes in which the theatrical images tend
to be monumental and stationary rather than fluid and mimetic.

Nearly all these features appear in the climactic episode of *The Winter's Tale*, the reunion of Hermione and Leontes. This is certainly the
most unexpected turn of any plot in Shakespeare's plays, depending as
it does on information concealed form the audience and therefore repro-
ducing a favorite Fletcherian device. (It is used in both *Philaster* and *A
King and No King*.) Moreover, the extraordinary balance of imaginative
engagement with esthetic detachment in this scene has long been admired. Hermione's animation is an undeniably effective moment in the
theater, fulfilling our hopes for Leontes' happiness beyond all expectation and yet at the same time calling attention to itself repeatedly as art.
Indeed, perhaps the best description of audience response to this scene
is James Shirley's description of the art of Beaumont and Fletcher, pre-
fixed to the 1647 folio:

> You may here find passions raised to that exellent pitch and by such
> insinuating degrees that you shall not choose but consent and go
> along with them, finding yourself at last grown insensibly the very
> same person you read, and then stand admiring the subtle tracks of
> your engagement.[64]

Yet differences between Fletcher and Shakespeare remain, and they can be specified in the purpose and function of detachment in the final scene of *The Winter's Tale*. We noticed earlier that characterization in Fletcher is determined largely by the ends of rhetorical declamation, with the result that the stage impression of the actor is heightened at the same time that the character is distanced from mimetic psychology or plot. The result is the Protean characterization and convoluted plots that are so often cited as a hallmark of this dramaturgy. Our detachment, then, serves the purpose of admiration—"to raise an act to full astonishment," as Robert Herrick put it in a commendatory poem to the Beaumont and Fletcher first folio;[65] "admiring the subtle tracks of your engagement," as Shirley says. What we admire is rhetorical display and the heroic proportions it suggests—a point that Dryden would learn from Beaumont and Fletcher in the Restoration, when their plays were the most popular of all those from before the closing of the theaters. Fletcherian tragicomedy is thus an important step in the transition from high-sounding *tyrants* like Herod and Pilate in the mystery plays to the high-sounding *heroes* of the Restoration heroic drama. The transition is not merely stylistic; it involves a changing ideology of power and a new conception of the human situation itself.

Shakespeare was also a transitional playwright, of course, but his plays are sensitive to what drama was moving away from as well as to what it was moving toward. Dramatic detachment in the climactic scene of *The Winter's Tale* thus functions much more as detachment does in the mystery plays than in Fletcherian tragicomedy. As V. A. Kolve has pointed out, when sacred subjects were mimetically represented (not, that is, ritually reenacted, as in the mass), detachment created constant reminders that this was "play" and not the real thing, however serious the play might be.[66] Shakespeare's subject in *The Winter's Tale* is not sacred, but the detachment he creates nonetheless works in much the way Kolve describes, while at the same time it italicizes the scene as art.

When Hermione's "statue" comes to life, the situation in the theater is closely analogous to medieval representations of miracles of the Host. While the best known example of these dramatized miracles is the Croxton *Play of the Sacrament*, Leah Marcus has pointed out that the mystery plays frequently use close parallels to sacramental miracle.[67] In any case, the stage miracle effectively contributes to the purpose of the plays themselves in providing visual evidence of the sacred presence. Invariably, such miracles are designed to answer skeptical disbelief, which is often expressed in abuse of eucharistic elements. The Croxton play is a case in point, where Aristorius steals the Host in order to sell it for a large sum to the cynical Jonathas and his cohorts, who mock and stab it. The same motif informs Mak's and Gil's parody of the Nativity in the Wakefield *Second Shepherd's Play*, and Joseph's abuse of the preg-

nant Mary in plays of Joseph's doubt. In every case, the audience witnesses blasphemous and often comical skepticism about the Host or the
Christ child and sees that skepticism answered with a visual representation of a miracle that produces belief: the crucified Christ rises from a
vat of boiling oil and wins the astonished belief of acquisitive merchants
and lapsed priests; the angel appears to the shepherds, who obediently
proceed to Bethlehem; the angel warns Joseph to cease his doubt about
his wife's miraculous pregnancy, and he does so, asking her to forgive
his earlier abuse of her. No angel appears in *The Winter's Tale*, but Hermione's statue comes to life in a moment when audience engagement is
intense because we believe her to be dead, and the initial impact of this
moment is therefore very close to the miraculous moments in medieval
drama. This parallel reinforces other parallels between Joseph and
Leontes that give the two a common metaphorical context: Leontes'
sexual jealousy, his abuse of Hermione, her serene endurance, his repentance, the awaking of his "faith," her loving forgiveness, and their
eventual reconciliation through the agency of the child Leontes had rejected.

Our response to this scene thus involves more than detached admiration for rhetorical display. Whether we recognize the parallel to traditional stage miracle or not, our initial response to Hermione's waking is
precisely the same as any audience's response to "visual proof" of miracle on stage. When blood poured in a steady stream from the risen
Christ's side in a 1983 production of the Chester Cycle's play of the
ascension, very few people laughed at the obvious mechanism that produced the "blood," and their laughter did not spread: engagement was
too intense.[68] For an audience that readily accepted miracles as a possible part of workaday reality, a stage miracle would be even more stunning, and it is therefore noteworthy that Shakespeare reinforces the un-
avoidable detachment of the bare stage with additional reminders that
this is play and not the real thing. Thus we are repeatedly assured that
the statue's animation is not the result of witchcraft. When Paulina offers to make the statue move, she hesitates because she fears "you'll
think— / Which I protest against—I am assisted / By wicked pow'rs"
(5.3.89–91). She bids those depart who think the business is "unlawful"
(96–97); she assures her audience that Hermione's actions "shall be
holy, as / You hear my spell is lawful" (104–5); and when Leontes embraces Hermione, he exclaims, "If this be magic, let it be an art / Lawful
as eating" (110–11).

But while this scene is admirable for more than mere rhetorical display, it also disengages our response by something more than the simple
devices of medieval drama. Only the most naive auditor would need to
be literally warned that the scene was not witchery—yet such auditors
the play has undoubtedly had. For a modern audience, the covert allu-

sions to black magic (if only to deny it) probably heighten the scene's imaginative intensity, and for those who have eyes and ears for them, the scene offers an almost endless series of reflections: the immediate recognition that this is not a represented miracle, since Hermione never really died; the further reflection that the statue is not a statue but a boy (or actress) playing Hermione playing a statue; the realization that the fine chisel that cut the lines on this statue's forehead was wielded not by Julio Romano but by an imaginative playwright who thus repudiated once more the unity of time.[69] If the magic of the scene is an art indeed lawful as eating, it is also some of the most compelling imaginative theater ever devised.

Yet that theater employs illusion in a manner that is quite distinct from courtly dramaturgy, as we have seen, and this distinction in itself points to Shakespeare's resistance to the ruling taste and its political implications. "Let me pass / The same I am, ere ancient'st order was / Or what is now received," urges Time (4.1.9–11), in lines that irresistibly suggest the voice of the playwright.[70] "Ancient'st order" and "what is now received" are phrases that precisely describe the courtly standard—classical and neoclassical alike. What follows these lines is equally precise as a description of archaic dramaturgy in *The Winter's Tale*, its durability, and its contemporary disrepute:

> I witness to
> The times that brought them in. So shall I do
> To the freshest things now reigning, and make stale
> The glistering of this present, as my tale
> Now seems to it.
> (4.1.11–15)

These lines are the play's most explicit deviation from the reigning fashion that condemned its stale dramaturgy—the critical fashion that would triumph with Rymer. Ignoring art as an explicit concern of *The Winter's Tale* is equivalent to the neoclassical rejection of popular drama in Shakespeare. What distinguishes the art of this play from estheticism is Shakespeare's openness to a wide range of taste: both what the court approved and what Shakespeare's popular heritage bequeathed him, including its naïveté and political skepticism. This art, in short, does not pretend it is apolitical, because its catholicity is an open declaration of independence from the ruling taste. At the same time, however, art is not ashamed to be more than nature—to include a playfulness and disinterested delight that sometimes offends Puritan and radical populist alike. Shakespeare's ability to plant and o'erwhelm custom is no less real now than it was four hundred years ago, and for once Jonson agreed with him: he was not of an age but for all time.

AFTERWORD ❧ POWER AND ART

The difference between Shakespeare's early romantic comedies and his late romances can be understood, to a very considerable extent, as a difference in the ruling taste. The static dramaturgy and rhetorical virtuosity of *Love's Labors Lost* are a response to the fashion created by John Lyly, whose linguistic preciosity, in turn, sums up the Tudor endorsement of literacy as an innovative sign of social privilege. Evidence of a similar preoccupation with language appears in the mature romantic comedies as well, particularly *As You Like It* and *Much Ado about Nothing*. The spectacular dramaturgy of the romances, on the other hand, often recalls that of the court masque or plays by Beaumont and Fletcher, who catered to the taste of an exclusive playgoing clientele. The romances thus respond to a criterion of privilege that is even more important for the Stuarts than literacy, namely, esthetic refinement. Prospero clearly represents this criterion: his booklearning is important primarily as a means to mastering "art," and art is his principal means to power. Prince Henry's coterie included the kingdom's most brilliant artists, and he was the first English royal personage, as we have just seen, to have himself painted in a heroic equestrian pose. He did so because he knew that that pose was reserved for emperors in Roman art: the refinement of his esthetic taste was in fact a taste for power.

The argument of this book, however, is that only part of Shakespeare's story is told in his sensitivity to the ruling taste: equally important, if not more so, is his dependence on a culturally residual tradition that strongly qualified what the ruling taste stood for. This residual tradition remained alive for him in the popular religious drama that gave rise to the public theater he worked in all his life. Thus, while the romantic comedies and the romances can be distinguished by their sensitivity to historical changes in the center of power, both kinds of play are alike in the way they *qualify* political power and social privilege. The self-awareness gained by Proteus in *Two Gentlemen of Verona* is essentially the same as the self-awareness gained by Posthumus Leonatus in *Cymbeline*: though both are gentlemen and courtiers, the nobility they acquire in the end derives not from inviolate social status but from the discovery and affirmation of their profound vulnerability. This discovery resembles Christian conversion because the sense of self at the heart of medieval religious drama correlates with a vision of political and social order as an order of mere power, with no redemptive capacity in its own right. This order of things prevails at the beginning of all the comedies and romances, and it is transformed not by structural changes in society but by the transformation of individuals within society. The framework of Shakespearean comic structure is thus essentially continuous with the framework of the divine comedy Shakespeare inherited from his immediate predecessors on the English stage.

While the dramaturgy of power in Shakespearean comedy and romance is strikingly neomedieval, what Shakespeare does in the history plays is unlike anything that preceded them. Without a ruling taste to determine what playwrights should do in history, Shakespeare seems to have derived a pattern of his own, based on the real dynamics of centralized power as he observed them in late Elizabethan England. What this pattern owes to medieval religious drama it owes chiefly by default, because Shakespeare's secular sense of history is very different from the providential history that emerges in the cosmic story of the mystery plays—the only other dramatic version of history he could have known. Yet one must be cautious in concluding from this difference that Shakespeare's histories are the product of emergent materialism, because the histories' picture of political order as an endless struggle for power is consistent with Augustine's description of the *Civitas Terrena*, which is caricatured in the mystery plays' portrayal of powerful worldlings. Society is not transformed in the history plays, as it is in the comedies and romances, because the end of human activity in these plays is not self-knowledge but power. Even when a character like Prince Hal models his career closely on the development of a morality play protagonist, the plays suggest that he does so not as a sign of spiritual self-transformation but in the interest of securing political advantage—that is, in the interest of power.[1] While this grim sense of political reality undoubtedly looks forward to the explicit materialism of Hobbes, it also looks back to Augustine's idea that social and political relations are defined by *libido dominandi*.[2] Whether Shakespeare had direct access to Augustine's idea or not, he had indirect access to it through those characters who possess political power in medieval religious drama, whose rhetorical bombast is a stylistic sign of the prideful "new fashion."

All's Well That Ends Well and *Measure for Measure* can be fruitfully understood as comedies in which Shakespeare experimented with the innovative dramaturgy of power he had invented in the history plays. The social and political realism of these "problem" plays is reminiscent of the history plays' realism about human relations in the arena of power: Bertram's class consciousness and Helena's and Duke Vincentio's recourse to the dissimulating exercise of power are more precise reenactments of contemporary social and political reality than anything in the romantic comedies. On one hand, Helena and the duke owe something to the mystery plays' interpretation of the Atonement as God's deception of Satan in order to defeat him. Traceable to patristic theology, this interpretation originally gained acceptance in part because of its compatability with the folklore motif of the Trickster, a motif that clearly animates the peasant Christ in the mystery plays, despite a prevailing scholastic redefinition of the atonement in terms that make the patristic doctrine look naive by comparison. On the other hand, the social implications of the medieval Christ as a peasant trickster are very different from the Renaissance advocacy of dissimulation as a means of gaining and maintaining power. In keeping with what he does in the comedies and romances, Shakespeare uses the medieval motif in the "problem" plays to qualify innovative defenses of coercive power. Helena and Vincentio are thus comparable to Portia in *The Merchant of Venice*: all three characters espouse a spiritual standard that implicitly weighs their own behavior and finds it wanting.

Shakespeare's neomedieval qualification of the Renaissance "new fashion" is nowhere more powerful than in his mature tragedies. Indeed, these plays can be distinguished from an early tragedy like *Titus Andronicus* by their relative distance from the ruling taste. In *Titus* the standard for tragic stature reinforces Elizabethan visions of social privilege. Here an established nobleman stoically endures unimaginable inflictions from duplicitous upstarts, and his endurance therefore provides a self-satisfying vision of suffering for those who craved to have their status vindicated in the face of contemporary upward mobility. When Shakespeare came to his mature tragedies, however, he abandoned fashionable neo-Roman expectations (or what contemporaries took to be Roman expectations, with all that they implied socially) and developed a distinctive tragic mode out of native dramatic tradition. The self-knowledge gained by Hamlet, Lear, Othello, and Macbeth is modelled in each case on the transforming self-discovery that usually distinguishes the powerless from the powerful in medieval religious drama. The tragic effect in these plays derives in the first place not from Stoic endurance but from its opposite: the enlightening encounter with one's own irreducible vulnerability. What makes such an encounter tragic rather than comic (as in the comedies and romances) is the symbolic collapse of its traditional informing context. Macbeth's self-awareness is greater than any other character's in *Macbeth*: no one speaks with greater insight or more haunting eloquence on the subject of Macbeth's destruction than Macbeth himself. Yet Macbeth is the means of his own undoing, and we therefore witness an increase in self-knowledge that ought to be spiritually salutary (both for the subject and his society) but in fact is just the opposite. This innovative tragic effect is indeed radical, but in its dependence on the expected vitality of familiar redemptive symbols, such as forgiveness, self-discovery, or reconciliation, it derives its power from a culturally residual tradition, not from what was culturally emergent.

Indeed, Shakespeare's dependence on residual Christian realism as a means of qualifying Renaissance power may well be crucial to understanding why his drama fell out of favor with the emergence of absolute monarchy in the seventeenth century and the triumph of art as a sign of power. To be sure, English drama under James I and his son embodied considerable resistance to absolute power, as recent critics have pointed out.[3] But with the restoration of the monarchy in 1660, the early humanist penchant for neoclassical decorum was finally vindicated, and as a consequence Shakespearean drama inevitably looked "inartificial," to borrow Sidney's quaint but revealing term.[4] Significantly, the late seventeenth-century model of decorum was France, which was not only the dominant European power but also the residence of Louis XIV, who created a milieu for both the tragedy of Racine and the theoretical criticism of Boileau. In England, Boileau inspired Rymer's fulminations against *Othello*, which provide striking evidence of neoclassicism's appeal to rigid social stratification. Rymer accurately identifies medieval drama as the source of Shakespeare's failure to achieve an artful separation of styles: in effect, Rymer thus prescribes for drama what architects like Sir Christopher Wren were achieving in architecture, namely, the transformation of style from "Gothic" barbarity to neoclassical refinement.

What actually happened in Restoration drama is not what Rymer prescribed, but it nonetheless points to the triumph of power in art. Dryden's "heroic drama" and his championing of the heroic couplet as the appropriate form of the high style are both products of drama's preoccupation with the newly restored monarchy.[5] As semiotic declarations of power, the balance and harmony of the heroic couplet are directly analogous to the balance and harmony of Vitruvian architecture, and it is no coincidence that the two forms began to move toward their future hegemony in the early Stuart years, under the influence, respectively, of Inigo Jones and Ben Jonson.[6] Indeed, Dryden's penchant for rhyme in the first years of the Restoration is part of his attempt to restore a distinctively Stuart art, and rhyme is essential to his dramaturgy of power. "But that benefit which I consider most in [rhyme]," he writes in 1664, "is that it bounds and circumscribes the fancy. For imagination in a poet is a faculty so wild and lawless that, like a high-ranging spaniel, it must have clogs tied to it lest it outrun the judgment."[7] Dryden establishes more than a commonplace of neoclassical criticism here: his positive assessment of judgment in binding and circumscribing the energy of the imagination is a stylistic tribute to the monarch's power over his wild and lawless people. The heroic couplet is the logical outcome of what is celebrated in Renaissance horsemanship—not merely reason containing passion but the learned and rational humanist courtier astride the brutish commons or an esthetically sophisticated monarch directing the chaotic energy of those he rules. Van Dyke's huge equestrian portrait of Charles I is meant to be understood this way, and the ironic disjunction between what that portrait asserts and what Charles actually faced politically is a close parallel to the disjunction between the idealism of the Caroline court masque and the world outside the court.

The revaluation of Shakespeare in such a context is paralleled, not surprisingly, by the revaluation of another writer much influenced by residual Christian realism: Bartolomé de las Casas, with whom this book began and with whom it can appropriately end. For Las Casas' *Most Brief Account of the Destruction of the Indies* is one of the sources for Dryden's *The Indian Emperor* (1665), which was Dryden's first important stage success and one of his most enduringly popular plays.[8] The emperor of Dryden's title is Montezuma, but he is not the play's principal character; that honor is reserved for his Spanish conqueror, Cortez. The play, in short, deals with successful European expansion in the New World, and the arguments Cortez uses to defend his actions are the arguments used by Restoration royalists to defend the actions of Charles II.[9] To be sure, the play is more complex than this summary suggests. Montezuma is a noble primitive, possessed of natural reason and heroic fortitude: he is, after all, a king. Cortez, at the same time, is cruel, coercive, and ruthless, for at one level the play is anti-Catholic and anti-Spanish. This is why Las Casas' exposé of Spanish cruelty was relevant to Dryden, and Dryden's play in fact spins a filament between the residual Christian realism of Las Casas and the dominant secular rationalism of the Enlightenment, given Voltaire's admiration for *The Indian Emperor*, which he saw in the 1770s and on which he based his own play, *Alzier*.[10]

For all its complexity, however, *The Indian Emperor* indubitably belongs to the ideology of centralized power that became dominant in the Renaissance, for Dryden's Cortez most importantly symbolizes royal authority restraining untamed natural energy. Shakespeare's precursor to such an image is Prospero, who controls the chaotic energy of Caliban in another New World setting. But Prospero learns things about himself that Cortez never learns—and cannot be conceived as learning, given his ideological context. By the same token, Dryden's use of Las Casas is a profound historical irony, since Las Casas had appealed to Augustine against the kind of claims made by Dryden's Cortez: "Monarchs may err, but should each private breast / Judge their ill acts, they would dispute their best" (*Indian Emperor*, 2.2.30–31). Such a doctrine requires private citizens, in effect, to grant the monarch infallibility, which is a grant Shakespeare never makes to anyone. If Milton heard this couplet (as he may well have done), he would unquestionably have understood it as a characteristic Stuart blow at Christian liberty, and had Shakespeare taken the ideology of Dryden's couplet as seriously as Dryden did, we would not have Shakespearean drama in the form we know it.

ABBREVIATIONS

CompD	*Comparative Drama*
CompL	*Comparative Literature*
DNB	*Dictionary of National Biography*
EETS	**Early English Text Society**
ELR	*English Literary Renaissance*
ES	*English Studies*
HLQ	*Huntington Library Quarterly*
JEGP	*Journal of English and Germanic Philology*
LeedsSE	*Leeds Studies in English*
MLQ	*Modern Language Quarterly*
MLN	*Modern Language Notes*
N&Q	*Notes and Queries*
RenQ	*Renaissance Quarterly*
RenD	*Renaissance Drama*
REL	*Review of English Literature*
RES	*Review of English Studies*
SQ	*Shakespeare Quarterly*
ShakS	*Shakespeare Studies* (Knoxville, Tennessee)
ShS	*Shakespeare Survey*
SP	*Studies in Philology*
TRHS	*Transactions of the Royal Historical Society*
YES	*Yearbook of English Studies*

NOTES

Preface

1. While the New Historicism is no longer so new, an excellent introduction to it (even for those already familiar with it) is the essay by Herbert Lindenberger, "Toward a New History in Literary Study," *Profession 84* (1984), 16–23. The New Historicist studies that have been most influential in the present book are by Stephen Greenblatt, *Renaissance Self-Fashioning* (Chicago: Univ. of Chicago Press, 1980); Jonathan Dollimore, *Radical Tragedy* (Chicago: Univ. of Chicago Press, 1984); Frank Whigham, *Ambition and Privilege: The Social Tropes of Elizabethan Courtesy Theory* (Berkeley and Los Angeles: Univ. of California Press, 1984), and several articles by Louis A. Montrose (see Works Frequently Cited, below). An important theoretical critique of New Historicism is the article by Edward Pechter, "New Historicism and Its Discontents: Politicizing Renaissance Drama," *PMLA* 102 (1987), 292–303.

2. Raymond Williams, *Marxism and Literature* (Oxford: Oxford Univ. Press, 1977), pp. 121–27.

3. R. A. Markus, *Saeculum: History and Society in the Theology of St. Augustine* (Cambridge: Cambridge Univ. Press, 1970), pp. 1–21.

4. See especially Oliver O'Donovan, *The Problem of Self-Love in Augustine* (New Haven, Conn.: Yale Univ. Press, 1982).

5. Paul Ricoeur, *Freud and Philosophy* (New Haven, Conn.: Yale Univ. Press, 1970), pp. 32–36.

6. Pechter, "New Historicism and Its Discontents," 301.

7. The quoted phrase is from Markus, *Saeculum*, p. 84.

8. Max Weber, *From Max Weber: Essays in Sociology*, trans. and ed. H. H. Gerth and C. Wright Mills (London: Kegan, Paul, Trench, Trübner, 1948), p. 123.

Chapter 1. Centralized Power and Christian Political Realism: Fifth Century and Sixteenth

1. Margaret M. McGowan, "Forms and Themes in Henri II's Entry into Rouen," *RenD*, n.s. 1 (1968), 218–20. For pertinent interpretive comments on the Brazilian village, see Steven Mullaney, "Strange Things, Gross Terms, Curious Customs: The Rehearsal of Cultures in the Late Renaissance," in *Representing the English Renaissance*, ed. Stephen Greenblatt (Berkeley and Los Angeles: Univ. of California Press, 1988), pp. 70–73.

2. Quentin Skinner, *The Foundations of Modern Political Thought* (Cambridge: Cambridge Univ. Press, 1978), 2:3–19. The ambiguities of Luther's position have been explored in a provocative article by Stephen Greenblatt, "Murdering Peasants: Status, Genre and the Representation of Rebellion," in *Representing the English Renaissance*, pp. 1–29. Corroborating Greenblatt's reading of Dürer's

satirical memorial to a peasant is Keith P. F. Moxey's essay, "The Function of Peasant Imagery in German Graphics of the Sixteenth Century: Festive Peasants as Instruments of Repressive Humor" in *Print and Culture on the Renaissance*, ed. Gerald P. Tyson and Sylvia S. Wagonheim (Newark: Univ. of Delaware Press, 1986), pp. 151–88. Greenblatt's attempt to deal with Shakespeare's *2 Henry VI* in light of Luther's response, however, is not entirely convincing, because the revolt Shakespeare stages is the English peasants' revolt, which occurred before the Reformation. This does not mean Shakespeare could not have responded to peasants in the same way Luther did, but it does mean that Shakespeare knew the Reformation was not the only incitement to peasant uprising. For a different way of understanding Shakespeare's early histories in the context of Renaissance social change, see chapter 5, below.

3. Mullaney, "Strange Things," p. 69.

4. *Bartolomé de las Casas*, trans. and ed. George Sanderlin (New York: Alfred A. Knopf, 1971), pp. 86–91.

5. This debate has been studied in two books by Lewis Hanke, *Aristotle and the American Indians* (London: Hollis and Carter, 1959) and *All Mankind is One* (Dekalb: Northern Illinois Univ. Press, 1974).

6. Hanke, *Aristotle and the Indians*, p. 96.

7. I am adapting "emergent" (along with "residual" and "dominant") in a technical sense as described by Raymond Williams and explained above in the Preface.

8. Augustine's influence on Las Casas has been argued most explicitly by David A. Brading, *Prophecy and Myth in Mexican History* (Cambridge: Cambridge Univ. Press, [1984]), pp. 7–27.

9. Skinner, *Foundations*, 2:302–48. See also William J. Bouwsma, "The Two Faces of Humanism: Stoicism and Augustinianism in Renaissance Thought," in *Itinerarium Italicum*, ed. Heiko A. Oberman and Thomas A. Brady (Leiden: E. J. Brill, 1975), pp. 45–46.

10. P.R.L. Brown, "St. Augustine's Attitude to Religious Coercion," *Journal of Roman Studies* 54 (1964), 107–16. For an incisive discussion of Augustine's differences with his contemporaries in regard to coercion, see Elaine Pagels, *Adam, Eve, and the Serpent* (New York: Random House, 1988), pp. 98–126.

11. Augustine, *City of God*, trans. Henry Bettenson (Harmondsworth: Penguin Books, 1972), 1.1. This edition is cited hereafter in the text by book and chapter number.

12. I am indebted here to R. A. Markus, *Saeculum: History and Society in the Theology of St. Augustine* (Cambridge: Cambridge Univ. Press, 1970), pp. 72–104. On the Renaissance humanist reversal of Augustine's redefinition, see Skinner, *Foundations*, 1:91–94.

13. Brading, *Prophecy and Myth*, pp. 25–26.

14. "According to Saint Augustine, what are great kingdoms without justice, but great *latrocinos*, which is to say, dwellings of thieves." Bartolomé de las Casas, *Obras escogidas*, ed. Juan Pérez de Tudela Beuso, 5 vols. (Madrid, 1957), 5:50. Quoted by Brading, *Prophecy and Myth*, p. 16.

15. Markus, *Saeculum*, pp. 45–71.

16. The affinity between Augustine and Hobbes was first pointed out by Herbert A. Deane, *The Political and Social Ideas of St. Augustine* (New York: Columbia Univ. Press, 1963), pp. 46, 47, 50, 56, and 234–36. M. J. Wilks develops

the idea at much greater length in "St. Augustine and the General Will," *Texte und Untersuchungen der Altchristlichen Literatur* 94 (1966), 478–522. Wilks's interpretation of the City of God as a temporal reality, however, is a distortion of Augustine's idea.

17. *City of God* 2.18. Cf. 3.17, where Augustine quotes Sallust on class warfare that issued in the plebeians being granted rights they had not enjoyed before. Augustine knew, in other words (because he read it in Sallust), that class struggle can ameliorate unjust social conditions.

18. Markus describes Thomistic interpretations of Augustine's political ideas as a "conservative deformation" of his thought (*Saeculum*, p. 103), and surveys representative examples on pp. 211–30.

19. Walter Benjamin, *Illuminations*, ed. Hannah Arendt, trans. Harry Zohn (New York: Schocken, 1969), p. 256.

20. *City of God* 5.19. For discussion and further references, see Deane, *Political and Social Ideas*, pp. 143–53.

21. Junius Brutus [Philippe de Mornay], *A Defense of Liberty against Tyrants*, ed. and trans. Harold J. Laski (London: G. Bull and Sons, 1924), p. 78. J. W. Gough points to a parallel instance in the writing of the Spanish humanist, Marius Salamonius, whose *De principatu libri septem* (1544) relates a contract theory of government to Augustine (*The Social Contract* [Oxford: Clarendon Press, 1936], pp. 45–47). On De Mornay and other radical Calvinists, see Skinner, *Foundations*, 2:309–48.

22. For complete references, see Paul Salmon, "The Site of Lucifer's Throne," *Anglia* 8 (1963), 118–23.

23. David Norbrook, *Poetry and Politics in the Renaissance* (London: Routledge and Kegan Paul, 1984), pp. 157–74; Jonathan Dollimore, *Radical Tragedy* (Chicago: Univ. of Chicago Press, 1984), pp. 120–33.

24. *The Prose Works of Fulke Greville, Lord Brooke*, ed. John Gouws (Oxford: Clarendon Press, 1986), pp. 68–69. Like De Mornay, Greville also speaks in the same breath of the tyrant trying "to be equal or above his master, and so to imprison divine laws within the narrowness of will" (p. 67).

25. Frances A. Yates, *Astraea: The Imperial Theme in the Sixteenth Century* (London: Routledge and Kegan Paul, 1975), pp. 29–87.

26. Manuel M. Martinez, "Las Casas on the Conquest of America" in *Bartolomé de las Casas in History*, ed. Juan Friede and Benjamin Keen (Dekalb, Ill.: Northern Illinois Univ. Press, 1971), pp. 326–28.

27. Richard Marius, *Thomas More: A Biography* (London: J. M. Dent, 1984), p. 36. Unfortunately, Marius is interested only in Augustine's impact on More's ascetic psychology, not his politics. See also R. W. Chambers, *Thomas More* (London: Jonathan Cape, 1935), pp. 82–83. I completed this brief discussion of More before discovering Martin W. Raitere's important article, "More's *Utopia* and *The City of God*," *Studies in the Renaissance* 20 (1973), 144–68. While Raitere's treatment is much fuller than mine, both make essentially the same point about Augustine and More, and Raitere does not consider R. A. Markus's careful analysis of Augustine's intellectual growth. Alsitair Fox deals briefly with *The City of God* in his discussion of More's *History of Richard III* in *Thomas More History and Providence* (New Haven, Conn.: Yale Univ. Press, 1982), pp. 96–98.

28. Thomas More, *Utopia*, ed. Edward Surtz and J. H. Hexter, in *The Com-*

plete Works of St. Thomas More (New Haven, Conn.: Yale Univ. Press, 1965), p. 241.

29. On the ambivalence of *Utopia*, see David M. Bevington, "The Dialogue in *Utopia*: Two Sides to the Question," *SP* (1961), 496–509.

30. Surtz and Hexter, eds., *Utopia*, p. 101.

31. Surtz and Hexter, eds., *Utopia*, p. cxiii. Stephen Greenblatt notes that Marx also originally conceived of communism "less as a coherent economic program than as a weapon against certain tendencies in human nature: selfishness and pride. . . ." (*Renaissance Self-Fashioning* [Chicago: Univ. of Chicago Press, 1980], p. 37). In some respects, it is therefore true to say that Marx also looks back to Augustine.

32. Deane, *Political and Social Ideas*, pp. 45–48.

33. R. H. Tawney, *The Agrarian Problem in the Sixteenth Century* (London: Longmans, Green, 1912), pp. 72–139.

34. Theodore H. DeWelles, "The Social and Political Context of the Towneley Cycle" (Ph.D. diss., Univ. of Toronto, 1980), p. 147. DeWelles's section on the Towneley *Mactacio Abel* is called "A Study of the Anti-Communal Character" (pp. 139–70). DeWelles outlines the rising resistance to late medieval communism and its association with millenarian reform (pp. 212–30). This resistance was very strong and persisted into the sixteenth century, when communism became associated with extreme Protestant groups—as it had been with Wycliffe. See Helen C. White, *Social Criticism in Popular Religious Literature of the Sixteenth Century* (New York: Macmillan, 1944), pp. 110–31 and passim.

35. Peter Martyr D'Anghiera, *De orbo novo*, ed. F. A. MacNutt, 2 vols. (New York and London: G. P. Putnam's Sons, 1912), 1:104. Quoted by Brading, *Prophecy and Myth*, p. 8.

36. Surtz and Hexter, eds., *Utopia*, pp. cv–cxxiv.

37. Greenblatt, *Renaissance Self-Fashioning*, pp. 11–73, explains More's ambivalence in terms of an infinitely adaptable irony that he was forced to adopt in the pursuit of power. Greenblatt's perceptive analysis of More's fallibility is sobering and noteworthy, but the thesis of More's infinite adaptability founders on his willingness to die for the sake of what he believed in, a decision that bestows authenticity on his ultimate action, at least. This decision is anticipated, moreover, in More's firm stand against what he saw as heresy in Luther and Tyndale, for religious tyranny (deplorable though it is) is clearly more consistent with religious belief than with ironic agnosticism. One must regret that More was not more charitable, but if he lacked the gift of Enlightenment toleration (which we enjoy), he also lacked a corresponding skepticism that sees through everything and therefore finally sees nothing at all.

Chapter 2. *Libido Dominandi* and *Potentia Humilitatis*: **The Medieval Dramaturgy of Power**

1. Hardin Craig, ed., *Two Coventry Corpus Christi Plays* (2d ed., London: Oxford Univ. Press, 1957), EETS, e.s. 87, *Shearmen and Taylors Pageant*, l. 783s.d. The probability of Shakespeare's seeing this cycle has long been recognized; its most recent authoritative mention is by Samuel Schoenbaum, *Shakespeare: A Documentary Life* (New York: Oxford Univ. Press in association with Scolar Press, 1977), pp. 88 and 121.

2. *The Service for Representing Herod*, in *Medieval Drama*, ed. David M. Bevington (Boston: Houghton Mifflin, 1975), p. 63.

3. Augustine, *City of God*, trans. Henry Bettenson (Harmondsworth, Eng.: Penguin Books, 1972), 1.1. This edition is cited hereafter in the text by book and chapter number.

4. K. S. Block, ed., *Ludus Coventriae* (London: Oxford Univ. Press, 1922), EETS e.s. 120, *Fall of Lucifer*, ll. 58–61.

5. George England, ed., *The Towneley Plays* (London: Kegan Paul, Trench, Trübner, 1897), EETS e.s. 71, *The Creation*, ll. 81–86.

6. For discussion of Augustine's idea of volition in the Fall, its relation to his political and social context, and its bearing on his advocacy of coercion, see Elaine Pagels, *Adam, Eve, and the Serpent* (New York: Random House, 1988), pp. 98–126. Pagels exaggerates Augustine's influence, however, in arguing that his analysis of guilt in the Fall is responsible for the cultural association of sexual intercourse with privacy (and by inference with shame). This is a little like arguing that Columbus' discovery of America is responsible for the world being round.

7. Jonathan Dollimore, *Radical Tragedy* (Chicago: Univ. of Chicago Press, 1984), p. 116. A more acute response to the social dimensions of Christ's life can be found in Peter Burke, *Popular Culture in Early Modern Europe* (N.Y.: Harper and Row, 1978), p. 193. Cf. Walter Cohen, *Drama of a Nation* (Ithaca, N.Y.: Cornell Univ. Press, 1985), pp. 71–72.

8. Cohen, *Drama of a Nation*, pp. 65–72.

9. Arnold Williams, *The Characterization of Pilate in the Towneley Plays* (East Lansing: Michigan State Univ. Press, 1950), p. 38.

10. John 18:36. For authoritative commentary that qualifies a narrowly spiritualized reading of Jesus' statement, see Raymond E. Brown, ed., *The Anchor Bible Gospel According to John*, 2 vols. (Garden City, N.Y.: Doubleday, 1970), 2:852–53.

11. Mervyn James, *Society, Politics, and Culture: Studies in Early Modern England* (Cambridge: Cambridge Univ. Press, 1986), p. 46.

12. England, ed., *Towneley Plays, Salutation of Elizabeth*, ll. 64–72.

13. For discussion and references, see Raymond E. Brown et al., eds., *Mary in the New Testament* (Philadelphia: Fortress Press; New York: Paulist Press, 1978), pp. 137–43. God's championing of the oppressed has been the basis for the recent movement called liberation theology. Among many books, see for example, Gustavo Gutierrez, *A Theology of Liberation*, trans. and ed. Caridad Inda and John Eagleson (Maryknoll, N.Y.: Orbis Books, 1973) and Jürgen Moltmann, *The Power of the Powerless*, trans. Margaret Kohl (San Francisco: Harper and Row, 1983).

14. R. M. Lumiansky and David Mills, eds., *The Chester Mystery Cycle* (London: Oxford Univ. Press 1974), EETS s.s. 3, *Wright's Play*, ll. 189–92; my emphasis. For thematic discussion of *potentia humilitatis* in the Chester Nativity, see Ruth M. Keane, "Kingship in the Chester Nativity Play," *LeedsSE* 13 (1982), 74–84.

15. *The Service for Representing the Slaughter of the Innocents*, in Bevington, ed., *Medieval Drama*, p. 68.

16. For arguments regarding the subversive effect of comic caricature, see Robert Weimann, *Shakespeare and the Popular Tradition in the Theater*, ed. Robert Schwartz (Baltimore: Johns Hopkins Univ. Press, 1978), pp. 64–72, and Mi-

chael D. Bristol, *Carnival and Theater* (New York: Methuen, 1985), pp. 59–71 and 107–55.

17. Clifford Geertz, "Ideology as a Cultural System" in *The Interpretation of Cultures* (New York: Basic Books, 1973), pp. 193–233.

18. David Bevington thus overstates the case in asserting that "medieval drama reveals few traces of political activity . . . because most religious drama concerned itself simply with the soul of the ordinary man or priest" (*Tudor Drama and Politics* [Cambridge, Mass.: Harvard Univ. Press, 1968], p. 27).

19. The principal proponents of this argument are E. K. Chambers, *The Medieval Stage*, 2 vols. (Oxford: Clarendon Press, 1903); Karl Young, *The Drama of the Medieval Church*, 2 vols. (London: Oxford Univ. Press, 1933); A. P. Rossiter, *English Drama from the Early Times to the Elizabethans* (London: Hutchinson's Univ. Library, 1950); Hardin Craig, *English Religious Drama of the Middle Ages* (London: Oxford Univ. Press, 1955).

20. See particularly O. B. Hardison, *Christian Rite and Christian Drama in the Middle Ages* (Baltimore: Johns Hopkins Univ. Press, 1965); V. A. Kolve, *The Play Called Corpus Christi* (Stanford, Calif.: Stanford Univ. Press, 1966); Rosemary Woolf, *The English Mystery Plays* (London: Routledge and Kegan Paul; Berkeley and Los Angeles: Univ. of California Press, 1972); Peter Travis, *Dramatic Design in the Chester Cycle* (Chicago: Univ. of Chicago Press, 1982).

21. Kolve, *Play Called Corpus Christi*, pp. 206–64. The quotation is from p. 207.

22. Hardison, *Christian Rite and Christian Drama*, pp. 1–34.

23. The quoted phrase is Michael Bristol's, *Carnival and Theater*, pp. 140–55. The chief critical inspiration for this position comes from Mikhail Bakhtin, *Rabelais and His World*, trans. Helene Iswolsky (Cambridge, Mass.: MIT Press, 1968), though Bakhtin says very little about drama. While not explicitly indebted to Bakhtin, Weimann takes a similar position in *Shakespeare and the Popular Tradition*. Cohen's argument in this vein in *Drama of a Nation* is chiefly indebted to Weimann, though Cohen acknowledges Bakhtin as well (p. 61).

24. *Peter Idley's Instructions to His Son*, ed. Charlotte D'Evelyn (Boston: D. C. Heath; London: Oxford Univ. Press, 1935), pt. 2, pp. 435–39.

25. *Wisdom*, ed. Mark Eccles in *The Macro Plays* (London: Oxford Univ. Press, 1969), EETS 262, ll. 344s.d. and 380s.d.

26. For topical considerations of Herod in the Towneley plays, see Theodore H. DeWelles, "The Social and Political Context of the Towneley Cylcle" (Ph.D. diss., Univ. of Toronto, 1980), pp. 255–318.

27. Roger H. Marijnissen and M. Seidel, *Bruegel* (New York: Harrison House, 1984), p. 29, plate numbers 248–49. For printed analogues of polemical peasant realism in German art contemporary with Bruegel, see Christiane Anderson, "Popular Imagery in German Refomation Broadsheets" in *Print and Culture in the Renaissance*, ed. Gerald P. Tyson and Sylvia S. Wagonheim (Newark: Univ. of Delaware Press, 1986), pp. 120–50.

28. Quoted in G. R. Owst, *Literature and Pulpit in Medieval England*, 2d ed., rev. (Oxford: Clarendon Press, 1961), p. 404. Hereafter cited as Owst in the text.

29. J. E. Neale, *Queen Elizabeth I* (1934; reprint, London: Jonathan Cape, 1952), pp. 309–10.

30. Dollimore, *Radical Tragedy*, p. 83.

31. In addition to *Literature and Pulpit* (above, n. 28), *Preaching in Medieval England* (Cambridge: Cambridge Univ. Press, 1926).

32. Owst's organization of chapters 5 and 6 in *Literature and Pulpit* is designed to reflect the wide range of social response and respondents on the late medieval homiletic scene; in both cases, Owst proceeds hierarchically from top to bottom, first in regard to the preachers and second in regard to their homiletic targets. Walter Cohen's allusion to the influence of the Mendicant friars is therefore misleading, since it implies that only the Mendicants were serious social critics (*Drama of a Nation*, p. 71).

33. For Gregory's polemical letter to Herman of Metz (written at the height of the Pope's controversy with Henry IV), see Sidney Ehler and John Morrall, *Church and State through the Centuries* (London: Burns and Oates, 1954), pp. 29–39. Walter Cohen sees the possible impact of this controversy in twelfth-century liturgical drama, but he reckons without the enduring influence of Augustine (*Drama of a Nation*, p. 53).

34. Lynn B. Squires, "Law and Disorder in *Ludus Coventriae*," *CompD*, 12 (1978), 210–11. The reprint of this article in *The Drama of the Middle Ages*, ed. Clifford Davidson et al. (New York: AMS Press, 1982) contains substantial printing defects and cannot be reliably consulted.

35. On the popularity of the Coventry plays, see Richard Ingram, *Coventry Records of Early English Drama* (Toronto: Univ. of Toronto Press, 1981), pp. xv–xvii.

36. Lynn B. Squires, "Legal and Political Aspects of Late Medieval English Drama" (Ph.D. diss., Univ. of Washington, 1977), pp. 171–93.

37. The morality play background of these characters is studied by Bernard Spivack, *Shakespeare and the Allegory of Evil* (New York: Columbia Univ. Press, 1958). For a recent refinement of Spivack's argument, see Alan C. Dessen, *Shakespeare and the Late Moral Plays* (Lincoln: Univ. of Nebraska Press, 1986).

Chapter 3. Tudor Power and the New Fashion

1. Francis Meres, *Palladis Tamia* (1598), in *Elizabethan Critical Essays*, ed. G. Gregory Smith, 2 vols. (London: Oxford Univ. Press, 1904), 2:17–18.

2. C. S. Lewis, *English Literature in the Sixteenth Century Excluding Drama* (Oxford: Clarendon Press, 1954), p. 2.

3. "The ideas of the ruling class are in every epoch the ruling ideas, i.e. the class which is the ruling *material* force of society, is at the same time its ruling *intellectual* force" (Karl Marx and Frederick Engels, *The German Ideology*, ed. C. F. Arthur [London: Lawrence and Wishart, 1970], p. 64).

4. The recognized authority on social transformations accompanying the centralization of power in England is Lawrence Stone, *The Crisis of the Aristocracy* (Oxford: Clarendon Press, 1965). For a recent and more specialized study, see Penry Williams, *The Tudor Regime* (Oxford: Clarendon Press, 1979), esp. pp. 421–56, where Williams discusses the transfer of power from provinces to crown and from old aristocracy to new humanists by examining the changing make-up of the Privy Council and regional elites.

5. Among other studies, see J. H. Hexter, "The Education of the Aristocracy in the Renaissance," *Journal of Modern History* 22 (1950), 1–20; Lawrence Stone,

"The Educational Revolution in England, 1560–1640," *Past and Present* 28 (1964), 41–80; Kenneth Charlton, *Education in Renaissance England* (London: Routledge and Kegan Paul, 1965); and Joan Simon, *Education and Society in Tudor England* (Cambridge: Cambridge Univ. Press, 1967). For a witty and engaging essay on learning and privilege, see Terence Hawkes, "Swisser-Swatter: Making a Man of English Letters," in *Alternative Shakespeares*, ed. John Drakakis (London: Methuen, 1985), pp. 26–46.

6. William Caxton, *The Book of the Ordre of Chyvalry* (1484), ed. Alfred T. P. Byles (London: Oxford Univ. Press, 1926), EETS o.s. 168, p. 122.

7. Roger Ascham, *The Schoolmaster* (1570), ed. Lawrence V. Ryan (Charlottesville: Univ. Press of Virginia, 1967), p. 69.

8. Richard Pace, *De fructu qui ex doctrina percipitur* (1517), ed. and trans. F. Manley and R. S. Sylvester (New York: Ungar Publishing Company, 1967), p. 23.

9. David Cressy, *Literacy and the Social Order in Tudor and Stuart England* (Cambridge: Cambridge Univ. Press, 1980) offers a statistical and tabular analysis of the growth of literacy in early modern England. His book is not helpful on upper-class competition in the early sixteenth century, however, because it focuses on the whole range of society over the course of two centuries and particularly on the formation of the middle class.

10. K. J. Wilson prefaces his edition of Elyot's letters with a brief summary of Elyot's career, "The Letters of Sir Thomas Elyot," *SP* 73 (1976). See particularly letter no. 11, to Thomas Cromwell, in which Elyot seeks to distance himself from the newly disgraced Thomas More and also petitions Cromwell for a portion of land seized from the monasteries.

11. Sir Thomas Elyot, *The Boke Named the Governour* (1531), ed. Henry H. S. Croft, 2 vols. (London: Kegan Paul, 1880), 1:5–6.

12. For the social implications of the Italian Platonic revival, see Lauro Martines, *Power and Imagination: City-States in Renaissance Italy* (New York: Alfred A. Knopf, 1979), pp. 301 and 325–28.

13. Thomas Wilson, *The Arte of Rhetorique* (1553), ed. Thomas J. Derrick (New York and London: Garland Publishing Co., 1982), p. 18.

14. Frank Whigham, *Ambition and Privilege: The Social Tropes of Elizabethan Courtesy Theory* (Berkeley and Los Angeles: Univ. of California Press, 1984), p. 3. I am indebted to Whigham's interpretation of Tudor courtly mannerism as a "rhetorical radiation of power," but I would add that rhetoric itself is one of the most important such radiations, because it so clearly indicates how style was socially transformed.

15. Sir Philip Sidney, *An Apology for Poetry*, in *Elizabethan Critical Essays*, ed. G. Gregory Smith, 2 vols. (Oxford: Clarendon Press, 1904), 1:199. The room Sidney leaves for "wide-ranging wit" is frequently construed as evidence that he really took neo-Aristotelianism less strictly than he appears to. But that is to impose on Sidney the later historical stand-off between the Enlightenment and Romanticism. In fact, the neo-Platonic basis for Sidney's defense of imagination involves an appeal to high-minded classicism that has the same social implications as his appeal to Artistotle.

16. Erich Auerbach, "*Sermo Humilis*," in *Literary Language and Its Public*

in Late Latin Antiquity and in the Middle Ages, trans. Ralph Manheim (Princeton, N.J.: Princeton Univ. Press, 1965), pp. 25–81.

17. Augustine, *De doctrina christiana* 4.12.34–4.19.38.

18. Auerbach, "*Sermo Humilis,*" pp. 39–41.

19. Sir Thomas More, *Utopia,* ed. Edward Surtz and J. H. Hexter in *The Complete Works of Thomas More* (New Haven, Conn.: Yale Univ. Press, 1965), pp. 131–33.

20. I take this point from John King, *English Reformation Literature: The Tudor Origins of the Protestant Tradition* (Princeton, N.J.: Princeton Univ. Press, 1982), pp. 42–46. See also David Norbrook, *Poetry and Politics in the English Renaissance* (London: Routledge and Kegan Paul, 1984), pp. 18–31.

21. *The Byble in Englyshe* (London, 1540), sigs. +ᵛ–+ii.

22. Elyot, *Governour,* p. 16.

23. Whigham's study of Elizabethan sumptuary laws reveals the enormous importance attached to clothing as a "limiting definition" of social status. See *Ambition and Privilege,* pp. 155–69.

24. Thomas Wilson, *Arte of Rhetorique,* p. 340. For Bishop Bromyard's comments, see above, p. 35.

25. Hugh Latimer, *Selected Sermons,* ed. Allan G. Chester (Charlottesville: Univ. Press of Virginia, 1968), pp. 29–30. For an argument that Latimer deliberately adopted the persona of plowman for prophetic purpose, see R. L. Kelly, "Hugh Latimer as Piers Plowman," *SEL* 17 (1977), 13–26.

26. W. Carew Hazlitt, ed., *Remains of the Early Popular Poetry of England,* 4 vols. (London: John Russell Smith, 1866), 3:274–75.

27. Thomas Cranmer, "A Sermon concerning the Time of Rebellion" (1549), in *The Remains of Thomas Cranmer,* ed. Henry Jenkyns, 4 vols. (Oxford: Oxford Univ. Press, 1833), 2:248–73; Latimer, *Selected Sermons,* pp. 147–50. Both Cranmer and Latimer preached these sermons at court. For a sensitive discussion of how reformers were compelled to embrace royal power, see Helen C. White, *Social Criticism in Popular Religious Literature of the Sixteenth Century* (New York: Macmillan, 1944), pp. 132–88.

28. Robert Crowley, *The Way to Wealth Wherein Is Plainly Taught a Most Present Remedy for Sedicion* (London, 1550).

29. *Philargyrie of Greate Britayne,* ed. John King, *ELR* 10 (1980), 47–75.

30. *DNB,* 13:243.

31. George Puttenham, *The Arte of English Poesie,* ed. Gladys D. Willcock and Alice Walker (Cambridge: Cambridge Univ. Press, 1936), p. 62. Daniel Javitch first pointed out that Puttenham's book is essentially an "art of conduct." See "Poetry and Court Conduct: Puttenham's *Arte of English Poesie* in Light of Castiglione's *Cortegiano,*" *MLN* 87 (1972), 865–82, and *Poetry and Courtliness in Renaissance England* (Princeton, N.J.: Princeton Univ. Press, 1978). Javitch's argument has been refined and expanded by Whigham in *Ambition and Privilege.*

32. The quotation is from Joyce Youings, *Sixteenth-Century England,* The Pelican Social History of Britain (Harmondsworth, Eng.: Penguin Books, 1984), p. 53.

33. John Ferne, *The Blazon of Gentrie* (London, 1586), p. 23, sig. ciiii. Columell's status is actually somewhat ambiguous: while he is called a plowman and given a peasant dialect, he seems to have acquired sufficient wealth to purchase

a coat of arms (part 2, p. 10, sig. Aa5ᵛ), though pronoun references in this passage are unclear and are probably intended to refer to Columell's landlord, rather than Columell himself.

34. Thomas Smith, *De Republica Anglorum* (1583), ed. Mary Dewar (Cambridge: Cambridge Univ. Press, 1982), pp. 71–72. My emphasis. For an analysis of the social transformation of pastoral as a parallel to the fall of the plower outlined here, see Louis A. Montrose, "Of Gentlemen and Shepherds: The Politics of Elizabethan Pastoral Form," *ELH* 50 (1983), 415–59.

35. The war of the theaters has been variously interpreted since it was first studied by Roscoe A. Small in *The Stage-Quarrel between Ben Jonson and the So-Called Poetasters* (Breslau: Verlag M. and H. Marcus, 1899), but the prevailing opinion is that it was a product of competition between the "rival traditions," as Alfred Harbage called them, that is, a relatively exclusive as opposed to a relatively nonexclusive theatrical tradition (*Shakespeare and the Rival Traditions* [London: Macmillan, 1952]). That Harbage overstated his case for the social distinction between public and private theaters has been recently argued by Ann Jennalie Cook, *Shakespeare's Privileged Playgoers* (Princeton, N.J.: Princeton Univ. Press, 1981), who incisively identifies Harbage's populist bias. But Cook's thesis has been seriously challenged in turn. See especially Martin Butler, *Theatre and Crisis 1632–1642* (Cambridge: Cambridge Univ. Press, 1984), pp. 293–306 (in which he refutes Cook in defense of his own comments about the Caroline audience [pp. 100–140] and the survival of the popular tradition [pp. 181–250]) and Andrew Gurr, *Playgoing in Shakespeare's London* (Cambridge: Cambridge Univ. Press, 1987), who takes a middle position between Harbage and Cook in his introduction (pp. 1–12) but offers ample evidence that Shakespeare's audience was socially mixed (see esp. pp. 59–79).

36. David M. Bevington, *From "Mankind" to Marlowe* (Cambridge, Mass.: Harvard Univ. Press, 1962). Bevington's argument has been substantiated from quite a different point of view by Robert Weimann, *Shakespeare and the Popular Tradition in the Theater*, ed. Robert Schwartz (Baltimore: Johns Hopkins Univ. Press, 1978). See also Walter Cohen, *Drama of a Nation* (Ithaca, N.Y.: Cornell Univ. Press, 1985), pp. 136–85.

37. *"Mankind" to Marlowe*, pp. 190–98. Bevington cites Stephen Gosson in opposition to popular dramaturgy, but Gosson's critique closely parallels Sidney's in *The Apology for Poetry*. As still another parallel, Harbage cites George Whetstone's Preface to *Promos and Cassandra* (1578), one of the sources for Shakespeare's *Measure for Measure* (*Rival Traditions*, pp. 62–63).

38. On the auspices of these plays, see David M. Bevington, "Popular and Courtly Traditions on the Early Tudor Stage" in *Medieval Drama*, ed. Neville Denny (London: Edward Arnold, 1973), pp. 90–107.

39. David M. Bevington, *Tudor Drama and Politics* (Cambridge, Mass.: Harvard Univ. Press, 1968), pp. 77–82.

40. Richard Axton, ed., *Three Rastell Plays* (Cambridge: D. S. Brewer; Totowa, N.J.: Rowman and Littlefield, 1979), ll. 567–613. My paraphrase conflates two speeches by the knight and the plowman.

41. Joel Altman, *The Tudor Play of Mind* (Berkeley and Los Angeles: Univ. of California Press, 1978), pp. 124–29.

42. The history of this commonplace has been outlined by George McGill

Vogt, "Gleanings for the History of a Sentiment: *Generositas virtus, non sanguis*," *JEGP* 24 (1925), 102–24. See also Albert B. Friedman, " 'When Adam Delved . . .': Contexts of an Historic Proverb," in Larry D. Benson, ed., *The Learned and the Lewd* (Cambridge, Mass.: Harvard Univ. Press, 1974), pp. 213–30. For self-interested Italian uses of the commonplace, see Martines, *Power and Imagination*, pp. 212–14.

43. Henry Medwall, *Fulgens and Lucrece*, in *The Plays of Henry Medwall*, ed. Alan H. Nelson (Cambridge: D. S. Brewer; Totowa, N.J.: Rowman and Littlefield, 1980), 1.730.

44. The three plays are Kyd's *Spanish Tragedy* (1587), Shakespeare's *Comedy of Errors* (1592), and Jonson's *Everyman in His Humour* (1598). These are all late in the century, at a time when the high style was making an important impact on popular drama. For suggestions that *The Comedy of Errors* may be less committed to an explorative model than Altman suggests, see chapter 4 below.

45. Rosemary Woolf, *The English Mystery Plays* (London: Routledge and Kegan Paul; Berkeley and Los Angeles: Univ. of California Press, 1972), pp. 312–23.

46. Ruth H. Blackburn, *Biblical Drama under the Tudors* (The Hague and Paris: Mouton, 1971), pp. 66–68.

47. Louis A. Montrose, "Gifts and Reasons: The Context of Peele's *Araygnement of Paris*," *ELH* 47 (1980), 443. For comments about Italian courtly precedents to this Elizabethan social exchange, see Martines, *Power and Imagination*, pp. 210–11 and 241–76.

48. Udall's dramatic business during Mary's reign is recorded in *Documents Relating to the Revels at Court in the Time of King Edward VI and Queen Mary*, ed. Albert Feurillat (Louvain: A Uystpruyst, 1914), pp. 159, 166, 167, 169. Evidence and various arguments about Udall's ambition were published by William Peery and William Edgerton in *N&Q* 194 (1949), 119–21 and 138–41; and 195 (1950), 223–26.

49. Puttenham, *Arte of English Poesie*, pp. 184–85. Whigham notes that "The element 'curry' is connected with the currycomb, and with 'clawing,' the Elizabethan slang equivalent of our term 'stroking.' We still speak of 'currying favor' " (*Ambition and Privilege*, p. 41).

50. *Peter Idley's Instructions to His Son*, ed. Charlotte D'Evelyn (Boston: D. C. Heath; London: Oxford Univ. Press, 1935), 1.580–81.

51. Harold Gardiner, *Mysteries' End* (New Haven, Conn.: Yale Univ. Press, 1946); Glynne Wickham, *Early English Stages 1300–1660* (London: Routledge and Kegan Paul, 1959), 1:112–76.

52. My count is based on Alfred Harbage, revised by S. Schoenbaum, *Annals of English Drama* (Philadelphia: Univ. of Pennsylvania Press, 1964), but it should be noted that no count can be absolutely precise, because for many plays we have nothing but a title, and in addition to the fact that titles do not always indicate a play's content, similar titles can sometimes refer to the same play (as in the case of a stage revival or reprint), sometimes to different plays.

53. *Sapienta Solomonis*, ed. and trans. Elizabeth R. Payne (New Haven, Conn.: Yale Univ. Press, 1938).

54. Anthony Esler, *The Aspiring Mind of the Elizabethan Younger Generation* (Durham, N.C.: Duke Univ. Press, 1966). Esler focuses on the serious con-

tenders for power, such as Robert Sidney and the earl of Essex, but his argument applies equally to those who were even less successful.

55. Henry Peacham, *The Compleat Gentleman* (1622; facsimile reprint, Amsterdam and New York: DaCapo Press, 1968), pp. 11–12.

56. G. K. Hunter *John Lyly: The Humanist as Courtier* (London: Routledge and Kegan Paul, 1962).

57. See, for example, Stephen Greenblatt, *Renaissance Self-Fashioning* (Chicago: Univ. of Chicago Press, 1980), pp. 193–221, and Jonathan Dollimore, *Radical Tragedy* (Chicago: Univ. of Chicago Press, 1984), pp. 109–19.

58. Karl Marx and Frederick Engels, *Selected Works*, 2 vols. (London: Lawrence and Wishart, 1950), 2:407. Cf. 1:328–29.

Chapter 4. Deconstructive Comedy

1. Sir Thomas Smith, *De Republica Anglorum* (1583), ed. Mary Dewar (Cambridge: Cambridge Univ. Press, 1982), p. 72. The passage quoted here immediately follows Smith's comment about gentlemen being "made good cheap in England," quoted above, p. 53. The phrase in square brackets is the wording of the 1583 printed edition (the copy text of Dewar's edition being a reconstruction of the original manuscript). Shakespeare may well have known this passage, since it also appears in William Harrison's *Description of England* in the 1577 edition of Holinshed's *Chronicles*, which Shakespeare consistently used. For discussion of precedence between Smith and Harrison, see Dewar's edition of Smith, pp. 157–62.

2. Robert Greene, *Greene's Groats-worth of Wit* (1592; facsimile reprint, Menston, Eng.: Scolar Press, 1969), sigs. Fᵛ–F2. For a perceptive reading of Greene's complaints about Shakespeare in the context of Shakespeare's life, see Muriel C. Bradbrook, *Shakespeare: The Poet in His World* (London: Weidenfeld and Nicolson, 1978), pp. 47–64.

3. Sir Philip Sidney, *An Apology for Poetry*, in *Elizabethan Critical Essays*, ed. G. Gregory Smith, 2 vols. (Oxford: Clarendon Press, 1904), 1:197.

4. Elizabethan response to Italian fashion was ambivalent—admiration and mistrust in roughly equal proportions. Courtly imitation of Italy, however, probably indicates the sincerest form of response. For cogent arguments that even Roger Ascham's forthright condemnation of Italian influence "resulted in conversion rather than dismissal," see Frank Whigham, *Ambition and Privilege: The Social Tropes of Elizabethan Courtesy Theory* (Berkeley and Los Angeles: Univ. of California Press, 1984), pp. 175–83.

5. Joel Altman, *The Tudor Play of Mind* (Berkeley and Los Angeles: Univ. of California Press, 1978), p. 166. My emphasis.

6. David M. Bevington, *From "Mankind" to Marlowe* (Cambridge, Mass.: Harvard Univ. Press, 1962), pp. 190–98.

7. On sumptuary laws as an expression of changing power relations, see Whigham, *Ambition and Privilege*, pp. 155–69.

8. "Enter in at the strait gate: for it is the wide gate and broad way that leadeth to destruction, and many there be which go in thereat, because the gate is strait and the way narrow that leadeth unto life, and few there be that find it." Chapter 7 below considers the medieval dramatic heritage of *All's Well* at greater length.

9. The modesty *topos* is described by Ernst R. Curtius, *European Literature and the Latin Middle Ages*, trans. Willard R. Trask (London: Routledge and Kegan Paul, 1953), pp. 83–85. Michael D. Bristol's discussion of *The Praise of Folly* in *Carnival and Theater* (New York and London: Methuen, 1985), pp. 130–33, misleadingly places Erasmus' satire in the context of the popular "serio-comic" tradition. The elaborate rhetorical structure of the work and Erasmus' explicit debt to Lucian point to high culture, not popular.

10. Stephen Greenblatt, *Renaissance Self-Fashioning* (Chicago: Univ. of Chicago Press, 1980), pp. 1–2.

11. Stephen Greenblatt, *Sir Walter Ralegh: The Renaissance Man and His Roles* (New Haven, Conn.: Yale Univ. Press, 1973), p. 41.

12. For opportunistic humanist use of the printing press, see two essays by Arthur J. Slavin, "The Tudor Revolution and the Devil's Art: Bishop Bonner's Printed Forms," in *Tudor Rule and Revolution*, ed. D. J. Guth and J. W. McKenna (Cambridge: Cambridge Univ. Press, 1982), pp. 3–23, and "The Gutenberg Galaxy and the Tudor Revolution," in *Print and Culture in the Renaissance*, ed. Gerald P. Tyson and Sylvia S. Wagonheim (Newark: Univ. of Delaware Press, 1986), pp. 90–109.

13. Whigham, *Ambition and Privilege*, p. 5.

14. George Puttenham, *The Arte of English Poesie*, ed. Gladys Willcock and Alice Walker (Cambridge: Cambridge Univ. Press, 1936), p. 299.

15. La Rochefoucauld, *The Maxims*, trans. Constantine FitzGibbon (London: Millington, 1974), maxim 254. My discussion is indebted here to Jonas Barish, *The Antitheatrical Prejudice* (Berkeley and Los Angeles: Univ. of California Press, 1981), pp. 210–20. Barish drew my attention to La Rochefoucauld and Daniel Dyke and greatly assisted my understanding of the Renaissance Protean self.

16. J. E. Neale, "The Elizabethan Political Scene," in *Essays in Elizabethan History* (London: Jonathan Cape, 1958), pp. 59–84.

17. *Cynthia's Revels*, 3.4.42–52, in *Ben Jonson*, ed. C. H. Herford and Percy Simpson, 11 vols. (Oxford: Clarendon Press, 1932), 4:90. My emphasis. The phrase "centered self" is Thomas M. Greene's, in "Ben Jonson and the Centered Self," *The Vulnerable Text: Essays on Renaissance Literature* (New York: Columbia Univ. Press, 1986), pp. 194–217.

18. Jonas Barish, *Antitheatrical Prejudice*, pp. 132–54. See also Katharine E. Maus, *Ben Jonson and the Roman Frame of Mind* (Princeton, N.J.: Princeton Univ. Press, 1984), pp. 22–46.

19. This tradition is described by Daniel Javitch, *"The Philosopher of the Court*: A French Satire Misunderstood," *CompL* 23 (1971), 97–124. Javitch's point is that in 1575 the English translator of Philibert de Vienne's *Le Philosophe de court* (1547) failed to understand the anticourtly satire in what he was translating because English response to courtesy literature was so overwhelmingly positive.

20. *Mankind*, in *Medieval Drama*, ed. David M. Bevington (Boston: Houghton Mifflin, 1975), l. 289.

21. Stanley Fish, *Self-Consuming Artifacts* (Berkeley and Los Angeles: Univ. of California Press, 1972). Fish treats Plato and Augustine as contributors to "self-consuming" without distinguishing between them. Close attention to so-

cial change in the Renaissance suggests that these two ancient authorities have very different legacies.

22. Paul Ricoeur, *Freud and Philosophy* (New Haven, Conn.: Yale Univ. Press, 1970), pp. 32–36. The two other principal representatives of the "school of suspicion" are Marx and Nietzsche.

23. Daniel Dyke, *The Mystery of Selfe-Deceving* (London, 1616), p. 35, sig. D2.

24. Puritan piety created its own kind of self-deception, of course, which became culturally entrenched when the Puritan legacy became socially dominant, as the Romantic poets, Freud, and Weber discovered in different ways. In the sixteenth and early seventeenth centuries, however, Puritanism was far from dominant, and its demystifying response to the ruling ideas in personal and social psychology anticipates in some ways that of Freud.

25. Thomas Wilson, *Arte of Rhetorique* (1553), ed. Thomas J. Derrick (New York and London: Garland Publishing Co., 1982), p. 323.

26. Ernest Jovy, "Deux inspirateurs inconnus jusqu'ici des Maximes de La Rochefoucauld: Daniel Dyke et Jean Vernueil," *Bulletin du Bibliophile* (15 Oct. 1909), 433–46.

27. For further discussion of Shakespeare and Lyly, see G. K. Hunter, *John Lyly: The Humanist as Courtier* (London: Routledge and Kegan Paul, 1962), pp. 298–349.

28. Louis A. Montrose, " 'Eliza, Queene of Shepheardes,' and the Pastoral of Power," *ELR* 10 (1980), 153–82. Montrose argues "that the symbolic mediation of social relationships was a central function of Elizabethan pastoral forms; and that social relationships are, intrinsically, relationships of power" (p. 153).

29. On Proteus and the theatrical self, see Barish, *Antitheatrical Prejudice*, pp. 98–103.

30. Puttenham, *Arte of English Poesie*, p. 184. For more on this point, see above, p. 56, and chapter 3, note 49.

31. For the background of Iago and Edmund in the morality play Vice, see Bernard Spivack, *Shakespeare and the Allegory of Evil* (New York: Columbia Univ. Press, 1958).

32. Robert G. Hunter, *Shakespeare and the Comedy of Forgiveness* (New York: Columbia Univ. Press, 1965).

Chapter 5. Inventing Secular History: The *Henry VI* Plays

1. See especially E.M.W. Tillyard, *Shakespeare's History Plays* (New York: Barnes and Noble, 1944). Other important studies in the same vein include Lily B. Campbell, *Shakespeare's Histories: Mirrors of Elizabethan Policy* (San Marino, Calif.: Huntington Library, 1947); Irving Ribner, *The History Play in the Age of Shakespeare* (rev. ed., London: Methuen, 1965); M. M. Reese, *The Cease of Majesty* (London: Edward Arnold, 1961).

2. Particularly important is H. A. Kelly's *Divine Providence in the England of Shakespeare's Histories* (Cambridge, Mass.: Harvard Univ. Press, 1970), but see also Robert Ornstein, *A Kingdom for a Stage* (Cambridge, Mass.: Harvard Univ. Press 1972), Moody Prior, *The Drama of Power* (Evanston, Ill.: Northwestern Univ. Press, 1973), H. R. Coursen, *The Leasing out of England* (Washington, D.C.: University Press of America, 1982), and C. G. Thayer, *Shakespearean Politics*

(Athens: Ohio Univ. Press, 1983). Especially good on the *Henry VI* plays is a series of articles by A. L. French, "Joan of Arc and Henry VI," *ES* 49 (1968), 425–29; "*Henry VI* and the Ghost of Richard II," *ES* 50 (1969), xxxvii–xlviii; and "The Mills of God and Shakespeare's Early History Plays," *ES* 55 (1974), 313–24. New Historicism has introduced a different kind of skepticism into discussion of the histories. See particularly Jonathan Dollimore and Alan Sinfield, "History and Ideology: The Instance of *Henry V*," in *Alternative Shakespeares*, ed. John Drakakis (New York and London: Methuen, 1985), pp. 206–27; Leonard Tennenhouse, *Power on Display* (New York and London: Methuen, 1986), pp. 72–101; Stephen Greenblatt, *Shakespearean Negotiations* (Berkeley and Los Angeles: Univ. of California Press, 1988), pp. 21–65.

3. David S. Kastan, *Shakespeare and the Shapes of Time* (Hanover, N.H.: Univ. Press of New England, 1982), pp. 15–16.

4. Joel Hurstfield, *The Illusion of Power in Tudor Politics*, The Creighton Lecture in History, 1978 (London: Athlone Press, 1979), p. 19. Hurstfield's comment is relevant here: "When once I suggested in a broadcast talk, that since in my own reading of the [Armada] episode the wind kept changing direction it was hard to determine its religious convictions, I stirred up some angry and scornful observations. One of my correspondents told me that I ought to have known that there were half a million documents in the Public Record Office which proved that God fought on the side of the English. Now that the Public Record Office has new and more commodious premises perhaps it will make accessible to scholars this hitherto unknown cache of records" (p. 32).

5. R. B. Wernham, *After the Armada: Elizabethan England and the Struggle for Western Europe* (Oxford: Clarendon Press, 1984), pp. 1–9.

6. Raphael Holinshed, *The First and Second Volumes of Chronicles* (London, 1587), pp. 1134–36.

7. J. E. Neale, *Elizabeth I and Her Parliaments*, 2 vols. (London: Jonathan Cape, 1957), 2:55–56.

8. For a thematic study of this movement in the *Henry VI* plays, see Edward Berry, *Patterns of Decay: Shakespeare's Early Histories* (Charlottesville: Univ. Press of Virginia, 1975).

9. Frank Whigham, *Ambition and Privilege: The Social Tropes of Elizabethan Courtesy Theory* (Berkeley and Los Angeles: Univ. of California Press, 1984), pp. 78–79.

10. Thomas Wilson, *The Arte of Rhetorique* (1553), ed. Thomas J. Derrick (New York and London: Garland Publishing Co., 1982), p. 18.

11. Whigham, *Ambition and Privilege*, pp. 63–82.

12. George Puttenham, *The Arte of English Poesie*, ed. Gladys Willcock and Alice Walker (Cambridge: Cambridge Univ. Press, 1936), p. 299.

13. Lawrence Stone, *The Crisis of the Aristocracy, 1558–1641* (Oxford: Clarendon Press, 1965), pp. 242–50.

14. For the argument regarding emergent materialism, see Jonathan Dollimore, *Radical Tragedy* (Chicago: Univ. of Chicago Press, 1984), p. 171.

15. Emrys Jones, *The Origins of Shakespeare* (Oxford, Clarendon Press, 1977), p. 31.

16. On early Tudor iconography, see John King, *English Reformation Literature: The Tudor Origins of the Protestant Tradition* (Princeton, N.J.: Princeton

Univ. Press, 1982), pp. 161–206. For the idealizing of the monarchy in early Tudor drama, see David M. Bevington, *Tudor Drama and Politics* (Cambridge, Mass.: Harvard Univ. Press, 1968), pp. 96–113.

17. John Foxe, *Actes and Monuments of These Latter and Perillous Dayes* (London, 1563), pp. 445–48 sigs. Ssi–Ssiiᵛ. The list of banned books with Fish's *Supplication* at its head is on p. 450, sig. Ssiiiᵛ. For More's reply to Fish, see Richard Marius, *Thomas More* (London: J. M. Dent, 1984), pp. 351–57. Helen C. White discusses Fish's book in *Social Criticism in Popular Religious Literature of the Sixteenth Century* (New York: Macmillan, 1944), p. 87.

18. Kastan, *Shapes of Time*, pp. 3–55.

19. *The Chester Mystery Cycle*, ed. R. M. Lumiansky and David Mills (London: Oxford Univ. Press, 1974), EETS s.s.3, *The Fall of Lucifer*, ll. 110–111.

20. *2 Henry VI*, 1.1.237 and 246. For other references to York's dilatory tactics, see *1 Henry VI*, 2.5.97, 101, 118–19; 3.1.61–64; 4.1.180–86; *2 Henry VI*, 2.2.64–68, and 3.1.331–40.

21. *The Towneley Plays*, ed. George England and A. W. Pollard (London: Kegan Paul, Trench, Trübner, 1897), EETS e.s. 71, *The Creation and Fall of the Angels*, ll. 8off.

22. Geoffrey Bullough, *Narrative and Dramatic Sources of Shakespeare* (London: Routledge and Kegan Paul; New York: Columbia Univ. Press, 1957–75), 3:210.

23. *The Towneley Plays*, *The Scourging*, l. 74. Only Chester omits the game motif. For commentary see V. A. Kolve, *The Play Called Corpus Christi* (Stanford, Calif.: Stanford Univ. Press, 1966), pp. 175–206.

24. H. M. Richmond, *Shakespeare's Political Plays* (New York: Random House, 1967), p. 61.

25. *The Chester Mystery Cycle*, *The Slaughter of the Innocents*, ll. 137– 216. For commentary see Rosemary Woolf, *The English Mystery Plays* (London: Routledge and Kegan Paul; Berkeley and Los Angeles: Univ. of California Press, 1972), pp. 202–11.

26. The fullest study of Marlowe's influence on Shakespeare's early histories is by David Riggs, *Shakespeare's Heroical Histories: "Henry VI" and Its Literary Tradition* (Cambridge, Mass.: Harvard Univ. Press, 1971).

27. Gabriel Harvey's ambivalence is recorded in copious *Marginalia*, ed. G. C. Moore Smith (Stratford-upon-Avon: Shakespeare Head Press, 1913). For commentary on the pattern Harvey represents, see Whigham, *Ambition and Privilege*, pp. 22–24.

28. Henry V's arrest and execution of Cambridge is a sore point with York in *Henry VI*. See *1 Henry VI*, 2.4.90–99 and 2.5.53ff. Shakespeare later dramatized the story in *Henry V*, 2.2. Cf. Moody Prior's comment: "One strong inference seems to emerge [in *Henry VI*], that although an undisputed legal succession provides the strongest moral support for the exercise of sovereign power, the right to govern cannot be separated from the ability to govern—from the capacity and talent for the exercise of power in the person of the man who occupies the sovereign office" (*Drama of Power*, p. 118). For useful comments on power *de jure* and *de facto* in *Henry VI*, see Richmond, *Shakespeare's Political Plays*, p. 61.

29. See Ernst H. Kantorowicz, *The King's Two Bodies: A Study in Medieval*

Political Theology (Princeton, N.J.: Princeton Univ. Press, 1953) and Marie Axton, *The Queen's Two Bodies* (London: Royal Historical Society, 1977).

30. Rosemary Woolf has traced the sources of some of these arguments (*English Mystery Plays*, pp. 105–13).

31. *Utopia*, ed. Edward Surtz and J. H. Hexter (New Haven, Conn.: Yale Univ. Press, 1965), p. 101.

32. Michael Mannheim argues that Humphrey Duke of Gloucester represents humanist interests in *Henry VI* and that he is crushed by Machiavellians, along with his saintly sovereign, in *The Weak King Dilemma in the Shakespearean History Plays* (Syracuse, N.Y.: Syracuse Univ. Press, 1973), pp. 90–95. This argument assumes a false dichotomy between the social interests of humanism and Machiavelli and ignores the extent to which Henry VI's weakness contributes to the problems of his kingdom.

33. Louis A. Montrose, " 'Elizabeth, Queene of shepheardes,' and the Pastoral of Power," *ELR* 10 (1980), 153–82, and "Of Gentlemen and Shepherds: The Politics of Elizabethan Pastoral Form," *ELH* 50 (1983), 415–59.

34. Ornstein, *Kingdom for a Stage*, p. 56; Reese, *The Cease of Majesty*, p. 200.

35. Bernard Spivack, *Shakespeare and the Allegory of Evil* (New York: Columbia Univ. Press, 1958), pp. 368–407.

36. Among others who take a critical view of the providentialism in *Richard III*, see A. L. French, "The World of *Richard III*," *ShakS* 4 (1968), 25–39; Wilbur Sanders, *The Dramatist and the Received Idea* (Cambridge: Cambridge Univ. Press, 1968), pp. 72–109; Prior, *Drama of Power*, pp. 42–58.

37. Wallace MacCaffrey, *Queen Elizabeth and the Making of Policy, 1572–1588* (Princeton, N.J.: Princeton Univ. 1981), pp. 12–13.

Chapter 6. The Elizabethan Hal

1. Peter Ure discusses "The Question of Political Allegory" in his New Arden edition of *Richard II*, 5th ed. (London: Methuen; Cambridge, Mass.: Harvard Univ. Press, 1961), pp. lvii–lxii. We cannot be certain that the play revived for Essex was Shakespeare's, but Ure agrees with E. K. Chambers that it probably was.

2. The only unambiguously Catholic allusion in *Henry V* is Henry's promise to establish two chantries for the soul of Richard II (4.1.297–99), since chantries had been banned in 1547. In context, this allusion nevertheless seems vaguely anti-Catholic and therefore contributes to the distance from Henry that the passage as a whole creates.

3. See John D. Cox, "*Henry VIII* and the Masque," *ELH* 45 (1978), 390–409.

4. The first serious study of economic pressure on the Elizabethan church was by Christopher Hill, *Economic Problems of the Church* (Oxford: Clarendon Press, 1956), but a new generation of historians has taken Hill's methods much further. See especially Felicity Heal, *Of Prelates and Princes: A Study of the Economic and Social Position of the Tudor Episcopate* (Cambridge: Cambridge Univ. Press, 1981). Joel Berlatsky concludes that the living standard of Elizabethan bishops declined over the course of the queen's reign, "The Elizabethan Episcopate: Patterns of Life and Expenditure," in *Princes and Paupers in the English Church, 1500–1800*, ed. Rosemary O'Day and Felicity Heal (Leicester: Leicester Univ.

Press, 1981), pp. 111–27. On Elizabethan patronage, see J. E. Neale, "The Elizabethan Political Scene," British Academy Raleigh Lecture for 1948, in *Essays in Elizabethan History* (London: Jonathan Cape, 1958), pp. 59–84, and Wallace MacCaffrey, "Place and Patronage," in *Elizabethan Governement and Society*, ed. S. T. Bindoff et al. (London: Athlone Press, 1961), 95–126.

5. John Strype, *Annals of the Reformation* (Oxford: Clarendon Press, 1824), vol. 1, pt. i, pp. 142–43, and *DNB*, 15:260.

6. C. J. Kitching, "The Quest for Concealed Lands in the Reign of Elizabeth I," *TRHS*, 5th ser., vol. 24 (1974), 63–78, and Heal, *Of Prelates and Princes*, pp. 232–33.

7. Whitgift's letters to Burghley in 1578 are in BL Lansdowne MS. 27, nos. 72 and 73. The list of "Inconveniences" is in Inner Temple Petyt MS. 538, no. 38, fols. 95–96.

8. Strype, *Annals*, vol. 2, pt. i, p. 538.

9. By the same token, profit may have prompted the queen to fill the vacancy again in 1599. Strype prints a scheme outlined in a letter to Elizabeth by the Lord Keeper, Sir John Puckring, in 1595, to enrich the queen (and himself) by appointing a new bishop and granting Puckring the income from some of the bishopric's leases. See *Annals*, 4:343–46.

10. Claire Cross, *The Royal Supremacy in the Elizabethan Church* (London: George Allen and Unwin; New York: Barnes and Noble, 1969), pp. 21–27.

11. This letter was published by White Kennet, *The Case of Impropriations* (London, 1704), appendix, p. 23.

12. Wallace MacCaffrey, *The Shaping of the Elizabethan Regime* (Princeton, N.J.: Princeton Univ. Press, 1968), pp. 22–63.

13. Joyce Youings, *The Dissolution of the Monasteries* (London: George Allen and Unwin; New York: Barnes and Noble, 1971), p. 135.

14. In a letter to Burghley in 1573, Parker backed up his opposition to Thomas Cartwright's antiepiscopal arguments by citing the Corpus Christi scholarships as evidence that he fruitfully used "the living that her majesty hath committed to my trust" (*Correspondence of Matthew Parker*, ed. J. Bruce and T. T. Perowne [1853; reprint, New York: Johnson Reprint Corporation, 1968], pp. 453–55).

15. On the conflation of fifteenth-century personified abstractions in the Vice, see David M. Bevington, *From "Mankind" to Marlowe* (Cambridge, Mass.: Harvard Univ. Press, 1962), pp. 121–23. Bevington does not deal with the social dimensions of these characters or with devils from the mystery plays as parallels to personified abstractions in the morality. My reservations about socialist interpretations of the Vice are stated above in chapter 2. For these interpretations, see particularly Robert Weimann, *Shakespeare and the Popular Tradition in the Theater*, ed. Robert Schwartz (Baltimore: Johns Hopkins Univ. Press, 1978), and Walter Cohen, *Drama of a Nation* (Ithaca, N.Y.: Cornell Univ. Press, 1985).

16. J. E. Neale, *Queen Elizabeth* (London: Jonathan Cape, 1934), p. 41.

17. Quoted by Alison Plowden, *The Young Elizabeth* (London and Basingstoke: Macmillan, 1971), p. 143.

18. Quoted by Neale, *Queen Elizabeth*, p. 67.

19. George Puttenham, *The Arte of English Poesie*, ed. Gladys Willcock and

Alice Walker (Cambridge: Cambridge Univ. Press, 1936), p. 186. For earlier discussion of this maxim, see pp. 56 and 86.

20. Puttenham, *Arte of English Poesie* p. 299.

21. Everard Guilpin, *Skialetheia*, ed. D. Allen Carroll (Chapel Hill: Univ. of North Carolina Press, 1974), Satire 1.67–76, p. 65. Carroll notes similar descriptions of courtly hypocrisy in *Richard II* and *Edward II*, and in satires by Marston, Nashe, and an anonymous satirist of Raleigh (pp. 157–59). For this reference to *Skialetheia* I am indebted to G. B. Harrison, *The Life and Death of Robert Devereux, Earl of Essex* (London: Cassel and Co., 1937), p. 193.

22. Ray Heffner, "Essex, The Ideal Courtier," *ELH* 1 (1934), 7–36.

23. La Rochefoucauld, *The Maxims*, trans. Constantine FitzGibbon (London: Millington, 1974).

24. Harrison, *Life of Essex*, p. 304. This biography is cited hereafter in the text as Harrison.

25. Beach Langston, "Essex and the Art of Dying," *HLQ* 13 (1950), 128. This article is cited hereafter in the text as Langston.

26. For Raleigh, see Stephen Greenblatt, *Sir Walter Ralegh: The Renaissance Man and His Roles* (New Haven, Conn.: Yale Univ. Press, 1973). Greenblatt writes pertinently about Queen Elizabeth to the same effect in *Renaissance Self-Fashioning* (Chicago: Univ. of Chicago Press, 1980), pp. 166–69.

27. W. P. Haugaard, "Elizabeth Tudor's Book of Devotions: A Neglected Clue to the Queen's Life and Character," *Sixteenth-Century Journal* 12 (1981), 70–106.

28. Wallace MacCaffrey, *Queen Elizabeth and the Making of Policy, 1572–1588* (Princeton, N.J.: Princeton Univ. Press, 1981), pp. 23–153.

29. Sir Arthur Quiller-Couch seems to have been the first to notice the morality play structure of Hal's story, *Shakespeare's Workmanship* (London: T. Fisher Unwin, 1918), pp. 140–44. A more recent argument, including later references, is Alan C. Dessen's article, "The Intemperate Knight and the Politic Prince: Late Morality Structure in *Henry IV*," *ShakS* 7 (1974), 147–71.

30. Emrys Jones, *The Origins of Shakespeare* (Oxford: Clarendon Press, 1977), p. 56, my emphasis.

31. Neale, *Queen Elizabeth*, passim.

32. For apt comments on "Petrarchan politics," see Greenblatt, *Renaissance Self-Fashioning*, pp. 165–66. David Norbrook argues that Fulke Greville's *Caelica* sonnets deliberately exploit the politicization of love poetry (*Poetry and Politics in the English Renaissance* [London: Routledge and Kegan Paul, 1984], pp. 157–74). See also Louis A. Montrose, " 'Shaping Fantasies': Figurations of Gender and Power in Elizabethan Culture," in *Representing the English Renaissance*, ed. Stephen Greenblatt (Berkeley and Los Angeles: Univ. of California Press, 1988), pp. 31–64, and an essay that depends heavily on Montrose's, Leonard Tennenhouse, *Power on Display* (New York and London: Methuen, 1986), pp. 17–44.

33. Walter B. Devereux, *Lives and Letters of the Devereux, Earls of Essex* (London: John Murray, 1853), 1:249–50.

34. Falstaff's debt to Tarlton has been discussed by J. A. Bryant, "Shakespeare's Falstaff and the Mantle of Dick Tarlton," *SP* 51 (1954), 149–62, and by Weimann, *Shakespeare and the Popular Tradition*, pp. 189–91. Bryant summarizes the parallels (p. 159) but without addressing their social context. My difference with Weimann's interpretation of the social parallels is indicated below.

35. Tarlton's uniqueness has been frequently noted. In *A Dictionary of Actors* (New Haven, Conn.: Yale Univ. Press; London: Oxford Univ. Press, 1929), Edwin Nungezer comments: "No other Elizabethan actor has been the object of so many notices in contemporary and later writing, or has been remembered with such various and practical tokens of esteem" (p. 355). Muriel Bradbrook remarks, in *The Rise of the Common Player* (Cambridge, Mass.: Harvard Univ. Press, 1962): "By the seventies, Tarlton was a national figure, the first actor to achieve stardom; perhaps the first man to be known all over England simply in terms of his personality" (p. 162). To similar effect is Andrew Gurr's description in *Playgoing in Shakespeare's London* (Cambridge: Cambridge Univ. Press, 1987): "Tarlton's fame, which made him a legend for sixty years after his death, is significant more for the phenomenon he represented than any jokes he actually created. It is hardly too much to say that, as much as the Virgin Queen herself, he became the chief emblem of the emerging national consciousness at the end of the sixteenth century" (p. 121).

36. The best collection of comments about Tarlton is Nungezer, *Dictionary of Actors*, pp. 347–65. Tarlton's writings have been edited by J. O. Halliwell, *Tarlton's Jests and News out of Purgatory* (London: Shakespeare Society, 1844).

37. For reports of Tarlton's origin, see Nungezer, *Dictionary of Actors*, pp. 347–48.

38. Tarlton's social context is well described by Bradbrook, *Rise of the Common Player*, pp. 162–77.

39. Gurr, *Shakespearean Playgoing*, p. 128.

40. Gary Taylor argues that the immediate epic influence on *Henry V* was Chapman's translation of Homer, published in 1598. (*Henry V*, ed. Gary Taylor [Oxford: Clarendon Press, 1982], pp. 52–58).

41. Frances A. Yates, *Astraea: The Imperial Theme in the Sixteenth Century* (London and Boston: Routledge and Kegan Paul, 1975), pp. 38–59; Roy C. Strong, *The Cult of Elizabeth* (London: Thames and Hudson, 1977), pp. 153–54.

42. Tennenhouse also comments on *Henry V* as romantic comedy (*Power on Display*, pp. 68–71). Tennenhouse's conception of romantic comedy as inspired by the court—and more specifically, by Philip Sidney (p. 18)—ignores the popular dramatic tradition, to which Shakespeare indisputably belongs, though Sidney had little use for it.

43. John Bakeless, *Christopher Marlowe* (New York: William Morrow, 1937), pp. 80–84.

44. *Shakespeare and the Problem of Meaning* (Chicago: Univ. of Chicago Press, 1981), pp. 33–62. This chapter first appeared as "Rabbits, Ducks, and Henry V," *SQ* 28 (1977), 279–96.

45. R. B. Wernham, *After the Armada* (Oxford: Clarendon Press, 1984), p. 143.

Chapter 7. Power and Archaic Dramaturgy in *All's Well That Ends Well*

1. F. S. Boas, *Shakespere and his Predecessors* (1896; reprint, New York: Haskell House, 1968), pp. 344–408.

2. Lawrence Danson traces the "problematic" perception of *The Merchant of Venice* to the Romantics, but its real vitality, as he acknowledges, has emerged

since the Holocaust. See *The Harmonies of "The Merchant of Venice"* (New Haven, Conn.: Yale Univ. Press, 1978), pp. 1–18.

3. The fullest and most careful exposition of the old and new law in *The Merchant of Venice* is Barbara Lewalski's article, "Biblical Allusion and Allegory in *The Merchant of Venice*," *SQ* 13 (1969), 327–43, though Lewalski does not take account of ambiguities of power in the play. For a more complex view, see Danson, *Harmonies*, pp. 56–81 and 126–69.

4. See particularly Richard Wheeler, *Shakespeare's Development and the Problem Comedies* (Berkeley and Los Angeles: Univ. of California Press, 1981) and Marilyn Williamson, *The Patriarchy of Shakespeare's Comedies: The Plays in History* (Detroit: Wayne State Univ. Press, 1986).

5. Kathleen M. Ashley, "The Guiler Beguiled: Christ and Satan as Theological Tricksters in Medieval Religious Literature," *Criticism*, 24 (1982), 126–37.

6. Gregory of Nyssa, *The Great Catechism*, chapter 26, in *Nicene and Post-Nicene Fathers*, ed. Philip Schaff and Henry Wace, 2d ser. (1892; reprint, Grand Rapids, Mich.: Wm. B. Eerdmans, 1983), 5:495. The passage quoted here is cited in a different translation by Gustaf Aulén, to whom I owe the reference, *Christus Victor: An Historical Study of the Three Main Types of the Idea of the Atonement*, trans. A. G. Herbert (London: SPCK, 1931), p. 69.

7. John Scott Colley, "Launcelot, Jacob, and Esau: Old and New Law in *The Merchant of Venice*," *YES* 10 (1980), 181–89. Colley recognizes the problems surrounding Portia: "She uses the trickery, the guile, and the cunning appropriate to a Shylock in order to defeat the trickery, cunning, and guile of the actual Shylock" (p. 185).

8. The earliest study of the idea in medieval drama is by Timothy Fry, who sees it as the primary unifying motif of the N-Town Cycle, "The Unity of the *Ludus Coventriae*," *SP* 48 (1951), 527–70. Alan H. Nelson's Ph.D. dissertation is the fullest study, "The Contest of Guile in the Middle English Corpus Christi Plays" (Univ. of California, Berkeley, 1966), a portion of which, dealing with the temptation plays, can be found in "The Temptation of Christ; or, The Temptation of Satan" in *Medieval English Drama*, ed. Jerome Taylor and Alan H. Nelson (Chicago: Univ. of Chicago Press, 1972), pp. 218–29. Nelson's summary is worth considering with Helena in mind: "Reflection upon the Temptation scene in this perspective suggests that Christ rather than Satan is the real tempter. Masking his identity from Satan, and refusing to reveal it, in spite of Satan's wiles, Christ gives him no alternative but to set out on a disastrous course which will end with the release of souls from Satan's power" (p. 229). For other studies of the "guiler beguiled" in medieval drama, see Ashley, "Guiler Beguiled," p. 135, n. 24.

9. *Towneley Plays*, ed. George England and A. W. Pollard (London: Kegan Paul, Trench, Trübner, 1897), EETS, e.s. 71, *Second Shepherds' Play*, ll. 710–13.

10. V. A. Kolve, *The Play Called Corpus Christi* (Stanford, Calif.: Stanford Univ. Press, 1966), pp. 156–58.

11. I take this point from Ashley, "Guiler Beguiled," pp. 132–33.

12. Francis Bacon, *Works*, ed. James Spedding et al., 14 vols. (Boston: Brown and Taggard, 1861), 4:323–24.

13. Stephen Greenblatt, *Renaissance Self-Fashioning* (Chicago: Univ. of Chicago Press, 1980), p. 224.

14. Robert G. Hunter, *Shakespeare and the Comedy of Forgiveness* (New York: Columbia Univ. Press, 1962), p. 118.

15. Frank Whigham, *Ambition and Privilege: The Social Tropes of Elizabethan Courtesy Theory* (Berkeley and Los Angeles: Univ. of California Press, 1984), p. 148.

16. John Ferne, *The Blazon of Gentrie* (London, 1586), pp. 9–10, sigs. Bv–Bv^v. In Ferne's imagined conversation, this remark by the lawyer is followed by one from the knight, which is even more abusive. Neither interlocutor imagines the unimaginable: that a socially superior woman might marry a man of ungentle standing. What makes this possibility unimaginable is that the most direct threat to the dominance of socially dominant males was for "their" women to marry a social subordinate. The parallel in modern experience is the white racist fear of black men with white women. That Shakespeare staged precisely this relationship in *Othello* is as striking as Webster's staging of a duchess's marriage with her master of horse in *The Duchess of Malfi*.

17. Howard Cole, *The "All's Well" Story from Boccaccio to Shakespeare* (Urbana: Univ. of Illinois Press, 1981), pp. 95–100.

18. Muriel C. Bradbrook, "Virtue Is the True Nobility: A Study of the Structure of *All's Well that Ends Well*," *RES*, n.s. 1 (1950), 293.

19. For topical commentary on these plays, see David M. Bevington, *Tudor Drama and Politics* (Cambridge, Mass.: Harvard Univ. Press, 1968), pp. 42–53.

20. M. E. Moeslein, ed., *The Plays of Henry Medwall: A Critical Edition* (New York and London: Garland Publishing Co., 1981), p. 81.

21. Thomas More, *Utopia*, in *The Complete Works of Thomas More*, ed. Edward Surtz and J. H. Hexter, (New Haven, Conn.: Yale Univ. Press, 1965), pp. 131–33. See above, p. 47.

22. Prudentius, *Peristephanon*, trans. H. J. Thomson in *Prudentius*, 2 vols. (London: William Heinemann; Cambridge, Mass.: Harvard Univ. Press, 1961), 2:237.

23. Augustine, *The City of God*, trans. Henry Bettenson (Harmondsworth: Penguin Books, 1984).

24. Augustine, *Ennarationes in Psalmos* 96.4, quoted by Erich Auerbach, *Literary Language and Its Public in Late Latin Antiquity and in the Middle Ages*, trans. Ralph Manheim (Princeton, N.J.: Princeton Univ. Press, 1965), p. 42.

25. *York Plays*, ed. Lucy Toulmin Smith (Oxford: Clarendon Press, 1885).

26. *The Chester Mystery Cycle*, ed. R. M. Lumiansky and David Mills (London: Oxford Univ. Press, 1974), EETS s.s. 3, *Trial*, ll. 355–56.

27. Rosemary Woolf, *The English Mystery Plays* (London: Routledge and Kegan Paul; Berkeley and Los Angeles: Univ. of California Press, 1972), pp. 258–60. See also Raymond St. Jacques, "Langland's Christ-Knight and the Liturgy," *Revue de l'Université d'Ottawa* 37 (1967), 146–58.

28. *The Service for Representing the Slaughter of the Innocents*, in *Medieval Drama* ed. David M. Bevington (Boston: Houghton Mifflin, 1975), ll. 8–11.

29. John W. Velz, "Sovereignty in the Digby *Mary Magdalene*," *CompD* 2 (1968), 32–41.

30. *Mary Magdalene* (from the Digby MS), in *Medieval Drama*, ed. Beving-

ton, ll. 1005–1010. Bevington translates line 1010: "Lord, bow down your heavens and descend" (Ps. 144:5).

31. *The Conversion of St. Paul* (from the Digby MS), ed. Bevington, *Medieval Drama*, ll. 545–51.

32. The paraphrase quoted here is G. K. Hunter's gloss on *All's Well*, 1.2.41–45, in the New Arden Edition of *All's Well* (London: Methuen, 1959).

33. For an illuminating discussion of sexuality in *All's Well*, see Arthur C. Kirsch, *Shakespeare and the Experience of Love* (Cambridge: Cambridge Univ. Press, 1981), esp. pp. 118–27, where Kirsch relates the play to Montaigne's essay, "Upon Some Verses of Virgil." Kirsch's interpretation begins with Freud but arrives at very different conclusions from those of another perceptive Freudian reading by Richard Wheeler, in *Shakespeare's Development and the Problem Comedies*, pp. 34–91.

34. John W. Velz, "From Jerusalem to Damascus: Biblical Dramaturgy in Medieval and Shakespearian Conversion Plays," *CompD* 15 (1982), 311–26.

35. Helena's background in folklore was first described by William W. Lawrence, *Shakespeare's Problem Comedies* (New York: Macmillan, 1931), pp. 32–77.

36. Ambrose, *Expositio Evangelii secundum Lucam* in *Corpus Christianorum Series Latina*, 14:31, quoted from the translation by Margaret E. Goldsmith, *The Figure of Piers Plowman* (Cambridge: D. S. Brewer, 1981), p. 75.

37. George Kane and E. Talbot Donaldson, eds., *Piers Plowman: The B. Version* (London: The Athlone Press, 1975), Passus 18, ll. 354–60.

38. Bertrand Evans, *Shakespeare's Comedies* (Oxford: Clarendon Press, 1960), pp. 145–66.

39. See especially James Calderwood, "Styles of Knowing in *All's Well*," *MLQ* 25 (1964), 283–94; Michael Shapiro, " 'The Web of Our Life': Human Frailty and Mutual Redemption in *All's Well That Ends Well*," *JEGP* 71 (1972), 514–26; Frances M. Pearce, "In Quest of Unity: A Study of Failure and Redemption in *All's Well That Ends Well*," *SQ* 25 (1974), 71–88.

40. Clifford Leech, "The Theme of Ambition in *All's Well That Ends Well*," *ELH* 21 (1954), 17–29; Bertrand Evans, *Shakespeare's Comedies*, pp. 145–66 (the most careful study of the plot to elucidate Helena's role as a deceiver); Howard Cole, *The "All's Well" Story*; Richard A. Levin, "*All's Well That Ends Well* and 'All Seems Well,' " *ShakS* 13 (1980), 131–44.

Chapter 8. Style, Goodness, and Power in *Measure for Measure*

1. Jonathan Goldberg, *James I and the Politics of Literature* (Baltimore: Johns Hopkins Univ. Press, 1983), p. 235.

2. Geoffrey Bullough, *Narrative and Dramatic Sources of Shakespeare*, 8 vols. (London: Routledge and Kegan Paul; New York: Columbia Univ. Press, 1952–75), 2:443–44.

3. The dedicatory epistles of Shakespeare's two narrative poems make an illuminating comparison with Whetstone's epistle. Shakespeare also seeks courtly patronage, of course, and he pays Southampton high compliments, but he is not obsequious, and he makes no allusion to style.

4. G. K. Hunter, "Italian Tragicomedy on the English Stage," *RenD*, n.s. 6 (1973), 123–48.

5. From King James's speech before Parliament in 1610, in *The Political Works of James I*, ed. C. H. McIlwain (Cambridge, Mass.: Harvard Univ. Press, 1918), pp. 307–8.

6. K. S. Block, ed., *Ludus Coventriae*, (London: Oxford Univ. Press, 1922) *EETS* e.s. 120, *The Trial of Mary and Joseph*, l. 201.

7. For studies of this motif in medieval drama, see chapter 7 above, n. 8.

8. M. C. Bradbrook, "Authority, Truth, and Justice in *Measure for Measure*," *RES* 17 (1941), 385.

9. Eph. 4:22. Cf. Col. 3:9 and Rom. 6:6. The Croxton *Play of the Sacrament* is the best-known example of identifying the old and new laws with Jew and Christian, respectively, but Gail Gibson argues persuasively that the same opposition also informs the figure of Joseph in plays of Joseph's doubt. See "Images of Doubt and Belief: Visual Symbolism in the Middle English Plays of Joseph's Troubles about Mary" (Ph.D. diss., Univ. of Virginia, 1975).

10. See, for example, *Measure for Measure*, 1.2.130–33 and 3.1.68–70. For illuminating commentary on scope and restraint, see Michael Goldman, *Shakespeare and the Energies of Drama* (Princeton, N.J.: Princeton Univ. Press, 1972), pp. 164–74.

11. Arthur Kirsch points out the details of Angelo's repression in *Shakespeare and the Experience of Love* (Cambridge: Cambridge Univ. Press, 1981), pp. 71–107.

12. Gail Gibson's comment on Joseph in this context is worth quoting in full: " 'Old' Joseph in the *Ludus Coventriae* play is not only a type of the Jews who did not believe, but also a type of unbelieving humanity in general. St. Paul had urged all Christians to 'put off the old man' and 'be renewed' (Eph. 4:22ff.); we see that process of individual spiritual renewal enacted by Joseph. Joseph, like all sinful, doubtful men, is *the* Old Man. His lament about the conflict between youth and old age sets up the terms of the struggle between the man who tests the apple or the pregnant womb and the man who believes. That lament may have been presented in the language of fabliau comedy, but the spectators were meant to consider it in terms of a larger divine comedy—the soul's struggle for salvation" ("Images of Doubt and Belief," p. 132). Joseph's coming to the end of himself in a believing response to divine miracle is thus an important precedent to Angelo's eventual recognition of his vulnerability.

13. The centrality of the Virgin's forgiveness in these plays offers extant precedent for what R. G. Hunter calls "the comedy of forgiveness" in Shakespeare. See *Shakespeare and the Comedy of Forgiveness* (New York: Columbia Univ. Press, 1962), pp. 24–41, where Hunter turns to precedents in French miracle plays because he could find so few precedents in English.

14. A similar idea appears in the key text of the story of the woman taken in adultery: "Let him that is among you without sin cast the first stone at her" (John 8:7). It is therefore not surprising that the "measure for measure" idea appears in medieval dramatic versions of the woman's story. See, for example, *The Cappemakers*, ll. 83–93, in *York Plays*, ed. Lucy Toulmin Smith (Oxford: Clarendon Press, 1885). In Shakespeare's day theologians were still associating the Sermon on the Mount with the story in John 8. Cf. Augustine Marlorate, *A Catholike and*

Ecclesiasticall Exposition of the Holy Gospel after S. John, trans. Thomas Timme (London, 1575): "Christ requireth perfect innocency to be in the witnesses, to the end that no man might take upon him to convince another of any crime, but such a one as should be pure and perfect and without all fault himself" (sig. Bb4).

15. In Wager's play, the Vice, Infidelitie, compares his actions to those of "obstinate friars," recalling the N-Town cycle's association of Jesus' enemies with corrupt ecclesiastics (*The Life and Repentance of Mary Magdalene*, ed. F. I. Carpenter [Chicago: Univ. of Chicago Press, 1904], ll. 413–14). This kind of continuity between medieval and Renaissance drama is damaging to Daryl Gless's argument that *Measure for Measure* is inspired by anti-Catholic satire. See *Measure for Measure: The Law and the Convent* (Princeton, N.J.: Princeton Univ. Press, 1979). Like the medieval playwrights, Wager identifies Jesus' enemies with the "old law" (ll. 1480, 1513, 1516–17, 1735, etc.), emphasizes the importance of tempering justice with mercy (ll. 1318–21, 1346–49, 1674–75, etc.), and cites Mary Magdalene as a model of repentance (ll. 1218–21, 2010–11).

16. See John W. Velz, "Sovereignty in the Digby *Mary Magdalene*," *CompD* 2 (1968), 32–41; Clifford Davidson, "The Digby *Mary Magdalene* and the Magdalene Cult of the Middle Ages," *Annuale Mediaevale* 13 (1972), 70–87; David L. Jeffrey, "English Saints' Plays," in *Medieval Drama*, ed. Neville Denny (London: Edward Arnold, 1973), pp. 75–89.

17. Pagina 12, ll. 1–2, in *The Chester Mystery Cycle*, ed. R. M. Lumiansky and David Mills, EETS s.s. 3 (London: Oxford Univ. Press, 1974). For commentary on the temptation play, see Rosemary Woolf, *The English Mystery Plays* (London: Routledge and Kegan Paul; Berkeley and Los Angeles: Univ. of California Press, 1972), pp. 219–23, and Peter Travis, *Dramatic Design in the Chester Cycle* (Chicago: Univ. of Chicago Press, 1982), pp. 152–56.

18. *Lectures or Tractates on the Gospel of John*, trans. John Gibb and James Innes, in *Nicene and Post-Nicene Fathers*, ed. Philip Schaff (New York: Christian Literature Company, 1888), 7:197–98.

19. Michel Foucault, *The History of Sexuality*, trans. Robert Hurley (New York: Vintage Books, 1980). Marilyn Williamson studies Shakespeare's comedies in light of Foucault's theories in *The Patriarchy of Shakespeare's Comedies: The Plays in History* (Detroit: Wayne State Univ. Press, 1986).

20. McIlwain, ed., *Political Works of James I*, p. 20.

21. A convenient summary of these parallels can be found in a highly critical review of them by Richard Levin, *New Readings vs. Old Plays* (Chicago: Univ. of Chicago Press, 1979), p. 171–93.

22. Norman Holland, "*Measure for Measure*: The Duke and the Prince," *CompL* 11 (1959), 16–20.

Chapter 9. Tragedy: Noble Weakness

1. "As Plautus and Seneca are accounted the best for comedy and tragedy among the Latins, so Shakespeare among the English is the most excellent in both kinds for the stage" (Francis Meres, *Palladis Tamia* [1598], in *Elizabethan Critical Essays*, ed. G. Gregory Smith, 2 vols. [London: Oxford Univ. Press, 1904], 2:317–18).

2. J. W. Cunliffe, *The Influence of Seneca on Elizabethan Tragedy* (New York: Macmillan, 1893). For an incisive critique of Cunliffe's methodology, see

G. K. Hunter, "Seneca and the Elizabethans: A Case-Study in 'Influence' " in *Dramatic Identities and Cultural Tradition* (Liverpool: Liverpool Univ. Press, 1978), pp. 159–73. "Seneca and English Tragedy" in the same volume (pp. 174–213) is also valuable.

3. Katharine Eisaman Maus, *Ben Jonson and the Roman Frame of Mind* (Princeton, N.J.: Princeton Univ. Press, 1984). Cf. G. K. Hunter, "A Roman Thought: Renaissance Attitudes to History Exemplified in Shakespeare and Jonson," in *An English Miscellany*, ed. Brian S. Lee (London: Oxford Univ. Press, 1977), pp. 93–118. Unlike Maus, Hunter does not reckon with the social motives that produced Elizabethan adulation of Rome, and he therefore tends to dichotomize attitudes to the Republic and the Empire too strongly. Gordon Braden argues persuasively that imperial attitudes were a logical extension of the idealized moralism of the Republic. See *Renaissance Tragedy and the Senecan Tradition* (New Haven, Conn.: Yale Univ. Press, 1985), pp. 5–27 et passim.

4. George Puttenham, *The Arte of English Poesie*, ed. Gladys D. Willcock and Alice Walker (Cambridge: Cambridge Univ. Press, 1936), p. 26.

5. Sir Philip Sidney, *An Apology for Poetry*, in *Elizabethan Critical Essays*, ed. Smith, 1:177.

6. Maus's discussion of Ben Jonson's "On My First Son" illuminates Renaissance adaptations of Roman Stoicism regarding the filial relationship. See *Ben Jonson and the Roman Frame of Mind*, pp. 119–22.

7. Virgil, *Aeneid* 10.517–20 and 11.81–82. Cf. *Aeneid* 6.819–23, where Brutus is praised for condemning his own sons to death. The likelihood that Shakespeare recalled Virgil in the Alarbus incident is increased by the fact that Alarbus' death is not part of the chapbook account of Titus's life (presuming, of course, that the chapbook represents a reliable version of Shakespeare's source).

8. Braden, *Renaissance Tragedy*, p. 57.

9. Lawrence Stone, *The Crisis of the Aristocracy 1558–1664* (London: Oxford Univ. Press, 1967), chapter 5.

10. "The Metamorphosis of Violence in *Titus Andronicus*," *Shakespeare Survey* 10 (1957), 46.

11. I am indebted here to Braden's account in *Renaissance Tragedy*, p. 102.

12. A. C. Hamilton reads the mythological background in *Titus* neo-Platonically as a suggestion of the Age of Saturn (cf. "Saturninus"), i.e., of a fallen world (*The Early Shakespeare* [San Marino, Calif.: The Huntington Library, 1967], pp. 63–89). For more recent assertions about the play's political realism, see Robert S. Miola, "*Titus Andronicus* and the Mythos of Shakespeare's Rome," *Shakespeare Studies* 14 (1981), 85–98 and Jacqueline Pearson, "Romans and Barbarians: The Structure of Irony in Shakespeare's Roman Tragedies" in *Shakespearean Tragedy*, ed. Malcolm Bradbury and David Palmer (London: Edward Arnold, 1984), pp. 159–82.

13. On the complementarity of Jonson's tragedies and masques, see Maus, *Ben Jonson*, pp. 57–58.

14. Roy Battenhouse, *Shakespearean Tragedy: Its Art and Christian Premises* (Bloomington: Indiana Univ. Press, 1969).

15. Thomas Rymer, *A Short View of Tragedy* (1692) in *The Critical Works*

of Thomas Rymer, ed. Curt A. Zimansky (New Haven, Conn.: Yale Univ. Press, 1956), pp. 113–16. Cited hereafter in the text as *Works*.

16. Rymer's dogmatic appeal to classical rhetoric in criticizing *Othello* has been interpreted by Joel Altman in the context of emerging canons of probability in the Renaissance (" 'Preposterous conclusions': *Eros, Enargeia*, and the Composition of *Othello*," *Representations* 18 [1987], 129–57). Rymer's social rejection of medieval religious drama is comparable to the social prejudice against actors that Pope frequently betrays in emending *King Lear* in his edition of Shakespeare. See Steven Urkowitz, "The Base Shall to th' Legitimate: The Growth of an Editorial Tradition" in *The Division of the Kingdoms. Shakespeare's Two Versions of "King Lear*," ed. Gary Taylor and Michael Warren (Oxford: Clarendon Press, 1983), pp. 26–28.

17. Nahum Tate, *The History of King Lear* (1681), ed. James Black (Lincoln: Univ. of Nebraska Press, 1975), p. 1.

18. Maynard Mack, *"King Lear" in Our Time* (Berkeley: Univ. of California Press, 1965), pp. 9–11.

19. On continuity between heroic drama and the sentimental tragedy that replaced it, see Robert D. Hume, *The Development of English Drama in the Late Seventeenth Century* (Oxford: Clarendon Press, 1976), p. 179.

20. Franco Moretti, " 'A Huge Eclipse': Tragic Form and the Deconsecration of Sovereignty" in *The Power of Forms in the English Renaissance*, ed. Stephen Greenblatt (Norman, Okla.: Pilgrim Books, 1982), pp. 7–8. For an application of Moretti's idea to the history plays, see David S. Kastan, "Proud Majesty Made a Subject: Shakespeare and the Spectacle of Rule," *SQ* 37 (1986), 459–75.

21. *Calendar of State Papers Relating to Scotland, 1547–1603*, ed. William K. Boyd, 13 vols. (Glasgow: HM Stationery Office, 1915), 9:247.

22. In Spenser's allegorization of Mary's trial and execution, one of her advocates is "Nobility of Birth, that bred / Great ruth through her misfortune's tragic stour" (*Faerie Queene*, 5.9.45). Mercilla sweeps this advocate aside, however, as she does all the others. Spenser's reduction of Erastian ideology to mere sentimentality strikingly anticipates later arguments favoring the execution of Charles I—and is an extremely risky move, in view of Spenser's ideological defense of monarchy in *The Faerie Queene*.

23. *Calendar of State Papers Relating to Scotland*, 9:251–56.

24. *The Tenure of Kings and Magistrates* (1649), in *Complete Prose Works of John Milton*, ed. Merritt Y. Hughes (New Haven, Conn.: Yale Univ. Press, 1962), 3:110–25.

25. Mack, *"King Lear" in Our Time*, pp. 49–56.

26. E. K. Chambers, *The Medieval Stage*, 2 vols. (Oxford: Clarendon Press, 1903), 2:151, 205, 356, 378, and Lawrence M. Clopper, ed., *Records of Early English Drama Chester* (Toronto: Univ. of Toronto Press, 1979), pp. 26 and 484.

27. *Robert of Sicily*, in *Middle English Metrical Romances*, ed. Walter H. French and Charles B. Hale (New York: Prentice-Hall, 1930), ll. 45–46.

28. Jonathan Dollimore, *Radical Tragedy* (Chicago: Univ. of Chicago Press, 1984), pp. 10–17.

29. Stephen Greenblatt, "The Cultivation of Anxiety: King Lear and His Heirs," *Raritan* 2 (1982), 92–114.

30. Lillian H. Hornstein, "*King Robert of Sicily*: Analogues and Origins," *PMLA* 79 (1964), 13–21. Alexandra H. Olsen challenges Hornstein's analysis, proposing instead that Robert belongs to Vladimir Propp's category of "victimized heroes." This argument would appear, however, merely to substitute a broader category for a narrower (and historically more carefully defined) category. See "The Return of the King: A Reconsideration of *Robert of Sicily*," *Folklore* 93 (1982), 216–19.

31. *Nichomachean Ethics*, 1122b, trans. Martin Ostwald (Indianapolis, Ind.: Bobbs-Merrill, 1962), pp. 90–91.

32. *Hymenaei*, in *Ben Jonson: The Complete Masques*, ed. Stephen Orgel (New Haven, Conn.: Yale Univ. Press, 1969), ll. 9–12.

33. See, for example, William R. Elton, *King Lear and the Gods* (San Marino, Calif.: The Huntington Library, 1968) and Dollimore, *Radical Tragedy*, pp. 189–203.

34. Rymer argues that "poetical justice" was invented by Sophocles and Euripides specifically as a means of vindicating divine Providence in tragedy. See *Tragedies of the Last Age* (1678) in *Works*, p. 22.

35. This is Paul Jorgensen's argument in *Lear's Self-Discovery* (Berkeley and Los Angeles: Univ. of California Press, 1967). Jorgensen overlooks the centrality of self-recognition in medieval religious drama, however, and focuses exclusively on humanist tradition.

36. What in another vanity would seem,
    Appears but noble confidence in him.
    No haughty boasting; but a manly pride:
    A soul too fiery, and too great a guide:
    He moves eccentric, like a wandring star;
    Whose motion's just; though 'tis not regular.
The Conquest of Granada, Part 1 (5.1.203–8) in *The Works of John Dryden*, ed. H. T. Swendenberg et al. (Berkeley and Los Angeles: Univ. of California Press, 1956–), 11:88.

37. Edward Bond, *Lear* (New York: Hill and Wang, 1972); Dollimore, *Radical Tragedy*, p. 193.

38. J. F. Danby, *Shakespeare's Doctrine of Nature: A Study of "King Lear"* (London: Faber and Faber, 1949); G. Wilson Knight, *The Wheel of Fire* (London: Oxford Univ. Press, 1930), pp. 160–206. For Dollimore's critique of "essentialist humanism," see *Radical Tragedy*, pp. 191–94. Examples include A. C. Bradley, *Shakespearean Tragedy* (London: Macmillan, 1905); Nicholas Brooke, *Shakespeare: "King Lear"* (London: Edward Arnold, 1963); Mack, *"King Lear" in Our Time*; Wilbur Sanders, *The Dramatist and the Received Idea* (Cambridge: Cambridge Univ. Press, 1968).

39. Howard Felperin, *Shakesperean Romance* (Princeton: Princeton Univ. Press, 1972), pp. 97–139. Felperin's argument regarding the structure of Shakespeare's mature tragedies is informed by Maynard Mack's classic essay, "The Jacobean Shakespeare: Some Observations on the Construction of the Tragedies" in *Jacobean Theatre*, ed. John Russell Brown and Bernard Harris (New York: St. Martins Press, 1960), pp. 11–41.

40. Rosalie L. Colie, "Reason and Need: King Lear and the 'Crisis' of the

Aristocracy," in *Some Facets of "King Lear,"* ed. Rosalie L. Colie and F. T. Flahiff (London: Heinemann, 1974), pp. 185–219.

41. Emrys Jones, *The Origins of Shakespeare* (Oxford: Clarendon Press, 1977), p. 52.

42. I follow the common emendation here of "top" for "to," though I am aware of recent arguments that the Folio is Shakespeare's revision of the First Quarto edition and both editions use "to." My reason for following the emendation is that it appears in the text I am using and does not alter the argument I am making. The same is true for other passages I cite from *King Lear* and for my argument about the play as a whole. For recent textual discussion, see Steven Urkowitz, *Shakespeare's Revision of "King Lear"* (Princeton: Princeton Univ. Press, 1980), Peter W. M. Blayney, *The Texts of "King Lear" and Their Origins*, 2 vols., vol. 1, *Nicholas Okes and the First Quarto* (Cambridge: Cambridge Univ. Press, 1982), vol. 2, forthcoming; and Taylor and Warren, ed., *Division of the Kingdoms* (above, n. 16).

43. K. S. Block, ed., *Ludus Coventriae* (London: Oxford Univ. Press, 1922), EETS e.s. 120, *Passion Play 1*, l. 93.

44. Joyce Youings, *Sixteenth-Century England*, The Pelican Social History of Britain (Harmondsworth, Eng.: Penguin Books, 1984), p. 53.

45. *Peter Idley's Instructions to His Son*, ed. Charlotte D'Evelyn (Boston: D. C. Heath; London: Oxford Univ. Press, 1935), pt. 1, ll. 580–81.

46. Robert Weimann, *Shakespeare and the Popular Tradition in the Theater*, ed. Robert Schwartz (Baltimore: Johns Hopkins Univ. Press, 1978); Walter Cohen, *Drama of a Nation* (Ithaca, N.Y.: Cornell Univ. Press, 1985).

47. Stephen Greenblatt, *Sir Walter Ralegh: The Renaissance Man and His Roles* (New Haven, Conn.: Yale Univ. Press, 1973) and *Renaissance Self-Fashioning* (Chicago: Univ. of Chicago Press, 1980).

48. Clifford Geertz, "Religion as a Cultural System" in *The Interpretation of Cultures* (New York: Basic Books, 1973), p. 99. The tragedy of King Lear is also illuminated by another comment in the same essay: "Bafflement, suffering, and a sense of intractable ethical paradox are all, if they become intense enough or are sustained long enough, radical challenges to the proposition that life is comprehensible and that we can, by taking thought, orient ourselves effectively within it—challenges with which any religion, however 'primitive,' which hopes to persist, must attempt somehow to cope" (p. 100).

Chapter 10. Ruling Taste and the Late Plays

1. If they love lees and leave the lusty wine,
   Envy them not: their palate's with the swine.
      No doubt some moldy tale,
      Like *Pericles*, and stale
   As the shrieve's crusts, and nasty as his fish-
      scraps out of every dish,
   Thrown forth and rak'd into the common tub
      May keep up the play-club.

Epilogue to *The New Inn* (1629), in *Ben Jonson*, ed. C. H. Herford and Percy and Evelyn Simpson, 11 vols. (Oxford: Clarendon Press, 1925–52), 6:429–93.

2. Jonathan Dollimore's reading of Jacobean tragedy suggests a predominantly social motive (*Radical Tragedy* [Chicago: Univ. of Chicago Press, 1984], especially pp. 139–50).

3. For discussion of James's entry, see Graham Parry, *The Golden Age Restored: The Culture of the Stuart Court, 1603–42* (New York: St. Martins Press, 1981), pp. 1–39.

4. Cicero is actually quoting the poet Antimachus, who recalls an incident when he was deserted by everyone except Plato at a reading of Antimachus' *Thebais* (*Brutus* 51.191, trans. G.L. Hendrickson [Cambridge, Mass.: Harvard University Press; London: William Heinemann, 1952]). I am indebted to Michael Murrin, *The Veil of Allegory* (Chicago: Univ. of Chicago Press, 1968), p. 9, for this reference and the one below to Sir John Harrington. Murrin cites both in his discussion of exclusive rhetoric in the Renaissance. His comparison with exclusive prophetic rhetoric in the Bible can be misleading, however, since the prophets never exclude on a social basis, whereas a stratified society is assumed as the context in classical and Renaissance rhetoric.

5. *Part of the King's Entertainment in Passing to His Coronation*, in *Ben Jonson*, ed. Herford and Simpson, 7:91.

6. *Tethys Festival*, in *Inigo Jones: The Theatre of the Stuart Court*, ed. Stephen Orgel and Roy Strong, 2 vols. (London: Sotheby, Parke, Bernet; Berkeley and Los Angeles: Univ. of California Press, 1973), 1:196.

7. *Neptune's Triumph*, in *Inigo Jones*, ed. Orgel and Strong, 1:365, ll. 59–68.

8. Sir John Harrington, *A Brief Apology for Poetry*, in *Elizabethan Critical Essays*, ed. G. Gregory Smith, 2 vols. (London: Oxford Univ. Press, 1904), 2:204. Despite his allusion to ancient authority, Harrington actually took this point from Sidney's *Apology for Poetry*, as Smith points out: ". . . there are many mysteries contained in poetry, which of purpose were written darkly, lest by prophane wits it should be abused" (1:206).

9. David M. Bergeron, *Shakespeare's Romances and the Royal Family* (Lawrence: Univ. of Kansas Press, 1985).

10. This painting has been recently cleaned and its original allegory has therefore been clarified. See Roy Strong, *Henry, Prince of Wales and England's Lost Renaissance* (London: Thames and Hudson, 1986), p. 115 and illus. 45.

11. Roy Strong, *Charles I on Horseback* (London: Allen Lane The Penguin Press, 1972), p. 49.

12. William Crashaw, *A Sermon Preached before the Right Honorable the Lord Lavarre, Lord Governor and Captain General of Virginia, Feb. 21, 1609* (London, 1610), sig. C4ᵛ. On Prince Henry's expansionist ambitions, see Strong, *Henry Prince of Wales*, pp. 60–63.

13. That Crashaw was probably responding to royal taste is suggested by very similar terms used in Pierre Erondelle's dedication to Prince Henry in Erondelle's translation of Marc Lescarbot's *Nova Francia* (London, 1609), sigs. ¶¶–¶¶ᵛ.

14. For reproductions of Jones's drawing, see Orgel and Strong, *Inigo Jones*, 1:158 and 216–17; for commentary, Strong, *Henry, Prince of Wales*, pp. 148–50.

15. Parry, *Golden Age*, p. 75; cf. Strong, *Henry, Prince of Wales*, p. 49.

16. Orgel and Strong, *Inigo Jones*, 1:204, 223, 224. Also illustrated in Strong, *Henry, Prince of Wales*, illus. 78, with commentary on pp. 170–71.

17. Jill Finsten, *Isaac Oliver: Art at the Court of Elizabeth I and James I*, 2 vols. (New York and London: Garland Publishing Co., 1981), 2:105 and fig. 66.

18. Louis A. Montrose, "Of Gentlemen and Shepherds: The Politics of Elizabethan Pastoral Form," *ELH* 50 (1983), 426.

19. *Oberon, The Fairy Prince*, in *Inigo Jones*, ed. Orgel and Strong, 1:127, lines 49–60.

20. *The Vision of Delight*, in *Inigo Jones*, ed. Orgel and Strong, 1:273, lines 193–96. For commentary, see Orgel, *The Illusion of Power* (Berkeley and Los Angeles: Univ. of California Press, 1975), pp. 51–55.

21. Orgel and Strong, *Inigo Jones*, 2:483.

22. C. H. McIlwain, ed., *The Political Works of James I* (Cambridge, Mass.: Harvard Univ. Press, 1918), pp. 307–8.

23. From a letter by Sir John More, reprinted in Robert Ashton, *James I by His Contemporaries* (London: Hutchinson, 1969), pp. 67–68. More's emphasis.

24. Joseph Hall, *The Works of Joseph Hall* (London, 1625), fol. 280, sig. Bb2. Jerry W. Williamson, *The Myth of the Conqueror: Prince Henry Stuart, A Study of 17th-Century Personation* (New York: AMS Press, 1978), p. 81.

25. *The Dramatic Works in the Beaumont and Fletcher Canon*, ed. Fredson Bowers (Cambridge: Cambridge Univ. Press, 1970), 2:29, 1.1.6–11.

26. Evelyn M. Simpson and George R. Potter, ed., *The Sermons of John Donne*, 10 vols. (Berkeley and Los Angeles: Univ. of California Press, 1953–62), 6:290. This passage is cited by Parry, *Golden Age*, p. 240. John B. Gleason has pointed out that Donne's annotations in his copy of More's *Utopia* reveal Donne's ambivalence about his role as court preacher. "Dr. Donne in the Courts of Kings: A Glimpse from Marginalia," *JEGP* 69 (1970), 599–612.

27. For courtly dramaturgy in *The Tempest*, see Gary Schmidgall, *Shakespeare and the Courtly Aesthetic* (Berkeley and Los Angeles: Univ. of California Press, 1981).

28. Ernest B. Gilman, " 'All Eyes': Prospero's Inverted Masque," *RenQ* 33 (1980), 214–30.

29. Robert G. Hunter, *Shakespeare and the Comedy of Forgiveness* (New York: Columbia Univ. Press, 1962), pp. 227–41.

30. *Sermons*, ed. Simpson and Potter, 6:289.

31. Daniel Dyke, *The Mystery of Selfe-Deceving* (London, 1616), p. 41, sig. D5.

32. Inga-Stina Ewbank notes that this scene so thoroughly embodies the spirit of the masque as to have been actually imitated in masques written by Beaumont and Campion, respectively, soon after *The Winter's Tale*. "The Triumph of Time in *The Winter's Tale*," *REL* 5(2) (1964), 98, n. 1.

33. *The Magnificent Entertainment Given to King James*, in *The Dramatic Works of Thomas Dekker*, ed. Fredson Bowers, 4 vols. (Cambridge: Cambridge Univ. Press, 1955), 2:278, ll. 35–39. For a detailed discussion of how Shakespeare uses music in *The Tempest* to qualify the assumptions of courtly dramaturgy, see David Lindley, "Music, Masque, and Meaning in *The Tempest*," in *The Court Masque*, ed. David Lindley, (Manchester: Manchester Univ. Press, 1984), pp. 47–59.

34. Thomas Rymer, *The Critical Works of Thomas Rymer*, ed. Curt A. Zimansky (New Haven, Conn.: Yale Univ. Press, 1956), pp. 169–70.

35. Gail M. Gibson, "The Images of Doubt and Belief: Visual Symbolism in the Middle English Plays of Joseph's Troubles about Mary" (Ph.D. diss., Univ. of Virginia, 1975), pp. 58–60 and 101–10.

36. Hardin Craig, ed., *Two Coventry Corpus Christi Plays*, 2d ed. EETS, e.s. 87 (London: Oxford Univ. Press, 1957), *Shearmen and Taylors' Pageant*, ll. 126–29.

37. *Winter's Tale*, 1.2.197, 201, 124. In the N-Town Cycle, Joseph is much bawdier than his Coventry counterpart, and therefore closer to Leontes:

Alas! Alas! My name is shent!
All men may me now dyspyse
And seyn, "Olde cokwold, thi bow is bent
Newly now after the Frensche gyse!"

K. S. Block, ed., *Ludus Coventriae*, EETS, e.s. 120 (London: Oxford Univ. Press, 1922), p. 110, ll. 53–56.

38. Craig, ed., *Two Coventry Corpus Christi Plays*, p. 5, ll. 133–35. Similar direct address appears in the N-Town Cycle's version of Joseph's doubt, p. 110, ll. 49–52.

39. Gibson, "Images of Doubt and Belief," pp. 104–23.

40. *Coleridge's Shakespearian Criticism*, ed. Thomas M. Raysor, 2 vols. (Cambridge, Mass.: Harvard Univ. Press, 1930), 1:110–11.

41. *The Chester Mystery Cycle*, ed. R. M. Lumiansky and David Mills, EETS, s.s. 3 (London: Oxford Univ. Press, 1974), Pagina 6, ll. 97–98.

42. S. L. Bethell, *"The Winter's Tale": A Study* (London: Staples Press, [1947]), pp. 60–61, and Barbara Mowat, *The Dramaturgy of Shakespeare's Romances* (Athens: Univ. of Georgia Press, 1976), p. 19. In *Henry V*, 3.3.38–41, Shakespeare alludes to "Herod's bloody-hunting slaughtermen" and "naked infants spitted upon pikes," which may be a reminiscence of a theatrical scene. The Chester author specifies "super lancea accipiet" ("let it be thrust on a lance") in a stage direction concerning one of the slaughtered infants (Pagina 10, 334 s.d.).

43. On Macbeth's destruction of innocence, see Paul Jorgensen, *Our Naked Frailties* (Berkeley and Los Angeles: Univ. of California Press, 1971), pp. 94–109.

44. Maurice J. Valency, *The Tragedies of Herod and Mariamne* (New York: Columbia Univ. Press, 1940), pp.75–87.

45. For Middleton's part, see Valency, *Tragedies*, pp. 87–91 and Anne Lancashire, ed., *The Second Maiden's Tragedy* (Manchester: Manchester Univ. Press; Baltimore: Johns Hopkins Univ. Press, 1978), pp. 23–32. Rasmussen's article, "Shakespeare's Hand in *The Second Maiden's Tragedy*," is forthcoming in *Shakespeare Quarterly*.

46. Valency, *Tragedies*, p. 16 and Gordon Braden, *Renaissance Tragedy and the Senecan Tradition* (New Haven, Conn.: Yale Univ. Press, 1985), pp. 156–71.

47. The stage direction for *Measure for Measure* 5.1.482 is "Enter . . . Juliet," with no mention of the baby she is reported as being near to delivering in 2.1.18–19. Whether or not she brings the baby with her in act 5 is therefore a director's choice. My point is that a production that includes the baby in act 5 (as the BBC Television version of the play does, for instance) inevitably reinforces a quality of reconciliation and hope in the play's conclusion. Conversely, the baby is invariably excluded from act 5 in productions that emphasize ambiguity and disappointment in the play's close.

48. Hunter, *Comedy of Forgiveness*, pp. 185–203.

49. Eugene M. Waith, *The Pattern of Tragicomedy in Beaumont and Fletcher* (New Haven, Conn.: Yale Univ. Press, 1952), pp. 86–98.

50. John Fletcher, *The Faithful Shepherdess*, ed. Cyrus Hoy, in *Dramatic Works*, 3:497. The connection between Fletcher's comment and *The Winter's Tale* has been noticed by Hallett Smith, *Shakespeare's Romances* (San Marino, Calif.: Huntington Library, 1972), p. 95.

51. Bernard Weinberg, *A History of Literary Criticism in the Italian Renaissance*, 2 vols. (Chicago: Univ. of Chicago Press, 1961), 2:1074–1105.

52. *Bartholomew Fair* in *Ben Jonson*, ed. Herford and Simpson, 6:16, ll. 127–32.

53. Orgel and Strong, *Inigo Jones*, 1:207, l. 30. Bacon's comment about antimasques indicates that he understood the decorum of Jonson's practice: "They have been commonly of fools, satyrs . . . antics. . . . As for angels, it is not comical enough to put them in antimasques" ("Of Masques and Triumphs" in *The Works of Francis Bacon*, ed. James Spedding et al., 15 vols. [Boston: Brown and Taggard, 1861], 12:210).

54. This is the speculation of Dennis Bartholomeusz, *The Winter's Tale in Performance* (Cambridge: Cambridge Univ. Press, 1982), p. 16.

55. Mowat, *Dramaturgy of Shakespeare's Romances*, pp. 75–76. Cf. pp. 35–94 and 121–28.

56. Bertolt Brecht, *The Messingkauf Dialogues*, trans. John Willett (London: Methuen, 1965), pp. 76–83.

57. Recent British productions have been more politically self-conscious than the American. For an example of the kind of critical pressure that has been brought to bear on the Royal Shakespeare Company, see Alan Sinfield, "Royal Shakespeare: Theatre and the Making of Ideology," in *Political Shakespeare*, ed. Jonathan Dollimore and Alan Sinfield (Manchester: Manchester Univ. Press, 1985), pp. 158–81.

58. Thomas Campion, *The Discription of a Maske*, in *The Works of Thomas Campion*, ed. Walter R. Davis (Garden City, N.Y.: Doubleday, 1967), pp. 214–15.

59. Bacon, "Of Masques and Triumphs," *Works*, 12:210.

60. For Inigo Jones's drawing of this headdress and an explication of its symbolism, see Orgel, *Illusion of Power*, pp. 61 and 63.

61. William O. Scott, "Seasons and Flowers in *The Winter's Tale*," SQ 14 (1963), 411–17.

62. My point here is not disallowed by recorded performances of *The Winter's Tale* at court on 5 November 1611, and again in the winter of 1612–13. Even if artificial flowers were used in these performances (as they must have been in midwinter productions of court masques), the fact remains that the scene in question emphasizes a princess's determined *submission* to nature, not her godlike domination of it, and while that fact would not have been denied by the use of artificial flowers in a court performance, it would have been reinforced by the use of natural flowers on the popular stage.

63. For examples of this discussion, see John Danby, *Poets on Fortune's Hill* (London: Faber and Faber, n.d.), pp. 152–83; Rolf Soellner, "Baroque Passion in Shakespeare and His Contemporaries," *ShakS* 1 (1965), 394–402; Arthur C.

Kirsch, *Jacobean Dramatic Perspectives* (Charlottesville: Univ. Press of Virginia, 1972), pp. 52–74 and 127–31.

64. *The Works of Beaumont and Fletcher*, ed. A. Glover and R. Waller (Cambridge: Cambridge Univ. Press, 1905–12), 1:xii.

65. Glover and Waller, ed., *Works of Beaumont and Fletcher*, 1:xii.

66. V. A. Kolve, *The Play Called Corpus Christi* (Stanford, Calif.: Stanford Univ. Press, 1962), pp. 8–32.

67. Leah Sinanoglou [Marcus], "The Christ Child as Sacrifice: A Medieval Tradition and the Corpus Christi Plays," *Speculum* 48 (1973), 491–509.

68. This was a production sponsored by the University of Toronto, 21–23 May 1983.

69. For further comments in this vein, see Howard Felperin, *Shakespearean Romance* (Princeton, N.J.: Princeton Univ. Press, 1972), pp. 211–45.

70. David Young, *The Heart's Forest* (New Haven, Conn.: Yale Univ. Press, 1972), pp. 140–45.

Afterword: Power and Art

1. In "Martial Law in the Land of Cockaigne" (*Shakespearean Negotiations* [Berkeley and Los Angeles: Univ. of California Press, 1988], pp. 129–63), Stephen Greenblatt argues insightfully that Elizabethan society tended to use religious anxiety as a means of enforcing social and political conformity. In effect, what Greenblatt notices is the Elizabethan attempt (though it is virtually ubiquitous in religious cultures) to institutionalize the private recognition of spiritual vulnerability and to harness it in the interest of political advantage. Such an attempt to institutionalize one's personal life for the sake of public gain is precisely the procedure Prince Hal follows. Shakespeare might therefore be said to have preceded Greenblatt in recognizing this phenomenon.

2. For Augustine and Hobbes, see Herbert A. Deane, *The Political and Social Ideas of St. Augustine* (New York: Columbia Univ. Press, 1963), pp. 234–37, and chapter 1, above.

3. See particularly Margot Heinemann, *Puritanism and Theatre: Thomas Middleton and Opposition Drama under the Stuarts* (Cambridge: Cambridge Univ. Press, 1980) and Martin Butler, *Theatre and Crisis, 1632–1642* (Cambridge: Cambridge Univ. Press, 1984). Keith Stavely has even extended the argument to the court masque, in *Criticism and Compliment: The Politics of Literature in the England of Charles I* (Cambridge: Cambridge Univ. Press, 1987), but his revisionist thesis that the Caroline masque maintained a critical independence of power runs afoul of Milton, who understood the court masque very differently.

4 ". . . where the stage should always represent but one place, and the uttermost time presupposed in it should be, both by Aristotle's precept and common reason, but one day, there is [in *Gorboduc*] both many days and many places, inartificially imagined" (*An Apology for Poetry*, in *Elizabethan Critical Essays*, ed. G. Gregory Smith, 2 vols. [London: Oxford Univ. Press, 1904], 1:197).

5. For further development of this argument, see John D. Cox, "Renaissance Power and Stuart Dramaturgy: Shakespeare, Milton, Dryden," *CompD* 22 (Winter, 1988–89).

6. David Norbrook, *Poetry and Politics in the English Renaissance* (London: Routledge and Kegan Paul, 1984), pp. 271–72. Cf. Arthur Kirsch, *Dryden's Heroic*

Drama (Princeton, N.J.: Princeton Univ. Press, 1965), pp. 30–32. Norbrook's phrase for the aim of Charles I's personal rule—"a harmonious pattern of ritualised submission" (p. 238)—is an apt description of politized esthetics in the Restoration as well.

7. *The Works of John Dryden*, ed. H. T. Swedenberg et al. (Berkeley and Los Angeles: Univ. of California Press, 1956–), 8:101. Cited below as CD (for "California Dryden").

8. On the popularity of *The Indian Emperor*, see CD 9:294–95; on Las Casas as Dryden's source, CD 9:309 and 315. For further discussion, see John Loftis, *The Spanish Plays of Neoclassical England* (New Haven, Conn.: Yale Univ. Press, 1975), pp. 178–208.

9. C. R. Kropf, "Political Theory and Dryden's Heroic Tragedies," *Essays in Theatre* 3 (1985), 130–32.

10. CD 9:315.

WORKS FREQUENTLY CITED

Primary

Ascham, Roger. *The Schoolmaster* (1570). Edited by Lawrence V. Ryan. Charlottesville: Univ. Press of Virginia, 1967.

Augustine. *City of God.* Translated by Henry Bettenson. Harmondsworth, Eng.: Penguin Books, 1972.

Bacon, Francis. *Works.* Edited by James Spedding et al. 14 vols. Boston: Brown and Taggard, 1861.

Bevington, David M., ed. *Medieval Drama.* Boston: Houghton Mifflin, 1975.

Bullough, Geoffrey. *Narrative and Dramatic Sources of Shakespeare.* London: Routledge and Kegan Paul; New York: Columbia Univ. Press, 1957–75.

The Chester Mystery Cycle. Edited by R. M. Lumiansky and David Mills. London: Oxford Univ. Press, 1974. EETS s.s.3.

Clopper, Lawrence M., ed. *Records of Early English Drama Chester.* Toronto: Univ. of Toronto Press, 1979.

Cranmer, Thomas. *The Remains of Thomas Cranmer.* Edited by Henry Jenkyns. 4 vols. Oxford: Oxford Univ. Press, 1833.

Crowley, Robert. *Philargyrie of Greate Britayne.* Edited by John King. *ELR* 10 (1980), 47–75.

———. *The Way to Wealth Wherein Is Plainly Taught a Most Present Remedy for Sedicion.* London, 1550.

D'Evelyn, Charlotte, ed. *Peter Idley's Instructions to His Son.* Boston: D. C. Heath; London: Oxford Univ. Press, 1935.

Dyke, Daniel. *The Mystery of Selfe-Deceiving.* London, 1616.

Elyot, Sir Thomas. *The Boke Named the Governour.* Edited by Henry H. S. Croft. 2 vols. London: Kegan Paul, 1880.

Ferne, John. *The Blazon of Gentrie.* London, 1586.

Holinshed, Raphael. *The First and Second Volumes of Chronicles.* London, 1587.

Ingram, Richard. *Coventry Records of Early English Drama.* Toronto: Univ. of Toronto Press, 1981.

Jonson, Ben. *Ben Jonson.* Edited by C. H. Herford and Evelyn Simpson. Oxford: Clarendon Press, 1925–52.

Las Casas, Bartolomé de. *Bartolomé de las Casas.* Translated and edited by George Sanderlin. New York: Alfred A. Knopf, 1971.

Latimer, Hugh. *Selected Sermons.* Edited by Allan G. Chester. Charlottesville: Univ. Press of Virginia, 1968.

Ludus Coventriae. Edited by K. S. Block. London: Oxford Univ. Press, 1922. EETS e.s. 120.

WORKS CITED

The Macro Plays. Edited by Mark Eccles. London: Oxford Univ. Press, 1969. EETS 262.

McIlwain, C. H., ed. *The Political Works of James I.* Cambridge, Mass.: Harvard Univ. Press, 1918.

Meres, Francis. *Palladis Tamia.* Edited by G. Gregory Smith. In *Elizabethan Critical Essays.* 2 vols. London: Oxford Univ. Press, 1904.

More, Sir Thomas. *Utopia.* Edited by Edward Surtz and J. H. Hexter. In *The Complete Works of Thomas More.* New Haven, Conn.: Yale Univ. Press, 1965.

Peacham, Henry. *The Compleat Gentleman.* 1622. Facsimile reprint. New York: DaCapo Press, 1968.

Puttenham, George. *The Arte of English Poesie.* Edited by Gladys D. Willcock and Alice Walker. Cambridge: Cambridge Univ. Press, 1936.

Rymer, Thomas. *The Critical Works of Thomas Rymer.* Edited by Curt A. Zimansky. New Haven, Conn.: Yale Univ. Press, 1956.

Sidney, Sir Philip. *An Apology for Poetry.* Edited by G. Gregory Smith. In *Elizabethan Critical Essays.* 2 vols. London: Oxford Univ. Press, 1904.

Smith, G. Gregory, ed. *Elizabethan Critical Essays.* 2 vols. Oxford: Clarendon Press, 1904.

Smith, Sir Thomas. *De Republica Anglorum.* Edited by Mary Dewar. Cambridge: Cambridge Univ. Press, 1982.

Strype, John. *Annals of the Reformation.* Oxford: Clarendon Press, 1824.

The Towneley Plays. Edited by George England. London: Kegan Paul, Trench, Trübner, 1897. EETS e.s. 71.

Two Coventry Corpus Christi Plays. Edited by Hardin Craig. 2d ed. London: Oxford Univ. Press, 1957. EETS e.s. 87.

Wilson, Thomas. *The Arte of Rhetorique* (1553). Edited by Thomas J. Derrick. New York and London: Garland Publishing Co., 1982.

Secondary

Altman, Joel. *The Tudor Play of Mind.* Berkeley and Los Angeles: Univ. of California Press, 1978.

Ashley, Kathleen M. "The Guiler Beguiled: Christ and Satan as Theological Tricksters in Medieval Religious Literature." *Criticism* 24 (1982), 126–37.

Auerbach, Erich. "*Sermo Humilis*" in *Literary Language and Its Public in Late Latin Antiquity and in the Middle Ages.* Translated by Ralph Manheim. Princeton, N.J.: Princeton Univ. Press, 1965.

Barish, Jonas. *The Antitheatrical Prejudice.* Berkeley and Los Angeles: Univ. of California Press, 1981.

Bevington, David M. *From "Mankind" to Marlowe.* Cambridge, Mass.: Harvard Univ. Press, 1962.

———. *Tudor Drama and Politics.* Cambridge, Mass.: Harvard Univ. Press, 1968.

Braden, Gordon. *Renaissance Tragedy and the Senecan Tradition.* New Haven, Conn.: Yale Univ. Press, 1985.

Brading, David A. *Prophecy and Myth in Mexican History.* Cambridge: Cambridge Univ. Press, [1984].

Chambers, E. K. *The Medieval Stage.* 2 vols. Oxford: Clarendon Press, 1903.

Cohen, Walter. *Drama of a Nation.* Ithaca, N.Y.: Cornell Univ. Press, 1985.

Cole, Howard. *The "All's Well" Story from Boccaccio to Shakespeare*. Urbana: Univ. of Illinois Press, 1981.

Cook, Ann Jennalie. *Shakespeare's Privileged Playgoers*. Princeton, N.J.: Princeton Univ. Press, 1981.

Cross, Claire. *The Royal Supremacy in the Elizabethan Church*. London: George Allen and Unwin; New York: Barnes and Noble, 1969.

Deane, Herbert A. *The Political and Social Ideas of St. Augustine*. New York: Columbia Univ. Press, 1963.

DeWelles, Theodore H. "The Social and Political Context of the Towneley Cycle." Ph.D. diss., Univ. of Toronto, 1980.

Dollimore, Jonathan. *Radical Tragedy*. Chicago: Univ. of Chicago Press, 1984.

Drakakis, John, ed. *Alternative Shakespeares*. London: Methuen, 1985.

Esler, Anthony. *The Aspiring Mind of the Elizabethan Younger Generation*. Durham, N.C.: Duke Univ. Press, 1966.

Evans, Bertrand. *Shakespeare's Comedies*. Oxford: Clarendon Press, 1960.

Felperin, Howard. *Shakespearean Romance*. Princeton, N.J.: Princeton Univ. Press, 1972.

Gardiner, Harold. *Mysteries' End*. New Haven, Conn.: Yale Univ. Press, 1946.

Geertz, Clifford. *The Interpretation of Cultures*. New York: Basic Books, 1973.

Gibson, Gail M. "The Images of Doubt and Belief: Visual Symbolism in the Middle English Plays of Joseph's Troubles about Mary." Ph.D. diss., Univ. of Virginia, 1975.

Greenblatt, Stephen. "The Cultivation of Anxiety: King Lear and His Heirs." *Raritan* 2 (1982), 92–114.

———. *The Power of Forms in the Renaissance*. Norman, Okla.: Pilgrim Books, 1982.

———. *Renaissance Self-Fashioning*. Chicago: Univ. of Chicago Press, 1980.

———. *Representing the English Renaissance*. Berkeley and Los Angeles: Univ. of California Press, 1988.

———. *Shakespearean Negotiations*. Berkeley and Los Angeles: Univ. of California Press, 1988.

———. *Sir Walter Raleigh: The Renaissance Man and His Roles*. New Haven, Conn.: Yale Univ. Press, 1973.

Gurr, Andrew. *Playgoing in Shakespeare's London*. Cambridge: Cambridge Univ. Press, 1987.

Hardison, O. B. *Christian Rite and Christian Drama in the Middle Ages*. Baltimore: Johns Hopkins Univ. Press, 1965.

Heal, Felicity. *Of Prelates and Princes: A Study of the Economic and Social Position of the Tudor Episcopate*. Cambridge: Cambridge Univ. Press, 1981.

Heffner, Ray. "Essex, The Ideal Courtier." *ELH* 1 (1934), 7–36.

Hunter, G. K. *Dramatic Identities and Cultural Tradition*. Liverpool: Liverpool Univ. Press, 1978.

———. "Italian Tragicomedy on the English Stage," *RenD*, n.s. 6 (1973), 123–48.

———. *John Lyly: The Humanist as Courtier*. London: Routledge and Kegan Paul, 1962.

Hunter, Robert G. *Shakespeare and the Comedy of Forgiveness*. New York: Columbia Univ. Press, 1965.

WORKS CITED

Javitch, Daniel. *Poetry and Courtliness in Renaissance England*. Princeton, N.J.: Princeton Univ. Press, 1978.

Jones, Emrys. *The Origins of Shakespeare*. Oxford: Clarendon Press, 1977.

Kastan, David S. *Shakespeare and the Shapes of Time*. Hanover, N.H.: Univ. Press of New England, 1982.

Kelly, H. A. *Divine Providence in the England of Shakespeare's Histories*. Cambridge, Mass.: Harvard Univ. Press, 1970.

King, John. *English Reformation Literature: The Tudor Origins of the Protestant Tradition*. Princeton, N.J.: Princeton Univ. Press, 1982.

Kirsch, Arthur C. *Dryden's Heroic Drama*. Princeton, N.J.: Princeton Univ. Press, 1965.

———. *Shakespeare and the Experience of Love*. Cambridge: Cambridge Univ. Press, 1981.

Kolve, V. A. *The Play Called Corpus Christi*. Stanford, Calif.: Stanford Univ. Press, 1962.

Langston, Beach. "Essex and the Art of Dying." *HLQ* 13 (1950).

Leech, Clifford. "The Theme of Ambition in *All's Well That Ends Well*." *ELH* 21 (1954), 17–29.

Lindley, David, ed. *The Court Masque*. Manchester: Manchester Univ. Press, 1984.

MacCaffrey, Wallace. *Queen Elizabeth and the Making of Policy, 1572–1588*. Princeton, N.J.: Princeton Univ. Press, 1981.

Mack, Maynard. *"King Lear" in Our Time*. Berkeley: Univ. of California Press, 1965.

[Marcus], Leah Sinanoglou. "The Christ Child as Sacrifice: A Medieval Tradition and the Corpus Christi Plays." *Speculum* 48 (1973), 491–509.

Marius, Richard. *Thomas More: A Biography*. London: J. M. Dent, 1984.

Markus, R. A. *Saeculum: History and Society in the Theology of St. Augustine*. Cambridge: Cambridge Univ. Press, 1970.

Martines, Lauro. *Power and Imagination: City-States in Renaissance Italy*. New York: Alfred A. Knopf, 1979.

Marx, Karl. *The German Ideology*. Edited by C. F. Arthur. London: Lawrence and Wishart, 1970.

Marx, Karl and Frederick Engels. *Selected Works*. 2 vols. London: Lawrence and Wishart, 1950.

Maus, Katharine Eisaman. *Ben Jonson and the Roman Frame of Mind*. Princeton, N.J.: Princeton Univ. Press, 1984.

Montrose, Louis A. " 'Eliza, Queene of Shepheardes,' and the Pastoral of Power." *ELR* 10 (1980), 153–82.

———. "Gifts and Reasons: The Context of Peele's *Araygnement of Paris*." *ELH* 47 (1980).

———. "Of Gentlemen and Shepherds: The Politics of Elizabethan Pastoral Form." *ELH* 50 (1983), 415–59.

———. " 'Shaping Fantasies': Figurations of Gender and Power in Elizabethan Culture." In *Representing the English Renaissance*, edited by Stephen Greenblatt, pp. 31–64. Berkeley and Los Angeles: Univ. of California Press, 1988.

Neale, J. E. *Elizabeth I and Her Parliaments*. 2 vols. London: Jonathan Cape, 1957.

———. *Essays in Elizabethan History*. London: Jonathan Cape, 1958.

———. *Queen Elizabeth I*. 1934. Reprint. London: Jonathan Cape, 1952.

Norbrook, David. *Poetry and Politics in the Renaissance*. London: Routledge and Kegan Paul, 1984.

Orgel, Stephen. *The Jonsonian Masque*. 2d ed. New York: Columbia Univ. Press, 1982.

Orgel, Stephen and Roy Strong, eds. *Inigo Jones: The Theatre of the Stuart Court*. Berkeley and Los Angeles: Univ. of California Press; London: Sotheby, Parke, Bernet, 1973.

Owst, G. R. *Literature and Pulpit in Medieval England*. 2d ed., rev. Oxford: Clarendon Press, 1961.

Pagels, Elaine. *Adam, Eve, and the Serpent*. New York: Random House, 1988.

Parry, Graham. *The Golden Age Restor'd: The Culture of the Stuart Court, 1603–42*. New York: St. Martins Press, 1981.

Pechter, Edward. "New Historicism and Its Discontents: Politicizing Renaissance Drama." *PMLA* 102 (1987), 292–303.

Prior, Moody. *The Drama of Power*. Evanston, Ill.: Northwestern Univ. Press, 1973.

Richmond, H. M. *Shakespeare's Political Plays*. New York: Random House, 1967.

Ricoeur, Paul. *Freud and Philosophy*. New Haven, Conn.: Yale Univ. Press, 1970.

Sanders, Wilbur. *The Dramatist and the Received Idea*. Cambridge: Cambridge Univ. Press, 1968.

Schoenbaum, S. *Shakespeare: A Documentary Life*. New York: Oxford Univ. Press, in association with Scolar Press, 1977.

Skinner, Quentin. *The Foundations of Modern Political Thought*. 2 vols. Cambridge: Cambridge Univ. Press, 1978.

Spivack, Bernard. *Shakespeare and the Allegory of Evil*. New York: Columbia Univ. Press, 1958.

Squires, Lynn B. "Law and Disorder in *Ludus Coventriae*," *CompD*, 12 (1978).

———. "Legal and Political Aspects of Late Medieval English Drama." Ph.D. diss., Univ. of Washington, 1977.

Stone, Lawrence. *The Crisis of the Aristocracy, 1558–1641*. Oxford: Clarendon Press, 1965.

Strong, Roy. *Henry, Prince of Wales and England's Lost Renaissance*. London: Thames and Hudson, 1986.

Tennenhouse, Leonard. *Power on Display*. New York and London: Methuen, 1986.

Travis, Peter. *Dramatic Design in the Chester Cycle*. Chicago: Univ. of Chicago Press, 1982.

Tyson, Gerald P., and Sylvia S. Wagonheim, eds. *Print and Culture in the Renaissance*. Newark: Univ. of Delaware Press, 1986.

Weimann, Robert. *Shakespeare and the Popular Tradition in the Theater*. Edited by Robert Schwartz. Baltimore: Johns Hopkins Univ. Press, 1978.

Weinberg, Bernard. *A History of Literary Criticism in the Italian Renaissance*. 2 vols. Chicago: Univ. of Chicago Press, 1961.

Wernham, R. B. *After the Armada: Elizabethan England and the Struggle for Western Europe*. Oxford: Clarendon Press, 1984.

WORKS CITED

Whigham, Frank. *Ambition and Privilege: The Social Tropes of Elizabethan Courtesy Theory.* Berkeley and Los Angeles: Univ. of California Press, 1984.

White, Helen C. *Social Criticism in Popular Religious Literature of the Sixteenth Century.* New York: Macmillan, 1944.

Wickham, Glynne. *Early English Stages 1300–1660.* London: Routledge and Kegan Paul, 1959.

Williams, Raymond. *Marxism and Literature.* Oxford: Oxford Univ. Press, 1977.

Williamson, Jerry W. *The Myth of the Conqueror. Prince Henry Stuart, A Study of 17th-Century Personation.* New York: AMS Press, 1978.

Woolf, Rosemary. *The English Mystery Plays.* London: Routledge and Kegan Paul; Berkeley and Los Angeles: Univ. of California Press, 1972.

Yates, Frances A. *Astraea: The Imperial Theme in the Sixteenth Century.* London and Boston: Routledge and Kegan Paul, 1975.

Youings, Joyce. *Sixteenth-Century England.* The Pelican Social History of Britain. Harmondsworth, Eng.: Penguin Books, 1984.

INDEX

Act of Abolishing Diversity of Opinions (1539), 50
Adam and Eve: and free will, 25; and political power, 15
Aeneas (*Aeneid*), 174
agricultural labor, sixteenth-century, 52
All's Well That Ends Well, 128–50; medieval dramaturgy in, 68; pregnancy in, 212
Altman, Joel, 54, 65, 257n.16
Ambrose, Saint, 146
Antony and Cleopatra, 177
Aristotle, 12, 15
Armada, the: and the history plays, 83–84
Ascham, Roger, 42–43
Ashley, Kathleen, 129, 131
As You Like It, 77, 80
atonement, doctrine of, 131
Auerbach, Erich, 46
Augustine, Saint: and Aquinas, 15, 233n.18; and Christian political realism, *xii*, 12–15; *City of God, xi*, 12–15, 23–24, 88; on class struggle, 233n.17; compared to Marx, 13–14, 234n.31; comparison of two Cities, 14, 20; *Confessions, xiii, xiv*, 10, 74; contrasted with Freud, 14; on Earthly City, *xii*, 12, 14; and empirical observation, *xii*, 14, 88, 91; on free will, 25; and Hobbes, 13, 17, 232–33n.16; influence on Thomas More, 18, 20, 233n.27; and Las Casas, 11–12; on levels of style, 46; on *libido dominandi*, 15, 23–24; and materialism, 14; on natural order, 15; and neo-Platonism, 14; and N-Town *Fall of Lucifer*, 25; *On Christian Doctrine*, 46; and political coercion, 12, 232n.10; on *potentia humilitatis*, 26; on power relations, 26–27; on property, 19; *Retractiones*, 12; on rhetorical decorum, 46; on Rome, 13–14; on Romulus and Remus, 24; on secular history, 88, 91; his sense of self, *xiii, xiv*, 74; on *sermo humilis*, 46; and Shakespearean tragedy, 178; on transcendent humility, 30, 138–39; on woman taken in adultery, 163

Bacon, Sir Francis, 132, 163, 216
Bakhtin, Mikhail, 236n.23
Baldwin, William, 56
Bale, John, 55, 92
Ball, John (medieval preacher), 37, 61
Barish, Jonas, 73, 243n.15
Bartholomew Fair (Jonson), 214
Battenhouse, Roy, 178
Beaumont, Francis, and John Fletcher: *A King and No King*, 212, 218; *The Maid's Tragedy*, 200–201; *Philaster*, 218
Benediktbeuern: Christmas Play, 23
Benjamin, Walter, 15
Bergeron, David, 197
Berlatsky, Joel, 247–48n.4
Berry, Edward I., 87
Bevington, David M., on "popular canon," 53; on popular dramaturgy, 66; on topicality in medieval drama, 236n.18; on the Vice, 248n.15
Beza, Theodore (reformer), 56